Asian Political Cartoons

University Press of Mississippi / Jackson

Asian Political Cartoons

John A. Lent

The University Press of Mississippi is the scholarly publishing
agency of the Mississippi Institutions of Higher Learning:
Alcorn State University, Delta State University, Jackson State
University, Mississippi State University, Mississippi University
for Women, Mississippi Valley State University, University of
Mississippi, and University of Southern Mississippi.

www.upress.state.ms.us

The University Press of Mississippi is a member
of the Association of University Presses.

First printing 2023
∞

Library of Congress Cataloging-in-Publication Data

Names: Lent, John A., author.
Title: Asian political cartoons / John A. Lent.
Description: Jackson : University Press of Mississippi, 2023. |
Includes bibliographical references and index.
Identifiers: LCCN 2022047086 (print) | LCCN 2022047087
(ebook) | ISBN 9781496842527 (hardback) | ISBN
9781496842534 (trade paperback) | ISBN 9781496842541 (epub)
| ISBN 9781496842558 (epub) | ISBN 9781496842565 (pdf) |
ISBN 9781496842572 (pdf)
Subjects: LCSH: Political cartoons. | Politicians—Asia—
Caricatures and cartoons. | Political culture—Asia—
Caricatures and cartoons.
Classification: LCC NC1680 .L46 2023 (print) | LCC NC1680
(ebook) | DDC 320.9502/07—dc23/eng/20221115
LC record available at https://lccn.loc.gov/2022047086
LC ebook record available at https://lccn.loc.gov/2022047087

British Library Cataloging-in-Publication Data available

It's winter 1954 and I'm hitchhiking home on my first holiday as a freshman at Ohio University. After getting a couple of rides, I am dropped off at a not-too-well-traveled stretch of road along the Ohio River. It is bitter cold, and I am wearing only a thin trench coat over my shirt and trousers. Freezing. On the hillside of the river is a small makeshift house spewing smoke from a pot-bellied stove. After a while, a middle-aged man in overalls comes out of the house, approaches me, and simply says, "Come down to the house and get warm and I will take you to the next town where you will have a better chance of hitching a ride." I warmed myself around the stove. We did not talk much. On the floor near me were this man's children playing when they were not taking a peek at this stranger. By the looks of their clothing and the room's furnishings, it was obvious that this man was struggling financially. As he and I got into his beat-up truck, I noticed his name on his mailbox. He had not told me his name, nor had I introduced myself. When he dropped me off in the next town, I thanked the man and said, "Mr. Potts, if I live to be one hundred, I will always remember you." I am eighty-six now, and Earl Potts still occupies a special place in my mind.

This book is dedicated to Mr. Potts and all the other Earl Pottses I have had the good fortune to have known. They are the soil and soul of the earth.

—John A. Lent

Contents

I owe my deepest gratitude to many kind people who helped me with this book. Some of them lent a hand earlier during my research trips to Asia in the 1980s and 1990s; they were acknowledged in the previous two books in this set—*Asian Comics* (2015, Mississippi) and *Comics Art in China*, with Xu Ying (2017, Mississippi)—and most are acknowledged here as well.

Top of the list are the hundreds of cartoonists and comic art individuals I have interviewed all over Asia. To the man/woman, they were generous with their time and materials; in some cases, they helped me get to destinations through maddening traffic, warmly welcomed me into their homes, studios, and offices, helped in interpretations, and steered me to other sources. In my considerably long career interviewing media, popular culture, political, and other figures on every continent (except Antarctica), I have found the cartoonists to be the most hospitable, cooperative, and friendly to be around.

Especially helpful were: **Bangladesh**: Mehedi Haque, Nasreen Sultana Mitu, Zahid Hasan Benu, Shishir Bhattacharjee, Sharier Khan, M. A. Kuddus, Tanmoy (Syed Rashad Imam), Harunoor Rasheed Harun, Nazrul Islam, Kazi Abul Kasem, Rafiqun Nabi, Ahsan Habib, Khondokar Abu Sayeed and wife, Gemy, Asiful Huda, and Saiful Alam; **Cambodia**: John Weeks, the Our Books staff, and Uth Roeun; **China**: He Wei, Chen Jianyu, Liao Bingxiong, Pang Bangben, Li Binsheng, Feng Yiyin, Fang Cheng, Wang Fuyang, Zhan Tong, Hong Jin Feng, Zheng Xinyao, Ding Cong, Zheng Huagai, Xu Pengfei, Hua Junwu, Te Wei, Chen Huiling, Miao Yintang, Wang Wei, Xia Dachuan, Huang Yuanlin, Quan Yingsheng, Ying Tao, Bi Keguan, Mai Fei, Chen Yuli, Jiang Yousheng, and Li Qingai; **Hong Kong**: Zunzi (Wong Kei-kwan), Chan Ya, Lily Lau, Larry Feign, Paul Best, and Ma Long (Ma Shing-yuen); **India**: Abu Abraham, R. K. Laxman, Suresh Sawant, Sudhir Tailang, Pran Kumar and family, Ramesh Chande, Prakash Shetty, Raju Nair, Gokul Gopalakrishnan, E. P. Unny, Sudhir Dar, V. R. P. Keshav, P. K. S. Kutty, Ajit Ninan, Rajinder Puri, and C. J. Yesudasan; **Indonesia**: Iwan Gunawan, Toni Masdiono, Dwi Koendoro, G. M. Sudarta, Dwinita Larasati and the CAB staff,

Acknowledgments

Ramli Badrudin, Mahtum and the *HumOr* staff, Beng Rahadian, Pramono R. Pramoedjo, Arwah Setiawan, Dominto M. Sudarno, Priyanto Sunarto, and Wagiyono Sunarto; **Japan**: Hayakawa Sadabumi, Kato Yoshiro, Kosuge Riyako, Kurata Shin, Nishida Toshiko, Nishizawa Yuzi, Sasaki Tomoko, Satō Sampei, Sugiura Yukio, Suzuki Yamato, and Tokoro Yukiyoshi; **Korea, South**: Park Jae-Dong, Yoon Young-Ok, Kim Song-Hwan, Park Soo-Dong, Chong Un-Gyong, Ahn Ui-Sup, Cho Kwan-Je, Choi Kyu-Seok, Keum Suk Gendry-Kim, Kim Pan-Kook, Kim Jae-Jung, Kim Soo-Bak, Kim Sung-Hee, Lee Hee-Jae, Lee Woo-Bok, and Park Kun-Woong; **Malaysia**: Lat (Mohd. Nor Khalid) and wife, Fauzi, Rejabhad, Muliyadi Mahamood and wife, Brigette, Jaafar Taib, Zunar (Zulkifli Anwar Ulhaque), and Muhamad Azhar Abdullah and wife, Vovi; **Mongolia**: Dan Erdenebal, Nambaral Erdenebayar, and Samandariin Tsogtbayar; **Myanmar**: the entire cartoonists' club of Myanmar, Aw Pi Kyeh, Crab (Su Myat Htwe), Joker (Nyan Myint), Kyaw Thu Yein, Maung Maung Fountain, Nay Myo Aye, Shwe Bo, and Win Aung; **Nepal**: Ram Kumar Panday and family, Dharma Raj Baral, Ashok Man Singh, Yubaraj Ghimire, Mohan Shyam Maharjan, and Abin Shrestha; **the Philippines**: Boboy and Guia Yonzon III and family, Gerry Alanguilan, Norman B. Isaac, Nonoy Marcelo, Larry Alcala, Roni Santiago, and A. V. H. Hardendorp; **Singapore**: Heng Kim Song, Deng Coy Miel, Cheah Sin Ann, Hup (Lee Hup Kheng), Manny Francisco, Ludwig Ilio, Sonny Liew, Don Low, José Ruiz, James Tan, and Dan Wong; **Sri Lanka**: Camillus Perera, Winnie Hettigoda, W. R. Wijesoma, S. C. Opatha, Jiffry Yoonoos, Dharshana Karunathilake, K. M. K. Medagama, Janaka Ratnayake, and Wasantha Siriwardena; **Taiwan**: Zola Zu, Li Shan, Ao Yao-hsiang, Chao Ning, Hoong Tei-lin, Hsiao Yen-chung, Jen (Chung Sung-wei), Ji Ching, L. C. C. (Lo Ching-chung), Ling Qun, Tang Jian-feng, and Wang Peng; **Thailand**: Chai Rachawat, Sudjai Bhromkoed, Arun Watcharasawat, Bancha Sangthunchai, Kamin (Chukiat Jaroensuk), Chuchart Mueningul, Pon, Teerapongsack Sungkatip, Yodpongsakul, and Yoottachai Kaewdee; and **Vietnam**: Chi (Chi Do Huu), Le Phuong, Ly Truc Dung, and Nguyen Thanh Phong.

There were so many others who helped, such as spouses and offspring of premier Chinese cartoonists, all of whom Xu Ying and I interviewed: Bi Weimin (Bi Keguan), Liao Ling-er (Liao Bingxiong), Wayne Cong (Ding Cong), Zhan Yong (Zhan Tong), Sun Yanhua (Sun Zhijun), Li Yan (Li Kuchan), Zhang Weijun (Zhang Leping), Zhang Weide (Zhang Wenyuan), Zhang Linchun (Zhang Guangyu), Zhu Jilin (Mi Gu), Huang Dagang (Yu Feng and Huang Miaozi), Charles Zee (A Da), Li Weiwei (Wang Zimei), and Shen Jun (Ding Cong); and many doctoral and master's students I supervised either at Temple University or at the Communication University of China, who helped while they were abroad or when I visited their home countries, such as: **China**: Dr. Hong-Ying Liu-Lengyel and husband, Dr. Alfonz Lengyel, Zhang Huilin, Dr. Wang Lei, Dr. Wang Jizhong, and Dr. Jia Fou; **Hong Kong**: Dr. Charles Elliott; **India**: Aruna Rao and Dr. John V. Vilanilam; **Japan**: Dr. Rei Okamoto and Dr. Fusami Ogi; **Korea**: Dr. HaeLim Suh, Dr. Sueen Noh, Dr. Daiwon Hyun, Dr. Myung Jun Kim, Dr. Hoon Soon Kim, Sang Kil Lee, Dr. Yu Kie-Un, Dr. Jae Woong Kwon, and Dr. Kim Chunhyo; **Nepal**: Fungma Fudong; **Taiwan**: Dr. Hong-Chi Shiau, Dr. Hsiao Hsiang-wen, Chyun-Fung Shi, Dr. Chang-De Liu, Peng Hui Ching, and Chu-Fen Tang; and **Thailand**: Dr. Warat Karuchit, Dr. Monsinee Keeratikrainon, and Oranuj Lertchanyarak and husband, Kanongdej.

Besides those already mentioned, academicians, media personnel, and other professionals who were tremendously useful were: Mike Rhode, Lim Cheng Tju, Kosei Ono, Ryan Holmberg, Ronald Stewart, Nishida Toshiko, Tomoko Sasaki, Liu Jinan, Connie Lam, Isao Shimizu, Annemari de Silva, Htet Lwin Lwin Aung, Orvy Jundis, Domini Torrevillas, Samuel Meshack, Josephine Joseph, Jhosephine Tanuwidjaya, Sankaran Ramanathan, Hane Latt, Keiko Tonegawa, Laura Barrett, Noh Kwang-Woo, Wang Jing, Jiang Meiying, Song Zufen, and Denise Gray.

Gurpreet Kochar, MD, kept me on the "straight and narrow" with his superior medical knowledge and skills, sound advice, and compassionate care, for which I am very grateful.

I wish to thank my wife, Xu Ying, who has aided in so many ways, keeping alive friendships with Chinese cartoonists, setting up interview appointments, serving as photographer and as interpreter in Chinese-speaking areas, and providing much overall support. My children, Laura Barrett, Andrea Murta, John V., Lisa, Shahnon, and Xian Liu, helped in various ways, for which I am grateful.

Working with the University Press of Mississippi on three books so far has been an excellent experience, going back to Seetha Srinivasan, but with this volume, predominantly with Vijay Shah and Lisa McMurtray. Thank you immensely for being a high-quality, fair, and author-friendly press.

The research for this book was entirely funded by the author.

—John A. Lent

Asian Political Cartoons

The political (editorial) cartoon has grabbed the global spotlight a few times in recent years, but usually the beam focused on situations and factors not favorable to this vaunted element of journalism. High among these attention-getting events were the free but not responsible Danish newspaper images mocking the prophet Mohammad and the disastrous fallout of their publication, and the provocation-for-the-sake-of-provocation *Charlie Hebdo* cartoons that led to the bombing of its Paris headquarters on one occasion and the murder of twelve staff members in January 2015.

Not garnering as much of the international stage as it should is the plight of the political cartoon itself. For a few days in 2019, criticism was heaped on the *New York Times* for discontinuing the use of political cartoons in its international edition, after it drew fire for publishing a drawing labeled as anti-Semitic in some quarters. Although a serious matter (despite the historical fact that the *New York Times* was never very cartoon friendly), its importance pales in comparison to the blight that has struck the political cartoon more generally and internationally—the serious depletion of newspaper staff political cartoonists (e.g., in the United States, from 275 in 1957 to 84 in 2007, and fewer than 30 now; and in Japan, only *Mainichi Shimbun* of the big three dailies still retains a political cartoonist); the increased victimization of political cartoonists worldwide, with killings, death threats (as in India recently), arrests, jailings, and long sentences (as in Malaysia, Turkey, Bangladesh, and Iran); forced and/or volunteer exile (as in Iran, Bangladesh, and China); and a what-can-I-do attitude as endemic among many apathetic, frightened, and/or oppressed publics of the world.

Why should one care about the fate of the political cartoon? First, because it has served as a vigilant watchdog on the powers that be. Ask former South African president Jacob Zuma, who continually fought off the visual barbs of Jonathan "Zapiro" Shapiro; or former Malaysian prime minister Najib Razak, who spent considerable time during his tenure in office fending off the strong cartoon attacks of Zunar (Zulkifli Anwar Ulhaque) and unsuccessfully trying to bring him to his knees; or William "Boss" Tweed of the corrupt politics

Introduction

3

of nineteenth-century New York City, who could not escape Thomas Nast's caricatures even when he fled to Europe. The political cartoon has been effective as a voice, having advantages over textual editorials, in that it is visual, direct to the point, and easy to comprehend.

Functions and Definitions of Political Cartoons

Besides its function as a watchdog of government and the political system, the political cartoon is also a social consciousness–raising instrument that can bring attention to social problems and then campaign to change them. This type of cartoon takes different forms and subjects—comic books that tackle social issues, such as those in the Philippines in the 1960s promoting family planning; Stella So's contemporary graphic novels about urban development-turned-historic-destruction in Hong Kong, and others in South Africa through the Storyteller Group of the 1990s that brought awareness to HIV/AIDS, women's rights, and other issues; newspaper strips that deal with the ravages of war (*Doonesbury* in the United States); and standard one-panel newspaper political cartoons that focus on the environment, government incompetence, the disparity between the rich and the poor, bureaucracy, or corruption, readily visible in the press of Asia and other parts of the world.

Because of the political and sociocultural backgrounds of Asian countries, the political cartoon is an important vehicle of public opinion and social change. By its visual nature, it is able to communicate effectively to large groups of illiterate or barely literate people found in many sections of the continent, assuming they have access to media. If unhindered (which it seldom is), the political cartoon is the voice of the unheard masses, as it was (or is) during the times of Abu and Laxman in India, Kim Song-Hwan and others in South Korea, Zunar in Malaysia, and Zunzi in Hong Kong. If heeded by policy makers, the political cartoon can be a viable agent of social change, as it has been during various campaigns across Asia.

On paper, the importance of the political cartoon stands out. However, for the political cartoon to stand front and center in reality, it must contend with a number of conditions implied above and discussed more fully in the rest of this volume.

At the top of the list of conditions are the motives of editors and cartoonists, and how well they can carry them out and how far they are willing to go to do so. Likely, the majority of Asian political cartoonists, at some time in their careers, had visions of changing the world. In nearly all cases, these lofty ambitions were dampened, or more likely completely washed away, by various restrictions and guidelines from government and religious officials, traditional norms and values, unwritten ways of doing things, or public outcries. In a not-so-steady and low-paying field such as political cartooning, cartoonists realize that to keep the rice bowl full, they have to toe the line.

Also, figuring in the delineation of political cartoons are the issues and problems they take on; although labeled political, these cartoons extend outward, encompassing sociocultural, economic, and even historical topics. In my view, South Korean graphic novels bringing to light past happenings (civilian massacres, comfort women, corporate-induced illnesses) covered up by a long run of dictatorships deserve a place under the heading of political cartooning.

A broad interpretation of political cartoons includes multiple platforms in addition to newspapers, such as magazines, comic books, graphic novels, the internet, animation, television, posters, and even street art. It also goes beyond the traditional one-panel format and includes tiny, one-column panel cartoons (pocket) very visible in South Asia, four-panel horizontal strips, and four-panel vertical cartoons, the latter extremely popular in South Korea at one time.

Generally, cartoonists describe the political cartoon simply as a vehicle carrying a message to sway public opinion. Professor and cartoonist Roy Paul Nelson makes a distinction between the weakest of them, which "merely restate the news in graphic form," and the strongest, which "depict a political, social, or economic problem and, by implication, offer some solution" (Nelson 1975, 7). He makes an interesting comparison between an ordinary painting, which he says whispers, and a political cartoon, which screams. The editorial page editor of the Minneapolis *Star Tribune*, Susan Albright, is more vivid, stating that political cartoons represent, "sometimes all at once and sometimes by turns, biting opinions, gentle ribbing, excruciating truths, shared grief, a belly laugh of recognition, a societal relief valve, a Mr. Hyde to our Dr. Jekyll, our outrageous cousin—the one we love, but whose audacity scares us" (American Press Institute 1998, 46).[1]

The political cartoon is defined broadly in this volume. Meant to be inclusive, the definition entails a range of purposes, issues/problems discussed, and platforms and formats used. I don't attempt to provide a one-sentence description of a political cartoon for fear of omitting some of its characteristics and slighting other dimensions through airtight compartmentalization. On these pages, the purposes of the political cartoons that are provided overlap with one another; in other words, they cannot be all inclusive and mutually exclusive, the usual formula for category formation.

With this caveat in mind, the purposes of the political cartoon usually are:

- To criticize politicians and other public figures and institutions for their statements, policies, and actions;
- To point out societal situations and conditions potentially harmful to the public welfare and call for remedial action and change;
- To satirize, mock, and make fun of public figures with or without any specific motive;
- To honor a noteworthy person upon his/her demise; and
- Infrequently, to praise an action, event, or individual for serving the public interest in exemplary fashion.

The "Freedom to Cartoon"

In nearly every region of the world, the purposes political cartoons serve are heavily dependent upon the processes by which they are created and sanctioned. In very rare cases, and virtually nowhere in Asia, does the cartoonist have "complete" freedom, from idea conception to appearance in print. It is safe to say that in Asia, and in a large part of the rest of the world, political cartoons are either what I term "house" cartoons, merely illustrating the day's editorial, or "collaborative," whereby the content and slant of the cartoon are determined and approved by the publisher and/or editor, with or without the cartoonist's input, or in a daily editorial board meeting where ideas are germinated or nourished and approved either directly or indirectly. Of course, in countries such as China, Myanmar, Singapore, and Vietnam, among others, political cartoons are banned outright or strictly controlled by powers much higher up than newspaper managements, through regulations, restrictions, and guidelines. A large portion of *Asian Political Cartoons* details the dangers to the "freedom to cartoon."

At various points in this book, the terms "self-censorship" and "guided cartooning" occur. Both are serious threats to the "freedom to cartoon" in Asia and deserve clarity. They are similar but have different perpetrators. Cartoonists in all parts of the world have told me that self-censorship is the worst type of control, rightly thinking that when some entity other than oneself attempts to restrict expression, one can try to find clever ways to get around the suppression. However, when a person censors him or herself, such recourse disappears.

"Guided cartooning" is my coinage adapted from the concept of a "guided press," initiated about a half century ago predominantly in Asia. What this entails is the press getting onside with the government, on the surface, to help authorities carry out their programs and campaigns to better the country. Underneath, it is a sneaky control mechanism, with the press required to accept guidance from the government. In the long run, the concept helped to kill freedom of the press in much of Asia, as it is likely to do with the freedom to cartoon.

In either scenario, the boundaries of acceptability sometimes are purposely left vague by authorities, who work on the assumption that editors and cartoonists will

5

be even more cautious, not knowing exactly where the red line is. However, in most instances, it is common knowledge who owns and controls the press, its political stance, and its vested interests that are to be protected.

The "freedom to cartoon" has had major setbacks in twenty-first-century Asia, as these pages will reflect. Using a schema I drew up in 2017, infringements on Asian "freedom to cartoon" have resulted through government suppression by legislative means (use/misuse of libel and sedition laws [e.g., Zunar in Malaysia] and laws regulating copyright, intellectual property, piracy, obscenity, and child pornography) and by unwritten restrictions and guidance policies (e.g., Maoist and Marxist doctrine in communist China and Vietnam, and Pancasila and Rukunegara ideologies in Indonesia and Malaysia, respectively), as well as by martial law and/or emergency measures (most recently in Myanmar). A second infringement has been through intolerance by religious groups (e.g., the arrest, jailing, further harassment, and forced exile of Bangladeshi cartoonist Mohammad Arifur Rahman), and hate groups. Third, cartooning has often been controlled by corporate/conglomerate ownership of the print media, which cartoonists must depend on for venues (South Korea, the Philippines, Malaysia, Singapore, and India, among others). In many countries (Bangladesh, for example), advertising far outweighs cartoons in bidding for valuable space; in other areas—the Philippines, Malaysia, Singapore, India, and Bangladesh—publishers and editors favor nonopinion illustrations over political cartoons. The wide range of companies that media conglomerates own and control can, and does, represent a threat to the "freedom to cartoon," as cartoonists are warned or know by experience or instinct the vested interests that are untouchable (Lent 2017, 1–35).

The means by which political cartoonists of Asia have been victimized include killings and disappearances (C. Irfan Hussain of India and Prageeth Eknaligoda of Sri Lanka), terroristic threats (e.g., Jiffry Yoonoos in Sri Lanka and Karnika Kahen of India), suspensions of publications (e.g., *Apple Daily* of Hong Kong, and *7 Day*

News and *Eleven* of Myanmar, all in 2021, and *Cambodia Daily* in 2017), arrests, imprisonments, harsh punishment, fines, and firings (e.g., Mana Neyistani and Atena Farghadani of Iran and Arifur Rahman of Bangladesh) (Lent 2017, 35–50).

Scope of *Asian Political Cartoons*

Structural Dimensions

Asian Political Cartoons is designed to be a companion to *Asian Comics*, also published by the University Press of Mississippi (2015). As such, it is structured by three geographical regions, each made up of countries that are alphabetically ordered. Countries/territories included are those covered in *Asian Comics*, with the addition of a chapter on Japan and shorter vignettes on Brunei, Iran, Mongolia, and North Korea. This new book shifts the focus from comics (comic strips, comic books, and gag [humor] cartoons) to political cartoons.

As with *Asian Comics* and other continent- or region-wide books I have authored or edited, *Asian Political Cartoons* uses a country-by-country approach. I favor this organization scheme, because each country or territory is distinct culturally, politically, linguistically, and economically, and lumping countries/territories thematically integrates them in ways that are neither realistic nor appropriate and could lead to manipulation.

Orientational Dimensions

The concentration in this volume is on printed newspapers and magazines (almost always products of the West historically) that carry political cartoons. I am very much aware that these media are on the downswing, that political satire comes in other forms, and that it predates what came from the West. Other forms are discussed throughout *Asian Political Cartoons*, such as posters and street protest art in Hong Kong to oppose tightening Chinese control; online and social media in various countries (examples being the splurge of webtoons in South Korea and other online cartooning in places such as Malaysia, Singapore, and Vietnam); comic books, comic strips, and graphic novels (particular examples being graphic novels that uncover corruption and violence committed by dictatorial governments and corporations in South Korea, comic books that glorify the leaders of North Korea, and the comic strip *Ikabod*, which mocked the Marcos dictatorship in the Philippines); humor magazines that have flooded Malaysia since 1978 and revitalized the country's satire tradition; and memes used to promote religious and political ideas in Indonesia and Malaysia.

Asian Political Cartoons does include some examples of precolonial satire (scrolls, *shunga*, *ukiyo-e*, and *kibyōshi* in Japan, wayang [puppet theater] in Indonesia, and Kalighat prints in India), but this content is limited because it is treated more fully in my previously published companion volumes, *Asian Comics* (2015) and *Comics Art in China* (2017) with Xu Ying.

Geographical Dimensions

Asian Political Cartoons is further delineated geographically. The countries and territories examined in this book were not chosen arbitrarily, nor from an orientalist perspective. Rather, they were selected to, first, account for the majority of countries and territories making up three of the five regions of Asia as outlined by the United Nations. The regions selected are: East Asia, consisting of China, Hong Kong, Macao, Japan, Mongolia, North Korea, South Korea, and Taiwan; Southeast Asia, encompassing Brunei, Cambodia, Indonesia, Laos, Malaysia, Myanmar, the Philippines, Singapore, Thailand, Timor-Leste, and Vietnam; and South Asia, including Afghanistan, Bangladesh, Bhutan, India, Iran, the Maldives, Nepal, Pakistan, and Sri Lanka.[2]

Central and Western Asia were excluded because: (1) their inclusion would have expanded the time span and size of the project enormously, necessitating many more years of research and certainly more than one volume; and (2) except for Cyprus, Turkey, and the United

Arab Emirates, I am relatively unfamiliar with the other twenty countries of these two regions, never having traveled in or researched them.

The second criterion for selection of countries and territories is a reiteration of the point just made: they were places where I had interviewed political cartoonists. During the past more than thirty-five years, I have interviewed political cartoonists of twenty of the twenty-eight countries and territories listed above. The eight where such interviews did not occur were Afghanistan, Bhutan, Brunei, Laos, Macao, the Maldives, North Korea, and Pakistan.

Research Dimensions

During my more than half a century of global research, I have depended on the interview as a chief tool of investigation. This came naturally as I completed my bachelor's and master's degrees in a journalism program that emphasized interviewing, and I devoted much of my academic career teaching reporting and writing. Almost all of my research on any topic has been based on the principle that it is essential to find out directly from those who lived through certain events what they know, believe, and experienced. This maxim was strengthened while I was teaching in an English department at the beginning of my career, hanging out with colleagues who enjoyed pontificating in the most obtuse language on symbolic meanings they concocted for various authors' works. During those occasions, I was sometimes reminded of the retort I heard the great American poet Robert Frost give at a small gathering I attended in 1960. Asked by an audience member if Frost repeated the line "And miles to go before I sleep," from "Stopping by Woods on a Snowy Evening," because he had much to do before he died, the elderly poet unhesitatingly shot back, "No. That was those damn professors. I repeated the line because I liked it."

Although I place much importance on the interview as a research method, I also realize that it is not foolproof (nor is any other method for that matter), having as it does issues relating to interviewee bias, credibility, and memory veracity. However, getting a source on record before memory fades or death occurs is an important first step; appraising, debunking, amending, or otherwise altering the information of an interview can follow as other statements, data, and opinions are forthcoming. In *Asian Political Cartoons*, I have tried to account for some of these pitfalls by backing up the interview with other information gathered through observation, textual analysis, and secondary sources; and by cross-checking with other interviewees.

Usually, I loosely constructed the interviews around topics or questions that allowed interviewees leeway in how they answered and at what length. I made an effort not to influence interviewees by the manner in which I posed my questions. Interviews took place wherever interviewees suggested: their homes, offices, corporate headquarters, a park, my hotel, restaurants, or tea shops, as well as at festivals, conferences, universities, or museums where I was invited to speak.

Interviews were recorded manually with pen and legal pad to provide a more natural setting and allow candidness by the interviewees. After each interview, I rewrote the notes, making some points clearer and recapturing others that may not have gained my attention earlier.

Interviews were held in English (especially in India, Malaysia, the Philippines, and Singapore) and in the native languages of the interviewees. In some countries/territories (China, Japan, Nepal, South Korea, Taiwan, and Thailand), former PhD advisees under my supervision at Temple University provided interpretation; in other places, individuals who helped arrange interviews also acted as interpreters. In Myanmar, I hired a professional interpreter. My wife, Xu Ying, usually interpreted/translated in Chinese-speaking areas. In nearly every case, interpreters were either cartoonists or comic art scholars, and therefore knowledgeable about terms and conditions of the field. These individuals are identified in the acknowledgments.

My interviewing of cartoonists started in the mid-1980s, first in the Philippines and Malaysia, and accelerated in the summers of 1992 and 1993, when I made

research trips specifically to interview cartoonists, first in South Korea, Taiwan, Hong Kong, the Philippines, Indonesia, and Singapore, and the second time all over India, Sri Lanka, Bangladesh, Myanmar, Thailand, Malaysia, Vietnam, and China. Numerous other research trips were made to Asia (probably more than eighty between 1986 and 2019) to interview cartoonists. During the past decade (2009–2019) alone, I made about three dozen separate trips to Asia to interview cartoonists (many political) in twenty-one countries and territories: Bangladesh (2016), Cambodia (2010), China (at least yearly), Hong Kong (2012, 2018), India (2009), Indonesia (2013), Iran (2011, 2013), Japan (2019), South Korea (2010, 2018), Malaysia (2014, 2016), Mongolia (2018), Myanmar (2018), Nepal (2016), the Philippines (2009, 2012, 2017, 2018), Singapore (2011, 2016), Sri Lanka (2018), Taiwan (2019), Thailand (2014), Turkey (2011), the United Arab Emirates (2015), and Vietnam (2010, 2018). Of 209 interviews between 1986 and the end of 2019 that are cited in *Asian Political Cartoons*, 99 occurred between 2009 and 2019. Although I have interviewed political cartoonists multiple times in Turkey and on one occasion in the UAE, these conversations are omitted here because this book does not include those regions, as already explained. The above-listed interviews updated and supplemented information and views I had obtained earlier. At a number of interviews, I was accompanied by my wife, Xu Ying, who participated, especially in Chinese-speaking situations where she served as interpreter.

Interviewees were chosen in different ways, sometimes by a cartoonist friend or acquaintance who either set up the meetings through his or her contacts or provided me with contact information and let me organize the meeting. Some of these individuals were Park Jae-Dong in Korea; Zola Zu in Taiwan; Tomoko Sasaki, Toshiko Nishida, and Ronald Stewart in Japan; Mehedi Haque in Bangladesh; Ram Kumar Panday in Nepal; Nguyen Thanh Phong in Vietnam; Carolyn Wong and Lim Cheng Tju in Singapore; Warat Karuchit in Thailand; Iwan Gunawan and Toni Masdiono in Indonesia; and Dan Erdenebal in Mongolia. At other times, the choosing of interviewees was by the snowball effect, whereby a cartoonist led me to others who also suggested still others to be interviewed, and sometimes through my continuing or renewing acquaintance with cartoonists I had interviewed in the past through new contacts I found by research or at chance meetings during conferences and festivals.

By design and/or happenstance, the political cartoonists interviewed represented a cross section of the field—male and female, senior and junior, and very prominent and less known. They have worked for newspapers of different political persuasions, owned by conglomerates, government and/or military ministries or units, political parties, and local interests. Many of the artists have been the best known in their countries—such as Nazrul Islam, Kazi Abul Kasem, Rafiqun Nabi, Ahsan Habib, and Shishir Bhattacharjee in Bangladesh; Zhang Ding, Liao Bingxiong, Ding Cong, Hua Junwu, Te Wei, and Fang Cheng in China; Zunzi (Wong Kei-kwan) in Hong Kong; Abu Abraham, R. K. Laxman, Pran Kumar, and Sudhir Tailang in India; Pramono Pramoedjo, Priyanto Sunarto, G. M. Sudarta, and Dwi Koendoro in Indonesia; the Neyistani brothers (Mana and Touka) and Massoud Shojai Tabatabei in Iran; Yukiyoshi Tokoro, Yoshiro Kato, Sampei Satō, and Yukio Sugiura in Japan; Kim Song-Hwan, Park Jae-Dong, and Chong Un-Gyong in Korea; Zunar (Zulkifli Anwar Ulhaque) and Lat (Mohd. Nor Khalid) in Malaysia; Satso (Samandariin Tsogtbayar) in Mongolia; Aw Pi Kyeh and Win Aung in Myanmar; Ashok Man Singh, Mohan Shyam Maharjan, and Abin Shrestha in Nepal; Nonoy Marcelo, Roni Santiago, Larry Alcala, and Norman Isaac in the Philippines; Heng Kim Song and Deng Coy Miel in Singapore; W. R. Wijesoma, S. C. Opatha, Jiffry Yoonoos, and Winnie Hettigoda in Sri Lanka; Lo Ching-chung, Li Shan, and Ling Qun in Taiwan; and Arun Watcharasawat, Chuchart Mueningul, and Chai Rachawat in Thailand.

In nearly all chapters, the contemporary focus is on those political cartoonists I interviewed, most of whom are major cartoonists—those who edge toward national treasure status (e.g., Lat in Malaysia; Abu and Laxman in India), or those who make attacking the government their lifetime passion no matter the cost (e.g., Zunar in

Malaysia; Kim Song-Hwan in Korea; Jiffry Yoonoos in Sri Lanka), or those who best identify a large segment of the political cartooning community. The latter category is represented by many interviewees who cannot eke out an existence by cartooning alone and use cartooning more like a hobby.

I supplemented interviews with visits to studios and other workplaces, exhibitions, museums, and comics libraries. When available, I looked at primary materials such as newspaper clippings, artists' and other personal collections, sketchbooks, scrapbooks, and archival papers. I conducted on-location research in many libraries in the United States, Canada, Europe, and Asia, and kept current by referring to hundreds of books and periodicals and the internet. I made useful contacts and gathered information by participating in many conferences worldwide and by founding and chairing the Asian Research Center of Animation and Comic Art (ARCACA) at the Communication University of China, Beijing, in 2006 and the Asia-Pacific Animation and Comics Association at Guiyang, China, in 2008; by cofounding and cochairing the annual Asian Youth Animation and Comics Contest (AYACC) in Guiyang, China, for eleven years beginning in 2007; and by founding, publishing, and editing the *International Journal of Comic Art* twice yearly since 1999.

Two questions and three statements will be addressed in these pages:

1. Are there common threads throughout the history of Asian political cartooning, and if they exist, what are they?
2. What, if any, outside factors played roles in the development and nourishment of Asian political cartooning?
3. Most of Asia has had, at best, a halting history of political cartooning.
4. Political cartooning as traditionally understood is facing hard times and a bleak future.
5. Political cartoonists in Asia continue to keep their profession alive by meeting crippling setbacks with ingenious comebacks while seeking other means to make a living.

Common Themes

Based on the questions and arguments to be addressed, *Asian Political Cartoons* takes up common themes in the country/territory chapters. Broadly, they are history and development, demographics, professionalism, "freedom to cartoon," the economics of political cartooning, and alternative platforms. Obviously, the themes emphasized depend upon a country's political cartoon situation.

Detailing these themes more sharply, history traces visual political messages from ancient times, then follows through the colonial era when foreign influences helped start political cartooning with multiple reincarnations of the British *Punch* and American *Puck*; the independence campaigns of the mid-twentieth century and the political cartoons and cartoon periodicals that supported them; the times of war political cartooning; and the authoritarianism of most postindependence governments that wreaked havoc on political cartooning.

The demographics theme refers to the quantity of cartoons produced under different types of circumstances, their quality, frequency, format, and placement, and the professionalism encompassing country and regional associations, networking apparatuses, training programs, and recognition and award schemes.

The theme "freedom to cartoon" broaches topics related to the perpetuation of controls on Asian political cartooning by government regulations and restrictions, religious intolerance, public outcries, in-house policies about off-limits topics, and self-censorship; the punishments suffered by cartoonists for crossing the line; and the ways they cope and continue to function. The economics of political cartooning includes the journalism profession more broadly, including the financial standing of newspapers, the impacts of their ownership arrangements, the effects of distracting forces (e.g., internet platforms) on their survival, and the circumstances of the individual political cartoonist, including working conditions (staff or freelance, workload, payment method, and ability to survive solely on cartoon work).

Alternative means to keep political cartoons alive and political cartoonists active are the publication of humor/cartoon magazines, a phenomenon dating to the nineteenth century, and the more recent multiple uses of the internet as a political cartoon platform. The latter includes South Korean investigative graphic novels, some of which started online, websites used by Chinese dissident political cartoonists abroad, and Facebook postings by a Vietnamese political cartoonist to a select group of family and friends.

Limitations and Partial Solutions

What I have attempted to do with this work is to shed light on Asian political cartoons as gleaned primarily from my interactions with cartoonists throughout three regions of the continent and from many secondary sources. As far as I can determine, *Asian Political Cartoons* is the first book on the topic.

It would be unreasonable to expect all country chapters to be of the same length. First of all, the countries differ widely in how long they have had political cartoons and the emphasis they have given them. Mongolia is a case in point. Traditionally a nomadic people, Mongolians historically have moved about, taking only the bare essentials with them. They were not in the habit of preserving materials that could be used for research later. Second, in some instances, information is difficult to obtain because of denial of access to government documents and individuals, limitations on entry and/ or movement in tightly closed countries (North Korea) and those under warlike conditions (e.g., Sri Lanka and Myanmar in recent years), or cultural factors, such as some women cartoonists' hesitancy to meet with a foreign interviewer.

Having written about Asian cartoons and comics for more than thirty-five years and Asian mass media since 1965, it is inevitable that I would repeat some of the information in my earlier books and articles in *Asian Political Cartoons*. Asian gag cartoons, comic strips, and comic books grew out of satirical magazines and political cartoons, so some of the historical accounts in my earlier *Asian Comics* and *Comics Art in China* (with Xu Ying) are repeated here. However, I am confident that most of the information in *Asian Political Cartoons* is newly found, and what was written earlier has been heavily modified through organizational reshuffling and adding to and updating existing information.

To expand the range of coverage and include countries for which limited amounts of information are available, four capsular vignettes are included covering North Korea and Mongolia in East Asia, Brunei in Southeast Asia, and Iran in South Asia. The vignettes on Mongolia and Iran are based on interviews I conducted.

Notes

1. For additional definitions and purposes of political cartoons—mostly from the perspectives of famous US political cartoonists—see Colldeweih and Goldstein 1998; for global views, see Szabo and Lent 1994.

2. The other two regions are: Central Asia (Kazakhstan, Kyrgyzstan, Tajikistan, Turkmenistan, and Uzbekistan) and West Asia (Armenia, Azerbaijan, Bahrain, Cyprus, Georgia, Iraq, Israel, Jordan, Kuwait, Lebanon, Oman, Qatar, Saudi Arabia, Palestine, Syria, Turkey, the United Arab Emirates, and Yemen).

Bibliography

American Press Institute. 1998. *Drawing Fire: The State of Political Cartooning.* Reston, VA: American Press Institute.

Colldeweih, Jack, and Kalman Goldstein, eds. 1998. *Graphic Opinions: Editorial Cartoonists and Their Art.* Bowling Green, OH: Bowling Green State University Popular Press.

Lent, John A. 2015. *Asian Comics.* Jackson: University Press of Mississippi.

Lent, John A. 2017. "Global Infringements on the 'Right to Cartoon': A Research Guide." *International Journal of Comic Art* 19, no. 1 (Spring–Summer): 3–70.

Lent, John A., and Xu Ying. 2017. *Comics Art in China.* Jackson: University Press of Mississippi.

Nelson, Roy Paul. 1975. *Cartooning.* Chicago: Henry Regnery.

Szabo, Joe, and John A. Lent. 1994. *Cartoonometer: Taking the Pulse of the World's Cartoonists.* North Wales, PA: WittyWorld Books.

East Asia

Historical Roots

Visual humor through caricature, satire and parody, and wit and playfulness has a long, rich history in dynastic China, represented in *nianhua*, popular New Year's pictures; the erotic Spring Palace paintings; grotesque figures adorning burial paraphernalia; and the illustrated "poetry of complaint" and "sarcastic quatrain" (Lent 2015, 9–25).

Modern cartooning—usually meaning coming from the West—entered China at the juncture of the nineteenth and twentieth centuries through cartoon/humor magazines, pictorial magazines, newspapers, and *lianhuanhua* (palm-size narrative picture books). Major catalysts for this transformation were the growing dissatisfaction with the Qing Dynasty[1] and increased contact with the outside world.

Four cartoon/humor periodicals are known to have been published in China during its formative period of comic art: the *China Punch* (1867–1868, 1872–1876), *Puck, or the Shanghai Charivari* (1871–1872), *Raoshe Zazhi* (the Rattle, 1896–1903), and *Shanghai Puck* (aka *Bochen Huaji Huabao*, or Bochen's Comic Pictorial, 1918–1919). These magazines had a few things in common; they were named after and emulated the British *Punch* or American *Puck*, and had short lives and small circulations. The *China Punch* was published in Hong Kong; the others in Shanghai (see chapter 2 on Hong Kong for more on the *China Punch*).

The pictorial magazines resulted from advances in printing that came to China in the last quarter of the nineteenth century. Although these magazines carried many cartoons, they differed from cartoon/humor magazines in layout, visual composition, and content (Rea 2013, 419). A British businessman, Ernest Major, pioneered the production of these illustrated magazines with *Yinghuan Huabao* (Yinghuan Pictorial, 1877–1880). By the early 1900s, many such magazines appeared, loaded with cartoon-like political drawings attacking the Qing Dynasty. Chinese cartoonists also took advantage of the increasing number of newspapers in the late Qing Dynasty. The growth of dailies was phenomenal: from

Chapter 1

China

1.1. "The Old Chinese Official and New Morals," H. K. Chun. *Shanghai Puck*, December 1918.

15

1.2. *The Story of Three Kingdoms*, illustrated by Chen Danxu. An early *lianhuanhua* published by Shanghai World Bookstore, 1925.

19 in 1895 to 500 in 1912 to 628 by 1926 (Hung 1994, 40). A large proportion of them were tabloids, and judging from some of their titles, were humor newspapers, for instance *Laughter Stage*, *Addled-Brained*, *Xiasan Huasi* (Shooting the Breeze), *Nonsense*, and two different versions of *Chaplin* (Rea 2015, 10).

Because of nomenclature and cultural factors, it is difficult to pinpoint the earliest political cartoon in China. Generally thought to be the first Western-style political cartoon drawn by a Chinese artist was "The Situation in the Far East," created on July 19, 1899, by revolutionary organizer Xie Zantai (see more details in chapter 2). The cartoon depicted encroaching dangers to China using animals to represent threatening countries: frog, France; eagle, United States; bear, Russia; dog, Britain.

Lianhuanhua, as with comic books, newspaper strips, posters, and the like, are not political cartoons per se, but they can and do function in similar ways by taking sides on issues, sparking debate and discussion, and dealing with current events. *Lianhuanhua* have been compared to US-style comic books; however, they differ considerably in size, format, message, and purpose. They are palm-size (five inches long, three and a half inches wide, and a quarter of an inch thick), contain one image per page, carry a paragraph description usually at the page's bottom, and are used to dispense messages to promote government political and social campaigns and educate and mobilize people.

Justifications for *lianhuanhua* to be classified as comic art are that they combine the verbal and visual and converge *gushihua* (storytelling) with *lianxuhua* (sequential pictures) to tell stories. The beginnings of *lianhuanhua* are up for debate, but they are usually identified with the early twentieth century.

At various times in the twentieth century, *lianhuanhua* were used to propagandize causes and campaigns, thus serving as government mouthpieces and functioning much like political cartoons. They were especially popular at the beginning of communist rule; between 1949 and 1963, 12,700 different titles with a combined circulation of 560 million appeared. Their themes emphasized "praising the Party, Chairman Mao, socialism, heroes of the new era, workers, peasants, and soldiers" (Ma Ke 1963). Their numbers decreased at the beginning of the Cultural Revolution in 1966 when *lianhuanhua* of the previous Seventeen-Year Period (1949–1966) were criticized and burned as "poison weeds." A revival occurred in 1971, spurred on by Premier Zhou Enlai and reaching peaks in 1983, when 2,100 titles appeared, surmounting 630 million copies, or about one-fourth of China's total book production that year (Jie 2004, 33; also Pan 2008, 706), and in 1984, when total circulation rose to 800 million.

The turbulent and troubling nature of the 1920s and 1930s was ideal for political cartoonists, whose vitriol spewed out toward a multitude of issues—territorial and political fragmentation, coups and purges, advancing fascism at home and abroad, and economic depression. They recognized that the May Fourth Movement of 1919 pushed China to look at a number of factors in a new light—for instance, the country's international status, its national identity and consciousness, and its cultural traditions. This period is called "*manhua*'s golden age" for its many contributions to Chinese comic art. Among them were the modernization of humor, art, and language; the commercialization of culture and the media; the positioning of humor as a "wellspring of national identity" (Kushner 2013, 52); and the orientation of art and cartoons toward the peasantry. Specific to comic art, the period yielded China's first newspaper comic

1.3. The second issue of *Modern Sketch*, cover by Ye Qianyu.

strips by Ye Qianyu, Zhang Leping, and Huang Yao; their main characters—Wangxiansheng (Mr. Wong), Sanmao, and Niubizi, respectively—did not shy from commenting on contemporary issues. Also, "firsts" to emanate from this era were China's first female cartoonists, Yu Feng and Liang Baibo, in the early 1930s; and the earliest attempts at professionalism with the first cartoon associations (the Shanghai Sketch Society in 1927, Manhua Yanjiuhui [the Cartoon Study Association], Cartoon Service, and Zhonghua Quanguo Manhua Zuojia Xiehui [the All-China Cartoon Association of Writers and Artists]), exhibitions, and training schemes.

Not to be forgotten as products of the 1930s were about twenty cartoon and humor magazines heavily loaded with political cartoons, and the all-important second generation of political cartoonists, a number of whom survived into contemporary times.

The progenitor of the magazines was *Shanghai Manhua* (Shanghai Sketch), published from 1928 to 1930 by Zhang Guangyu. However, the "centerpiece of China's

golden age of cartoon art" (Crespi 2011) was *Shidai Manhua* (Modern Sketch), started in 1934. The monthly featured the art of more than one hundred cartoonists, many destined to become the masters of Chinese cartooning, and was credited with capturing the "crises and contradictions that have defined China's twentieth century as a quintessentially modern era" (Crespi 2011). In its later life, *Shidai Manhua* ran otherwise censored information, which led to its suspension and its editor Lu Shaofei's detainment.

The cartoon/humor magazines launched the careers of most of China's second-generation master political cartoonists, including Ding Cong, Liao Bingxiong, Hua Junwu, Zhang Ding, Te Wei, Chen Huiling, and Mai Fei. What made these early cartoonists distinct were their political consciousness, sense of realism, anti-imperialist and antifeudalist inclinations, sympathy for the underdog, and utter disregard for classical Chinese and traditional Western art (J. Chen 1938, 308). Even the so-called father of Chinese cartooning, Feng Zikai, who saw cartoons as pure art and not propaganda and was known for idyllic drawings of children and "everyday life experiences of his hometown" (Feng 2002), also moved to social comment themes during the 1930s' politicization of art.

As Japan moved aggressively into China in 1931, 1932, and 1937, Chinese cartoonists became engaged in what they called "cartoon warfare." The pen combatants included older generation artists such as Ding Song (father of Ding Cong), Wan Laiming, and Feng Zikai, as well as young cartoonists such as Zhang Ding and Liao Bingxiong as teenagers, Te Wei, and Zhang E. Some of their depictions were shocking: a mother's head blown off by a bomb while nursing her infant, Japanese soldiers using Chinese for bayonet training, feeding Chinese to dogs, or having Chinese baby bayonet competitions.

By 1938, Chinese cartooning had changed significantly, from symbolic, indirect, government-abiding approaches to blunt and bold styles and content that was more realistic, politically charged, and appealing to the masses. Known as Xinmeishu Yundong (the New Art Movement), this style dominated the wartime years.

17

1.4. Political cartoonist Ding Cong, Beijing, December 20, 2002. Photo by Xu Ying. Courtesy of Ding Cong and his wife, Shen Jun.

1.5. Political cartoonist Liao Bingxiong with a version of his "Self-Ridicule," which he drew at the end of the Cultural Revolution. He was freed from government detainment but still afraid to move. Courtesy of Liao Ling-er, daughter of Liao Bingxiong.

1.6. Political cartoonist Hua Junwu in his Beijing home, May 31, 2006. Photo by Xu Ying. Courtesy of Hua Junwu.

1.7. "Japanese Enemy Killed Our Children Like That," Zhang Leping, 1938. Permission of Zhang Weijun.

The tasks of wartime cartoonists were daunting: they had to bring the cartoon to the people, not just to art galleries; make it reflect life; use it as a propaganda vehicle; and keep it both Chinese and genuinely artistic (Lent and Xu 2017). Various techniques, styles, and venues were used to implement cartoon warfare, such as *baodaohua* (reportage picture), an easily printed drawing using simple brushstrokes to describe real events; the use of simple, direct-language storytelling techniques and easy-to-understand titles and proverbs (Liao 2002); and producing cartoons in different forms and placing them in every conceivable space. Some of the ideas about cartoons' use were codified by Mao Zedong at the 1942 Yan'an Forum on Literature and the Arts, where he objected to the uncritical importation of foreign images and rejected art for art's sake. Mao implored artists to use the language of the masses, serve politics by following the Chinese Communist Party (CCP), and show positive aspects of peasant life.

Many of these tactics of "cartoon warfare" were taken up by the National Salvation Cartoon Propaganda Corps, a group initially of eight cartoonists led by Ye Qianyu whose mission was to persuade civilians to resist and to raise Chinese soldiers' morale at the front.[2] They used many cartoon forms, techniques, and venues in doing this: publishing their own magazines and journals, holding more than one hundred exhibitions, and producing thousands of cartoons displayed on billboards, banners, murals, trucks, and large posters (Lent and Xu 2017, 53, fig. 3.5). The corps started in Shanghai in 1937 and moved frequently, daringly staying ahead of Japanese troops, all the time gathering more cartoonists.

Other cartoonists opposed the Japanese, working for various newspapers and magazines (including about a dozen cartoon magazines, plus literary magazines), serving with military units, or acting independently. Military units (both Guomindang and Communist) had their own periodicals that contained cartoons, as well as their own teams of cartoonists drawing propaganda cartoons under very difficult conditions. Some cartoonists moved about with the Drama Propaganda Corps (a different group staging plays that warned about the Japanese presence), drawing anti-Japanese posters displayed at troupe performances. Propaganda leaflets dropped from aircraft imploring Japanese soldiers to surrender were also a part of "cartoon warfare" (Lent 2014).

In the post–World War II era, China experienced a shift from external to internal affairs, from patriotic and anti-imperialist to political and antigovernment (Hung 1994, 125). Cartoonists did not lack subject matter but were short on materials and even outlets when the Guomindang government closed all publications with Communist leanings. Some cartoonists resorted to exhibitions as outlets. The Guomindang had strong censorship laws, forcing antigovernment cartoonists to use subtlety or go underground.

When Mao Zedong and the CCP took control in 1949, the official line on art and cartooning was spelled out, its major contention being that *guohua* (traditional Chinese painting) had to be reformed to be realistic and socially useful with tinges of Western influences. With

1.8. Sketch of a Chinese plane dropping propaganda leaflets on Japan.

theory in place, the Communists concentrated on media organizations, collectivization, and specialization. The government implemented state ownership, and with it came the power to organize media by structure and function and determine the topics they covered. Much of the content of postliberation propaganda art (including cartoons) demonized the enemies of the new regime.

Political cartoons, known as *shishi manhua* (current affairs cartoons), and *lianhuanhua* were the main vehicles for reflecting government policies in the 1950s. The party line of anti-Americanism was followed by cartoonists during the Korean War; however, on the whole, what was expected of cartoonists and artists during the Seventeen-Year Period (1949–1966) either fluctuated, or was not understood, or was not heeded, the latter usually cited as a drummed-up charge against cartoonists. The various Mao campaigns of this time (opposing the writer Hu Feng, the Hundred Flowers Campaign, the Anti-Rightist Campaign, and the Great Leap Forward) resulted

1.9. An eight-page, accordion-folded flyer espousing the Great Leap Forward, late 1950s.

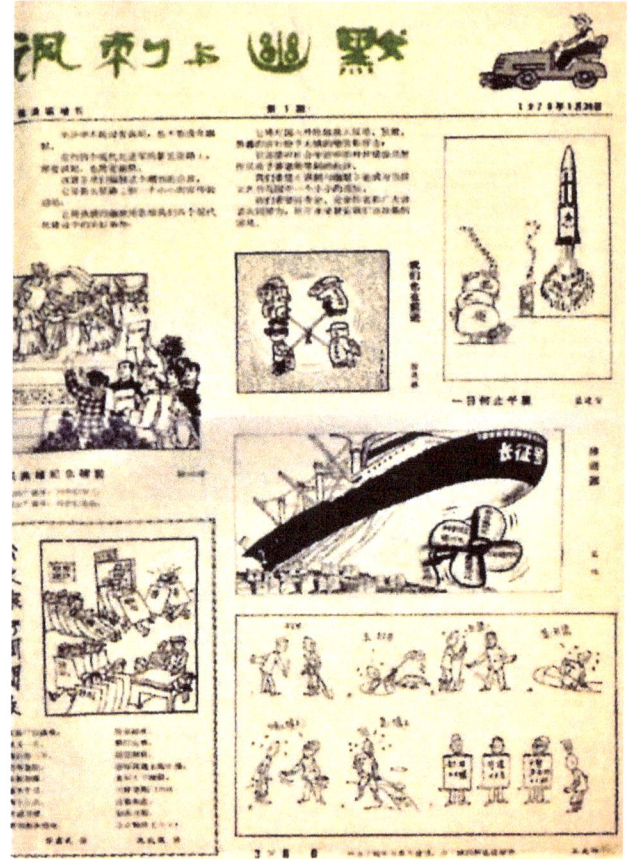

1.10. *Fengci Yu Youmo* (Satire and Humor), inaugural issue, January 20, 1979.

in many arrests, imprisonments, and banishments to the countryside for cartoonists and other artists and intellectuals. On the tail end of these campaigns came the even more restricting Cultural Revolution (1966–1976), which unleashed monstrous forces that negatively altered Chinese society and resulted in the deaths of millions of Chinese, the arrest, imprisonment, and banishment of many more, and the wiping out of teaching, cultural artifacts, and almost all cultural production. Many cartoonists were humiliated, arrested, imprisoned, and sent to the countryside to work manually with farmers. Cartoonists Ding Cong, Liao Bingxiong, and Wang Fuyang were forced to give up drawing and their lifestyles, each for at least twenty years; others were given shorter terms (Lent and Xu 2005). Such harsh treatment incapacitated the victims afterward; both Liao Bingxiong (2002) and Jiang Yousheng (2002) said that they hesitated going back to their normal lives and careers when the Cultural Revolution ended, for fear it would start up again or that its ending was a trick or hoax.

The comic art community came out of its shell, recovering (actually progressing) in the first half-dozen post–Cultural Revolution years, as it rallied against political interference, launched new periodicals such as *Satire and Humor* in 1979, reinstated pre–Cultural Revolution comic art leaders such as Hua Junwu, Ye Qianyu, and Cai Ruohong, drew and exhibited many cartoons vilifying the Gang of Four and the Cultural Revolution, and attacked impediments to modernity. Ralph Crozier

(1981) singles out 1979 as an important year for political cartoons in the drive toward liberalization, stating that political cartoons took on an unprecedented bite and much topical relevance, enlarged their scope of subject matter, received more space and prominence in newspapers, and drew unflattering portraits of the party leadership. Cartoons showed administrators as obstacles to modernization, revealing their traits of corruption, inefficiency, favoritism, and privilege (Bradley 1986). Julia F. Andrews (1994, 390) also chooses 1979 as significant in the transformation of Chinese art (including cartoons) because of these trends: (1) an art deco style for ornamental purposes; (2) a "new sympathetic realism identified with 'Scar' literature which lamented the personal tragedies of the Cultural Revolution"; and (3) the "politically engaged modernism of the Stars," an exhibition of unofficial dissident art, which she calls "the most notorious artistic event" of 1979, leading to many calls for "artistic democracy" (Andrews 1994, 396).

1.11. "Manhuajie Chongyang Denggaotu" (Cartoon World on a Hill in September), Wang Zimei. *Shanghai Manhua*, no. 6, October 10, 1936. Permission of Li Weiwei, daughter of Wang Zimei. A composite of China's top cartoonists in the 1930s. Back row: Zhang Yingchao, Lu Zhixiang, Ding Cong, and Cai Ruohong; middle row: Wang Zimei, Lu Fu, Zhu Jinlou, Te Wei, Huang Yao, and Zhang Leping; front row: Wang Dunqing, Liang Baibo, Ye Qianyu, and Huang Miaozi.

The changing of policies and practices in the Chinese art world as well as, to some degree, the developing infrastructure and the opening of the country to a market economy, had profound impacts on cartooning beginning in the 1980s. New professional and other cartoon-centric groups appeared, such as the Cartoon Art Committee of China's Artists' Association in 1986; the China Journalistic Caricature Society in 1987, dealing with news cartoons; and worker-specific groups such as the Qiu County Farmers Frog Cartoon Group, started in 1983, the Beijing Workers Cartoon Group (and its imitators), and the Military Camp Humor Cartoon Group in 1986. These groups have encouraged cartooning among their members through periodicals, competitions, training, and exhibitions (Li 2009; Y. Chen 2009; He 2009; Zheng 2002, 2005).

Besides *Satire and Humor*, other cartoon magazines came out of this period. By the late 1980s, there were six other cartoon magazines, about ten cartoon newspapers, and at least twenty regular cartoon columns in newspapers and magazines. Other important changes occurred in comic art education and other areas of professionalism, such as the exposure of Chinese cartoonists to the outside world, the increasing role of women, and the emergence of a new breed of outward-looking, sometimes entrepreneurial cartoonists. These phenomena did not occur overnight, and most came about in the first decade of the new millennium, when the Chinese government pumped huge amounts of money into comics and animation with the aim of making them valuable export products.

The Government and Cartooning

Given the schema-relegating roles a government can play relative to mass media—namely, facilitator, regulator, restrictor, and user—it is apparent that the Chinese government applied the first of these during the 2010s. Recognizing, as South Korea had in 1994, that comic art was an important cultural product for exportation, the Chinese government worked strenuously to upgrade and expand these soft industries. There were other reasons for developing this sector at the national level: (1) to offset the strong foreign influences brought in by manga, anime, and American animation, and (2) to help fill the programming schedules of the rapidly developing new television stations.

As for the government acting as regulator and censor of cartoons and comics, agencies and laws were in place that seemed to function well until the introduction of the internet. In 2013, two different agencies monitoring broadcast and print media merged to form the State Administration of Press, Publication, Radio, Film, and Television (SAPPRFT), to resolve the lack of a clear demarcation of roles. Outright censorship of cartoons occurred, but probably not as often as suspected, because it was not necessary for one or more of these reasons: (1) cartoonists know the precise boundary of what is and is not permissible and do not cross it; (2) alternately, the dividing line is too fuzzy, and cartoonists dare not take the chance of stepping over it; (3) editors specify the contents of cartoons, and when there is deviation from these specifications, they either ask the artists to alter the cartoons or they do not use them; (4) cartoonists follow the traditional custom that elders and leaders deserve respect and should not be held up to ridicule, and (5) China's long history of censorship and punitive repercussions keep editors and cartoonists on their toes (Lent and Xu 2017, 142). Actually, these five points apply to the situation for cartoonists in much of Asia.

Straightforward as all of this seems, occasionally Chinese leaders feel it necessary to point out shortcomings and to reinforce or reframe what is expected.

President Xi Jinping did this in 2014 while addressing a forum on art and literature. His speech struck out at vulgar popular culture, the fickleness of culture, and the commercialization of art at the expense of social value. Xi also called for a conservative and patriotic view of art, greater control of new art forms, and the sanitizing of foreign art forms (Canaves 2015, abstracted in Lent and Xu 2017, 137–38). Although Xi's points were well chosen and well expressed, that he felt he had to make them at a major meeting in the early part of his presidency seemed to suggest that he was about to tighten control over the arts and literature and mete out punitive actions against those who dared to dissent.

Cartooning under Xi Jinping

In the second half of the 2010s, President Xi's rule was greatly strengthened, first in October 2016, when the Communist Party awarded him the symbolically important title of "core leader," then in February 2018, when Xi abolished term limits for his chairmanship, clearing the way for him to lead China for life.

Fears mounted that this augmented power centered in one individual would boost China's already growing authoritarianism. There had been a few internationally recognized instances of cartoon suppression under Xi's leadership; of course, they did not occur in the mainstream print media, tightly controlled by the state and party, but on alternative platforms.

Two cartoonists who gained international attention for raising the ire of authorities were Rebel Pepper (Wang Liming) and Badiucao (real name not revealed). Both posted their cartoons on the internet.

By 2012, Rebel Pepper's cartoons had nearly a million followers on China's large microblog service Sina Weibo. His account had been erased 180 times, and each time he opened a new account under a different name, until his profile was deleted and his lucrative online store was closed (Langfitt 2012). While still in China, Rebel Pepper spent a night in detention and likely would have faced a long prison term for subversion had he not fled to Japan

1.12. "Cutting Off Your Tongues for Your Own Good," Rebel Pepper (Wang Liming). A comment on a heavy-handed Communist Party policy to expand the Chinese language at the expense of native languages in ethnic minority areas.

in 2014. He eked out a bare existence in Tokyo drawing cartoons for Japanese newspapers, and in 2017 he moved to the United States (Fish 2018).

Badiucao has lived in Australia since 2009; he has distributed scathing political cartoons on Weibo targeting China and continues his attacks, but they are no longer available in China. His Weibo account has been shut down thirty-seven times, and as this platform has become extremely insecure, he moved to Twitter (Carter 2016).[3] Aware of the severe punishments other Chinese dissidents had faced, Badiucao concealed his identity by wearing a ski mask, even though he no longer lived in China. He unmasked in 2019, after receiving death threats and learning that his family members in China had been detained; obviously, Beijing officials knew his identity (Gunia 2019). For a few years in Melbourne, he was a preschool teacher who, unbeknown to anyone, moonlighted as a dissident cartoonist. In his words: "During the day, I worked, changed nappies and sang lullabies to the kids; at night, I became a fighter in my little room, going through all the news of the day to find the topic to address with my pen" (Qin 2019). Badiucao was granted the 2019 Robert Russell Courage in Cartooning Award, given by Cartoonists Rights Network International, for courage in editorial cartooning in 2019.

Political cartoonist Jiang Yefei was not as fortunate as Rebel Pepper and Badiucao in fleeing China, although

he made a valiant attempt. In 2008, after being detained twice for criticizing the government's handling of the Sichuan earthquake, he fled to Thailand. Jiang was granted refugee status by the United Nations and was to be resettled in Canada. While in Thailand, Jiang criticized China's human rights record and other policies on the overseas Chinese-language news website Boxun as well as on his Facebook and Google+ pages. In 2015, as his cartoons grew in popularity, Jiang received anonymous phone calls demanding that he stop drawing Chinese authorities. In October of that year, he was arrested by the Thai police for breaking immigration laws and deported to China, despite having been approved for asylum in Canada. Jiang was detained incommunicado for nearly three years, and in July 2018 he was secretly tried and sentenced to six and a half years imprisonment for "inciting subversion of state power" and "illegally crossing a national border" (CPJ n.d.). A Reporters without Borders official blasted President Xi for showing an "unprecedented level of intolerance against independent voices" and Thai prime minister Prayuth Chan-ocha for allowing the extradition, knowing what fate held for Jiang (CPJ n.d.).

The fourth recent case of suppression involved a different medium—comic books—and a novel, but weird, offense, *jingzhen ribenren* (*jingri*, or "spiritually Japanese"). Twenty-two-year-old Zhang Dongning was held under criminal detention in 2019 for drawing more than three hundred comic books based on Chinese current events, depicting Chinese people—often those tied to the Communist Party—with heads of pigs. Her detention came on the heels of a nationwide crackdown on a recent movement in China celebrating Japanese culture and right-wing militarism, some adherents even defending Japan's invasion of China in the 1930s. The police accused Zhang of shaming China, distorting historical facts, trampling national dignity, and hurting the feelings of the Chinese people (J. Wong 2019). Her Weibo account was also deactivated by the police.

As if making "insulting China" or being "spiritually Japanese" criminal acts were not far-fetched enough, the authorities went after a far softer target, A. A. Milne's

Winnie-the-Pooh. The cuddly bear was censored from the internet in 2017 when the Chinese Communist Party, increasingly sensitive of any mockery of the very powerful Xi Jinping, bristled at online images suggesting a resemblance between Xi and Pooh. Winnie-the-Pooh had endured China's censorship on other occasions: in 2013, when images of Pooh and another Milne character, Tigger, appeared alongside Xi and US president Barack Obama after their meeting, and in 2014, when Xi and Japan's prime minister Abe Shinzo met (Hernández 2017).

Authorities were drumming up an even tougher stand against free expression in 2019, as state media reported on the issuance of directives asking local publicity (propaganda) offices to "stand on political high ground to modulate every television episode, even documentary, and every cartoon," and be watchful "every second" for anything that deviated from the "official main theme" or "sensitive topics" (Fu 2019). A cult of personality seems to be building around Xi as well as a drive toward revisioning recent Chinese history, sweeping events and eras such as the Tiananmen Square protests and the Cultural Revolution into the dustbin.

Bits of criticism of communism, censorship, and authoritarianism can be found in underground comics very deeply embedded in China's clandestine subculture. As an example of one artist's stealth, Wen Ling kept all of his comics on his zip drive, plugging the drive into his computer and printing out copies only on demand. His concern was that if his computer were confiscated, he would be arrested. Wen Ling's comics have been described as "pretty puerile, pretty sexual, pretty anticommunist" (Abrams 2019). Underground artist Yan Cong published the self-referential *Narrative Addiction*, much of which deals with repression in China and his interactions with the police and his professors. Underground comics have been "published" in one form or another for years, distributed in the 2000s on online graffiti boards and chat rooms with no intent to print or sell them, and then in *Special Comix*, a sporadically published anthology that appeared six times between 2005 and 2015. *Special Comix* could not sustain itself because of funding and publication restrictions (Yin 2018).

Concluding Remarks

The Chinese cartoonists I am acquainted with call themselves news cartoonists, not political or editorial cartoonists, and that is a more accurate and honest appellation, for they do not criticize and they avoid political spats; usually, they do no commentary at all. They are basically illustrators of some carefully selected news events.

Notes

1. Pinyin romanization is used in this chapter, because that is the system prevalent in China.

2. Of the original members of the corps, I interviewed five, either alone or with Xu Ying. They were: Te Wei, Zhang Ding, Liao Bingxiong, Han Shangyi, and Mai Fei. Their accounts are included in Lent and Xu 2017, 51–56; and Lent and Xu 2008.

3. Badiucao has claimed that Twitter has millions of viewers in China. He sees those viewers as "seeds to spread the message" (Roney 2017).

Bibliography

Abrams, Loney. 2019. "China's Underground Comic Scene Debuts at the Outsider Art Fair: Here the Curator Describes His Journey into the Clandestine Subculture." Artspace, January 17. https://www.artspace.com/magazine/interviews_features/qa/chinas-underground-comic-scene-debuts-at-the-outsider-art-fair-here-the-curator-describes-his-55892.

Andrews, Julia F. 1994. *Painters and Politics in the People's Republic of China, 1949–1979.* Berkeley: University of California Press.

Bradley, Jeff. 1986. "Chinese Political Cartoons Hit Corruption, Ineptitude." *Los Angeles Times*, July 6.

Canaves, Sky. 2015. "Xi Jinping on What's Wrong with Contemporary Chinese Culture." *China Film Insider*, October 26. https://www.chinafile.com/reporting-opinion/culture/xi-jinping-whats-wrong-contemporary-chinese-culture.

Carter, Jeremy Story. 2016. "Political Cartoonist Badiucao Challenges China's Great Firewall." Australian Broadcasting Corporation, February 25. https://www.abc.net.au/radionational/programs/drive/china-cartoonist-badiucao-pushes-political-envelope-past/7193556.

Chen, Jack. 1938. "China's Militant Cartoons." *Asia*, May, 308–12.

Chen, Yuli. 2009. Interviews with John A. Lent and Xu Ying, Qiuxian, China, May 28–30.

Committee to Protect Journalists (CPJ). n.d. "Jiang Yefei." https://cpj.org/data/people/jiang-yefei/.

Crespi, John A. 2011. "China's *Modern Sketch*, 1: The Golden Era of Cartoon Art, 1934–1937." Massachusetts Institute of Technology, Visualizing Cultures. https://visualizingcultures.mit.edu/modern_sketch/ms_essay_03.pdf.

Crozier, Ralph. 1981. "The Thorny Flowers of 1979: Political Cartoons and Liberalization in China." *Bulletin of Concerned Asian Scholars* 13, no. 3: 50–59.

Feng, Yiyin. 2002. Interview with John A. Lent and Xu Ying, Shanghai, January 10.

Fish, Isaac Stone. 2018. "Chinese Political Cartoonist Rebel Pepper Finds More Artistic Freedom in the US." *The World*, PRX, July 2. https://theworld.org/stories/2018-07-02/chinese-political-cartoonist-rebel-pepper-finds-more-artistic-freedom-us.

Fu, Eva. 2019. "China Jails 22-Year-Old for Drawing 'Insulting' Cartoons." *Epoch Times*, August 1. https://www.theepochtimes.com/china-jails-22-year-old-for-insulting-cartoons_3026474.html.

Gunia, Amy. 2019. "This Is a Fight! Meet Badiucao, the Dissident Cartoonist Taking On the Chinese Government." *Time*, August 27. https://time.com/5634635/badiucao-chinese-dissident-artist.

He, Wei. 2009. Interview with John A. Lent and Xu Ying, Beijing, May 24.

Hernández, Javier C. 2017. "Winnie-the-Pooh, Used to Mock President, Stirs Chinese Censors." *New York Times*, July 18, A7.

Hung, Chang-Tai. 1994. "The Fuming Image: Cartoons and Public Opinion in Late Republican China, 1945–1949." *Comparative Studies in Society and History* 36, no. 1 (January): 122–45.

Jiang, Yousheng. 2002. Interview with John A. Lent and Xu Ying, Beijing, December 17.

Jie, Ziping. 2004. *Lianhuanhua: Faded Memory*. Taiyuan, China: Shanxi Ancient Book Press.

Kushner, Barak. 2013. "Unwarranted Attention: The Image of Japan in Twentieth-Century Chinese Humour." In *Humour in Chinese Life and Culture: Resistance and Control in Modern Times*, edited by Jessica Milner Davis and Jocelyn Chey, 47–82. Hong Kong: Hong Kong University Press.

Langfitt, Frank. 2012. "Provocative Chinese Cartoonists Find an Outlet Online." *All Things Considered*, National Public Radio, March 16.

Lent, John A. 2014. "Allied, Japanese, and Chinese Propaganda Cartoon Leaflets during World War II." *International Journal of Comic Art* 16, no. 1 (Spring): 258–301.

Lent, John A. 2015. *Asian Comics*. Jackson: University Press of Mississippi.

Lent, John A., and Xu Ying. 2005. "Cartooning and China's Cultural Revolution." *International Journal of Comic Art* 7, no. 2 (Fall): 89–125.

Lent, John A., and Xu Ying. 2008. "Cartooning and Wartime China. Part 1: 1931–1945." *International Journal of Comic Art* 10, no. 1 (Spring): 76–139.

Lent, John A., and Xu Ying. 2017. *Comics Art in China*. Jackson: University Press of Mississippi.

Li, Qingai. 2009. Interviews with John A. Lent and Xu Ying, Qiuxian, China, May 28–30.

Liao, Bingxiong. 2002. Interviews with John A. Lent and Xu Ying, Guangzhou, January 4–5.

Ma Ke. 1963. "Cheers to the New Achievement of the Serial Picture." *People's Daily* (Beijing), December 29.

Pan, Lingling. 2008. "Post-Liberation History of China's *Lianhuanhua* (Pictorial Books)." *International Journal of Comic Art* 10, no. 2 (Fall): 694–717.

Qin, Amy. 2019. "Quietly Prodding China's Political Conscience with Cartoons." *New York Times*, June 5, A8.

Rea, Christopher. 2013. "'He'll Roast All Subjects That May Need the Roasting': Puck and Mr. Punch in Nineteenth-Century China." In *Asian Punches: A Transcultural Affair*, edited by Hans Harder and Barbara Mittler, 389–422. Heidelberg: Springer-Verlag.

Rea, Christopher. 2015. *The Age of Irreverence: A New History of Laughter in China*. Oakland: University of California Press.

Reporters without Borders. 2018. "Chinese Political Cartoonist Sentenced to 6 and a Half Years in Prison." July 25. https://www.refworld.org/docid/5bc6eee0a.html.

Roney, Tyler. 2017. "Badiucao: Challenging China with Political Cartoons." *The Diplomat*, March 2. https://thediplomat.com/2017/03/badiucao-challenging-china-with-political-cartoons/.

Wong, Lok-to. 2019. "'Spiritually Japanese' Artist Held in China's Anhui over Pig-Head Cartoons." Radio Free Asia, August 1. https://www.rfa.org/english/news/china/cartoons-08012019135537.html.

Yi Guo, James. 2015. "Conceptualizing the Freedom of the Press in Chinese Political Cartoons." *International Journal of Comic Art* 17, no. 2 (Fall–Winter): 217–37.

Yin, Yijun. 2018. "The Underground Artists Giving China Comic Relief." Sixth Tone, June 5. https://www.sixthtone.com/news/1002404/the-underground-artists-giving-china-comic-relief.

Zheng, Huagai. 2002. Interview with John A. Lent and Xu Ying, Beijing, December 16.

Zheng, Huagai. 2005. Interview with John A. Lent and Xu Ying, Beijing, June 12.

爐港督談他的富貴爐

天涯淪落兩叔侄

A cartoon drawn by famed Hong Kong political cartoonist Zunzi (Wong Kei-kwan) in 1997, at the time
of the colony's handover from Great Britain to China,
lends itself to this introduction. A duck representing
Hong Kong is forced from one cage (Great Britain) to
another (China), just as it had been chased in the reverse
direction over a century before. Zunzi's portrayal is
of a Hong Kong that was an in-between state lacking
self-autonomy.

This image is apropos when considering anything historical about the city; one must first separate the Hong
Kong portion from China's history. The same goes for
the history of political cartooning.

Chapter 2

Hong Kong

History: The British Period

As elsewhere in Asia (e.g., India, Japan), visual political
humor entered Hong Kong through a satirical magazine,
in this case introduced by a British journalist, W. N.
Middleton, and modeled after London's *Punch*. The
China Punch (1867–1868, 1872–1876) was China's first
cartoon magazine and the only one located in Hong
Kong. It was a subsidiary of the *China Mail* (founded in
1845), which the *China Punch* labeled "the China Snail."
Historian Christopher Rea (2013, 398) writes that the
China Punch took an interest in the "surreal official proceedings of the colonial government . . . , the fantasies
that the Oriental dream world engenders among Europeans . . . , [the] topsy-turvy world [where] government
officials can do no right, gender roles are suspended (if
not inverted) and Europeans are at the mercy of their
supposed inferiors, the Chinese." He describes the magazine's contents as "caricatures of colonial government
officials and their Chinese counterparts, roundups of
fictitious social events, parodic telegrams and letters to
the editor, witty rhymes on financial, political, commercial and social topics, and copious one-off puns" (Rea
2013, 399). The *China Punch* had a short life and a small
circulation, mostly among the Anglophone community.

Hong Kong was home to the first Western-style
political cartoon drawn by a Chinese artist. However,

2.1. The *China Punch* was Hong Kong's (and China's) first humor magazine.

27

the artist, Xie Zantai (Tse Tsan-tai), was born and raised in Australia, and the cartoon, "The Situation in the Far East" (*shiguk tu*), was printed in Japan in 1899 and published in a Shanghai publication in 1903. A revolutionary collaborator with Sun Yat-sen, Xie drew the cartoon to warn the Chinese of foreign powers' "aggressive ambitions" and "destructive intentions" (W. S. Wong 2002a, 13). The cartoon was a map of China showing foreign powers represented by animals (eagle, United States; bear, Russia; dog, Britain; frog, France), and one designated as a sausage (Germany), piecing up China as the Chinese showed no concern (Lent and Xu 2017, 15, fig. 1.13). Xie also cofounded, with Alfred Cunningham, the *South China Morning Post* (1903), the oldest surviving English-language paper in Hong Kong.

Because of its detachment from both the mainland and the Chinese government, Hong Kong has served as a publishing outlet, escape abode, and key base of support for political cartoonists in times of turmoil, such as the revolutionary movement from 1895 to 1911, World War II, the Civil War, and Mao Zedong's 1949 "liberation."

During the period leading up to the 1911 overthrow of the Qing Dynasty, and for a time after, Hong Kong was a haven for its own revolutionary newspapers and periodicals and, for short periods, publications that were banned and evicted from the mainland. When the cartoon-laden, Guangzhou-based *Shishi Huabao* (Journal of Current Pictorial) was banned for its very anti-Qing stand, the magazine moved to Hong Kong in 1907, lasting there for a few issues before the British authorities caved to Qing pressure and banned it. The trend continued when a few *Shishi Huabao* cartoonists started *Zhenxiang Huabao* (The True Record, 1912), published in Guangzhou and distributed in Shanghai. Harshly critical of the new government and the ruling Guomindang Party, *Zhenxiang Huabao* was stopped in 1913, at which time some of its cartoonists fled to Hong Kong. One of them, Zheng Nu-quan, earned the respect of a Hong Kong drugstore owner who financed his *Renjian Huahel* (Human Art Club), which published only one issue owing to Zheng's death (W. S. Wong 2002a, 14). Hong Kong was a refuge for banned periodicals and

2.2. The *True Record*, published in Guangzhou in 1912, was fiercely anti–Guomindang Party, the reason it was closed.

cartoonists from the mainland, but it was not a secure haven; British officials were known to bend to the mainland's pressure and carry out its bidding.

During the revolutionary era and through the 1940s, Hong Kong continued its role as a spillover place for unwelcome Republic of China periodicals and artists. Although Shanghai was the center of Chinese cartoon magazines and satirical and political cartooning in the 1920s and 1930s, Hong Kong had its historical moments: for example, one of China's two earliest women cartoonists, Yu Feng, had her work first published in Hong Kong periodicals in 1934–1935; the initial six-month run of the cartoon magazine *Bun-gok Manhua* (the Sketch) was printed in the colony; and Zhonghua Quanguo Zuojia Xiehui (the All-China Cartoon Association of Writers and Artists), begun in Shanghai in 1937, had a branch in Hong Kong (Lent and Xu 2017, 35, 37–43). Wendy Siuyi Wong (2002a, 39) reports that the National Cartoon

Association also set up a branch in Hong Kong, led by Ye Qianyu. In 1939, it organized an exhibition of antiwar cartoons and comics called Xiandai Zhongguo Manhua Zhan (Modern Chinese Cartoonist Exhibition). Also of note is that *Jiuwang Manhua*, the periodical of the mobile Jiuwang Manhua Xuanchuandui (the National Salvation Cartoon Propaganda Corps), published briefly in Hong Kong when the Japanese occupied Shanghai, its initial publication location, in 1937. When the corps was dissolved a few years later, some cartoonists, notably Liao Bingxiong (2002) and Te Wei (2001), fled to Hong Kong, as did others later during the civil war (e.g., Liao [2002] and Ding Cong [2002]). Kin Wai Chu (2018, 475) claims that more than twenty Communist cartoonists had moved to Hong Kong by 1939. Liao stayed from 1947 to 1950, leaving Guangzhou "under intensifying white terror in the area ruled by China's regime" (Liao 2002). In Hong Kong, he satirized politics and culture at break-neck speed, producing drawings he later did not admire: "I published more than 3,000 in Hong Kong; I drew too many daily. I had more than ten pennames. Hong Kong was a cultural desert and enjoyed a low cartoon level. I followed them; I drew the way they liked. But, in Chongqing, I drew high-quality cartoons" (Liao 2002).

In 1948, some of these self-exiled cartoonists organized a club (Renjian Huahui), a cartoon studies department, and a journal, *Zheshi Yige Manhua Shidai* (This Is a Cartoon Era), whose sole issue included works by Liao and Cheng Ka-chun on topics such as China-US relations, the Guomindang Party, and the unfairness of capitalism (W. S. Wong 2002a, 39).

Chinese-Language Cartooning

Political cartoons in Hong Kong did not cease with the 1949 Communist takeover of China; local cartoonists continued their interest in the mainland. Wong (2002b, 32) points out that in the late 1960s, at the height of China's Cultural Revolution, "the editorial cartoon pages in both [Hong Kong] pro- and anti-communist newspapers published cartoons criticizing the opposing position."

2.3. E-king Yen had much to do with reviving political cartooning in the 1960s and 1970s.

By the 1950s, according to Chu (2018, 476), nearly every newspaper had regular cartoons/comics, but most were entertaining, not political. This changed a bit when E-king Yen (Yim Yee-king) began to draw political cartoons for the *Tin Tin Daily News* in 1962, and then for the *Dai Jung Daily* and *Express Daily* as well. He is credited with reviving political cartoons in Hong Kong, although he called his drawings something else: "*manhua* about current affairs." E-king Yen described his political cartooning in the 1960s and 1970s as the "best" period of his career; he could use his drawings to "express whatever I liked and to criticize people harshly." However, by the 1980s, he grew tired of doing this, became depressed, and drank heavily, saying that he felt like "just some silly man standing on the street yelling and telling everybody off." At his wife's suggestion, they moved to Los Angeles, where he returned to his painting, described as a "simple, almost Zen-like style of drawing with freestyle illustrations in watercolor and ink, accompanying his calligraphic lines about nature

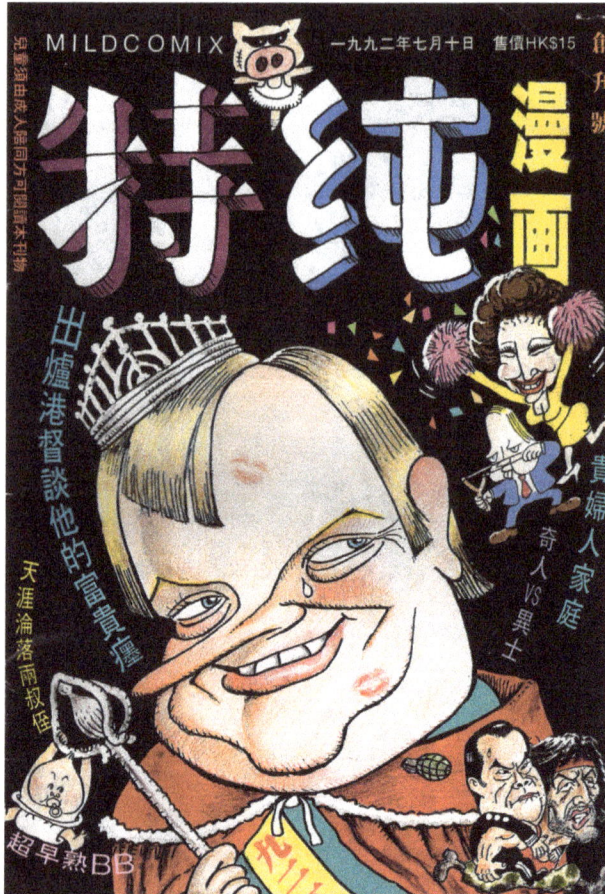

2.4. The cover of the inaugural issue of the political cartoon magazine *Mild Comix*, by Apink, July 1992. Courtesy of Apink.

2.5. Political cartoonist Ma Long (Ma Shing-yuen) in his office, March 20, 2012. Photo by Xu Ying. Courtesy of Ma Long.

and life, interpersonal relations, and search for mindfulness" (Su 2018).

Others followed Yen's lead, such as Wong Sze-ma, who died in 1983 before he could see his album of *Ming Pao* newspaper cartoons, *Debussy*, published; and beginning in the 1980s, Zunzi (Wong Kei-kwan), Ma Long (Ma Shing-yuen), Yuan Yat-mok (aka Local Boy), and Apink. Zunzi has been drawing political cartoons on a freelance basis for *Ming Pao* and other periodicals for more than four decades; Ma Long has drawn many political cartoons, founded and edited a political commentary magazine, *Fan Dou* (Rebellious), and founded and managed, with his wife, Fong She-mei, Century Culture, a publisher of children's comics they created; Yat-mok wrote a liberal political newspaper strip in 1988; and Apink was founder and editor of *Mild Comix*, a pictures-without-text magazine that dealt with current affairs and political matters with a large dose of humor.

The most persistent, hardest hitting of the Chinese-language press cartoonists have been Ma Long and Zunzi. Both kept a close watch on China and sharply criticized its leaders, particularly after the Tiananmen Square massacre of 1989 and as the 1997 transfer of Hong Kong's sovereignty approached.

In 1991, Ma Long anticipated the drying up of press freedom once China took over Hong Kong, and he started *Fan Dou*. By getting the magazine off the ground at that time, Ma Long anticipated that it would be a growing concern by 1997, with a greater chance of survival. He underestimated the fear that already existed in Hong Kong. The contracted distributor pulled out just before the inaugural issue, saying that he was "too old to make an enemy with China" (Ma Long 1992). He agreed to handle foreign distribution if his name was not used. Ma Long (1992) said that when the first issue appeared, the distributor canceled that agreement as well, frightened of possible ramifications. The only other foreign

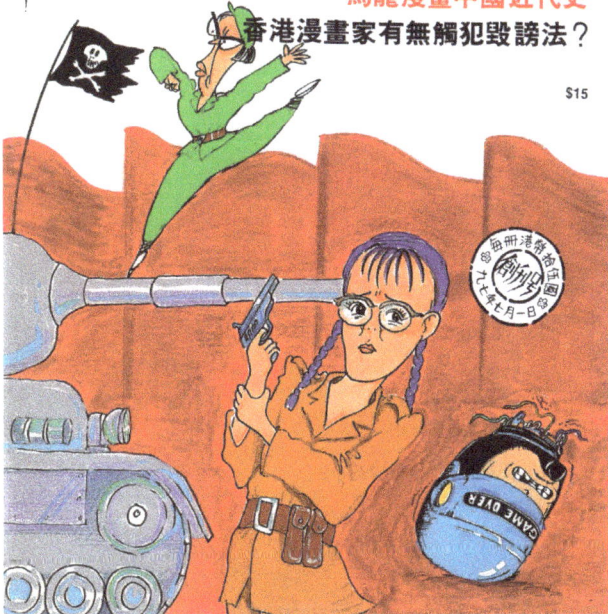

2.6. *Fan Dou* (Rebellious), inaugural issue, 1991. The main character of a Cantonese comedy, *Her Fatal Ways*, played by Mao Zedong's widow, Jiang Qing, is dancing in front of the tank. The cartoon concerns the 1997 turnover of Hong Kong.

2.7. Zunzi (Wong Kei-kwan), Hong Kong, March 20, 2012. Photo by Xu Ying. Courtesy of Zunzi

distributor leaned toward China, so Ma Long had to ditch his plan for overseas sales. *Fan Dou* lasted just seven issues, dying within six months (Ma Long 2012). Ma Long was also drawing political cartoons for the *Hong Kong Daily News* in 1992. He said that his editor did not want "too sharp" cartoons about China, even though, in his mind, Chinese cartoonists have a desire and tendency to "hit harder," because they are Chinese and have a "direct feeling."[1] Ma Long continued his political cartoon career, drawing for *Ming Pao* and *Apple Daily*.

Zunzi's political cartooning career began in 1980, drawing for *Ming Pao* and other newspapers and magazines[2] as well as serving as arts editor for *Ming Pao*. He said that for much of the 1980s, publishers shied away from using his cartoons because they "cut too close to the bone" (Mosher 1991, 28). His status increased as the public recognized his tough but tactical stance, which

he explained to Larry Feign (1986, 73): "If you can't give me the limit, I'll push it to the furthest limit I have. It's a game of position." In our first interview in 1991, Zunzi said already that political cartoonists were not "really free," working under many restrictions having to do with "who owns the newspaper" and with editors who "know how to choose cartoonists and know their standard" (Zunzi 1991). More direct control came when editors altered cartoonists' messages and censored them. He gave examples, one of which was: "A left-wing newspaper cartoonist drew a cartoon about a Hong Kong governor who died in Beijing. He drew him as a candle with the light flickering out. The editor stopped it, because he said it looked like a bomb. He stopped printing that edition and reran the paper without the cartoon. Editors don't want to upset the Chinese representatives in Hong Kong" (Zunzi 1991).

English-Language Cartooning

The English-language dailies *South China Morning Post* (*SCMP*) and *Hongkong Standard* also carried one-panel and strip cartoons with a political overlay—the *SCMP* from its 1903 beginnings and the *Standard* probably from 1985 (Feign 1992). By the 1950s and 1960s, there were a few strips that dealt with Hong Kong culture and politics, drawn by individuals who, according to veteran cartoonist Larry Feign (1992), were "told by someone they could draw well and decided they'd do cartoons." Feign, who drew for both dailies, described the *SCMP* as a "stuffy, colonist" paper; however, he did grant that it and the Hong Kong press generally shied away from using foreign, syndicated cartoons. He added: "If you had a good idea, you'd get a chance, but that means a lot of rubbish gets in too" (Feign 1992). The *SCMP* relinquished its stuffiness when Rupert Murdoch bought it in 1986.

Feign backed up his point that most of the cartoonists drew during lulls in their full-time jobs, by stating that the first regular *SCMP* strip, *Buzzy the Bee*, about a bee that eavesdrops on society, was drawn by a civil servant in the 1950s. Others followed. In 1974, accomplished South African French horn musician Napier Dunn, who had begun sketching caricatures while "waiting for string players to finish their segments," was in transit in Hong Kong on his way to Tokyo to accept a place in the Japan Philharmonic Orchestra when he decided to stay in the colony. He accepted a position on the *SCMP*, drawing *Pen Points*, about addiction centers, leper colonies, and prisons he had visited (Dunn 1996; Feign 1986, 67–70). In the 1980s, examples include former policeman Andy C. Neilson, with his conservative, single-panel political feature *Pen $ Inc.* (1983) in the *SCMP*; lawyer Christopher Young ("Templar"), who drew the politically oriented *Basher* (1984), also for the *SCMP*, to offset his courtroom boredom; and an accountant, Hung Mo Gwai, who created *Jackson Road*, hiring an artist to draw a four-panel template of people sitting at a bar, their backs to the reader, in which he simply inserted different word balloons to comment on the day's main issues (Feign 1992). In 1987, Stuart Allen introduced *Twigg* to the *Standard* as well as a front-page pocket cartoon shortly thereafter. The sole female cartoonist at the time was Hope Barrett, who in 1988 created *Spray* for

2.8. Larry Feign, home studio, Hong Kong, July 1992. Photo by John A. Lent. Courtesy of Larry Feign.

TV Times; it featured a bunch of cockroaches. She also drew the short-lived *Myopia* in the *Standard*'s children's section (Feign 1992).

By the late 1980s, both English dailies had professional political cartoonists. Australian Paul Best, as art editor of the *SCMP*, drew the daily's political cartoon and *Sunday Best* for years, while New York transplant Larry Feign, using the pseudonym Fong, drew a weekly political cartoon and daily strip, *Fong's Learn Chinese the Hard Way*, for the *Standard* and a strip, *The World of Lily Wong*, for the *SCMP*. *The World of Lily Wong* portrayed Hong Kong political and cultural pratfalls; it was very popular, as were Feign's cartoon books, which parodied the lives of expatriates in Hong Kong.

Feign (1992) identified 1985 as "the magic date," a time when professional cartoonists began replacing the "flashes in the pan," content was taking on a political edge, and the public was moving beyond its "make-money-and-shut-up" attitude toward politics. He explained his point, claiming that Hong Kong had been "one of the best-run, least-corrupt governments in the world, with a patriarchal attitude toward its people, who felt no need to speak out" (Feign 1992). But in the mid-1980s, matters changed significantly to awaken the public and ramp up the political cartooning scene. One major catalyst was the colonial government's refusal to ask China to consider scrapping a nuclear reactor plant it was planning to construct at Daya Bay near Hong Kong; this decision led to angry public discussions and genuine political cartooning. Leading the charge were Feign and newcomer Zunzi. Political thoughts on the Daya Bay controversy permeated all types of cartoons, including strips such as *The World of Lily Wong* and *Basher*. Feign (1992) said early on that he had settled on a 50/50 split between political and nonpolitical content in *Lily Wong*, but changed it to 70/30 in 1985; similarly, *Basher* moved from portraying the antics of a lawyer and a drunken judge (almost all the time) to much more content about Hong Kong–China relations.

Paul Best thought that, at the time of our interview in 1992, China was increasing its interference in Hong Kong affairs, and this was being lampooned in political cartoons. He also saw slightly more self-censorship on the part of his editor.

The China Period

Throughout the rest of the 1990s and into the twenty-first century, Hong Kong political cartooning could be likened to a sinking vessel, patched almost beyond recognition but determined to stay afloat.

There were increasingly fewer daily newspapers (Zunzi reported about fifteen in 2012), a number of which were owned by big business firms and nearly all being devoid of political cartoons. Self-censorship was common, and dissent was lacking in the press. Political cartooning was not an enticing profession for young artists, some of whom turned to the internet as a venue.

Zunzi, a longtime participant in and observer of Hong Kong political cartooning, sensed that most

2.9. Cover of *Postuticians*, 1993. One hundred Zunzi caricatures of leaders of China, Taiwan, and Hong Kong. Courtesy of Zunzi.

newspapers were "frozen," the exception being *Apple Daily*, which he said "makes some noise." He said that with "not much dissent in newspapers and many controlled by big business, ordinary people have no place to express themselves in the media" (Zunzi 2012).

Newspapers with political cartoonists in 2018 were *Ming Pao* and *Apple Daily* (Zunzi and Ma Long) and the *South China Morning Post* (Harry Harrison). The *SCMP*'s political cartoonist has been hemmed in by a culture of self-censorship that has existed for years at the daily; top editors "routinely rewrote, played down, or withheld critical stories for fear of offending influential Chinese officials or business executives," according to a former editor. The message of getting onside became more transparent after 2016, when China's mammoth technology and retail corporation, Alibaba, took over the *SCMP*, implementing a mission to improve China's image and promote Beijing's wishes and views (Hernández 2018, A8). As for *Ming Pao* and *Apple Daily*, China tolerated them as its "showcases of press freedom" in Hong Kong (Zunzi 2018). Actually, *Apple Daily* used to dedicate a much larger section to political and other cartoons; however, the space has shrunk significantly as the paper has attempted to salvage sales of business advertisements, much reduced because of local businesses' fear of political repercussions from Beijing (Zunzi, quoted in Qiao n.d.).

Apple Daily and its owner, Jimmy Lai, faced pressure from Beijing for years because of their critical commentary. Lai started *Next* magazine as part of his Next Media Group (now Next Digital) after the Tiananmen Square massacre. Initially, the Chinese government retaliated against his media's criticism by forcing Lai's retail clothing branches on the mainland to close. In 1995, Lai launched *Apple Daily* in Hong Kong and, later, Taiwan to serve as prodemocracy proponents. In June 2021, police raided *Apple Daily*, arrested five executives, and then closed the newspaper; Lai was imprisoned, denied bail, and charged with offenses against the mainland authorities that could keep him detained for life (CPJ 2021).

All other Hong Kong daily newspapers, according to Zunzi, are "either on China's side or owned by Chinese mainlanders." The internet has hosted a few politically inclined cartoonists, such as "Angry Angry," Cuson Lo, and Kong Biu. The latter announced at the time of my 2018 visit that he planned to post his cartoons on Facebook, each for ten minutes before they would disappear (Zunzi 2018).

Putting his observations in a post-1997-transfer-of-power perspective, Zunzi pointed out:

> The Hong Kong population is changing. To those born after 1997, China's policies are not agreeable to them. China people don't know civil rights; Hong Kong young people do. In the local democratic camp, there is a difference between the old and the new; the new are more radical.
>
> The Hong Kong rich give weight to China's rich. Bigger China companies are coming here, and more and more, the Hong Kong government is siding with China. (Zunzi 2018)

These comments tie in to earlier remarks by Zunzi that, since 1997, young people have exhibited greater

2.10. Political cartoon, Zunzi. Courtesy of Zunzi.

radicalness; their major motivation is not to make money but to live their own lives, to have interesting jobs, and to be supported by their parents (Zunzi 2012).[3]

It seems that Hong Kong popular culture leans in support of the moneyed, older class, restraining from criticism of China—promoting a favorable impression of the mainland among Hong Kong's people and those of the rest of the world. What Alibaba uses the *SCMP* for attests to this fact, as does an example on a more blatant scale that Zunzi provided: "There is a so-called 50 Cent Party here. The China government hires Hong Kong youngsters to say good things about China online, for which they are paid fifty Hong Kong cents per sentence" (Zunzi 2018).

Fears of China's design to dominate Hong Kong and possibly compromise or abandon the "one country, two systems" rule in effect since 1997 crescendoed in the 2010s, leading to a climate of self-censorship that blunted critical views while local authorities implemented the use of an "invisible hand of interference," added legislative restrictions, and strengthened business transactions that augmented China's presence.

The self-censorship, whether by publisher, editor, or cartoonist, was very worrisome, and the few remaining active political cartoonists increasingly identified and strongly denounced it. Of course, Zunzi had warned about the dangers of self-censorship for years, but by the late 2010s other cartoonists gave examples of being censored by cartoon producers rather than government regulators. One such artist was illustrator Ng Kap-chuen (aka Ah To), whose works have massive followings on Facebook and Yahoo News. Ah To was about to publish a book of his cartoons when the publisher, Ming Pao Publications, ordered him to remove strips referencing Xi Jinping and the Chinese national flag. He was flabbergasted. His publisher was part of the media conglomerate that owned the daily *Ming Pao*, and Ah To never expected an institution deemed prodemocracy "to self-censor out of concerns over . . . 'imaginary laws'" (Cheung 2018; also Lau 2016–2017; Cheng 2016). Ah To found another publisher to bring out his book.

When Beijing announced a new national security law for Hong Kong, bypassing the local government entirely in doing so, fears ran high that freedom of expression was doomed. The law proscribes seditious and subversive activities and, depending on how finely or loosely "seditious" and "subversive" are defined, can be a serious threat. The new legislation severely curtails freedoms guaranteed in Hong Kong's Basic Law and the Sino-British Joint Declaration and puts at risk anyone whose words or actions are deemed critical of the People's Republic of China or Hong Kong governments. The law applies to citizens and noncitizens regardless of where such words or actions take place.

Protest Art

In both 2014 and 2019–2020, parts of Hong Kong served as extended canvases adorned with protest art. In 2014, prodemocracy demonstrations seeking full universal suffrage for Hong Kong became known as the Umbrella Movement, named after the yellow umbrellas protesters used to deflect police pepper spray and tear gas. The movement took on an aesthetic quality as the areas occupied by protesters became on-street exhibition spaces for installations, mobiles, sculptures, banners, and message boards, some parodying Xi Jinping and the Hong Kong police, many others caricaturizing city leaders. Editorial cartoons became common street art, done by both professional and amateur political and

2.11. Protest illustration by Daxiong, Daxiong's Facebook page, 2019. Reprinted with permission of the *International Journal of Comic Art* 21, no. 2 (Fall–Winter 2019): 47–73. John A. Lent, publisher. Article by Justin Chiu-tat Wong.

nonpolitical cartoonists. Among the stalwarts were Zunzi, Ah To, Justin Wong, Cuson Lo, Kit Man, Brian Chan (aka Bak Shui), Mr. and Ms. HK People, Hello Wong, and DDED. They helped revive a dying political cartoon profession. However, as the Umbrella Movement ended and China's control tightened, so did the political cartoon mobilization peter out—that is, until new protests in 2019.

The 2019 protests, which began in June and extended well into 2020, were sparked by an extradition bill that would send criminal suspects to China. The months of upheaval led to a flourishing of political art drawn by what Zunzi called "a lot of actually real good cartoonists," simultaneously lamenting that "we can't see them normally in the daily newspaper" (Ore 2020).[4]

While the protests were outwardly leaderless, they were well organized and functional, as were the political cartoons that accompanied the movement. Prominent political cartoonist Wong Chiu-tat (Justin) carefully documented political cartooning for the first four months of the protests, relying on his on-site participation in the demonstrations and his analysis of more than four thousand cartoons he collected from social media and the streets. His findings confirmed:

1. The cartooning was functional, carried out by editorial cartoonists such as Zunzi, Ma Long, and himself; online political cartoonists such as Cuson Lo, Ah To, Kit Man, Hello Wong, DDED, and Mr. and Ms. HK People; nonpolitical illustrators; nonprofessionals and amateurs; the Creative/Public Relations Team; and overseas cartoonists.
2. Online cartoonists enjoyed more freedom, were more responsive to the movement, and had a much bigger following fanbase than print cartoonists.
3. More than one hundred illustrators joined the movement who, because of their diversity, added new ideas and graphic styles.
4. Nonprofessionals and amateurs contributed comments through stickers, posters, and notes posted on so-called Lennon Walls placed throughout the city.
5. The Creative/Public Relations Team, with thousands of anonymous members, used various visual techniques to influence public opinion, promote ideas, and mobilize the public.
6. Overseas cartoonists (e.g., Daxiong, Rebel Pepper, and Badiucao) joined the fray, portraying the movement as war against the Chinese Communist Party. (J. Wong 2019, 48–54)

Wong (2019, 57–64) broadly categorized the movement's political cartoons into those providing analytical commentary and those that were provocative, subdividing them further into commentary that served the function of a "political cartoon from the perspective of a commentator"; documentary; public relations, that aimed to give the public a positive feeling about the protests; and solidarity.

2.12. Demonstration banner with a caricature of Teresa Cheng, secretary for justice of Hong Kong, June 12, 2019. Reprinted with permission of the *International Journal of Comic Art* 21, no. 2 (Fall–Winter 2019): 47–73. John A. Lent, publisher. Article by Justin Chiu-tat Wong.

Writing about Wong's own political cartoons featured in *Ming Pao* and online, a *Financial Review* reporter told how they were re-created on huge banners unfurled by protesters, some using irony, some blending different themes to make a point, and "others borrow[ing] from the works of American painter and printmaker Edward Hopper and Belgian surrealist René Magritte" (Smith 2019).

The cartoons posted on city walls, in the subway system, or online sometimes were fast reactions to protest happenings, almost in breaking-news, journalistic fashion; other times, they were more deliberate. A number borrowed popular culture characters or their sayings to make a point. One cartoon drawn by Kit Da Sketch used martial arts master Bruce Lee's phrase "Be water, my friend," meaning be hard like ice, flow like water, and disappear like vapor (Sala 2019).

Other thought-out methods of deployment used in the protest art included repeated references to dates of important movement events on "protest calendars," urging the public to remember them; appeals and explanations denouncing vandalism and violence; and a strategy of extending "beyond the local context: from offline to online, domestic to abroad" (Ismangil 2020).

A Brief Conclusion

As the future of periodical political cartooning becomes more precarious, Hong Kong professional and amateur artists have paved new, or patched up old, pathways to get messages across. No doubt, China will put up roadblocks to mute free expression, and it is more than likely that dedicated political cartoonists will detour around them, find their position, and push to their furthest limit, using the modus operandi of Zunzi way back in 1986.

Notes

1. Ma Long (1992) said that another difference between foreign and local cartoonists in Hong Kong is that foreign artists take more time drawing, while the Chinese works are "more sketchy," the concentration being on the issues, not the art.

2. Zunzi's cartoon output was extraordinary. For example, in 1991, he was producing two political cartoons seven days a week for *Ming Pao*; one each daily for the *Hong Kong Economic Journal* and the *Economic Times*; three pages of prose and cartoons weekly for *Next* magazine; and one page each for the biweekly *Pai Shing* (Common People) and the English-language "Through the Tiger's Eye" column for the *Hongkong Standard*. He also wrote freelance features and played the key role in organizing the Hong Kong Cartoonists Association (Zunzi 1991). Between 1981 and 1987, Zunzi drew more than two thousand cartoons solely on the looming barrier to freedom that the 1997 handover posed. Some ended up in political literature and on posters.

3. On another occasion, in 2009, Zunzi described Hong Kong people as "smart, not politically indifferent: we know what politics is, so we know how to avoid it and when not to take it too seriously. For most of the not-so-important issues, we would applaud for two seconds if we are happy with them, otherwise we just concentrate on our own business and continue to watch TV and make money. But when it is necessary, we will stand up and make our voices heard."

4. *Ming Pao*, a daily for which Zunzi draws, found it almost impossible to cover firsthand the large number of demonstrations that broke out, and the paper increasingly depended on Zunzi to provide a suitable cartoon. Some even found their way onto the paper's front page (Ore 2020).

Bibliography

Apink. 1992. Interview with John A. Lent, Hong Kong, July 12.

Best, Paul. 1992. Interview with John A. Lent, Hong Kong, July 12.

Cheng, Kris. 2016. "Hong Kong Cartoonist Drops Publisher amid Charges of Self-Censorship." *Hong Kong Free Press*, May 27. https://hongkongfp.com/2016/05/27/hong-kong-comic-artist-find-new-publisher-political-satire-book-original-one-self-censors/.

Cheung, Rachel. 2018. "Hong Kong's Cartoonists Aren't Giving Up on Dissent." *Nation*, June 25.

Chu, Kin Wai. 2018. "A Forgotten Link in the History of the Chinese Newspaper Political Cartoon: The Cartoon Album of *The World of E-king Yen*." *International Journal of Comic Art* 20, no. 1 (Spring–Summer): 470–88.

Chun, Robert Qiao. 2017. "Zunzi's Hong Kong: Leading Political Cartoonist Looks Back." *News Lens*, July 20. https://international.thenewslens.com/article/74014.

Committee to Protect Journalists (CPJ). 2021. "CPJ Board Honors Hong Kong's Jimmy Lai with Gwen Ifill Press Freedom Award." Press release, June 21. https://cpj.org/2021/06/cpj-board-honors-hong-kongs-jimmy-lai-with-gwen-ifill-press-freedom-award/.

Ding, Cong. 2002. Interview with John A. Lent and Xu Ying, Beijing, December 20.

Dunn, Napier. 1996. Interview with John A. Lent, Durban, South Africa, July 11.

Feign, Larry. 1986. "Hong Kong Cartoonists." *Cartoonist Profiles*, June, 66–73.

Feign, Larry. 1992. Interview with John A. Lent, Hong Kong, July 11.

Hernández, Javier C. 2018. "Newspaper's New Goal: Change How the West Sees China." *New York Times*, April 1, A8.

Ismangil, Milan. 2020. "Surrounded by Slogans: Perpetual Protest in Public Space during the Hong Kong 2019 Protests." International Institute for Asian Studies *Newsletter* 85 (Spring). https://www.iias.asia/the-newsletter/article/surrounded-slogans-perpetual-protest-public-space-during-hong-kong-2019.

Lau, Betty. 2016–2017. "Award-Winning Hong Kong Political Cartoonist Refuses Self-Censorship." InMedia, December 17, 2016,

38

and January 23, 2017. https://hongkongfp.com/2017/02/25/ award-winning-hong-kong-political-cartoonist-refuses-self -censorship.

Lent, John A. 1993. "Cartoons in Hong Kong and South Korea." *Asian Culture Quarterly* 21, no. 2 (Summer): 16–32.

Lent, John A., and Xu Ying. 2017. *Comics Art in China*. Jackson: University Press of Mississippi.

Liao, Bingxiong. 2002. Interview with John A. Lent and Xu Ying, Guangzhou, January 4, 5.

Ma Long [Ma Shing-yuen]. 1992. Interview with John A. Lent, Hong Kong, July 12.

Ma Long [Ma Shing-yuen]. 2012. Interview with John A. Lent and Xu Ying, Hong Kong, March 20.

Mosher, Stacy. 1991. "Cocking Last Snooks." *Far Eastern Economic Review*, July 11, 28–30.

Nib. 2014.. "Hong Kong's Political Cartoonists Take On the Umbrella Revolution." October 7. https://medium.com/the-nib/ hong-kongs-political-cartoonists-take-on-the-umbrella-revo lution-4f12207a8580.

Ore, Jonathan. 2020. "Hong Kong Political Cartoonist Zunzi Says He Won't Back Down from China's New Security Law." CBC Radio, *Day 6*, May 29. https://www.cbc.ca/radio/day6/dysfunc tion-in-long-term-care-the-meaning-of-karen-zunzi-crispr -covid-19-tests-baroness-von-sketch-more-1.5588200/hong -kong-political-cartoonist-zunzi-says-he-won-t-back-down -from-china-s-new-security-law-1.5588367.

Qiao, Robert C. n.d. "Zunzi's Hong Kong: 20 Years Later." https:// robertcqiao.wordpress.com/zunzis-hong-kong-20-years-later/.

Rea, Christopher. 2013. "'He'll Roast All Subjects That May Need the Roasting': Puck and Mr. Punch in Nineteenth-Century China." In *Asian Punches: A Transcultural Affair*, edited by Hans Harder and Barbara Mittler, 389–422. Heidelberg: Springer-Verlag.

Sala, Ilaria Maria. 2019. "Hong Kong Has Become a Gallery of Protest Poster Art." *Quartz*, July 26. https://qz.com/ quartzy/1673655/see-the-poster-and-comic-from-hong -kongs-protest.

Smith, Michael. 2019. "Art in Action: Hong Kong's Political Unrest Sparks a Creative Fire." *Financial Review*, December 27. https:// www.afr.com/life-and-luxury/arts-and-culture/art-in-action -hong-kong-s-political-unrest-sparks-a-creative-fire -20191210-p53iq2.

Su, Xinqi. 2018. "Renowned Hong Kong Cartoonist Yim Yee-king, Also Known as Ah Chung, Dies at 85." *The Star* (Petaling Jaya, Malaysia), August 13. https://www.thestar.com.my/news/ regional/2018/08/14/renowned-hong-kong-cartoonist-yim -yeeking-also-known-as-ah-chung-dies-at-85/.

Te, Wei. 2001. Interview with John A. Lent and Xu Ying, Beijing, June 16.

Wong, Justin Chiu-tat. 2019. "Initial Investigation of Political Cartoons and Illustrations in the Anti-Extradition Bill Protest in Hong Kong." *International Journal of Comic Art* 21, no. 2 (Fall–Winter): 47–73.

Wong, Wendy Siuyi. 2002a. *Hong Kong Comics: A History of Manhua*. New York: Princeton Architectural Press.

Wong, Wendy Siuyi. 2002b. "Manhua: The Evolution of Hong Kong Cartoons and Comics." *Journal of Popular Culture* 35, no. 4 (Spring): 25–47.

Zunzi [Wong Kei-kwan]. 1991. Interview with John A. Lent, Drexel Hill, Pennsylvania, July 30.

Zunzi [Wong Kei-kwan]. 2012. Interview with John A. Lent and Xu Ying, Hong Kong, March 20.

Zunzi [Wong Kei-kwan]. 2018. Interview with John A. Lent, Hong Kong, May 24.

It is safe to say that Japan has one of the richest and oldest traditions of all Asian countries in the realm of comic art. Looking at what I consider to be the major elements of comic art and, by extension, political cartooning, Japanese culture has long brimmed with caricature, satire/parody, humor/playfulness, and narrative/sequence. In this presentation, narrative/sequence takes a back seat to the other three elements because it usually is not associated with political cartoons. It should be remembered, though, that Japan also pioneered in narrative/sequence with the comic book–like *kibyōshi*, which appeared in the late eighteenth century (Hibbett 2002; Kern 2007).

Historical Overview

Caricature, satire, and narrative go back to at least the twelfth-century picture scrolls by Tendai Sect Bishop Toba Sōjō; called *chōjū-giga* (humorous pictures of animals and birds), they satirized the religious hierarchy and noblemen through the funny actions of monkeys, rabbits, frogs, and foxes pretending to be humans. Bishop Toba may have been responsible for the *hōhigassen* (farting contest) and *yobutsu kurabe* (phallic contest) scrolls, the latter showing men comparing "their huge erect members and using them in ingenious feats of strength" (Schodt 1983, 30; Blyth 1959, 286). The caricature picture scroll gained popularity during the Kamakura period (1192–1333), depicting hell, ghosts, and disease with "sledgehammer realism" and much grotesqueness (Schodt 1983, 29).

The *ukiyo-e* woodblock prints of the Tokugawa period (1603–1868) brought forth a higher quality of caricature, impressive enough to regale European painters such as Van Gogh, Monet, Manet, Toulouse-Lautrec, and Dante Gabriel Rossetti (Schodt 1983, 28). *Ukiyo-e* caricature was wildly exaggerated (especially in *shunga*, or erotic prints [Fagioli 1997]), brightly colored, and often tied to the foibles of the times. The exaggeration of *ukiyo-e* was such, Richard Lane writes, that it could "distort reality and depart so much from it and yet still

Chapter 3

Japan

express a sensitive human beauty" (1982, 244). R. H. Blyth describes the Tokugawa period as "one of caricature, military and political resistance to it, and popular resistance to that resistance through caricature" (1959, 29). No doubt the authorities had concerns about the fallout from caricature, arresting and exiling caricature artist Hanabusa Itcho (1652–1724) to an island for twelve years as punishment for his book of pictures, *Hyakunin Joro*, which rashly depicted the fifth shogun (Chibbett 1977, 196).

As already mentioned, satire/parody was present in Bishop Toba's scrolls, as it was in the eighteenth-century *toba ehon* (Toba picture books) that carried his name. *Toba ehon*, along with *hanjimono* (visual puzzles and rebuses), parodied Japanese politics and society using amusing visual puns that had secret meanings (Duus 2001, 968). The first of these picture books was *Tobae Sankokushi*, created in 1702 by Shumboku Ōoka. Others followed, all in monochrome, often spoofing "drunken, pompous, and posturing samurai"; they continued to be printed into the early nineteenth century. Peter Duus (2001, 971) writes that *hanjimono* prints were meant to amuse, but their concealed political meanings revealed opinions otherwise "drastically restricted" at the time.

The *kibyōshi* (yellow covers), a five-by-seven-inch booklet similar to comics, was one of the most widely published genres of the last quarter of eighteenth-century Japan. Adam Kern calls it the "first form of prose literature to systematically satirize contemporary political figures," so effective in infuriating the government that the "senior councilor moved to censure most of the leading authors" (2007, 28, 29).

Ukiyo-e were also satirical, having grown out of a sense of social protest. Noted American novelist and *ukiyo-e* connoisseur James Michener (1954) called *ukiyo-e* an "art of gentle ridicule . . . that thumbed its nose at the Tokugawa dictatorship." Particularly in *shunga ukiyo-e*, the pompous samurai was made to look foolish: his wife was shown bedding the gardener while he contentedly snored (Michener 1954, 211–12). Frank Whitford (1977, 41) likens *ukiyo-e* prints to political cartoons, carrying a multiplicity of meanings and being politically motivated.

3.1. Utagawa Kuniyoshi (1797–1861), one of the four leading artists of the *ukiyo-e* school, who inserted humor and satire in his works. Memorial portrait by Utagawa Yoshiku, 1861. Courtesy of the British Museum.

Japanese art became even more satirical as the Tokugawa government began to topple and Western influences permeated the country. Bridging these significant changes in political systems and cultural forms were the artist Utagawa Kuniyoshi (1797–1861) and his student Kawanabe Kyōsai (1831–1889), both very adept at adding humor and playfulness with a sprinkling of satire to their drawings.

Kuniyoshi's vast, cleverly conceived oeuvre includes riddle pictures incorporating complex satires of the Tenpō reforms era, upside-down pictures in which a second picture is visible when a portrait is upended, composites combining human figures to form an assembled face, alphabets formed from bodies of fish, cats, and humans, visual puzzles such as an entanglement of fourteen men's bodies to look like thirty-five people, scratched graffiti, erotic drawings, anthropomorphic prints, and a drawing of sparrows acting out a brothel scene (depictions of courtesans were forbidden). Some of these works depicted political figures and events through Kuniyoshi's own "iconography of concealment," consisting of "visual hints, puns, and clues deployed in *hanjimono* . . . and other comical prints" (Duus 2001, 972; also Clark 2009).

The so-called demon of painting, Kawanabe Kyōsai, was also prolific as well as quick in his drawing style, in spite of (or because of?) his prodigious drinking of sake (Clark 1993, 17–18). Whereas Kuniyoshi produced an array of intricate forms, Kyōsai was known for painting on all types of surfaces and venues, for example scrolls, fans, huge theater curtains, book illustrations, picture lanterns for brothels, and newspapers, where he drew satirical cartoons covering a spectrum of subjects such as farts, ink battles, hell, demons, "proverbs," landscapes, gods, and animals (Oikawa 1996, 37). Mixing work with pleasure, he regularly held *shogakai* (calligraphy and painting parties) "at which he would turn out literally hundreds of small and medium-sized works at speed to order for paying guests at the event" (Clark 1993, 7). He relished painting humorous and satirical works, sometimes in the off-color manner of Toba Sōjō. In 1870, he was imprisoned for several months because he comically drew government officials while he was very drunk.

Western influences on comic art flowed into Japan in the mid-nineteenth century when the country ended nearly three hundred years of isolation. Introduced were different technologies such as zinc etching and copper plate printing, and cultural artifacts, one of the latter being the humor magazine. A British army officer turned foreign correspondent, Charles Wirgman, started the *Japan Punch* (1862–1887) to humorously report on Japanese political-societal news for the foreign population of Yokohama. In the inaugural issue, the editor wrote:

> It had been our intention to have published an "Overland Punch," but having remembered the very seedy appearance of some editors after the issue of theirs, we enquired the reason, and discovered that it arose from want of sleep. These infatuated men spent six nights in getting the

3.2. Japan's first humor magazine, the *Japan Punch*, started by Charles Wirgman in 1862.

"overland" published. They assured us that it was impossible to do it in the daytime. We at once resolved forever to abandon our original decision and adhere to our motto "Idleness is the Parent of Happiness!" We have consigned the midnight oil to perdition, and firm in our intentions of never taxing our constitutions with over-exertion, we intend to keep our minds in a perpetual state of vernal freshness, free from anxious thought or care, and happy as a bull terrier with a rat. We will never do today what we can put off till some future period of our sublunar career. "Honi soit qui mal y pense." Verb. Sap. (*Oriental Affairs* 1939, 259)

Renowned comics collector and researcher Shimizu Isao (1991, 29) credited the magazine as the originator of the concept of Japanese cartoons as a mass medium.

The *Japan Punch* spurred similar periodicals. Among them were the first to be published by a Japanese and the first to be filled with cartoons, *Eshimbun Nipponchi* (the Illustrated Newspaper of Japan), begun in 1874 by Kyōsai and a novelist;[1] and the weekly cartoon organ of a popular rights movement, *Marumaru Chimbun* (1877–1907), whose cartoon director, Honda Kinkichirō, mixed traditional Japanese and Western art styles and wrote captions in both English and Japanese (Shimizu 1989, 1991).[2] Not long after came the biweekly *Tobae* (Caricature) (1887–1890), published in Yokohama by French artist Georges Bigot, and an advertising-cum-humor-sheet,

3.3. *Tokyo Puck* cover by Kitazawa Rakuten, April 15, 1905.

The Box of Curios, initiated in 1889 as a monthly to advertise its owner's curio shop, but by 1892 converted into an advertising/humor weekly with the cartoons of Australian-born American Frank A. Nankivell (Stewart 2006). Bigot's satire before *Tobae* was biting, outspoken, and often offensive, as related in the December 11, 1886, *Chōya Shimbun*:

> The French artisan Bigot . . . is said to call into his home ragpickers loitering in the streets of Tokyo. . . . He sketches the most impoverished examples of Japanese low-life and sends the pictures back to his home country. Might there not be some way to prevent this practice as it will invite the contempt of foreigners toward our national customs. (quoted in Meech-Pekarik 1986, 187)

With the startup of *Tokyo Puck* (1905–1912) in the late Meiji period, Japan's cartoon world was greatly energized, yielding the country's first large color cartoon magazine; its creator, Kitazawa Rakuten, was the first Japanese cartoonist to devote his life to the profession. Kitazawa, influenced by American cartoons, thought of cartoons in the context of journalism, expanding the range of cartoon topics to include international affairs, adding the dimension of timeliness by soon publishing every ten days, and aiming for mass circulation. Previously, cartoon magazines had been published for small enclaves of foreign residents or to support a movement, thus circulating a mere two hundred copies in the case of the *Japan Punch* and fifteen thousand for *Marumaru Chimbun*. Quickly, *Tokyo Puck* circulated one hundred thousand copies. Kitazawa wished to uplift the quality of cartoons,[3] which had begun to decline, to be more like those of the West; to single out the new style, he renamed cartoons generally as *manga*, which replaced the generic *ponchi* (punch) (Okamoto 1996, 7; also Sakai and Shimizu 1985; Ishiko 1988; Shimizu 1989).

After Kitazawa left the magazine, three other versions of *Tokyo Puck* appeared between 1912 and 1941, serving as the launching pad for the careers of some of Japan's top cartoonists, such as Okamoto Ippei and Shimokawa Hekoten. In the 1920s and 1930s, cartooning was further politicized as artists were imbued with antiestablishment and Marxist viewpoints using the newly formed *Musansha Shimbun* (Proletariat News) and *Senki* (War Banner) as outlets for their Marxist cartoons and organizing groups such as Nihon Mangaka Renmei (the Japan Cartoonists Association) and Shin Manga-ha Shūdan (New Cartoonists Faction Group) to help cartoonists find outlets and strike a blow to the conservatism of the Japanese cartoon community.

Shin Manga-ha Shūdan, founded in 1932, sprouted from a group of young cartoonists who, in 1929, started *Manga Man* (Cartoon Man) magazine, which introduced more American cartoons as well as Japan's *ero guro nansensu* (erotic grotesque nonsense) cartoons of 1929–1931. This genre was associated with a "political, ironic humor that took on such themes as the transformation wrought by a modernity dominated by Euro-American mores" (Silverberg 2006, 30).

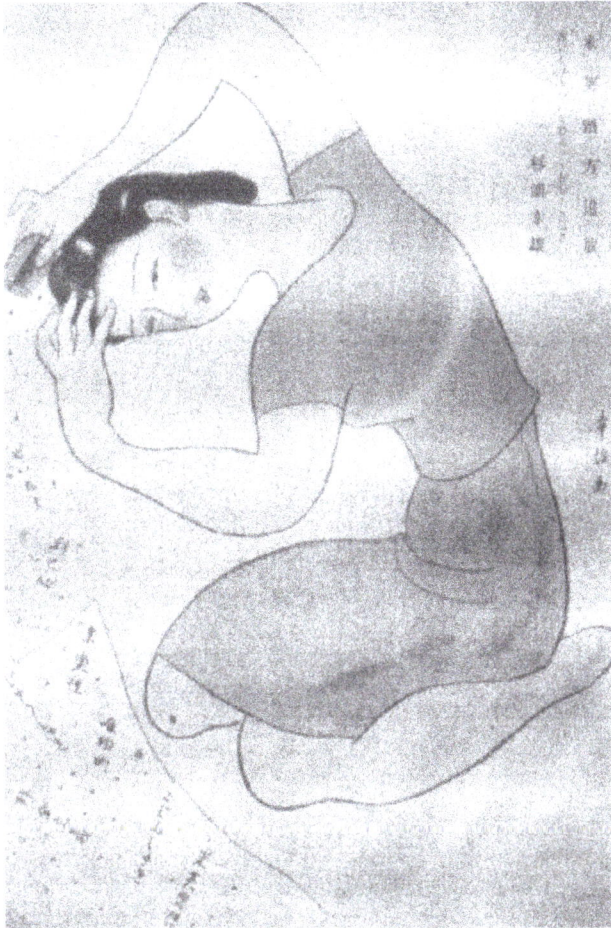

3.4. "Purging One's Head of Anglo-Americanism," Sugiura Yukio. *Manga Man* magazine, May 1942. Subtitled "Get rid of the dandruff encrusting your head," the image shows a woman combing out of her hair: extravagance, selfishness, hedonism, liberalism, materialism, money worship, and individualism. Courtesy of Sugiura Yukio.

Sugiura Yukio founded Shin Manga-ha Shūdan along with Kondō Hidezō and Yokoyama Ryūichi; Sugiura explained the purpose of the group and the relevance of the *ero guro nansensu* movement to cartoons of the times:

The purpose in organizing the group was because the condition of cartoonists was poor. Individually, if we went to the magazines seeking improvements, we'd be turned down. So, led by me, we thought it better to organize a group to negotiate with the magazine editors for payment. The beginnings of the 1930s was a bleak period. The mood of the people was very gloomy and desperate. The erotic, grotesque, nonsense cartoons became popular as a result. [These cartoons] were influenced by American and French cartoons. *Punch* influenced these types.

3.5. Sugiura Yukio, seated left with John A. Lent. Background, left to right: Ryuzan Aki, Yamato Suzuki, and Yuzi Nishizawa. Sugiura's home, Tokyo, November 6, 1993.

These were very sophisticated, modern cartoons using the pen. (Sugiura 1993)

Ero guro nansensu cartoons were popular among artists because they were considered modern, and they were safe to draw at a time when Japan, advancing toward war, attempted to control all forms of thought and expression.

The writing was on the wall, so to speak, in the early 1930s, as the proletarian cartoon movement died in 1934, suppressed by the "thought police"; *Manga Man* was closed by the government in 1931, and cartoonists and editors were arrested so often that some magazines "designated an employee as 'jail editor'—he who had the honor of taking the rap and saving the company" (Schodt 1983, 51). Among cartoonists affected by the crackdown were Yanase Masuma, a fervent champion of the masses, who was arrested, tortured, and jailed in 1932; Suyama Keiicha, co-organizer of Nihon Mangaka Renmei, arrested and imprisoned for two years in 1933; and Matsuyama Fumio, also critical of the government, imprisoned for three years in the early 1930s. In the mid- and late 1930s, the control was tightened, obliterating many periodicals under a restructuring mobilization law, closing most cartoonist organizations, and strictly enforcing government policy.

One of the major tasks of the Japanese Imperial Army in the 1930s and into the 1940s was to inculcate in Asian (particularly Chinese) societies the notion that the Japanese came in peace for their protection and to liberate them from the throes of colonialization. Major propaganda tools the Japanese used were political posters and political cartoons, the latter heavily influenced by Japanese cartoons of the 1920s. However, the scenario was far different by the late 1930s, according to Zhang Shaoqian (2014), as "Japan's colonial expansion complicated its cultural influence on China," and the Chinese worked to separate themselves from Japan's cultural heritage.

During the war, paper shortages hampered publications, leaving *Manga Man* and *Manga Nippon* nearly alone as cartoon magazines. Single-panel cartoons in newspapers and magazines became extremely propagandistic, viciously attacking enemies, particularly Roosevelt, Churchill, and Chiang Kai-shek, while comic strips portrayed the daily life of Japanese civilians, including messages that promoted national unity, conservation, production, loyalty, and harmony (Rhodes 1976, 253). Also serving Japanese propaganda aims were cartoon leaflets dropped by airplane on Asian civilians and Allied soldiers. Those meant for the local populace depicted the Japanese as friendly liberators fighting to free colonized Asians, while cartoon leaflets designed for Allied forces tried to divide and conquer the American, British, and Australian militaries, make soldiers long to return home to an enjoyable life with their families, and plant the idea in their minds that their wives back home were having sex with other men (Lent 2014, 258–301; Okamoto 1996, 5–17). Overall, one thing was for sure: the political cartoon's role had shifted gears, from subverting authority to supporting it.

The postwar era provided political fodder of different topics for cartoonists, such as American soldiers and local women, inflation, the black market, the wrecked economy and landscape, and the occupation. An example provided by a *New York Times* correspondent encapsulates a couple of these themes: "A cartoon shows

3.6. A Japanese wartime propaganda leaflet destined for China, showing US president Franklin D. Roosevelt with British prime minister Winston Churchill and Chinese Nationalist leader Chiang Kai-shek in his pockets, both injured by Japanese bullets.

a tall GI strolling with a little Japanese girl. Two Japanese men are lookers-on, and the first of them, according to the dialogue appearing below the picture, is annoyed at such conduct by an American soldier. 'Well, it all depends on how you look at it,' quips the second, 'after all, it's his country, isn't it?'" (Parrott 1946, 28).

Generally, the single-panel political cartoon lost its edge and was marginalized with the postwar rise of story comic books (manga),[4] whose lucrative market attracted most of the skilled cartoonists at a time when some cartoon-friendly periodicals were dying, and the increasing indecisiveness of politicians made for uninteresting drawings (Schodt 1983; also Illerbrun 2005).

The Weakening of Political Cartoons

These trends had a lot to do with the weakening of Japanese political cartoons, which led to the present state of the profession, as related by Ronald Stewart:

> Japanese political cartooning is widely considered to be weak: lacking in number and scope, and importantly, lacking in the aggression necessary to produce biting satire. A major reason for this low assessment is that the most publicly visible forum for political cartoons, the national daily newspapers, have, particularly in the 1980s, reduced the number and prominence of the cartoons they carry, and settled into using primarily mild, non-offensive cartoons. (Stewart 2016, 179)

Other researchers have attempted to find answers to why newspaper political cartooning has deteriorated. In a study of how the editorial cartoons of two national newspapers (*Yomiuri Shimbun* and *Asahi Shimbun*) covered six Japanese prime ministers who served between 1980 and 1993, Ofer Feldman concludes that the cartoons "portray and reflect political reality" (rather than comment or give an opinion) (1995, 579), and that there was virtually no difference in the number of cartoons the newspapers used, the days when they appeared, and their attitudes (573). Such uniformity in Japanese newspapers results from "consensus" news-gathering and reporting.

In another study of *Asahi Shimbun*, Kurt Illerbrun (2005, 45–46) reports that the *hanjimono* concealment in cartoons of the past was not present, that the prominent display of an artist's name under a cartoon assured the authorities it was that artist's and not the newspaper's opinion, and that metaphors were kept simple. Illerbrun added that state censorship combined with the mammoth Dentsu advertising agency's influence to mold popular culture and keep damaging cartoons out of the press, and cartoonists were unwilling to test the limits of censors.

The augmented temerity of Japanese political cartoonists was obvious when I interviewed a number of them in 1993. Veteran cartoonist Sugiura Yukio (1993) thought that the work of political cartoonists in Japan was not interesting or witty: "Japanese get nervous writing political cartoons," and they must coordinate their opinions with those of the editor. Suzuki Yamato (1993) agreed that political cartoonists were "always under the influence of the editor" and lamented that they did not draw cartoons "simply and to make people laugh," but tried to be "sophisticated." Nishizawa Yuzi (1993) criticized the tendency of fellow cartoonists to draw the "backstory" (behind the scene) of political figures, which, in his opinion, was not interesting, while Aki Ryūzan (1993), who drew his first cartoons while a postal worker, felt that he and other cartoonists could not criticize politicians, thus making for dull matter.

Kato Yoshiro (1993), then president of the Japan Cartoonists Association and a major comic strip cartoonist, compared the state of his country's cartooning in the 1940s and 1950s when his career started with the situation at the time of our interview in 1993. He said that political and strip cartooning was at "ebb tide" in 1993 while manga were rising, and that the quality of work and the number of readers sophisticated enough to grasp the essence of cartoons were both down. Kato's oeuvre consisted mainly of newspaper comic strips based on "social events and the news." His major strip and the oldest continuous strip in Japan was *Mappira-Kun* (Mr. No Way), which he started in *Mainichi Shimbun* in 1954.

Another of Japan's prominent cartoonists in 1993 was Satō Sampei, noted for his comic strips, especially *Yūhi-kun* (Mr. Setting Sun) in *Asahi* [Rising Sun] *Shimbun* and *Fuji Santarō*, about a *sararīman* (salaryman). Satō thought of himself as an editorial cartoonist, his strips wearing two faces, that of ordinary family life and that of big social problems. He said that his strips had no story line: "They are just to show people one moment of a social/political phenomenon, of a problem of society, or of family life" (Satō 1993). Reflecting on newspaper cartoons in 1950 when he started, Satō said that at that time editors were more interested in cartoons and were more capable of finding good cartooning talent. Because such editors had become rare, he continued, the number of skilled cartoonists had decreased by the 1990s. Satō's most popular strip, *Fuji Santarō*, about a middle-class office worker, went to great lengths to champion the cause of Japanese consumers, showing them being sold unsafe cars, protesting without results in front of the Diet (the national legislature), and being assured that "America's bugle-blowing economic cavalry will rescue [their] pocket books" (Wetherall 1980, 25).

Contemporary Political Cartooning

In the decades since the 1990s, the state of Japan's political cartooning has increasingly deteriorated. The statistics tell the story. The big three newspapers (*Asahi Shimbun*, *Yomiuri Shimbun*, and *Mainichi Shimbun*) reduced the weekly number of political cartoons they printed, initially in their evening editions. For example, *Yomiuri* dropped its weekly total from fourteen to seven by 2006, to three in 2011, and none in 2018. The same type of drop occurred at *Asahi* and *Mainichi*. By 2018, *Asahi*'s two assigned cartoonists each published eight cartoons a month and *Mainichi*'s sole cartoonist, four monthly. Other dailies with regular political cartoons were *Sankei Shimbun*, two cartoonists and a total of seven to nine cartoons monthly; *Komei Shimbun*, two, each with six monthly, and *Tokyo Shimbun*, one cartoonist and eight cartoons per month (Nishida 2019). These and other dailies have massive circulations, six of them in the millions, with *Yomiuri* at the top with almost 8.5 million, followed by *Asahi* at more than 5.9 million. Besides *Yomiuri*, *Nikkei Shimbun* (2.4 million) and *Chunichi Shimbun* (nearly 2.3 million) are the others of the six largest dailies without local cartoons (Nishida 2019).

Stewart (2016) conducted a survey of political cartoons in the big three dailies and Kyodo News concerning the 3/11 disaster of 2011 (the earthquake, tsunami, and nuclear power plant destruction at Fukushima), finding that the dailies were slow to react to the disaster with cartoons and that the cartoons used were mostly "bland calls for unity and for support for the government." He further said that the newspapers used the typical cartooning style found in national papers of "[p]eopling cartoons with cute-ish short statured figures with large, stylized heads, similar to many newspaper comic strip characters, and featuring non-offensive facial caricature, almost never made deliberately ugly. It is a style that is no doubt less insulting to its target, but one that can soften a cartoon's satirical punch on occasions when criticism is deployed" (2016, 187). On the other hand, according to Stewart (2016, 184, 197), cartoons in small magazines on the fringe of the mainstream and those on the internet were more aggressive with more biting commentary and broader perspectives. They also tackled taboo subjects and were quicker to react than mainstream dailies. Though not in abundance, there are a few examples of smaller, non-Tokyo-based dailies that have had combative cartoonists. One

is the regional *Fukushima Minpō* (circulation 250,000), whose cartoonist, Asakura Yūzō, began a weekly cartoon, *Disaster Picture-Diary*, dealing specifically with Japan's 3/11 disaster. Asakura's discourse deviated widely from that of the rather complacent cartoonists who made up the norm. As Stewart concluded from a survey he conducted, Asakura alone was "capable of elevating his subjects in depicting tragedy, celebrating life, and in deploying humor to highlight ironies of life in the disaster affected area. He is also capable of angrily cutting down subjects through satirizing those who are insensitive, incompetent, or immoral" (Stewart 2014a).

A less flattering portrait of Japanese political cartooning was painted for me in 2019 during interviews with four cartoonists and the chief editors of Kyodo Illustration,[5] as well as political cartoonists with *Mainichi Shimbun* and *Akabata Shimbun*.

Because cartoonist staff positions on Japanese newspapers are so rare these days, many newspapers rely on Kyodo Illustration for their political cartoons. As is the case worldwide, the benefits of syndication for the newspapers are that the cartoons are less expensive to produce and the subject matter is safer; the disadvantages are sameness of the subject matter and the neglect of local subjects and issues.

Kyodo Illustration is a branch of Kyodo News, founded in 1945 as the successor of the wartime Dōmei News Agency; the illustration branch was added in the 1970s. Kyodo overall has about 1,600 employees domestically and internationally. Seven cartoonists make up the cartoon staff, each designated a day of the week to draw. Cartoon editor Hayakawa Sadabumi (2019) said that the number of cartoonists they employ is adequate, because Kyodo sends out only one cartoon daily. The agency's cartoons are distributed only in Japan; overseas circulation would happen solely by request, of which there has never been any, he said.

Kyodo News is a nonprofit, cooperative news agency that is neither owned nor controlled by the government; it receives its financial support from the fifty member newspapers who pay for the services based on their circulations. Cartoonists are paid the same rate per cartoon, not by cartoonist seniority or prestige, or cartoon quality, Hayakawa (2019) said. Although the mission of Kyodo cartoons is "to criticize the power structure," according to Hayakawa, the syndicate has never had any complaint about its cartoons from the government or politicians. He said that the cartoonists avoid taboo topics such as victims of disasters, royalty, and the handicapped (Hayakawa 2019). Multiple checks are made on a Kyodo cartoonist's work at the idea and sketch stages, and, even after the editor approves a cartoon, there are three more checks, Hayakawa said; he added that those cartoons that are rejected are often dismissed at the idea stage.

The chief editor of Kyodo Illustration, Sasaski Tomoko, sketched out the routine of a designated cartoonist for the day:

> Arrive at Kyodo at 10 a.m. Some cartoonists . . . already know what they will draw about. They understand Kyodo's policies. About twice a month, a cartoonist knowledgeable about our policies will have his preconceived ideas rejected. The cartoonist then reads several newspapers here. By 11 a.m., I also know what the news is and will give ideas to those who seek them. By 1 or 2 p.m., the cartoonist should have an idea formed, at which time, he or she talks about it with Mr. Hayakawa. After 2 p.m., the cartoonist starts a rough draft, and at 3 p.m., the cartoon is shown to us [editors] again, and we check spelling and see if it is in the Kyodo style of writing. The Kyodo style is just a reversed way of saying the same thing. By 4 p.m., the cartoon is drawn by pen and completed by 5 p.m. (Sasaki 2019)

Commenting on the future of Japanese political cartooning, Sasaki (2019) said that newspapers should be the place to publish cartoons, because they use professionals, different from the internet, where amateur works appear alongside professional ones. But newspapers must use cartoons more often. She also felt that Kyodo cartoonists were older people who did not know the technology, and there was a need to recruit younger cartoonists who are savvy about technology.

Veteran Kyodo cartoonist Hazama Ryuji captured the essence of the country's political cartooning position,

saying that newspapers did not open much space for political cartoons; the ones they used were not strong or sharp but rather soft and funny, and young people were not interested in politics. His philosophy, which he claimed was similar to that of all Japanese cartoonists, is to "make people smile" and not "harm" them, his reasoning for that being: "All people are flawed with good and bad characteristics, so I want to show what is funny among them and seek harmony" (Hazama 2019). Toshi Hiko (2019), who has been a cartoonist for thirty years, ten of which were with Kyoto, said that the Japanese market was good for manga/anime/games but not for political cartoons, because there is no demand for them. Female cartoonist Kosuge Riyako (2019) described her style as "angry but soft," saying that she draws prominent male politicians in a "cute" way. In fact, the biggest problem she saw for cartoonists was their inability to portray the prime minister and other top politicians as "human beings like us, with humor." Kosuge made the connections between the public's disinterest in political cartoons and their diminished market: "People who grew up with political cartoons are getting older, and younger people are not interested in them. Why aren't they? During the older generation's time, magazines welcomed political cartoons. No more. There is no market for political cartoons. Four-panel cartoons used to use political themes. No more. Now, they deal only with everyday life." Drawing cartoons for Kyodo since 1990, Kosuge has seen only a very few female political cartoonists in Japan, which she claimed resulted from their disinterest in politics. "When I started at Kyodo, they expected a woman cartoonist to draw about women's topics," she said (Kosuge 2019). The overall scarcity of venues for political cartoons makes Kyodo a "cartoonist's paradise," Kyodo cartoonist Matsuzawa Hidekazu (2019) said, as he rehashed what his colleagues had said: audiences have dwindled and changed, and the humor component is essential in political cartoons.

The number of cartoons these artists create for Kyodo hardly seem adequate to keep them busy and their families comfortable. Hazama draws two a week; Toshi, one a month; Matsuzawa, fifty to sixty yearly for an average of

50

「危なっかしいな……」小菅りやこ

NBH
昭2A
802

2019
1/4

3.7. Political cartoon, Kosuge Riyako. Kyodo Illustration. Permission of Kosuge Riyako.

3.8. Self-caricature by political cartoonist Matsuzawa Hidekazu. Kyodo Illustration. Permission of Matsuzawa Hidekazu.

Japan

3.9. "I Wouldn't Dare Pull the Trigger." Tokoro Yukiyoshi. *Mainichi Shimbun*. Permission of Tokoro Yukiyoshi.

3.10. Political cartoon, Kurata Shin. *Akabata Shimbun*, 1999. Permission of Kurata Shin.

five monthly. Each is paid ¥50,000 per cartoon. Kyodo cartoonists are not permitted to submit political cartoons to other media, although they are free to draw and sell other types of cartoons and illustrations. Hazama has drawn baseball manga, crossword and other puzzles, and illustrations; Toshi, for a while, drew animated *sesō* manga (current news cartoons) for the 47 News website and continues to do illustrations and four-panel strips twice a week for magazines; Kosuge has supplemented her income by drawing a four-panel strip twice monthly; and Matsuzawa has drawn for in-house magazines dealing with security and shipbuilding.

Mainichi Shimbun's political cartoonist since 1985, Tokoro Yukiyoshi (2019) expressed some views parallel to those of his Kyodo colleagues: that magazine circulations have dropped (to almost one-half between 1996 and 2018) and that he prefers "humorous, easy-to-understand political cartoons rather than real strong ones used as weapons." Elaborating further, he said: "Because Japanese society is more communally organized, cartoonists and editors (as well as people more generally) are hesitant to speak out because to do so might hurt others" (Tokoro 2019). The mission of Japanese political cartoons differs from that of cartoons in

3.11. Political cartoon, Yoshiaki Yokota. Kyodo Illustration. Permission of Yoshiaki Yokota.

some parts of the West, he continued, because in Japan, the cartoons are meant "to make fun of a situation, not to try to recommend a solution."

Tokoro's cartoon appears weekly on Friday on *Mainichi*'s international news page. He said that the cartoon used to be one-panel but was switched to two panels when the international situation became more complicated. He also draws cartoons with universal themes for international periodicals. All of his work is on a freelance basis, including that for *Mainichi*, an arrangement he prefers. Tokoro gave Japanese political cartoons a "high probability" of surviving, but cartoonists need to find new ways (such as combining imaginary figures with those of politicians in manga format or creating games using political figures as subjects) and different venues, such as web magazines and smaller publications. The biggest problem of political cartoonists in Japan, he thought, was the difficulty of drawing about neighbors China and Korea because of leftover hard feelings from World War II (Tokoro 2019).

Since launching his career in 1978, Tokoro has had a variety of jobs, drawing phone cards for politicians who distribute them free to potential voters, two-panel cartoons for sports magazines, and cartoons about the week's events for a Nagoya television station. He continued to draw for Nagoya newspapers even after moving to Tokyo in 1983, sending his work by airmail. His decision to move to Tokyo at age thirty-six was based on his hunch that it was the right age to go, and "not wait until I was thirty-seven or older." Tokoro recalled his new beginnings in Tokyo:

There were many printing plants near where I lived in Tokyo. If, at the last minute before going to press, a publication had space needing to be filled, I drew cartoons to fill the space—in less than four hours. All printing companies knew of me and called upon me to fill space for them. Sometimes, I already had a cartoon ready before the printer sought one. I would work all night, then sleep with my sports coat on, ready to awaken and meet the editors, usually women, who came to my place to pick up the cartoon. (Tokoro 2019)

One newspaper that carries a political cartoon daily is *Akabata Shimbun*, the organ of the Communist Party of Japan (CPJ). Three cartoonists, working on a nonstaff basis, provide the drawings—two twice a week and one, a sole cartoon weekly. Kurata Shin,[6] the veteran among them, said that the newspaper's (and the CPJ's) policy is to "correct what is not good for the people, to follow the people's demands." The government does not like this policy, he said; "for example, our attacks on the government's purchase of expensive military equipment," but it does not retaliate. Kurata (2019) seldom checks with the editor, because he knows well the CPJ's policies and taboo topics; as an example, he said that he could not "draw women as unequal to men." Asked if *Akabata* ever praised capitalism or the United States, he answered: "We criticize Trump, but admire Lincoln and others. I criticize America for acting as if it is the top of the world, but not American democracy, and I contend that Japan should not always follow the US."

Kurata (2019) agreed that Japanese political cartooning is spiraling downward and is not appreciated as before. He thought that people "expected better cartoons, and maybe the cartoonists cannot meet the expectations. They are skillful enough, but the payment is not sufficient. They should be able to make a living without problems." Kurata's hopes are that the "cartoonist group can train younger aspirants and ensure their future and expand the space for political cartoons." He pointed out that contemporary political cartoonists, for lack of newspaper and magazine space, hold exhibitions and print pamphlets to expose their work (Kurata 2019).

A Brief Conclusion

The story is all too familiar, as it is mostly everywhere, that the task for Japanese political cartoonists to find ingenious ways to preserve this vital art is monstrously gigantic. With a long and rich history of satiric drawings, attended at times by creative readjustments to their form and style to keep them alive and thriving, Japan is likely up to the challenge.

Notes

1. *Nipponchi*'s cover displayed the "mocking pun" that the magazine was "licensed" but "forbidden," an unnecessary boast as its founders stayed clear of attacking the government (Duus 2001, 976).

2. The magazine's logo, *marumaru*, means "circles," derived from the small circles editors used for self-censorship in the galley proof stage, according to Julia Meech-Pekarik (1986, 181), who adds: "[S]ome books went into print with entire lines of little circles substituted for objectionable words." "Chimbun" was a pun on *shimbun*, implying "strange writings."

3. Kitazawa abhorred the use of the word *ponchi* to refer to comic art, regularly stressing his aim "to wipe out *ponchi*," because they had dropped in quality and were "old-fashioned, overly wordy, and incapable of direct expression" (Stewart 2014b).

4. Although manga are excluded from the main thrust of this book, a number of them over the years have been politically oriented. Prime examples are the best-selling books of far right author Kobayashi Yoshinori, which claim that "comfort" women were not the Japanese military's sex slaves but rather sex volunteers, and defended the "justness" of Japan's role in World War II (French 2001, 3). *Barefoot Gen* by Nakazawa Keiji qualifies as a politically themed series, portraying the author's experiences of the US atomic bombing of Hiroshima and the lingering aftereffects. In the 1970s and 1980s, pronuclear manga were issued by the government and power industry to offset rising antinuclear sentiment. Manga against nuclear power first appeared in 1970 and continued to be written for decades (Holmberg 2016).

5. Two other Kyodo cartoonists whom I did not interview in 2019 are Arai Taro, who became a cartoonist when the company for which he worked collapsed, and Yoshiaki Yokota. I met Yoshiaki briefly at Kyodo, but we could not talk long because he was leaving for a Melbourne exhibition of Japanese cartoons that day. The logo of Kyodo News and Kyodo Illustration does not include the macrons, though the Japanese word *kyōdō* does.

6. Kurata is known by the name Shin, but he signs as Sin.

Bibliography

Aki, Ryūzan. 1993. Interview with John A. Lent. Tokyo, November 6.

Blyth, R. H. 1959. *Oriental Humour*. Tokyo: Hokuseido Press.

Chibbett, David. 1977. *The History of Japanese Printing and Book Illustration*. Tokyo: Kodansha.

Clark, Timothy. 1993. *Demon of Painting: The Art of Kawanabe Kyōsai*. London: British Museum Press.

Clark, Timothy. 2009. *Kuniyoshi: From the Arthur R. Miller Collection*. London: Royal Academy of Arts.

Duus, Peter. 2001. "Presidential Address: Weapons of the Weak, Weapons of the Strong; The Development of the Japanese Political Cartoon." *Journal of Asian Studies* 60, no. 4 (November): 965–97.

Esselstrom, Erik. 2015. "Red Guards and Salarymen: The Chinese Cultural Revolution and Comic Satire in 1960s Japan." *Journal of Asian Studies* 74, no. 4 (November): 953–76.

Fagioli, Marco. 1997. *Shunga: The Erotic Art of Japan*. New York: Universe.

Feldman, Ofer. 1995. "Political Reality and Editorial Cartoons in Japan: How the National Dailies Illustrate the Japanese Prime Minister." *Journalism and Mass Communication Quarterly* 72, no. 3 (September): 571–80.

French, Howard W. 2001. "Japan's Resurgent Far Right Tinkers with History." *New York Times*, March 25, 3.

Hayakawa, Sadabumi. 2019. Interview with John A. Lent, Tokyo, February 4.

Hazama, Ryuji. 2019. Interview with John A. Lent, Tokyo, February 4.

Hibbett, Howard. 2002. *The Chrysanthemum and the Fish: Japanese Humor since the Age of the Shoguns*. Tokyo: Kodansha.

Holmberg, Ryan. 2016. "Pro-Nuclear Manga: The Seventies and Eighties." *Comics Journal*, February 26. https://www.tcj.com/pro-nuclear-manga-the-seventies-and-eighties.

Horn, Maurice, ed. 1976. *The World Encyclopedia of Comics*. New York: Chelsea House.

Illerbrun, Kurt. 2005. "The Japanese Political Cartoon: Development and Decline." Master's thesis, University of Oxford.

Ishiko, Jun. 1988. *Nihon Mangashi* [A History of Japanese Comics]. Tokyo: Shūkai Shisōsha.

Kato, Yoshiro. 1993. Interview with John A. Lent, Tokyo, November 6.

Kern, Adam L. 2007. "The Kibyoshi: Japan's Eighteenth-Century Comicbook for Adults." *International Journal of Comic Art* 9, no. 1 (Spring): 3–32.

Kosuge, Riyako. 2019. Interview with John A. Lent, Tokyo, February 4.

Kurata, Shin [Sin]. 2019. Interview with John A. Lent, Tokyo, February 6.

Lane, Richard. 1982. *Images from the Floating World: The Japanese Print*. New York: Dorset Press.

Lent, John A. 2014. "Allied, Japanese, and Chinese Propaganda Cartoon Leaflets during World War II." *International Journal of Comic Art* 16, no. 1 (Spring): 258–301.

Matsuzawa, Hidekazu. 2019. Interview with John A. Lent, Tokyo, February 4.

Meech-Pekarik, Julia. 1986. *The World of the Meiji Print: Impressions of a New Civilization*. New York: Weatherhill.

Michener, James A. 1954. *The Floating World: The Story of Japanese Prints*. New York: Random House.

Nishida, Toshiko. 2019. Correspondence with John A. Lent, January 13.

Nishizawa, Yuzi. 1993. Interview with John A. Lent, Tokyo, November 6.

Oikawa, Shigeru. 1996. *Comic Genius: Kawanabe Kyōsai*. Tokyo: Tokyo Shimbun.

Okamoto, Rei. 1996. "Portrayal of the War and Enemy in Japanese Wartime Cartoons." *Journal of Asian Pacific Communication* 7, nos. 1–2: 5–17.

Oriental Affairs. 1939. "Japan Punch." May, 259–70.

Parrott, Lindesay. 1946. "Laughs from Tokyo." *New York Times Magazine*, May 12, 28.

Rhodes, Anthony. 1976. *Propaganda: The Art of Persuasion, World War II*. New York: Chelsea House.

Sakai, Tadayasu, and Shimizu Isao. 1985. *Nisson Sensōki no Manga* [Comics during the Sino-Japanese War]. Tokyo: Shikuma Shobō.

Sasaki, Tomoko. 2019. Interview with John A. Lent, Tokyo, February 4.

Satō, Sampei. 1993. Interview with John A. Lent, Tokyo, November 8.

Schodt, Frederik L. 1983. *Manga! Manga! The World of Japanese Comics*. Tokyo: Kodansha.

Shimizu, Isao, ed. 1989. *Nihon Manga no Jiten* [Dictionary of Japanese Comics]. Tokyo: Sanseidō.

Shimizu, Isao, ed. 1991. *Manga no Rekishi* [A History of Japanese Cartoons]. Tokyo: Iwanami Shoten.

Silverberg, Miriam. 2006. *Erotic, Grotesque Nonsense: The Mass Culture of Japanese Modern Times*. Berkeley: University of California Press.

Stewart, Ronald. 2006. "An Australian Cartoonist in 19th Century Japan: Frank A. Nankivell and the Beginnings of Modern Japanese Comic Art." *International Journal of Comic Art* 8, no. 2 (Fall): 77–97.

Stewart, Ronald. 2014a. "Breaking the Mainstream Mold: The Birth of a Local Political Cartoonist in Post-3.11 Japan." *European Journal of Humour Research* 2, no. 4 (November): 74–94.

Stewart, Ronald. 2014b. "Manga Studies #2: Manga History; Shimizu Isao and Miyamoto Hirohito on Japan's First Modern 'Manga' Artist Kitazawa Rakuten." *Comics Forum*, June 14. https://comicsforum.org/2014/06/14/manga-studies-2-manga-history-shimizu-isao-and-miyamoto-hirohito-on-japans-first-modern-manga-artist-kitazawa-rakuten-by-ronald-stewart/.

Stewart, Ronald. 2016. "Post 3-11 Japanese Political Cartooning with a Satirical Bite: Non-Newspaper Cartoons and Their Potential." *Kritika Kultura*, no. 26: 179–220.

Sugiura, Yukio. 1993. Interview with John A. Lent, Tokyo, November 6.

Suzuki, Yamato. 1993. Interview with John A. Lent, Tokyo, November 6.

Tokoro, Yukiyoshi. 2019. Interview with John A. Lent, Tokyo, February 5.

Toshi, Hiko. 2019. Interview with John A. Lent, Tokyo, February 4.

Wetherall, William. 1990. "Bashers at Wits' End: Satirists Practise Democracy-by-Proxy." *Far Eastern Economic Review*, August 2, 25–26.

Whitford, Frank. 1977. *Japanese Prints and Western Painters*. New York: Macmillan.

Zhang, Shaoqian. 2014. "Combat and Collaboration: The Clash of Propaganda Prints between the Chinese Guomindang and the Japanese Empire in the 1930s–40s." *Journal of Transcultural Studies* 5, no. 1: 95–133. http://heiup-uni-heidelberg.de-journals/index.php/transcultural/article/.

Long before the Korean peninsula was split geographically, politically, and ideologically, the country had a rich legacy of satire and humor. During the Chosŏn Dynasty (1392–1897), *sohwa* (funny stories) were spread among many genres, including poetry, mask plays, and literary works. Much of the *sohwa* mocked government officials and Japan's imperialist ambitions in Korea.

Visual satire took on some importance with the arrival of newspapers and magazines, especially after the pro-independence 1919 movement. Mildly critical of the Japanese occupation, political cartoons took the form of *t'ongsokjŏk* (popular cartoons), drawn by professional cartoonists to entertain, and *minjunk manhwa* (readers' cartoons), which carried a political, critical tone (Shuster 2014, 39). In the late 1920s, the Japanese colonial government began to crack down on the press, resulting in cartoons being less critical.

Governance of the arts was a priority of leader Kim Il Sung, who in 1946, similar to Mao Zedong in Yan'an a few years earlier, defined the role of culture. In fact, the Federation of Literature and Arts, set up in 1946, predated the founding of the Democratic People's Republic of Korea (DPRK). One of the early goals of the state was to eradicate the long-held bias of North Korean writers against satire, which they viewed as low and vulgar. Satire, the officials contended, was the means to do away with old beliefs and customs while building a completely new infrastructure. To accomplish this, the state began to train satirists (Shuster 2014, 56).

Because of North Korea's low literacy rate at the time, visual satire through cartoons and posters was far more successful in addressing the state's aims than literary works. David Shuster (2014, 22) writes that North Korean culture in the 1950s was defined by the "massive production of social and political satire by the state" and a "pervasive practice of street play, or street jesting," both attributed to a lack of "leisure infrastructure" in the period following the Korean War, known as the "Fatherland Liberation War" in North Korea.

In August 1946, *Horang'i* (Tiger) was started as a satirical current events periodical; its name was changed to *Hwalsal* (Arrow) in January 1948. A sixteen-page

Vignette: North Korea

NK.1. *Hwalsal* culture magazine, volume 16, front cover.

magazine, *Hwalsal* was made up of "satirical and agitating cartoons, comic strips, and illustrations," with the aim, according to Martin Petersen, to

> mobilize their Korean readership to social revolution and criticize the Japanese, U.S., and South Korean enemies of the nation. The magazine mainly features various one-frame and full-page cartoons, juxtaposing life in the North and the South—the socialist and imperialist-capitalist worlds. In many cases, this juxtaposition is accentuated by rendering self and other, right and wrong, in disparate graphic styles. *Hwalsal* volume 15 (pp. 6–7) and volume 16 (pp. 8–9) also contain multi-panel sequential image narratives on the merits of socialist, pro-North guerillas operating in the South. (Petersen 2019, 28)

Foreign influences were evident in at least volumes 9, 15, and 16, all of which included editorial cartoons as "Soviet manhwa." After all, *Hwalsal* was modeled after the Soviet humor magazine *Krokodil* (Crocodile).

Hwalsal regularly supported cartoons as change agents, allowing its own comic art to be reprinted throughout North Korea, soliciting criticism and manhwa contributions from its readers, converting them into "active participants in the very act of turning the everyday into satire" (Shuster 2014), asking workers and farmers to publish accounts of workplace negligence and mistakes they observed as text or cartoons in local newspapers and *pyŏkpo* (wall gazettes), and writing a series of articles on how to make effective cartoons for workplace *pyŏkpo*.

Other venues for early DPRK satire cartoonists were the cultural magazines *Cho-Sso ch'insŏn* (Korean-Soviet Friendship), started by the Korean Soviet Friendship Society, and *Ch'ŏllima*, a monthly named after the Chŏllima Movement (1958) and started in 1959. As with *Hwalsal*, these magazines used much social satire that mocked old beliefs and customs, South Korea, and the United States, and turned mundane events into comical stories. Surveying six volumes of *Ch'ŏllima* from 1964, Petersen (2019, 34) identifies three types of image/text formats: illustrated stories, comic strips, and serialized

NK.2. *Kumsong Chongynon Chulpansa* (The True Identity of Pear Blossom), Kim Yong-hyon and Choe Chu'-sop, 2004.

manhwa. There were foreign touches in *Ch'ŏillima* as well, notably Hŏ Nŭngt'aek's *Kildoli: Namjŏsonŭl han koaŭi unmyong* (Kildoli: The Destiny of a South Korean Orphan), a running story of an orphan among the "downtrodden masses of the South," very similar to China's Sanmao the Vagrant, a character by Zhang Leping who suffered similarly during Guomindang rule.

A third cultural magazine, *Chosŏn Yesul* (Korean Art), carried a significant number of children's *kurimchaek* (picture books or comics) and manhwa. A monthly, *Chosŏn Yesul* discussed theater, films, music, art, and acrobatics for an audience of artists, other arts professionals, and the general public. *Chosŏn Yesul* featured three articles in 2005 and 2006 that framed its use of *kurimchaek* and manhwa: "a canon of *kurimchaek* that were told in person by and as such are emanations of the life and wisdom of the Three Generals" (Kim Il Sung, Kim Jong Il, and Kim Jong Suk); "Military First-era illustrations for children, influenced by the artistic

NK.3. *Mirror*, Kim Yong-suh and Ryang Ok-shil. *Korean Woman*, February 2010.

ideas and theory of Kim Jong Il, with the early achievements of Kim Il Sung in the field of manhwa"; and early satirical manhwa on the "relation between father and son in this cultural field, and on its function as a 'powerful weapon for propaganda and agitation'" (Petersen 2019, 258). In short, these comics deify the leaders and promote the state ideology.

Kurimchaek are popular and accessible, sold and rented at a reasonable fee at bookstores. The most popular genres are spy and military, for instance *Paekkot' ŭi changch'e* (The True Identity of Pear Blossom), which depicts US and Japanese spies as easy prey for Pyongyang's best special agents. Some military comics may have been based on the diaries of revolutionaries who fought alongside Kim Il Sung (James 2012). Other titles deal with Korean fables and legends. The plots have been described by a *Stars and Stripes* writer as "often wacky, usually pinning blame on loud-mouthed Americans and opportunist Japanese for cursing their promised land with vice" (Cain 2010, 15). Embedded in comics stories is the *juche* philosophy (affirming the radical self-reliance of the state) that is ever-present in all media. Ri Pyong-Jo (2010) gives an example of the *juche* spirit in a comic strip called *Mirror* in *Korean Woman* magazine, February 2010:

> PANEL 1: "Mother-in-law, I'm back from work."
>   "You've worked hard. Go inside and sit down."
> PANEL 2: "Today I cooked up something special."
>   "There you go again! I told you I would handle the cooking this evening."
> PANEL 3: "Hey, why are you already up, instead of resting longer?" "You're busy in the morning. I have to lend you a hand."
> PANEL 4: "How is it that you're always such an innovator?" "How can I not be, with a mother-in-law who treats me like her own daughter?"

What Alzo David-West wrote about North Korean literature is applicable to comic art: it is "firmly controlled by the political regime" and "bureaucratically controlled, functionally didactic, culturally nationalist, and politically Stalinist" (2009, 22). Some of the values promoted in *kurimchaek* are foreign to the Western mind: for example, the "nation-as-family values that allegorise and partly replace biological family values" (Petersen 2012, 34) and "paternal abandonment of family duties due to work duties for the sake of the Fatherland" (42).

58   Generally, comics in North Korea have been published by Kumsong Chongnyon Chulpansa (Kumsong Youth Publishing House), Munlak Yesul Chulpansa (Literature and Arts Publishing House), and Kullo Tanche Chulpansa; they are distributed to schools as gifts, use a "national narrator" (such as Kim Il Sung or Kim Jong Il) to introduce settings, are poorly produced but often aesthetically well developed and conceptually complex; and sometimes are well researched (Strangio 2011).

Bibliography

Cain, Geoffrey. 2010. "North Korea Illustrated: The Comic Books That Brainwash North Koreans." *Stars and Stripes*, March 9, 15.

David-West, Alzo. 2009. "The Literary Ideas of Kim Il Sung and Kim Jong Il: An Introduction to North Korean Meta-Authorial Perspectives." *Cultural Logic* 16. https://ojs.library.ubc.ca/index.php/clogic/article/view/191548.

James. 2012. "North Korean Comic Books: Propaganda or Propamanga?" *Korea Bang*, May 14. https://www.koreabang.com/2012/pictures/north-korean-comic-books-propaganda-or-propamanga.html.

Petersen, Martin. 2012. "Sleepless in the DPRK: Graphic Negotiations of 'Family' in *The True Identity of Pear Blossom*." *Scandinavian Journal of Comic Art* 1, no. 2 (Autumn): 30–58.

Petersen, Martin. 2019. *North Korean Graphic Novels: Seduction of the Innocent?* Abingdon, Oxon., England: Routledge.

Ri, Pyong-Jo. 2010. "In North Korea, Juche Iron vs. American Crows." *New York Times*, April 18.

Shuster, David. 2014. "A Jester with Chameleon Faces: Laughter and Comedy in North Korea, 1953–1969." PhD diss., Harvard University.

Strangio, Sebastian. 2011. "'You Are Followers of the Juche Philosophy, So I Can Put My Trust in You': Reading North Korean Comic Book Propaganda." *Slate*, June 21. http://www.slate.com/id/2296642.

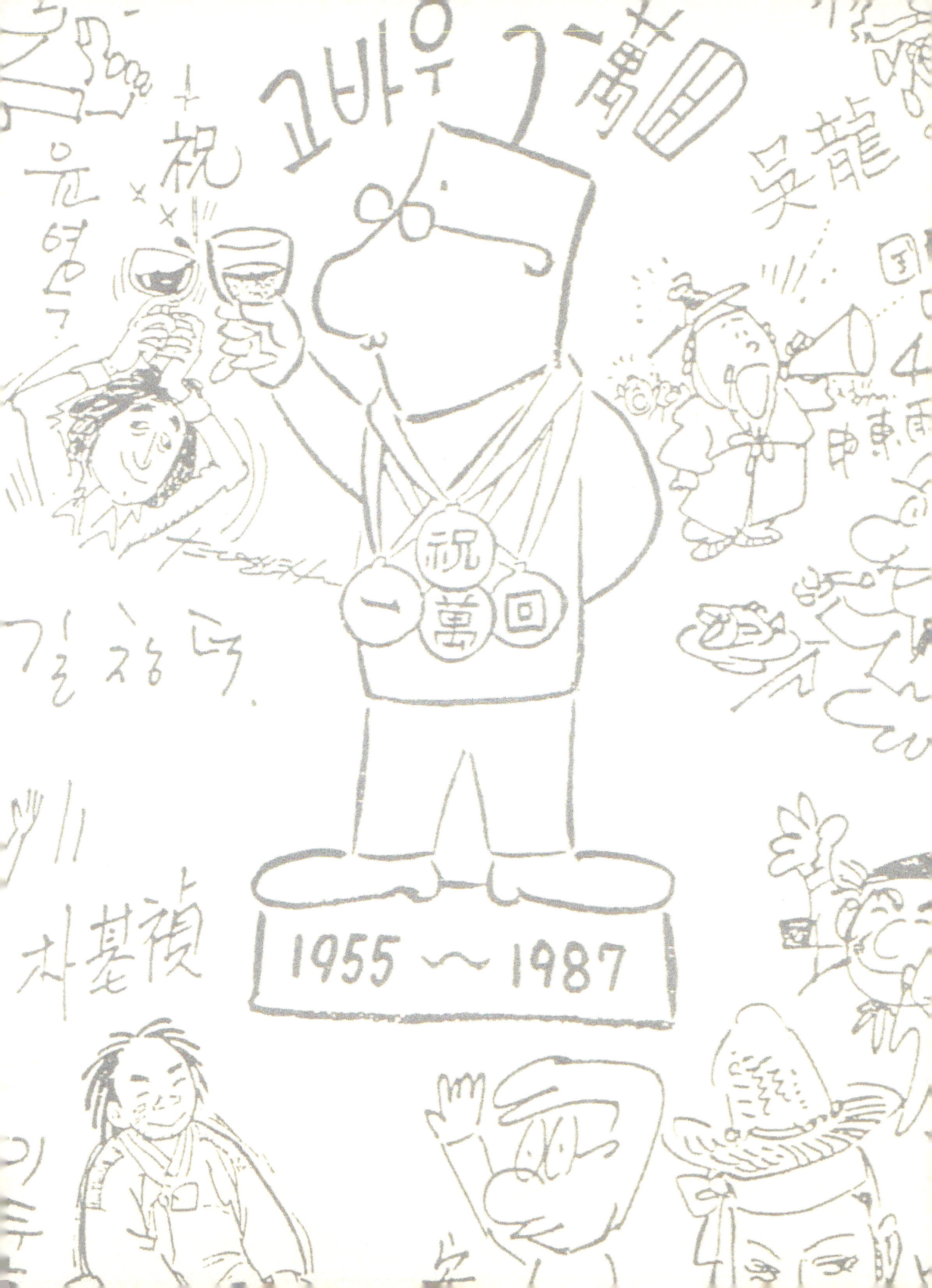
祝 고바우 一萬回
吳龍
祝
一 萬 回
1955 ~ 1987

Historical Overview

Illustrations appeared in the inaugural (October 1883) and at least two subsequent (January 30 and February 17, 1884) issues of Korea's first newspaper, *Hansong Sonbo*. Shortly after, three other newspapers used illustrations, but to label them cartoons would be stretching the point. For certain, their declared uses dismissed them as political cartoons: namely, to introduce Western science, advertise products, and beautify the newspaper (Y.-O. Yoon 1986).

A German traveler to Seoul, Ernst von Hesse-Wartegg, wrote that he saw locally drawn political caricatures during his 1884 visit; however, they circulated only among the intelligentsia. He did not disclose whether they appeared in newspapers. It is highly likely that only the intelligentsia had the literacy skills and income to appreciate newspapers. Hesse-Wartegg reported:

> I saw a political caricature which was drawn by a Korean. It described Korea as an unusually shaped person. The person's head was small and bald. His arms and legs were skinny and thin. However, his body was fat. Look, said a Korean, this is the poor figure of my country. This head means king, arms and legs are squeezed and suppressed people. But, the fat body is noblemen and bureaucrats in this country. (quoted in H.-C. Lee 1982, 9)

After the Korean newspapers *Hansong Sonbo* and *Hansong Chubo* were closed in 1894, satirical poetry, but not cartoons, appeared in the Japanese-operated newspapers that remained. Lee Hae-Chang (1982, 9–18) surmises that satirical drawings probably circulated informally in a limited number.

More likely, the first newspaper cartoon for the public appeared in *Taehan Minbo* on June 2, 1909. Drawn by Yi To-Yong, the cartoon shows a gentleman with top hat and cane spewing out four streams of words announcing the paper's missions: to promote the understanding of the national situation, to unite people by restoring the Korean spirit, to represent the real public opinion, and to report diverse facts on the basis of

Chapter 4

South Korea

4.1. "Saphwa" by Yi To-Yong, the first newspaper cartoon in Korea. *Taehan Minbo*, initial issue, June 2, 1909.

reality (H.-C. Lee 1982, 19–20). This almost reads like a definition of political cartoons.

Ironically, although *Taehan Minbo* was very critical of the Japanese occupation, the paper owed its very existence to the Japanese resident general, who, after the passing of the 1907 Newspaper Law and the suppression of another newspaper, *Taehan Maeil Sinbo*, allowed the start-up of *Taehan Minbo* and other private newspapers.

Taehan Minbo was often censored because of Yi To-Yong's strong cartoons, which satirized the cruelty of the Japanese and the traitorous activities of some Japanophile Koreans. *Taehan Minbo* editors alerted readers when a cartoon was censored, completely covering it with black ink. The authorities closed the newspaper on August 31, 1910 (Y.-O. Yoon 1986).

During the 1910s, it was mainly *Kyongsong Ilbo* that printed cartoons. Owned by Japanese businessmen and

marked by unwavering allegiance to the colonial authorities, *Kyongsong Ilbo* printed many cartoons glorifying Japanese culture and occupation policies and viciously attacking Korean underdevelopment.

The bloody March 1, 1919, independence movement changed nearly everything, and certainly the cartoon scene. At a higher level, the Japanese emphasized cultural over militaristic tactics; entertainment over propaganda. For example, *Kyongsong Ilbo* cartoons quit elevating Japanese culture and maligning that of Korea; instead, they offered entertainment and humor, especially through comic strips introduced in the 1920s. New dailies *Dong-A Ilbo* and *Chosun Ilbo* appeared and offered more venues for cartoonists, and a new phenomenon, readers' cartoons, allowed for wider and more diverse opinions. Daily newspapers allocated special sections for readers' cartoons, such as *Donga Manhwa* in *Dong-A Ilbo*, *Ch'ul P'il Sajin* in *Chosun Ilbo*, and *Chibang Manhwa* in *Sidae Ilbo*.[1]

By the mid-1920s, the situation changed again. Critical newspapers were suspended or closed, readers' cartoons disappeared for a while, and what political cartoons remained were replaced by children's and humor manhwa (comics) (Y.-O. Yoon 1992). Remaining dailies favorable to the Japanese used cartoons throughout the 1930s to legitimate Japan's buildup of militarism, boost soldier morale, and severely criticize the Allied forces. Many pre–World War II cartoonists were actually traditional brush painters who learned cartooning from Kim Dong-Sung, who had studied journalism in the United States (Y.-O. Yoon 1986).

Newspaper political and social commentary cartoons slowly returned after World War II. Kim Kyu-Taek, called the father of one-panel political cartoons by historian Yoon Young-Ok (1992), resumed his career, as did others, often with comic strips.

Among the issues the political cartoons dealt with were the ideological struggle between rightists and leftists, the thirty-eighth parallel that divided the peninsula, the cooperative China-Korea relationship, the housing crisis, the power shift from the US military to Korean civilian authorities, comparisons between US and

Korean products, and the reestablishment of the nation. The Public Affairs Office of the US military government published a weekly newsletter, which, through cartoons, encouraged support for the rebuilding of Korea (H.-C. Lee 1982).

The years 1945–1950 also yielded three cartoon magazines designed for the public and destined to be the breeding ground for future cartoonists of importance. All of the magazines had brief lives. The first, *Manhwa Hangjin* (Parade of Cartoons), started on September 15, 1949, ran into trouble from its first issue and was suspended by the Ministry of Education after three appearances. *Manhwa News* lasted longer, even gaining a peak circulation of forty-six thousand, before its main cartoonist, Kim Yong-Hwan (1912–1998), split and started *Manhwa Shinmun*, which published two issues before the Korean War. *Manhwa Shinmun* restarted when hostilities ceased, and it became the first home for Kim Song-Hwan's (1932–2019) very long-lived *Gobau* (High Firm Rock) (Oh 1981).

During the Korean War (1950–1953), cartooning continued, mostly used to support the war effort. Cartoonists drew for military publications such as the Ministry of National Defense's weekly *Manhwa Sungni* (Cartoon Victory) and the army's *Sabyong Manhwa* (Soldiers' Cartoons), created cartoon flyers used for propaganda against the enemy, published comic books that vilified the communists or praised the brave South Korean soldiers (Oh 1981), and issued a cartoon magazine, *Manhwa Sinbo*, that lasted for seven or eight issues. (For fuller treatments of the history of Korean political cartooning, see Lent 1995 and W.-B. Lee 1991).

The 1950s were a difficult time for cartoonists, not just because of the devastation caused by two major wars on Korean soil in fewer than fifteen years but also because of the lack of attention (and resultant insufficient pay) their work was given. Veteran political cartoonist Kim Song-Hwan remembered: "People asked, 'Why do cartoons?' The advertising manager of my paper asked, 'Why waste good advertising space for political cartoons?'" (Song-Hwan Kim 1992). Equally exasperating, according to Kim, was that cartoonists

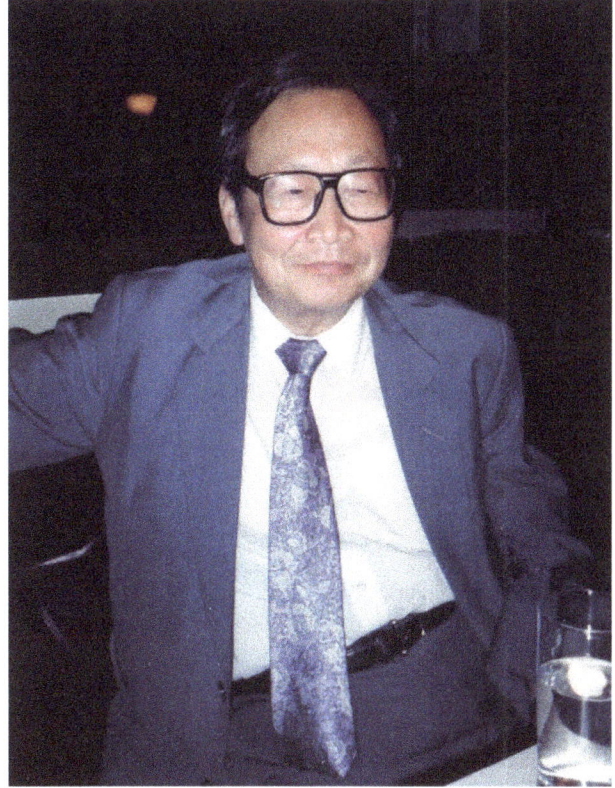

4.2. Kim Song-Hwan, veteran political cartoonist, *Manhwa Shinmun*, *Dong-A Ilbo*, and *Chosun Ilbo*, Seoul, July 1992. Photo by John A. Lent. Courtesy of Kim Song-Hwan.

were paid "only pennies at the papers—almost as bad as page boys got." He added: "When I started, cartoon reading was the hobby of children only. We had much difficulty at first. Many cartoonists dropped out, because their work was not popular" (Song-Hwan Kim 1992).

But hard times sometimes lead to bursts of energy and creativity and determined efforts to conquer adversity. That seems to have happened in the South Korean cartoon community, for, during the 1950s, a batch of vibrant political cartoonists made their presence known through both one- and four-panel works. The four-panel strips were enlarged interpretations of political cartoons, or as Oh Kyu-Won (1981, 24) distinguished between them: the one-panel political commentary cartoons centered on problematic issues, while the four-panel ones showed how the issues were adopted or rejected by society.

Vertically arranged four-panel commentary cartoons became more popular until they were the major attraction for readers, the first item they looked for when opening their newspapers (Y.-O. Yoon 1992).

Advertisers recognized their popularity, vying vigorously to purchase the one-column, one-inch space under them. That tiny space carried the most expensive rate in all dailies, four to five times the normal fees. Kim Song-Hwan, who introduced this type of cartoon with his strip *Gobau* on February 1, 1955, in *Dong-A Ilbo*, said that the revenue generated in one day by the one-inch advertisement under his cartoon could pay ten reporters' salaries for a month. He said that advertisers had to wait to be considered for that slot and to show that they had advertised consistently with large expenditures in other sections of the daily (Song-Hwan Kim 1992). Yoon Young-Ok (1992) claimed that some advertisers contracted by the year for the space under the four-panel cartoons.

Four-panel cartoons appeared on the cultural or social page (the next to last page of the paper), were displayed vertically stacked, carried a regular title that had a symbolic meaning, featured the same character every day, and were numbered consecutively. Usually, panel 1 was an introduction, panel 2 a reversion, panel 3 the emphasis, and panel 4 the punchline (Lee 1992).[2]

Besides Kim's *Gobau*, two other four-panel commentary cartoons debuted in 1955: Ahn Ui-Sup's *Dookobi* (Mr. Toad, a sign of good luck) and Chong Un-Gyong's *Auntie Walsun* (a tart-tongued housemaid). Subsequently, others followed, such as Yoon Young-Ok's *Kat'uri* (Mrs. Hen Pheasant, a symbol of diligence and intelligence) and Kim Pan-Kook's *Ch'onggaeguri* (blue frog, representing resistance) (Ahn 1992; Chong 1992; Y.-O. Yoon 1992; P.-K. Kim 1992). These cartoon characters are closely identified with their creators. Kim Song-Hwan (1992) spoke of himself and Gobau as synonymous, stating that because he had been drawing for about forty years, his character was popular, and Kim was broadly known by Koreans.

As previously mentioned, the ongoing four-panel cartoons addressed current political, social, and economic issues, therefore subjecting their creators to close public

4.3. A popular, vertical four-panel political strip, *Gobau*, by Kim Song-Hwan, *Chosun Ilbo*, July 4, 1992, no. 11,666. Courtesy of Kim Song-Hwan.

4.4. *Gobau* surrounded by other noted Korean cartoon characters on the occasion of the strip's ten-thousandth appearance, 1987. Courtesy of Kim Song-Hwan.

4.5. A popular 1990s political strip, *Auntie Walsun*, by Chong Un-Gyong, no. 5,435. Courtesy of Chong Un-Gyong.

and government scrutiny. For a large part of the second half of the twentieth century, South Korea was ruled by tough militarist and civilian governments, and during this time the public grew to appreciate political cartoons. Yoon Young-Ok explained: "Through the dictatorships, military governments closed people's ears and eyes. People wanted to know the truth, and the articles could not give it. The cartoons, even though fictional, gave a hint at the truth and people believed in them" (Y.-O. Yoon 1992). The Korean public grew savvy to implied messages in the four-panel works, sometimes reading messages into cartoons that were not intended by the artist. Kim Song-Hwan

included many messages in *Gobau* that upset the repressive Park Chung-Hee regime. He talked about this, saying that he drew democracy as it existed in foreign countries and that he often used symbols. On one occasion, for instance, he put sunglasses on Gobau; President Park was known for regularly wearing black sunglasses. Kim said that Park hated the implication that "because you can't see his eyes, you can't know if he is saying the truth" (Song-Hwan Kim 1992; also Y.-O. Yoon 1986, 299–322).

Other political cartoonists sidestepped government censorship any way they could, while enduring many indignities. Yoon Young-Ok lost his position on *Seoul*

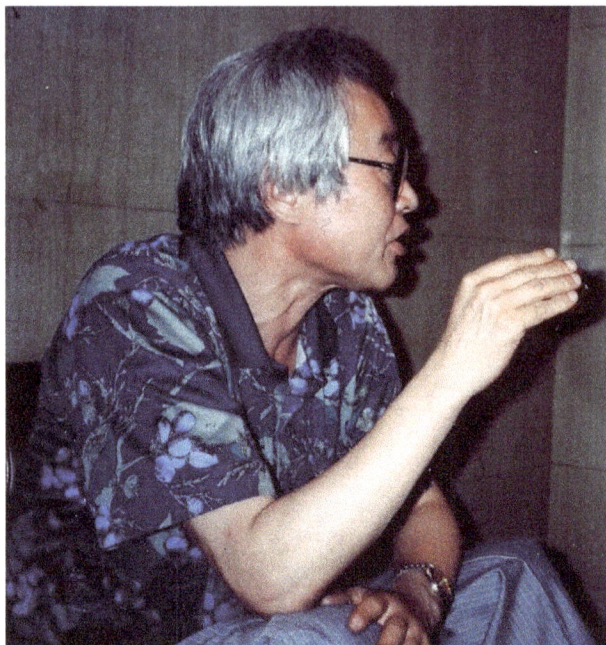

4.6. Political cartoonist Yoon Young-Ok, *Seoul Shinmun*, Seoul, July 1992. Photo by John A. Lent. Courtesy of Yoon Young-Ok.

Shinmun in 1972 because of a cartoon that the government thought was critical of Park's New Community Movement; Ahn Ui-Sup was fired by *Hankook Ilbo* because of government pressure; and Kim Ki-Baek lost his regular cartoon because of government interference (Y.-O. Yoon 1986, 304–5).

In a number of instances, the punishments were much more severe. The dean of political cartoonists, Kim Song-Hwan described his career while under the Park and Chun Doo-Hwan governments as living on "the edge of a razor blade." During those years, Kim said that he was censored, trailed by secret police, harassed by threatening phone calls, interrogated for long stretches without sleep, fined, and imprisoned under three dictators. The Korean Central Intelligence Agency constantly threatened him; in 1974, the year the first lady was assassinated, Kim was jailed twice. On one occasion, *Dong-A Ilbo* staff members forced his release from jail by staging a strike. Earlier, in 1957 and 1958, the police fined him; they also told him that they planned to inform higher officials that he was a "red." Kim said:

Also, I was called on occasion to the prosecutor's office where I had to write why I drew certain cartoons. I had to explain the implications of the cartoons, what I had in mind. Things were reported spontaneously and regularly to Park Chung-Hee. He knew everything about me. Once, when I drew a cartoon of Park, he let the *Dong-A Ilbo* Blue House [the president's residence] correspondent know he hated it and that I should be informed. I had to leave work early for a week as I feared what might happen to me. Similar things happened under Chun. He personally wanted to meet me. He said there were calls for reform because of *Gobau*, and he suggested that I emigrate to the United States. (Song-Hwan Kim 1992)

During his four decades of cartooning, Kim faced more than two hundred government attempts to change his work. Sometimes he had to redraw his cartoons many times in a day before they were approved. He said:

I hated to draw the cartoon four times a day so I would just do a humor cartoon, drop the political content. But the censors would ask me to draw again as they thought I had hidden meanings in the humor. I would just put in a dog or something that was funny, and the censors would misread it to think I was calling them or the government dogs. Seven censors looked at my work. Once, all seven approved a cartoon, but just before press time, they still asked me to redo it. (Song-Hwan Kim 1992)

Gobau was moved to *Chosun Ilbo* after the government instigated Kim's sacking at *Dong-A Ilbo* (Shim 1991, 54, also Koh 1988, 28–32).

Liberalization

For the most part, political cartooning became more robust when liberalization was ushered in during the late 1980s (Clifford 1988). In interviews in Seoul in July 1992, political cartoonists stated that they were freer, afforded much public respect, and enjoyed very comfortable lifestyles. Some of their salaries compared

4.7. Longtime political cartoonist Park Jae-Dong, Seoul, August 10, 2018. Photo by Kim Chunhyo. Courtesy of Kim Chunhyo and the *International Journal of Comic Art*. Permission of Park Jae-Dong.

favorably with those of the leaders of the dailies where they worked; a political cartoonist with ten or more years of experience drew an outlandish average of US$4,500 to $6,000 monthly (P.-K. Kim 1992; Y.-O. Yoon 1992). Also on the plus side was the noticeable increase of magazines since 1970, at least eight hundred new titles by 1980, almost all containing cartoons (K.-J. Park 1980, 5).

A few political cartoonists saw negative consequences of the liberalization. They pointed out that the issues were more complicated and equivocal (P.-K. Kim 1992); that newly vested special interest groups protected some of the political cartoonists' favorite targets; that treatment of societal issues lacked the "punch" of preliberalization (Shim 1991, 54–55); and that cartoonists were answerable to more constituencies, especially the chaebols (conglomerates) that own and/or control all major publications (Shim 1991, 55).

By the 1990s, South Korea had advanced to a semiperipheral place between highly industrialized and less developed countries, stimulating the growth of chaebols. Some of the chaebols, such as Samsung, Hyundai, and Han'guk Hwayak (later, Hanwha), purchased major dailies as good business policy to protect their interests. Cartoonist Park Jae-Dong (1992) said of this trend: "Many political cartoonists have to follow their newspaper's [and by extension, chaebol's] policy and they can't do their best work." Kim Pan-Kook, whose newspaper, *Kyunghyang Shinmun*, was owned by a giant explosives company, said that he showed the editor his finished cartoons but received neither direction nor approval from him. He said, actually, that the chaebol ownership had stabilized the daily and improved his personal status (P.-K. Kim 1992).

Political cartoonists solidified their rights to autonomy in the 1990s and into the twenty-first century. A few refused to steer away from issues related to the government or chaebols that owned their newspapers and resigned, claiming ideological differences; others used more direct attacks than in the past. In 1997, Choi Min-Sung led a strike at the *Segye Daily* because of frequent interference in the editorial rights of reporters and cartoonists. As a result, Choi was fired, coming back only after three years of litigation. When he returned to *Segye*, he began to use a small footprint trademark on all of his cartoons, indicating that he had been stomped on by higher powers (S.-K. Lee 2004).

Political cartoonists at that time attempted to attract younger readers by inserting gags and parodies of movies in their works. Many of the cartoonists, being relatively young themselves, had their own agenda. They lampooned conservative newspapers in their cartoons and started their own association, the National Editorial Cartoonists Association, in 2000.

Political cartoons in both one- and four-panel formats had ebbed in importance by the time of my next interviews in August 2018. The stalwarts of the latter twentieth century were deceased, retired (e.g., Kim Song-Hwan after 14,139 episodes of *Gobau* and Chong Un-Gyong after 8,829 installments of *Auntie Walsun*), or had moved to other careers (e.g., Park Jae-Dong to animation).

Park Jae-Dong (2018), who had participated in or observed the cartooning scene since the 1980s, claimed

67

4.8. One-panel political cartoon by Park Jae-Dong in *Hankyoreh*, July 7, 1992. Permission of Park Jae-Dong.

that political cartooning as it once was known was nearly nonexistent. First, the number of newspapers had decreased, and of those surviving, only *Kyunghyang Shinmun* and *Hankyoreh* still carried a daily political cartoon: *Kyunghyang*, a four-panel, and *Hankyoreh*, a one-panel.[3] Park said that a second reason for the death of political cartoons was the increasing conservatism of newspapers owners (chaebols), who wanted to avoid "punchy" cartoons and did not tolerate progressive cartoonists. The third cause for the diminishment of political cartoons, according to Park, related to new venues such as Facebook, Webtoons, and other ways of exhibiting work, which took on political dimensions (J.-D. Park 2018).

Sociopolitical Graphic Novels

Another venue for reporting and commenting on social and political issues that has surfaced are social/historical realism graphic novels. Certainly not political cartoons in the traditional definition of the form, these graphic novels serve as a type of comics journalism. They bring to the surface significant news happenings long buried during decades of authoritarian regimes and deemphasized by contemporary play-it-safe, chaebol-controlled

dailies. Investigative by nature, these books are not meant to have the timeliness of daily drawings of current events; they deal with recent history, or as cartoonist Park Kun-Woong put it, "the many hidden stories in modern Korean history that were not allowed to be told by the country's military regimes" (K.-W. Park 2018). Cartoonists uncover these stories by using the reporter's tools of interviewing and searching public and historical documents. Producing sociopolitical realism graphic novels is challenging: first, because it takes time to research, earn the trust of witnesses to get them to talk, and separate truth and facts from untruths, unsubstantiated information, and rumors; second, because many of the events took place in the distant past, the credibility of the sources must be determined; third, because of the sensitivity of the topics, the safety and privacy of the victimized must be respected; and fourth, the cartoonists must figure out where the red line is drawn by government, military, religious, and corporate authorities and whether or how to cross it. In some cases, cartoonists collaborate in reporting, writing, and drawing the stories. For example, six cartoonists cooperated in bringing out *Yongsan, Where I Once Lived*, the story of a 2009 fire in the Yongsan district of Seoul, where housing residents protesting their eviction without notice by the government clashed with huge regiments of police, resulting in the death of five protesters and one policeman in a fire of undetermined origins (*Hankyoreh* 2013). Five cartoonists gathered information from family members of each of the fire victims and witnesses, while a sixth wrote and drew an epilogue that synthesized the interview findings (S.-B. Kim 2018).

Other controversial stories buried or slighted by the South Korean government and media became subjects of graphic novels, including the more recent *Sewol* ferry disaster of April 16, 2016, which, as later investigations determined, was caused by inept management, negligence of duty, and abandonment of the ship by the captain and crew, resulting in the drowning of 304 passengers (e.g., Kim Sung-Hee's *Tale of a Sad and Funny Country*); Samsung's ongoing corporate denial and refusal to accept responsibility for the deaths and

4.9. *Dustfree Room*, Kim Sung-Hee. An investigative graphic novel exposing Samsung's history of industrial illnesses and deaths. Permission of Kim Sung-Hee.

4.10. A page from Park Kun-Woong's *Spring of the Dead Year*, a graphic novel uncovering stories of South Korean citizens wrongly accused of being North Korean spies by President Park Chung-Hee's regime. Permission of Park Kun-Woong.

illnesses of 138 of its semiconductor employees exposed to toxic materials (e.g., Kim Sung-Hee's *Dustfree Room* and Kim Soo-Bak's *The One Thing Missing at Samsung: The Feel of Humanity*); the "comfort women" sexually enslaved by the Japanese military during World War II (e.g., Keum Suk Gendry-Kim's *Grass*); and the 4-3 uprising (of April 3, 1948) during which 70 percent of Jeju Island's villages were destroyed and anywhere from fifteen thousand to sixty thousand people (most civilians) died in conflicts between Republic of Korea military and police (with the compliance of the US military), and communist insurgents (e.g., Park Kun-Woong's *Story of Hong*). For nearly fifty years, mere mention of the Jeju incident was punishable by beatings, torture, and long prison sentences (Johnson 2000, 99–101).

Investigative graphic novelists probed and exposed, or questioned, still other generally ignored stories,

among them the sad plight of Korean citizens working in Hiroshima and Nagasaki at the time of the US atomic bombings (e.g., Gendry-Kim's *A Day with Grandfather*); treasonous accusations wrongly brought against South Koreans during the Park Chung-Hee regime (e.g., Park Kun-Woong's *Spring of the Dead Year*); the torturing of civilians during the dictatorships; the killings of South Korean civilians by the South Korean military during the Korean War; the 1987 June Democracy Movement (e.g., Choi Kyu-Seok's *100 Degrees Celsius*); difficulties forming a labor union (e.g., Choi Kyu-Seok's *Songgot*); the massacre of hundreds of South Korean citizens by the US military at the Bridge at No Gun Ri during the Korean War; and the plight of dissidents Hur Young-Chul and Kim Geun-Tae (e.g., Park Kun-Woong's *Animal Time*).

As would be expected, gathering information about these topics often was an onerous task. In preparing

못 먹고 쉬지도 못하고 일만 하니까
병나서 죽는 사람도 많고……

사람이 죽었어요!

또?

여자 히니는 다쳐서 앓다가 죽었어.

여기 있다간 죽을
때까지 일만 할 거야.

맞아.

도망가다 잡히면
우릴 모두 죽일 거야.

여기서 죽으나
도망가다 죽으나……

어쩌려고?

어무이 아부지 얼굴
한 번만이라도 보고
죽으면 소원이 없겠어.

4.11. A page from the multi-award-winning graphic novel *Grass*, by Keum Suk Gendry-Kim, investigating the Korean "comfort" women (sex slaves) used by the Japanese military during World War II. Permission of Keum Suk Gendry-Kim.

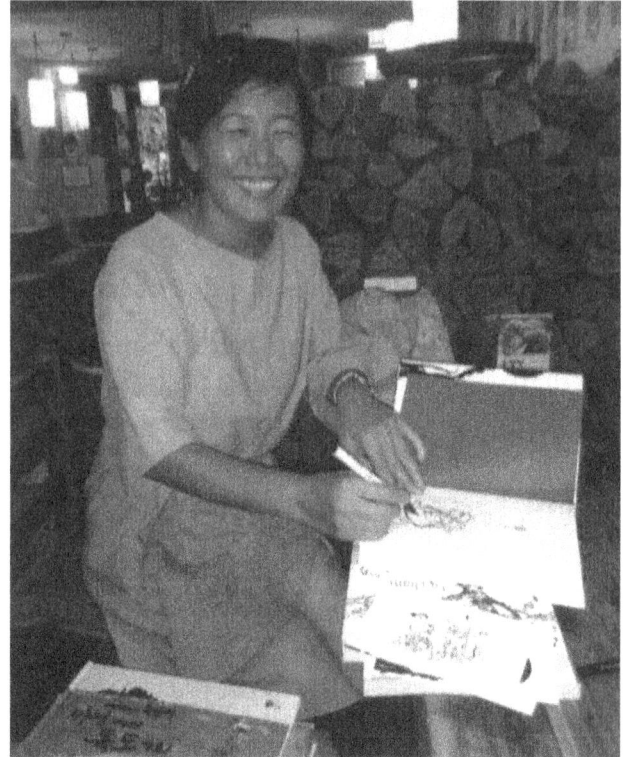

4.12. Prolific investigative graphic novelist Keum Suk Gendry-Kim, Seoul, August 8, 2018. Photo by Kim Chunhyo. Courtesy of Kim Chunhyo and the *International Journal of Comic Art*. Permission of Keum Suk Gendry-Kim.

Grass, Keum Suk Gendry-Kim spent parts of three years interviewing ten comfort women (one in China) and historians, as well as reading many books on the Japanese occupation. Her trip to China to interview a surviving comfort woman was fruitful, Gendry-Kim said, because the woman told her the stories of other comfort women. Although much has been written about comfort women, Gendry-Kim focused on specific aspects such as social class and gender, "generalizing for a world audience how authoritarian systems oppress women, especially poor women" (Gendry-Kim 2018). For *A Day with Grandfather*, she interviewed Korean victims of the atomic bombing now living in Korea and Japan.

Park Kun-Woong interviewed ten survivors wrongly accused of being North Korean spies for his *Spring of the Dead Year*. Although most of them "actively" recounted

what they had experienced, for some, the trauma was too overbearing, he said. Park dealt with his own emotions, he said, "by believing that what I was doing was right. So that I relieved any pain I had, and I could interview" (K.-W. Park 2018). Kim Sung-Hee and Kim Soo-Bak had similar emotional misgivings about doing books on the *Sewol* ferry disaster. Kim Sung-Hee, in researching *Tale of a Sad and Funny Country*, shied away from interviewing the families about their deceased children, depending instead on government sources and mainstream newspapers to see how they treated the disaster (Sung-Hee Kim 2018; also Gravett 2015). Kim Soo-Bak could not draw about that tragedy, because he did not want to intrude into the lives of victims' families (S.-B. Kim 2018). However, both artists published books about the health travesty and attempted cover-up at Samsung.

For *Dustfree Room*, Kim Sung-Hee covered the story from inside Samsung, first obtaining names from a semiconductor workers' solidarity organization and then interviewing workers, families of victims, and former engineers (Sung-Hee Kim 2018). Choi Kyu-Seok, claiming that his approach to handling such topics was different, said that he looked at the bigger picture, revealing the wrongs of the system rather than the emotions of the system's victims. He elaborated: "For example, stories with war usually are about soldiers and what they are engaged in. I want to deal with topics like why the war started, and with the generals, not the soldiers, not the issue of strength" (Choi 2018).

The audience reach of some of these investigative comics exceeds that of the few remaining newspaper political cartoons, a few selling tens of thousands of copies, being adapted into movies and television shows, and translated for overseas sales. Choi Kyu-Seok's *Songgot* (2015) is a three-book series, each volume selling fifty-thousand copies; both *Songgot* and Choi's *Record for the Wetland Ecosystem* (2012) were made into television dramas, and his books were translated into other languages (Choi 2018). Believing that there can be "many fruits from one seed," Park Kun-Woong has had his books adapted into a movie and Webtoons and translated into French (K.-W. Park 2018). Prolific Keum Suk Gendry-Kim published sixteen books (mostly historically or sociopolitically oriented) between 2012 and 2018, one of which, *Grass*, appeared in English, French, Italian, and Spanish editions (Gendry-Kim 2018); and a cartoonist of an earlier generation, Lee Hee-Jae (born 1952), sold large numbers of his multivolume titles, a handful in Chinese, French, and Japanese versions. Lee's books describe the "pain, fear, joys, [and] emotions of ordinary people like me" (H.-J. Lee 2018). Lee and Park Jae-Dong pioneered this realism-type of comics production and well remembered times when they had to resort to metaphorism. Lee told of the military's reaction to his comic book *Leading Player* (1986), in which he used a young boy beaten by a soldier as a metaphor for Kwangju citizens killed and injured by the military in the 1980 uprising. Lee said that the book's publisher was

4.13. Investigative graphic novelist Park Kun-Woong, Seoul, August 9, 2018. Photo by Noh Kwang-Woo. Courtesy of Noh Kwang-Woo and the *International Journal of Comic Art*. Permission of Park Kun-Woong.

warned by the military: "You want to die? Your company will be closed" (H.-J. Lee 2018).

Korean social/political realism cartooning, as with most investigative reporting, sets off sparks (sometimes explosions) that authorities feel a need to dowse. A way the administrations of Lee Myung-Bak (2008–2013) and Park Geun-Hye (2013–2017) attempted to squelch dissent was by maintaining artist blacklists. By February 2017, 9,473 artists, including Kim Soo-Bak and Park Kun-Woong, had made the list (Noh 2017). Park Kun-Woong said that he was proud to be on the list (despite being excluded from any government-funded projects[4]), being watched by the police, and knowing that his phone calls were recorded (K.-W. Park 2018). Kim Soo-Bak did not understand why he was not honored by being blacklisted a second time by the Park Geun-Hye presidency (S.-B. Kim 2018). The very few reactions from government recently have been annoying but relatively mild compared with the early days of the republic.

There were a few attacks on these cartoonists by conservative groups and the mass media. Park Kun-Woong's *Animal Time* was attacked by Park Geun-Hye supporters and removed from some libraries (Melikian 2016), and the books about Samsung by Kim Sung-Hee and Kim Soo-Bak were denied advertising space in some of the country's independent print and online periodicals. Stopsamsung (2012) reported: "One publication rejected the ad after the publisher [Bori] refused to remove the references to Samsung from copy. Another publication rejected it, citing a conflict of interest between sponsors because Samsung is also a sponsor. A third publication demanded high premiums for the ads. Samsung controls the lion's share of the advertisement market."

A number of conditions came together to set the stage for these cartoonists to take on the task of introducing this genre of cartoons. There was a more liberal government, a strong manhwa presence and audience, a diminished role for newspapers and their political cartoons, and a publisher, Bori, presided over by Yoon Gu-Byung, that was willing to risk bringing out these controversial titles in its Footprints of Peace series.

The major motivating factor that brought this disparate body of relatively young (almost all born in the 1970s and later) individuals to the drawing table was the economic downturn of 1997, when most of them entered the dried-up job market. They had similar experiences. An international trade major, Kim Sung-Hee despaired of finding a job in her field and turned to cartooning, alternately working three months in the food industry, ice cream factories, telemarketing, and other part-time jobs, followed by three months of only drawing (Sung-Hee Kim 2018). She also sought freedom from South Korea's family-centered, patriarchal society, as did Keum Suk Gendry-Kim. Majoring in Western painting, Gendry-Kim said that she became "bored standing in one place to paint" and decided to go to France to study sculpture and to free herself of the assigned roles of "getting married, sacrificing yourself and forgetting

your dreams" in Korea (Melikian 2017). In France, she graduated in fine arts from the University of Strasbourg and then went to Paris. Because of the city's high cost of living, she toiled as a babysitter, clothes saleswoman, museum keeper, and cashier, meaning she had no time or energy to do sculpture. Gendry-Kim then took a cartoonist position in a Parisian Korean-language newspaper, and then became a translator of Korean comics into French. At that point, she decided that she also could tell people's stories, and, after seventeen years abroad, returned to Seoul to do just that (Gendry-Kim 2018). Her books have been translated into many languages, made the best-of-the-year lists of the *New York Times* and the *Guardian*, and received international awards (E. J. Yoon 2021). Kim Soo-Bak and Choi Kyu-Seok also came to cartooning by necessity and accident after graduating about the time of the economic recession. Kim worked in construction for three years, simultaneously sharpening his drawing skills through cartooning (S.-B. Kim 2018), while Choi had a side job teaching drawing before he decided that it was possible to flavor popular entertainment comics with real social and political issues (Choi 2018).

A Brief Conclusion

One trait that comes to mind when describing the history of South Korean political cartooning is adaptability. These cartoonists have been adaptable to an assortment of degrees of freedom or suppression as different administrations entered and exited the Blue House; adaptable to new technologies with which to produce and distribute cartoons; adaptable to needs that demand a variety of forms and styles.

From the earliest days of Korean newspapers, cartoons appeared that brought strong reactions from the authorities. At first, they offended the Japanese occupation forces, followed by a string of repressive dictatorships. Cartoonists contended with the repression, keeping low profiles and employing metaphors and other subtle forms of hidden messages.

South Korean cartoonists also quickly adjusted to new technologies to carry forward their profession, outmaneuvering colleagues worldwide in finding ways to make Webtoons and other online apparatuses benefit cartooning. They were creatively flexible as well in using new forms and styles of presentation such as the four-panel sociopolitical cartoons of the latter part of the twentieth century and the more recent realism-based, investigative graphic novels. Because of this ability to bend, to adapt, to roadblocks put in their way and to explore new routes, South Korean political cartoonists are optimistic that their profession will survive in one form or another.

Notes

1. The most prosperous times for readers' cartoons were the 1950s and 1960s, when more experienced cartoonists commented upon and instructed the amateur drawers (Y.-O. Yoon 1986). In the 1970s, readers provided cartoons two or three times weekly; these soon-to-be freelancers eventually organized, and when dailies needed cartoons, they pulled from this group. Cartoonist Kim Pan-Kook (1992) credited the group with providing the "major cartoonists" of his time.

2. This structure derives from the classical Chinese essay on the civil service exam of introduction, development, twist, and punchline.

3. This was confirmed by a nonscientific check of six top dailies on August 7, 2018. The papers were *Hankyoreh, Kyunghyang Shinmun, Hankook Ilbo, Dong-A Ilbo, Chosun Ilbo,* and *JoongAng Ilbo.* All are national newspapers of twenty-eight to thirty-two pages. *Kyunghyang Shinmun* had a four-panel cartoon, *Hankyoreh* a one-panel, and *Hankook Ilbo,* the US strip *Blondie* in color. The others merely had nondescript, small drawings illustrating some stories.

4. K. J. Noh (2017) describes major drawbacks of being blacklisted: "[M]ade ineligible for government funding, subjected to tax audits, prevented from exhibiting or screening at government sponsored or public events, put under surveillance, harassed, threatened, starved of resources. Some [artists] became literally untouchable."

Bibliography

Ahn, Ui-Sup. 1992. Interview with John A. Lent, Seoul, July 3.
Cho, Joo-Chung. 1992. Interview with John A. Lent, Seoul, July 3.
Cho, Kwan-Je. 2003. Interview with John A. Lent, Seoul, August 16.
Choi, Kyu-Seok. 2018. Interview with John A. Lent, Seoul, August 11.
Chong, Un-Gyong. 1992. Interview with John A. Lent, Seoul, July 7.
Clifford, Mark. 1988. "A Funny Thing Happened on the Way to Democracy." *Far Eastern Economic Review*, May 26, 52–53.
Gendry-Kim, Keum Suk. 2018. Interview with John A. Lent, Seoul, August 8.
Gravett, Paul. 2015. "Sung-hee Kim: Seeking Truths in Korean Manhwa." July 20. http://paulgravett.com/articles/article/sung_hee_kim.
Hankyoreh. 2013. "After Four Years, Yongsan Disaster Is Still Unsolved." Editorial, January 21. http://www.hani.co.kr/arti/english-edition/e_editorial/570569.html.
Johnson, Chalmers. 2000. *Blowback: The Costs and Consequences of American Empire*. New York: Henry Holt.
Kim, Jae-Jung. 2003. Interview with John A. Lent, Seoul, August 15.
Kim, Pan-Kook. 1992. Interview with John A. Lent, Seoul, July 2.
Kim, Song-Hwan. 1992. Interview with John A. Lent, Seoul, July 4.
Kim, Soo-Bak. 2018. Interview with John A. Lent, Seoul, August 6.
Kim, Sung-Hee. 2018. Interview with John A. Lent, August 6.
Ko, Dong-Hwan. 2018. "Unfolding History, Coloring Humanity." *Korea Times*, July 6. http://www.koreatimes.co.kr/www/culture/2018/04/316_218371.html.
Koh, Sun-Ah. 1988. "Kim Song-Hwan, Spokesman for the People, Cartoonist of the Old Kobau." *Korea Today*, no. 4: 28–32.
Lee, Hae-Chang. 1982. *History of Korean Political Cartoons*. Seoul: Iljeesa.
Lee, Hee-Jae. 2018. Interview with John A. Lent, Seoul, August 10.
Lee, S.-K. 2004. "Controversy about Layoff of Political Cartoonist of *Segye Daily*." *Hankyoreh*, June 3.
Lee, Won-Bok. 1991. *The World of Cartoons and the Cartoons of the World*. Seoul: Mijinsa.
Lee, Won-Bok. 1992. Interview with John A. Lent, Seoul, July 2.
Lent, John A. 1995. "Korean Cartooning: Historical and Contemporary Perspectives." *Korean Culture* (Spring): 8–19.
Lent, John A. 2018. "The New Wave of Investigative Cartooning in South Korea." *International Journal of Comic Art* 20, no. 2 (Fall–Winter): 90–109.
Lim, Cheong-Sun. 1994. Interview with John A. Lent, Seoul, July 5.
Melikian, Laurent. 2016. "Park Kun-Woong ('Je suis Communiste'): 'Nous ne sommes pas libérés de la guerre des idéologies'" [Park Kun-Woong ("I Am Communist"): "We Are Not Free from the War of Ideologies"]. ActuaBD, March 16. https://www.actuabd.com/Park-Kun-woong-Je-suis-Communiste.
Melikian, Laurent. 2017. "Keum Suk Gendry-Kim: 'J'arrive chargée d'espoir'" [Keum Suk Gendry-Kim: "I'm Coming Full of Hope"]. ActuaBD, May 23. https://www.actuabd.com/Keum-Suk-Gendry-Kim-J-arrive-chargee-d-espoir.
Noh, K. J. 2017. "South Korea's Artist Blacklist." *Dissident Voice*, February 23. https://dissidentvoice.org/2017/02/south-koreas-artist-blacklist.

73

Oh, Kyu-Won. 1981. *The Reality of Korean Cartoons*. Seoul: Youl Hwa Dang.

Park, Jae-Dong. 1992. Interview with John A. Lent, Seoul, July 7.

Park, Jae-Dong. 1994. Interview with John A. Lent, Seoul, July 3, 5.

Park, Jae-Dong. 2003. Interview with John A. Lent, Seoul, August 15.

Park, Jae-Dong. 2018. Interview with John A. Lent, Seoul, August 10.

Park, Ki-Joon. 1980. "Caricature and Comic Strips: Essential to Korean Journalism." *Asian Culture Quarterly* 18, no. 1 (January): 4–5.

Park, Kun-Woong. 2018. Interview with John A. Lent, Seoul, August 9.

Park, Soo-Dong. 1992. Interview with John A. Lent, Seoul, July 7.

Shim, Jae Hoon. 1991. "A Hard Act to Follow." *Far Eastern Economic Review*, June 13, 54–55.

Stopsamsung. 2012. "The Comic Book Ads That Money Can't Buy." Stop Samsung, May 29. https://stopsamsung.wordpress.com/2012/05/29/the-comic-book-ads-that-money-cant-buy-2/.

Yi, Wonsoon. 1994. Interview with John A. Lent, Seoul, July 6.

Yoon, Emily Jungmin. 2021. "Interview with Keum Suk Gendry-Kim: Imagining the Collective Memory of History." *Korean Literature Now* 51 (Spring).

Yoon, Young-Ok. 1986. *The History of Korean Newspaper Cartoons*. Seoul: Youl Hwa Dang.

Yoon, Young-Ok. 1992. Interview with John A. Lent, Seoul, July 3.

With the limited amount of information available, political cartooning in Mongolia can be characterized as relatively young, sporadic in usage, and not particularly popular. This can be attributed to different factors. Producer-director of Nomadic Comics Luvsangaldan Erdenebalsuren (aka Dan Erdenebal) believes that comic art generally has not thrived because the Mongols are nomads who travel light, not settling long enough to establish many cultural institutions and shedding possessions, even their history in written form, as they move about (Erdenebal 2017, 148).

Also contributing to the slow development of political satire were the periods when Mongolia was under Chinese (Qing Dynasty), Japanese, and Soviet rule. Veteran painter and cartoonist Samandariin Tsogtbayar (Satso) said that during the Soviet times, it was very difficult to draw about the Mongolian government, Genghis Khan, and other entities and issues. He said that before 1990, "we could not draw Genghis Khan, because he was known as a cruel man, a murderer. In the past decade or so, he has been reimaged, for improving the postal system, giving women the right to divorce, and other advancements. So many things carry his name now—the airport, banks, huge statues, etc." (Tsogtbayar 2018).

Tsogtbayar emphasized that he has no problem with government authorities now, declaring that he has much freedom, actually that he is "totally free"; the editor accepts all of his cartoons, and he faces no editorial or self-censorship. He gave as an example a recent cartoon of his that portrayed a minister of justice killing justice (Tsogtbayar 2018).

Yet despite this high level of freedom, political cartoons are scarce in Mongolia. Tsogtbayar even claimed that he alone drew political cartoons in the country, putting them on Facebook and Twitter, despite no payment forthcoming. Although I saw no newspaper political cartoons the short time I was in Ulaan Baatar in 2018, another source, Alan J. K. Sanders, writes that most Mongolian newspapers run an "occasional" cartoon reflecting popular concerns, but usually shy away from mocking neighbors Russia and China and avoid depicting recognizable politicians, the latter because of strong

Vignette: Mongolia

M.1. Political cartoonist Samandariin Tsogtbayar (Satso), Drexel Hill, Pennsylvania, May 8, 2018. Photo by John A. Lent. Permission of Samandariin Tsogtbayar.

M.2. Self-explanatory cartoon, Satso. Permission of Samandariin Tsogtbayar.

M.4. Very early sequential cartoon poster explaining the revolution to the public. Courtesy of Dan Erdenebal and the *International Journal of Comic Art*.

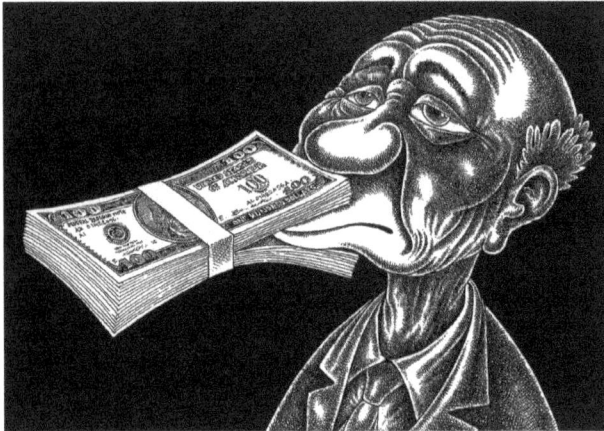

M.3. Cartoon by Satso. Permission of Samandariin Tsogtbayar.

M.5. Cartoon poster pointing out Japanese oppression in World War II. Courtesy of Dan Erdenebal and the *International Journal of Comic Art*.

defamation laws. Sanders refers to cartoons in *Ödriin Sonin* and *Önöödör* (Sanders 2017, 1016–17).

The reasons for the sparsity of Mongolian political cartoons, according to Tsogtbayar, are: (1) lack of a cartoon/humor periodical after the long-lived *Tonshuul* (Woodpecker) folded in 2008 (Tsogtbayar was a *Tonshuul* cartoonist from 1985 to 1992); (2) very few venues of any type for cartoons, the country not being rich in the number of newspapers and magazines;[1] (3) virtually no value put on cartoons, or on culture more generally; and (4) rates paid to cartoonists by the newspapers that are so minuscule that the hard work necessary to produce cartoons is not commensurate with the payment. Despite these serious limitations, Tsogtbayar

draws a cartoon daily because, as he said, it is his "life," his hobby; more importantly, because he can make a comfortable living through his paintings, advertising, and other illustration work (Tsogtbayar 2018) as well as his salary as director of Hiimori Publishing House (1992–1995) and vice director of Interpress Printing Company (1997–).

Nambaral Erdenebayar, sufficiently respected as an innovator in comic art that the Mongolian Foreign Ministry bestowed upon him the honorific title Cultural Envoy of Mongolia,[2] concurred that the "freedom to cartoon" has been broad since the establishment of democracy, adding: "We are always mocking the government, doing caricatures of the president and other officials." He, too, acknowledged the shortage of political cartoonists, attributing it to the scarcity of artists overall and there being "no wages, salaries for cartoonists of press

cartoons, so, no payment, no cartoons in the paper"
(Erdenebayar 2018).

Early semblances of Mongolian satirical art were the
sequential propaganda posters that explained and promoted the 1921 revolution. Attached to fences, outdoor
walls, and outside surfaces of *gers* (a type of yurt or
dwelling), the posters showed how the revolution would
affect the public, sometimes with daily life images; they
continued to appear into the 1930s (Erdenebal 2017, 148).

There may have been cartoons in Mongolia's earliest
newspaper, *Mongolyn Unen* (Mongolian Truth), started
on November 10, 1920, or the first magazine, *Shine Tol*
(New Mirror), beginning in 1913, but the few sources
available, such as D. Urjinbadaam, former secretary of
the Union of Mongolian Journalists, did not mention
any visual material in these periodicals. Initially, *Mongolyn Unen*, an organ of Mongolian revolutionaries led
by Damdin Sukhe-Bator, was published in Irkutsk, the
Soviet Union, and smuggled into Mongolia; it became
legal in Mongolia in April 1921. Other newspapers came
on the scene between 1921 and 1925, including *Namyn
Amdral* (Party Life), started in 1923 as the theoretical
organ of the Communist Party; *Ulaan-Od* (Red Star),
begun in 1924 as the army organ; and *Zaluuchuudiin
Unen* (Youth's Truth), also launched in 1924. All of them
stridently propagandized for the Mongolian People's
Revolutionary Party, befriended the Soviet Union,
attacked feudalists and foreign occupiers, and called for
unity among workers and peasants of the world (Urjinbadaam 1982, 154–55). Because these papers imitated
the Soviet press, it would be expected that they were
text-heavy and visuals-shy. The newspaper known to
have had almost daily cartoons and comic strips about
current events was *Zaluuchuudiin Unen* (Erdenebal
2017, 150).

There is no mention of visual content in *Shine Tol*,
which dates to March 6, 1913, and lasted until August 21,
1914. The forty-page periodical was devoted to science,
history, education, political science, and literature (Lent
1982, 157). By the 1940s, Mongolia had its own monthly
humor/cartoon magazine, *Matar* (Crocodile), named
and modeled after the Soviet Union's *Krokodil*.[3] The

M.6. Newspaper cartoon in *Zaluuchuudiin Unen* (Youth's Truth) depicting the Soviet Union stopping German oppression during World War II.
Courtesy of Dan Erdenebal and the *International Journal of Comic Art*.

M.7. *Matar* (Crocodile), no. 2, 1944, portraying the suppression of
Germany. Courtesy of Dan Erdenebal and the *International Journal of
Comic Art*.

77

M.8. Cover page of *Humuujil Jigshil* (Repugnance), successor to *Matar* and predecessor of *Tonshuul*, 1961. Courtesy of Dan Erdenebal and the *International Journal of Comic Art*.

Notes

1. Occasionally, a comic book will be launched, but most disappear after a brief existence. In 2020, Women for Change in Mongolia started a series of comic books to bring social consciousness to women's issues. The first issue dealt with women's political participation, the second with domestic violence, and the third with secrets of having great sex (Tali 2020).

2. Erdenebal credited Erdenebayar with introducing to Mongolia the first comics series of three books in 2004–2005; coming up with the idea of creating a series of 108 comic books called *Bumbardi* in 2007–2008 (the first issue appearing in 2013); creating what was probably the first comic book in Mongolia, *The Adventures of Borkhuu, Odkhuu, and Tumurkhuu*, in 1993; and producing in 2011 *Bongo* (nine books), very popular among children and also made into a television series (Erdenebalsuren 2018). At thirty-four years old in 2018, Erdenebayar said that he is the most veteran Mongolian comics series creator, having started when he was eighteen (Erdenebayar 2018).

3. It is worth pointing out that the names of Mongolian newspapers and periodicals often were adopted from the Soviet Union, examples being *Unen* (*Truth*, from *Pravda*), *Ulaan-Od* (Red Flag), and *Matar* (Crocodile). *Matar* changed its name to *Humuujil Jigshil* (Repugnance) and later to *Tonshuul*.

major venue for satirical and propaganda art and comic strips, *Matar*, in its early life, dealt with World War II and Mongolia's role in the war, the Yalta Conference, and recognition of independence for Mongolia, and then with socialist propaganda and the "transition to a socialist union, and the day-to-day lifestyle of working-class people, as well as historical events happening locally or internationally" (Erdenebal 2017, 150–54).

As alluded to earlier in this capsule perspective, political cartooning in Mongolia has had a wobbly past and looks to have an even shakier future, for reasons such as the advent of the market economy forcing cartoonists to fend for themselves, a lopsided heavy work level/low payment scale for press artists, and a disparate body of cartoonists with a dismal view of their profession.

Bibliography

Erdenebal, Dan. 2017. "Comics in an Unexpected Place: Mongolia." *International Journal of Comic Art* 19, no. 2 (Fall–Winter): 148–62.

Erdenebalsuren, Luvsangaldan [Dan Erdenebal]. 2018. Interview with John A. Lent, Ulaan Baatar, July 27, 30.

Erdenebayar, Nambaral. 2018. Interview with John A. Lent, Ulaan Baatar, July 27, 30.

Lent, John A. 1982. "Additional Information (Mongolia)." In *Newspapers in Asia: Contemporary Trends and Problems*, edited by John A. Lent, 157–59. Hong Kong: Heinemann Asia.

Sanders, Alan J. K. 2017. *Historical Dictionary of Mongolia*. Lanham, MD: Rowman and Littlefield.

Tali, Didem. 2020. "These Women Are Challenging Mongolia's Gender Norms with Comic Books." *The Lily*, December 7. https://www.thelily.com/these-women-are-challenging-mongolias-gender-norms-with-comic-books/.

Tsogtbayar, Samandariin [Satso]. 2001. *Best Cartoon Collection*. Ulaan Baatar: Interpress.

Tsogtbayar, Samandariin [Satso]. 2018. Interview with John A. Lent, Ulaan Baatar, July 31.

Urjinbadaam, D. 1982. "Mongolian People's Republic." In *Newspapers in Asia: Contemporary Trends and Problems*, edited by John A. Lent, 153–57. Hong Kong: Heinemann Asia.

Historical Overview

At the outset, it should be noted that cartooning existed in Taiwan before 1949, during Japanese rule, 1895–1945. In the early stage of the occupation, there were only three newspapers, used to advocate colonial rule; anything denigrating the Japanese was blocked. The Japanese-drawn editorial cartoons were meant to indoctrinate Taiwanese to follow colonial policy; those by local artists treated some social issues, but very mildly.

Under stringent censorship conditions, a few cartoonists dared to draw about current events and customs and employ social satire. Chen Ping-huang (pen name Chi Lung-sheng), a professional journalist for *Sing Ming-Pao* and *Feng Nien Monthly*, also drew for the two newspapers as an amateur cartoonist. In 1935, Chen published *Chi Lung-sheng's Comic Collection*, a book of his cartoons showing the dissatisfaction of Taiwanese people with Japanese colonialization (Liu Mei-min 1993). Another who drew social satire cartoons was Chen Kuang-hsi, whose work appeared in the Japanese magazine *Wang Yang*. He realized the danger he faced, telling my PhD student Hsiao Hsiang-wen: "Under such stern control of speech freedom, it's running a risk of execution to comment on current events by drawing political cartoons. No one will do that" (Chen 1993, quoted in Hsiao Hsiang-wen 1995).[1] A third who sneered at Taiwanese social conditions in the 1940s was Yeh Hung-chia, hailed at the time of his death in 1990 as the father of the political cartoon. He quit drawing political cartoons after a China-Taiwan conflict on February 28, 1947, and worked as a designer until 1956, when he turned to creating comic books, his biggest success being the fifty-five volume *Chuko Szu-lang* character series (Chiu 1990, 6; also Hsu 1990; Lent 1993, 3).

However, many of the earliest political cartoonists in Taiwan came with the Chinese Nationalists and their sympathizers, who fled China with Chiang Kai-shek[2] as Mao Tse-tung assumed power on the mainland.

Among them were the Liang brothers—Zhong-ming (1907–1982), Yiu-ming (1906–1984), and Ding-ming (1898–1959), known as the "Liang Family's Three

Chapter 5

Taiwan

81

5.1. Yeh Hung-chia, hailed as the father of Taiwanese political cartoons. Caricature by Hung Teh-lin. Courtesy of Hung Teh-lin.

Heavyweighters." While on the mainland, they carried out Chiang's bidding from the 1920s through World War II, and they continued in Taiwan. During the war, they drew mainly for *Army Graphic*, emphasizing Japanese atrocities and weaknesses, and the courage and sacrifice of Chinese soldiers and civilians. Ellen Johnston Laing (2004, 176) identified the eldest brother, Ding-ming, as the first to pay his allegiance to Chiang. A successful calendar poster artist for the British American Tobacco Company, Ding-ming forfeited some of his commercial fame, as his artistic career became "entwined with Chiang's Nationalist Party" after he met Chiang in 1925. His brother Yiu-ming, an official war artist for the Guomindang army, painted many works about air battles as tributes to the Republic of China Air Force (Yuan 2015).

The Liang brothers, along with Chang Ying-chao, Ching Ho (real name Chen Ching-ho), and Niu Ko (real name Li Fei-ming), continued attacking the Chinese Communist Party (CCP) in newspaper editorial cartoons and/or comics. In 1949, brothers Zhong-ming and Yiu-ming Liang established the *Graphic Journal* in Taipei, with the aim to publish international and domestic political cartoons, social satire, humor comics, and comics serials. Liang Zhong-ming provided the *Graphic Journal* with a ready pool of cartoons contributed by his military students in arts training classes he organized and taught. When the *Graphic Journal* folded after one year, Liang Yiu-ming and Liang Zhong-ming were invited to become editor-in-chief and arts editor, respectively, of the *Central Daily News* cartoon page. They continued to attack the CCP and its leaders and became better known through their signature cartoons—Yiu-ming's *Bumpkin Goes to the South* and *Dr. No*, and Zhong-ming's *Huang Hsing Autobiography*. Another periodical carryover from the mainland was *Youth Warrior Daily*, founded as *Soldier Weekly* in China in 1940 by the Guomindang Political Department of National Defense. In Taiwan, it, too, carried anti-CCP cartoons.

Cartoonists labored under many Guomindang government restraints: working under martial law restrictions, paper shortages, and the 1951 newspaper regulations that limited the number of printing licenses and pages. The cartoonists' mission changed from unifying and encouraging citizens during wartime to propagating the Guomindang messages denigrating the Communists.

Other mainland cartoonists moved to Taiwan, including Chang Ying-chao, Ching Ho, and Niu Ko. They and others such as Liu Han-yu and Hsu Mao-sung were "united to produce a literature that would keep alive anti-Communist sentiment, maintain the desire for counterattack and a return to the mainland, and convey the ideology of the Three Principles of the People" (Ching 1993),[3] and also to "serve the educational function to educate lots of peasants to cultivate" (Liu Han-yu 1991, 1993).

Besides the training provided early on by Liang Zhong-ming, the Guomindang's Political Military Academy with connections to the *Victory Journal*, and the Political Department of National Defense with its aligned *Youth Warrior Daily*, also instructed would-be cartoonists with the standardized anti-Communist slant and then published their editorial cartoons.

The 1950s were a heyday of political cartoons, newspaper strips, and comic books in Taiwan. Political cartoons were favored by mainland migrant cartoonists; children's comics and illustrations by local artists. A 1953 survey found that one-third of Taipei's 213 periodicals regularly published political cartoons and comics (Chang Yu-wei 1954). The increased readership generated by the use of cartoons spurred newspapers to hire staff cartoonists and to provide a comics column of political cartoons, as the *Great China Evening News* did in 1956. With the government-ordered limitations on newspaper licenses and number of pages, and newspapers' penchant to publish better-known cartoonists, there was spillover of political cartoons to the magazines. Singled out by Hsiao Hsiang-wen (1995) as a "creative voice to editorial cartooning" among periodicals, *Popular Custom Graphic Monthly*, starting up in 1953, innovated with a "how to draw cartoons" column, which set a particular theme each issue and solicited single-frame cartoons of various drawing styles. Many senior

5.2. "Sensational 1988." Yu Fu, *Independence Evening Post*, January 26, 1989. An advertisement for six books about 111 Taiwanese political figures. Courtesy of Yu Fu.

cartoonists freely contributed their work. Topics varied from issue to issue and included "If I Won the Major Lottery," "After Going Back to the Mainland," and "The Mobilization." Additionally, *Popular Custom Graphic Monthly* ran current events commentary cartoons (mostly domestic), social satire, and comics serials.

While comic books and newspaper strips were reaching their peak from 1956 to 1966, political cartoons were declining in frequency and popularity. Government-owned newspapers continued to publish a considerable quantity of political cartoons to keep up their anti-Communist propaganda, while other dailies only used humorous comic strips. A reason for the drop-off of interest in political cartoons related to the ingrained notion that leaders and elders should be respected and not mocked. Normally, under an authoritarian government such as the Guomindang, a drop in political cartoon activity would be blamed on censorship. However, in Taiwan, censorship affected comic books while they were at their peak in the late 1960s, and to

a lesser degree political cartoons, which already were restricted by martial law sanctions and carefully scrutinized by editors before publication. On the other hand, comic books, thought to be detrimental to children's development, were hit with strong regulations in 1967 that required them to be examined by the National Institute for Compilation and Translation. The NICT received much criticism, accused of being biased in favor of imported Japanese manga and of using a double standard that angered many cartoonists enough to quit drawing for a generation (Lent 2015).

Martial law mandates kept close watch on any undesirable content in mass media, such as questioning the government's legitimacy and not taking an anti-Communist stance, as well as on individuals considered pro-Communist or "slander leaders" who "harm social order" or ferment "social discord between the people and the government" (Hsiao Hsiang-wen 1995). Political cartoonists abided by these rules, in the process restraining themselves from taking a stance and allowing their work to be used as government propaganda. Often, they were in a quandary, trying to figure out where the fine line was between what was acceptable and unacceptable and verifying that it had not been moved. Under such uncertain situations, cartoonists questioned everything. For example, Liu Hsing-ching (1993) told how, on an occasion in the late 1960s, he had pondered whether to publish a humor cartoon he had drawn about a bald man, lest any official who had lost his hair be offended.

By the 1970s, with the rise of a middle class and a more favorable economic climate, there was more recognition of an emerging opposition. Cartoonists began to take sharp stabs at the shortcomings of the government, mainly through *tangwei* (politicians other than those of the Guomindang) magazines such as *Taiwan Political Review*, *Formosa*, and *The Eighties*. The late 1970s and early 1980s saw the flourishing of a new generation of political cartoonists, most notably Cheng Chai-pao of the *United Daily News*, L. C. C. (Lo Ching-chung) of the *China Times*, Yu Fu (Lin Kuei-yo)[4] of the *China Times*, and CoCo (Huang Yung-nan) of *Formosa*. They were joined by still other cartoonists, as many as one hundred between 1982 and 1984 (Dong 1985).

These cartoonists played key roles in the opposition journalism that was making strides in Taiwan. Forbidden topics began to be openly discussed; satire replaced propaganda in *tangwei* periodicals and some dailies. L. C. C. (1993) said of *tangwei* political cartoons, "They are not flattering but hostile to the authorities"; and senior cartoonist Yang Chi-hsien (1994) noted that "the target of satire had changed from the Communists to the ruling party; the comment, from praising the authorities to sharply criticizing them." Cartoonist Chao Ning (1986), who felt that "true" political cartoonists had not existed in Taiwan for years and that those who did work in the field were extremely cautious and not well versed in political affairs, said he saw that the situation was "changing a bit" by 1986. His conservatism about the rate of change was understandable, because, in 1986, a number of topics and techniques were still off-limits. For example, Yu Fu quit his job at the *China Times* that

5.3. Yu Fu, "What's in a Name?" *China Times*, July 20, 1990. Courtesy of Yu Fu.

year, when the paper restrained him from caricaturizing Taiwan's plastics tycoon, who was a friend of the paper's publisher. A year later, Yu Fu, while with the *Independent Evening News*, broke the barrier against doing caricatures of top political and business figures with his rendering of President Chiang Ching-kuo parting the Red Sea.

Yu Fu was no stranger to controversy; his cartoons were rejected a number of times in the early 1980s, prompting him to route his banned cartoons to other outlets (Yu Fu 1991). Outspoken about his cartooning responsibilities, Yu Fu thought that he should not illustrate the opposition's views, which others did, but instead take the role of the journalist and search for different perspectives on an issue. He made this clear in a collection of his editorial cartoons, stating: "I do not like to be too clear-cut about my stance. When people ask me if I belong to the 'tu-pai' (independence faction) or the 'tung-pai' (unification faction), I tell them I belong to the 'papai' ('Popeye,' as in the cartoon) group, the comic faction" (Yu Fu 1989).

L. C. C. began his career in the late 1970s, initially with the *China Times*. By the late 1980s, he had his own cartoon section in the *Commercial Times*, also drew for the *Independent Evening News*, and was one of five owners of the first comic strip weekly, *Cartoon Show* (begun in 1985). He said that the main reason for drawing cartoons was to "challenge authority and anything unreasonable," and that 1991 was the "right" time for political

5.4. Political cartoon by L. C. C., 2004. Courtesy of L. C. C.

cartoonists, because the country was in a "transitional stage of development of democracy" (*Independent Evening News* 1991). Also beginning his career in the late 1970s, CoCo had a cartoon feature, *A-Wa Biography*, in *Formosa* magazine. His work dealt with current events and the bureaucracy, but not individuals (Yu Fu 1991) or "simply ideology"; he believed that "absolute 'right-wrong' or 'yes-no'" does not exist in a political system (CoCo 1991). From 1982 to 1987, he was in the United States working as an editor and cartoonist. When the Guomindang began to clamp down in the mid-1980s, CoCo was told by government officials to stay there; in other words, he was not welcomed back to Taiwan.

The government did not sit idle as these younger cartoonists, *tangwei* magazines, and leading dailies made dents in the Guomindang armor. For example, the number of issues of newspapers and magazines (mainly *tangwei* periodicals) banned and confiscated rose from 9 in 1980 to 295 in 1986.

The End of Martial Law

The lifting of martial law and restrictions on newspapers in 1988 made for the most important transition period in Taiwan's political cartoon history. Newspapers expanded in number, as did space devoted to cartoons and strips. The *United Daily News*, *Min Shen Pao*, *Liberal Times*, and *China Evening Post* each provided a half page of cartoons. Nearly every major daily carried

political cartoons, a number of which dealt with hitherto forbidden topics such as domestic political conflicts and mainland China news. Both the public and the cartoonists felt more at ease to discuss sensitive issues without fear of being arrested. Generally, the frequency of political cartoons skyrocketed (for more on the changes, see Lim 1990). A study of four major dailies shows that their use of political cartoons jumped from 64 issues in eighteen months (July 1986–December 1987) before the end of martial law to 578 in eighteen months after martial law (January 1988–June 1989) (Yu 1991).

Another survey conducted in 1989–1990 determined characteristics of thirty-two cartoonists (political and nonpolitical, professional and freelance) whose works appeared regularly in newspapers. Nine lived solely from their cartooning job, two were women, and three were born on the mainland. The average age of the cartoonists was thirty-five. Seven of the artists did strictly political cartoons, and eleven drew both political and other types of cartoons. Significant tendencies one can draw from the survey are that most of the cartoonists were Taiwan-born and unlikely to be enamored with issues of the mainland, relatively few could live solely from cartooning, and comic art was predominantly a male domain dominated by drawers of comic strips and comic books.

By 1992, when I made my second of four major research trips to Taiwan, political cartooning on the island was in robust shape: more respect was being given to the profession, the subject matter had

他用閞愛的眼
神看我……

中央常會

5.5. Political cartoon by CoCo,
December 31, 1978. Courtesy
of CoCo.

5.6. Political cartoonist CoCo. Courtesy of CoCo.

The upbeat mood was tempered by some limitations political cartoonists faced in the 1990s: caricaturizing people in power and authority was slow to be accepted; editors using political cartoons did not know where to place them, as standard editorial and op-ed pages were scarce or did not exist; and many cartoonists were inept at drawing, especially of the human figure. There were calls for less-cluttered balloons, less labeling, more critical focus on issues, and a more thorough understanding of domestic and international issues (*Free China Review* 1992, 1). The recurring issue of insufficient space in newspapers for cartoons was a shortcoming mentioned by several cartoonists I interviewed (Ao 1992; Lao 1992; Hsiao Yen-chung 1992), as was editors' haphazard criteria for the selection and placement of cartoons. Wang Peng (1992) said that his cartoons sometimes were assigned to a page of commentary, other times to a section that dealt with the topic emphasized in the cartoon, and occasionally to a prominent or filler space, depending on his level of friendship with the editor.

The comic art scene had changed for the worse by the beginning of the twenty-first century and my next series of interviews in July 2005. The number of editorial cartoonists in Taiwan had dwindled to about twenty, only half of whom were active (Li Shan 2005); newspaper comic strips were very few; and Japanese manga had played havoc with the local comic book market.

Veteran political cartoonist Li Shan (2005) worried about the future of his profession, because newspapers had cut the space allowed for political cartoons and usually they did not use freelance drawings, only those of

broadened, criticism was more abrasive, and space was available for cartoons in most major newspapers (W. Chang 1992, 16). Also, a freer atmosphere existed, as verified by the cartoonists. L. C. C. (1992) said that the situation was "very different" from ten years prior, that he could draw "anything without limitations," and that he had "100 percent freedom to draw" what he wanted in his paper. He said that some cartoonists were restricted by newspaper policies, for instance being assigned topics by editors or having their work changed (L. C. C. 1992).

5.7. Veteran cartoonist Li Shan, Taipei, July 25, 2005. Photo by John A. Lent. Courtesy of Li Shan.

5.8. Political cartoonist Tang Jian-feng, Taipei, February 11, 2019. Photo by Xu Ying. Permission of Tang Jian-feng.

"their own editorial cartoonists." He labeled the country's political cartoon scene as "embarrassing," pointing out that it is a difficult task to become adept at interpreting the news, yet those who have mastered the task have no venues in which to print their work. The downturn had happened about five years earlier, with no obvious explanation (Li Shan 2005). Other political cartoonists tried to make sense of the abrupt change. Wang Peng (2005) thought that it was because the public had lost interest in politics, distracted by diversions such as cable TV and the internet; newspapers had gotten smaller; and keeping a cartoonist staff was costly, publishers' rationale being, "If the market does not need any, why keep them?" (Wang 2005). The president of the cartoonists' union, Tang Jian-feng (2005), said that as the government loosened its tight grip on news, many television stations appeared, reflecting news more quickly than print media; also, they had interactive potential through call-in programs.

An ironic twist was that while political cartooning was being given short shrift by the public, publishers, and editors, the government seemed to be abating its regulating and restricting functions while elevating its

facilitating capabilities.[5] In 1998, the government funded a two-floor cartoon library consisting of at least sixty thousand comic books, of which forty thousand were Taiwanese titles that had passed the censors. Some dated from the earliest efforts in the 1950s (Li Ying-hao 2005). The government also granted funds to ten individuals to create their comic books; supported two publications, *Dragon Youth* for fans and *Cartoon Creation Record*, the cartoonists' union periodical; and sponsored both the Golden Elephant Awards (established in 2002 for comics, cartoons, illustrations, and animation) and the Golden Cup Awards for publishing, with a category for cartoon books (Hoong 2005). There were also a couple of political cartoonists' associations registered by the government, but it is unclear whether they were government financed.

The Contemporary Situation

The contemporary climate that Taiwanese political cartoonists find themselves in reminds me of the status of Soviet-bloc cartoonists after the dissolving of the

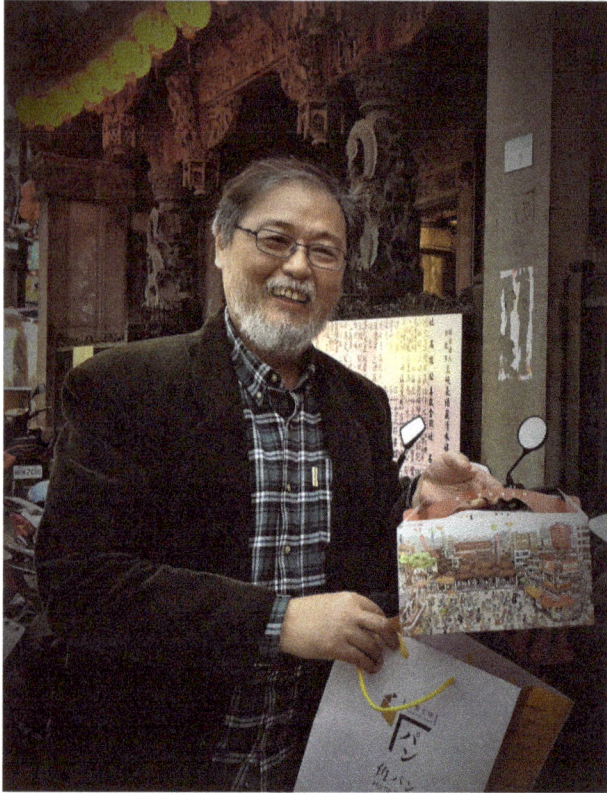

5.9. Ling Qun, Sanxia, Taipei, February 13, 2019. Photo by Xu Ying. Permission of Ling Qun.

5.10. Sanxia mural scene by Ling Qun, which is licensed to local merchants to use on packaging. Permission of Ling Qun.

USSR: under communism, they had no freedom but had work and adequate income; under capitalism, the exact opposite rang true. In Taiwan, political cartoonists have a higher degree of freedom than at any time in the country's history but are experiencing fewer opportunities to exercise that freedom with the drying up of venues.

Tang Jian-feng, who had served as president of the Taiwan Cartoonists Association in the 1990s and presided over the Art Society of China and the Confucius Institute when I interviewed him in 2019, found much fault with Taiwanese political cartooning. First of all, Tang said, not many young people draw political cartoons, because now there is a plethora of political parties, and "if you offend any one of them, you are sent to court. Artists only know art, and to be sent to court is unfathomable and a headache for them" (Tang 2019). He said that because almost all political cartoonists are

freelance and are paid by the cartoon (NT$1,000 each, or US$33), they find it nearly impossible to survive without other employment. Tang also took offense with Taiwanese peoples' indifference toward international events, and cartoonists' shying away from dealing with global commentary. He surmised that local cartoonists, not knowledgeable about other countries and their sensitive issues, play it safe and ignore foreign stories (Tang 2019).

Another veteran, Ji Ching (formerly staff cartoonist, now "invited" or freelance cartoonist for the *United Daily News*), considered himself the only Taiwanese political cartoonist who survives solely from his drawings. He also draws cartoons for *World Daily* in the United States and a web magazine, *Observation Station* (Ji 2019). Ji contended that although he draws for the major Guomindang daily, he can decide the news he will

emphasize and take a different stand from that of the Guomindang. He said that he has an amiable relationship with the editor, who seldom changes his cartoons. His main worry, though, is that "one day the newspaper will not carry political cartoons as circulations get smaller and smaller" (Ji 2019). Already, the only Taipei dailies carrying a regular political cartoon are the *United Daily News* and *Apple Daily*, with only the *United Daily News* printing one in its Sunday edition. Similarly, very few magazines are political cartoon–friendly, two that are being *Today Weekly* and *Commercial Weekly* (Ji 2019).

The diminished importance accorded printed political cartoons has motivated some cartoonists and newspapers to move in alternative directions to survive financially and keep some semblance of the profession alive.

Ling Qun (pen name for Yang Hsin-i) has been innovative in his efforts to continue drawing political cartoons and still survive financially. For thirty years, he drew a political cartoon daily for the *United Daily News*, and also did a four-panel political cartoon for the weekly *Du Jia Baodao* (Unique Report) magazine. But in recent years, the *United Daily News* dropped the staff position Ling held, and *Du Jia Baodao* folded. Although he continued submitting a daily political cartoon to the newspaper as a freelancer, the payment was low, and he felt it necessary to come up with other means to supplement his income. He figured that it might be profitable to tie in with businesses in the Sanxia district of Taipei, where he lived (Ling Qun 2019).

First, Ling painted an extended, cartoon-like wall mural in Sanxia, featuring the district's various storefronts. He then approached the merchants whose businesses are displayed on the mural and sold them the copyright for five years to use the mural scene in their

承認一個中國，中國即中共！

5.11. Political cartoon by Wang Peng. Courtesy of Wang Peng.

promotions and packaging boxes or bags (Ling Qun 2019). Ling has not run out of ideas on how to hook into a business model, sketching scenes of Sanxia on postcards, drawing the history of an old company on its wrapping paper and a biography of an official at his request, and envisioning drawing local buildings, such that with a card that people can purchase, they can see inside the building (Ling Qun 2019).

On the corporate level, too, an attempt was made to rescue the lowly political cartoon, although the manner in which it was done was unorthodox and even sleazy and would not meet the approval of "true" political cartoonists. In 2009, Hong Kong media tycoon Jimmy Lai, then headquartered in Taipei, launched the CG production house Next Media Animation to animate the news of the day, producing fifty to sixty original, animated 3-D news reenactments every twenty-four hours.[6] Next Media started out with strictly sensational, "crazy" content (crimes and scandals in Taiwan and Hong Kong, "salacious celebrity gossip . . . and scathing political commentary"), spiced with editorial cartoon metaphors and combining stylistic concepts of political cartoons, comic books, video games, and the nightly news (Kaplan 2010). Distribution of this animated news/opinion was through postings on the websites of Lai's newspapers and on YouTube (where brief advertisements were inserted), and through syndication deals similar to those of the Associated Press. Lai thought that what Next Media was doing was the future of journalism; it is "like watching a video game, but it is the news!" he said (Kaplan 2010).

By 2014, Next Media had attracted paying partners and clients such as Reuters, Kyodo News, MSN, and Univision with more serious content, but it continued its funny and "crazy" videos as "just a door to enter our world." In fact, the Next Media crew thought of its funnier content as "modern-day political cartoons" (Hu 2014).

A Concluding Remark

Taiwanese political cartooning for much of its early period was a contented lapdog of the Guomindang government; then changed into a snarling pit bull at times after martial law ended; and metamorphosed into an abandoned street mongrel, shelterless, dispirited, and worried about its survival. Its only consolation is knowing that it is not alone in its misery.

Notes

1. Hsiao Hsiang-wen (1995) surveyed a large segment of the cartooning community in Taiwan during the early 1990s. In her PhD dissertation, she relates what they said about editors' perceptions of editorial cartoons and cartoonists, both senior and contemporary cartoonists' perceptions of the transition of editorial cartoons (their role, content, function, and political disposition), and politicians' perceptions of the same. This is valuable information for that transitional period in Taiwanese political cartooning.

2. Wade-Giles romanization is used in this chapter, because that is the system prevalent in Taiwan.

3. The "Three Principles of the People" were to implement democracy, promote art research, and develop traditional morals.

4. The pen names cartoonists give themselves make for stories of their own. Lin Kuei-yo told Hsiao Hsiang-wen that his pen name, Yu Fu, meaning "fish's husband," came about because his wife is called "Fish" because of her activeness and cleverness (Yu Fu 1991).

5. This was not the first time that the government had lent support to comic art. The National Institute for Compilation and Translation, the bane of cartoonists for years, aided cartoonists in the 1990s, sponsoring a youth camp for cartooning, setting up schemes to encourage young talent, hiring cartoonists to draw comic books for schools, holding two competitions (each held twice yearly), and soliciting cartoons on varied topics and publishing them in books and newspapers (Lent 1993, 12).

6. Jimmy Lai (Lai Chee-ying) pushes a paparazzi style of journalism that is racy, gossipy, and politically hard-hitting, slanted against mainland China and advocating democracy. His main periodicals, *Apple Daily* and *Next* magazine, are published and wid8ely circulated in both Hong Kong and Taiwan.

Bibliography

Ao, Yao-hsiang. 1992. Interview with John A. Lent, Taipei, July 10.

Chang, Winnie. 1992. "From Knights Errant to Errant Couples." *Free China Review*, January, 4–17.

Chang, Yu-wei. 1954. *Comics Art*. Taipei: Chuan Ming Publishing.

Chao, Ning [Johnny]. 1986. Interview with John A. Lent, Taipei, August 8.

Chen, Kuang-hsi. 1993. Interview with Hsiao Hsiang-wen, Taipei, Summer.

Ching, Ho. 1993. Interview with Hsiao Hsiang-wen, Taipei, Summer.

Chiu, Jennifer. 1990. "Yeh's Cartoons Lived in Every Child's Dreams." *Free China Journal*, June 7, 6.

CoCo [Huang Yung-nan]. 1991. Interview with Hsiao Hsiang-wen, Taipei, January 8.

Dong, Yu-ching. 1985. "New Breed of Cartoonists Mirror the Modern Way of Chinese Life, Trends and Politics." *Free China Journal*, July 28.

Free China Review. 1992. "Satire Comes of Age." January, 1.

Hoong, Tei-lin. 2005. Interview with John A. Lent, Taipei, July 26.

Hsiao, Hsiang-wen. 1995. "Political Cartoons in Taiwan: Historical Profile and Content Analysis." PhD diss., Temple University.

Hsiao, Yen-chung. 1992. Interview with John A. Lent, Taipei, July 10.

Hsu, Hai-liang. 1990. "First Political Cartoonist Hung-Chia Yeh Dead." *Tzu-Li Early Newspaper*, April 25.

Hu, Elise. 2014. "For Taiwanese News Animators, Funny Videos Are Serious Work." National Public Radio, January 27. https:// www.npr.org/sections/alltechconsidered/2014/01/27/267018 900/for-taiwanese-news-animators-funny-videos-are-serious -work.

Independent Evening News. 1991. "Aesthetic Dagger in Taiwan." January 5.

Jen [Chung Sung-wei]. 2019. Interview with John A. Lent and Xu Ying, Taipei, February 13.

Ji, Ching. 2005. Interview with John A. Lent, Taipei, July 25.

Ji, Ching. 2019. Interview with John A. Lent and Xu Ying, Taipei, February 16.

Kaplan, Michael. 2010. "Taiwan Tabloid Sensation Next Media Re-Creates the News." *Wired*, August 30. https://www.wired .com/2010/08/mf_appledaily/.

L. C. C. [Lo Ching-chung]. 1992. Interview with John A. Lent, Taipei, July 9.

L. C. C. [Lo Ching-chung]. 1993. Interview with Hsiao Hsiang-wen, Taipei, Summer.

Laing, Ellen Johnston. 2004. *Selling Happiness: Calendar Posters and Visual Culture in Early-Twentieth-Century Shanghai*. Honolulu: University of Hawai'i Press.

Lao, Chung. 1992. Interview with John A. Lent, Taipei, July 10.

Lent, John A. 1993. "The Renaissance of Taiwan's Cartoon Arts." *Asian Culture Quarterly* 21, no. 1 (Spring): 3–17.

Lent, John A. 2015. *Asian Comics*. Jackson: University Press of Mississippi.

Li, Shan. 1992. Interview with John A. Lent, Taipei, July 9.

Li, Shan. 2005. Interview with John A. Lent, Taipei, July 25, 28.

Li, Ying-hao. 2005. Interview with John A. Lent, Taipei, July 28.

Lim, Ching-wen. 1990. "Editorial Cartoonists Enjoy Newfound Freedoms." *Free China Journal*, July 9.

Ling Qun [Yang Hsin-i]. 2019. Interview with John A. Lent and Xu Ying, Sanxia, Taipei, February 13.

Liu, Han-yu. 1991. Interview with Hsiao Hsiang-wen, Taipei, January.

Liu, Han-yu. 1993. Interview with Hsiao Hsiang-wen, Taipei, Summer.

Liu, Hsing-ching. 1993. Interview with Hsiao Hsiang-wen, Taipei, Summer.

Liu, Mei-min. 1993. "Chi Lung-shen Draws Life 60 Years." *United Evening Post*, April 9, 19.

Tang, Jian-feng. 2005. Interview with John A. Lent, Taipei, July 28.

Tang, Jian-feng. 2019. Interview with John A. Lent, Taipei, February 11.

Tseng, Chi-chun. 1991. Interview with Hsiao Hsiang-wen, Taipei, July 24.

Wang, Peng. 1992. Interview with John A. Lent, Taipei, July 9.

Wang, Peng. 2005. Interview with John A. Lent, Taipei, July 28.

Yang, Chi-hsien. 1994. Interview with Hsiao Hsiang-wen, Taipei, April.

Yu, O Yang. 1991. "Content Analysis of Political Cartoons in Daily Newspapers from July 1986 to June 1989." Master's thesis, Fu Jen Catholic University.

91

Yuan, Quan. 2015. "War Artist's Paintings Bring History to Life."
  Shanghai Daily, July 17. http://shanghaidaily.com/people/
  War-artists-paintings-bring-history-to-life.

Yu Fu [Lin Kuei-yo]. 1989. *Taiwan without Martial Law 1988
  Illustrated: A Collection of Yu Fu's Editorial Cartoons*. Taipei:
  Independence Evening Post.

Yu Fu [Lin Kuei-yo]. 1991. Interview with Hsiao Hsiang-wen,
  Taipei, January 6.

Zola, Zu. 2019. Interview with John A. Lent and Xu Ying, Taipei,
  February 11.

Southeast Asia

My only visit to Brunei Darussalam (hereafter, Brunei) was in November 1977. My mission was to interview key personnel at Radio Television Brunei about the recent launch of the country's first television station in March 1975. What was astonishing about this accomplishment was that only six months elapsed between the time the British protectorate first specified color television, along with a national airline and an agriculture advancement policy, as goals toward modernity, and the first telecasts. Also very noticeable was how the color television channel leapfrogged other stages of media development. In the 1970s, besides Radio Brunei, only one nondescript weekly newspaper existed in all of Brunei. Magazines were not visible, nor were many cartoons (Lent 1979).[1] Print media did not seem to be important in this oil- and natural gas–rich country.

In the intervening half century since, there has been some progress in the growth of print media and the use of comic art. About a half dozen newspapers exist today, led by the *Borneo Bulletin* (established in 1953), the only one publishing seven days weekly and the largest, circulating twenty-five thousand copies. The country has about a dozen newspapers in all, almost all nondaily.

Newspapers and magazines carry cartoons and strips, which are of a humor stripe and devoid of political content that would irritate the hardline government of Brunei. There are no accounts of the infringement of the "freedom to cartoon" coming out of Brunei, because cartoonists know very well the taut red line not to be crossed and the severe consequences if they do step over it.

Brunei is an absolute monarchy with strict press legislation that requires annual publishing permits and gives the government arbitrary power to shut down media at will. An updated Sedition Act of 2005 expands the list of punishable offenses to include "criticism of the sultan, the royal family, or the prominence of the national philosophy, the Malay Islamic monarchy concept." What little private press exists is owned or controlled by the sultan's family and/or practices self-censorship.

When Bruneian cartoonists speak of dealing with social issues and provoking thought, what they mean

Vignette: Brunei Darussalam

are more universal topics such as the importance of family, lifelong learning, and materialism, not criticism of government personnel and policies. The very few Bruneians who are referred to as editorial cartoonists, such as Rahim Jahit, stick with safe topics, in the process practicing a crippling self-censorship. To include Brunei's newspaper cartoonists among satirists and political cartoonists would be blasphemous to those who used their drawings to watch and criticize authority when necessary and attempt to bring about social and political change.

Though on a limited scale, social change is a goal of some comic book creators in Brunei, especially those working under the governmental Dewan Bahasa dan Pustaka (Language and Literature Bureau), a publisher of educational materials. The first comic strip in its children's magazine, *Mekar*, was *Kisah Alim* (Alim's Story), illustrated by Haji Ali Haji Raham in February 1998. The DBP has published other comic books that prioritize Islamic restrictions that forbid obscenity, violence, and vulgarity and reflect Bruneian identity such as the use of the Bruneian Malay language, culture, and tradition (Muhamad Norhadi 2021). Among these titles are *Daniel and Batu Ajaib* (Daniel and the Magical Stone), about a persevering boy who believes that nothing is impossible if one has knowledge; *Kemasyhuran Balkiah* (The Glory of Balkiah), recounting the epic tales of the fifth sultan of Brunei; *Lakak-Lakak*, a comics magazine created in 2020 to attract local cartoonists to show their work; and the popular *ZOY Topeng Sakti* (ZOY with the Powerful Mask), which since 2010 has related the fictional story of a boy who was bestowed powers to do good things for his country. The book also promotes the Malay language among Brunei's youth.

Among the handful of independent comic book creators, a university lecturer, Dr. Malai Yunos, is the most prolific with a count of six since he began in 1990. His books are "social commentary and autobiographical," meaning they relate to safe, everyday life experiences in a soft uncritical tone (Muhamad Norhadi 2021). Journalist Aaron Wong, in his account of one of

Malai Yunos's recent comics, *Apa Ada Noh?*, clarifies this meaning, pointing out that the book is written in the Bruneian Malay dialect and tries to "authentically replicate everyday, interpersonal scenarios that would be relatable to Bruneians, with the longer narratives usually ending with a moral message" (Wong 2018). The same can be said of the five books by Rahim Jahit, although their contents have a tint of social criticism, satire, and humor, because they were collected from his *Borneo Bulletin* "editorial" cartoons.

A Brief Conclusion

Having had one of the worst records of comic art advancement in nearly all of Asia, Brunei since the 1990s has been inching its way out of the doldrums, publishing a few comic books, organizing a small community of cartoonists, opening a comic book store, and holding an exhibition or two. However, no matter how far one stretches the meanings associated with political cartoons (as I have been doing in this vignette), Brunei comes up short.

Note

1. Among the few that were published in the 1970s was *Si-Tuyu* (The Idiot), drawn by Awang Md Salleh Ibrahim. Published in the government weekly *Pelita Brunei* (established in 1956), the character Si-Tuyu is an old man who "gives naïve views about the changes of social and political environment in Brunei" (Muhamad Norhadi 2021, 128). Muhamad Norhadi gives an example in which Si-Tuyu reasoned that if he arrived later to purchase a movie ticket, he would avoid a crowd, but all the tickets were sold by then. Of course, this is not really commentary on Brunei's social and political scene as a political cartoonist would define it.

Bibliography

Lent, John A. 1979. "Brunei: Television in a Rich Ministate." *BME's World Broadcast News*, March–April.

Muhamad Norhadi bin Ibrahim. 2021. "Comic Art: Towards the Development of Creative Publishing in Brunei Darussalam." Master's thesis, Universiti Brunei Darussalam.

Wong, Aaron. 2018. "Dr. Malai Yunus Launches Sixth Comic Book, Apa Ada Noh?" Biz Brunei, August 12. bizbrunei. com/2018/08/dr-malai-yunus-launches-sixth-comic-book -Apa-ada-noh/.

Recounting the career of Ung Bun Heang (1952–2014) gives a picture of the travails of being a cartoonist drawing about the fractious and volatile politics of Cambodia. Bun was a twenty-three-year-old art student and cartoonist at *Nokor Thom* when the Khmer Rouge seized power from Lon Nol's government on April 17, 1975, and set in motion one of humankind's worst genocidal campaigns. In fewer than four years, three million people were evacuated from the capital, Phnom Penh, to the countryside, there to toil and endure consciousness-building propaganda meetings. A third of the evacuees perished from torture and executions, malnutrition, disease, and overwork before Vietnamese forces liberated Cambodia on January 7, 1979.

Bun Heang kept a low profile during his enslavement, hiding the fact that he was educated and from a wealthy family, all the time working very long days in paddy fields and building dams. During civil disorder within the Communist Party in 1978, Bun Heang was able to get away, and he looked for relatives in the local reeducation camp. He later recounted: "All the guards had left, leaving only corpses, skeletons and evidence of starvation, torture and execution. Finding another killing field, [Bun Heang] saw young children having their heads smashed against trees, naked women slaughtered and tossed into pits, men kneeling at the edge of a pit to be killed" (Stephens 2014).

After the overthrow of Pol Pot and the Khmer Rouge, Bun Heang worked in the Ministry of Information and Propaganda and attended political reeducation classes; this time, they extolled the Vietnamese as liberators. He ran afoul of the authorities for portraying a heroic Vietnamese with protruding teeth in cartoons he drew for the ministry's propaganda films, and he, along with his wife, Phiny Ung, decided to escape, bribing their way through checkpoints to the Khao-I-Dang refugee camp in Thailand. They were given refugee status in Brisbane, arriving in May 1980.

In Australia, Bun Heang and Phiny Ung often discussed and anguished over the terrible experiences they and millions had suffered under the Khmer Rouge and agreed not to let them be forgotten or ignored. They

Chapter 6

Cambodia

began to take notes about their talks, which Bun Heang sketched. They said that because they had no photographs or documents, it was crucial that they remember everything accurately. It took more than two years (1980 and 1981) to draw ninety black pen drawings, most of which were published in *The Murderous Revolution: Life and Death in Pol Pot's Kampuchea* (1985), authored by Martin Stuart-Fox ("Statement of Bun Heang and Phiny Ung," n.d.).

For years, Bun Heang chronicled and severely criticized Cambodian politics from afar, until he died in February 2014. His sharp attacks, especially against Cambodian political corruption and abuses, appeared in the *Far Eastern Economic Review* (published in Hong Kong) for a number of years and his online blog Sacrava Toons (established in 2001). Cambodian authorities blocked his website and suspended KI Media, which also used his cartoons, in January 2011, the reason being his work's political sensitivity. He felt that he was unable to return to Cambodia for safety reasons, calling himself a "very ugly black sheep in Cambodia" (Brouwer 2006; also Crothers 2014; Nou 2015).[1]

As discussed in a few chapters of this book, political cartoonists in other authoritarian societies have fled their homelands in fear of reprisals and continued their attacks in neighboring countries, ready examples being China and Myanmar. In some instances, they are criticized for not staying in their home states and fighting it out. Perhaps public indignation in Cambodia about Bun Heang likewise resulted from his strong criticism from afar.

The Dismal Condition of Political Cartooning

To say that Cambodian politics has been tumultuous for at least the past half century is a fair assessment. The country has faced war on its own soil, struggled through a genocidal regime, and drastically changed forms of government and name designations multiple times: from independence from France in 1953 to the present, Cambodia has had communism, constitutional

monarchy, multiparty democracy, a unitary dominant party, and parliamentary elective constitutional monarchy and has carried ten different names. One-party rule under Prime Minister Hun Sen (in office as head of government since 1985) became effective in 2018, when the Supreme Court, dominated by the ruling Cambodian People's Party, dissolved the main opposition party, leading to the ruling party securing all 125 National Assembly seats. After the election, opposition party leaders were detained; some left Cambodia and others were barred from political activity for five years, while the number of people arrested and detained for political reasons increased sharply. What little freedom of the media had existed before now collapsed, as previously independent newspapers and broadcast outlets remained closed or were sold to allies of the government, social media outlets were closely watched and regulated, and other legislation was introduced on "cybersecurity" and "fake news."

Under such stringent conditions, political cartooning has all but vanished. Its downward spiral was very evident in June 2010 during my visit to Phnom Penh. Political cartoons (and other forms of comic art) were nearly nonexistent in three major Khmer-language and two English-language dailies I scanned during the latter part of June. Very bland artistically, the dailies did not carry domestic or foreign comic strips, or any illustrations of stories, even though they all had substantial numbers of pages with enough space to accommodate cartoons. In fact, only the *Kampuchea Thmey Daily* published locally drawn political cartoons, usually two daily, most often at the bottoms of the same pages. They were two or three columns wide, in the same rough style, and on domestic situations. Neither the *Rasmei Kampuchea Daily Newspaper* nor *Koh Sântepheap* (Peace) used any form of cartoons, and the English-language tabloid dailies did not fare any better. The *Phnom Penh Post* had two syndicated gag cartoons, and the *Cambodia Daily*, a political cartoon by Tom Toles of the *Washington Post*.

During the course of Cambodia's postindependence decades, the level of freedom to cartoon fluctuated, as would be expected with the frequent changes of types

100

of governance. As witnessed in the post-Marcos Philippines, post-dictatorial South Korea, and post-Sukarno and Suharto Indonesia, among others, when the valves of control are loosened, heretofore forbidden information, strong criticism, and pent-up feelings and opinions spout forth. Usually, sensationalism is a veneer printed over journalism. Eric Loo wrote in 2006 that Khmer newspapers, knowing that shock value sells, coated their front pages with "pejorative expressions, loaded headlines, and photographs of gore, nudity, violence, and bloodied corpses" (2006, 65), and, I might add, cartoons unrestrained in taking down opponents. Political cartoons by their very nature are not meant to be impartial, and in a mass media landscape such as that of Cambodia, where newspapers are normally party owned or backed, to expect impartiality is delusionary. Most of what Loo summarized about Cambodian journalism is easily adapted to political cartooning: "The road towards ethical professional journalism remain [sic] blocked by low salaries, culture of political patronage and impunity, the government's ambivalent relationship with the media, and low literacy rate, which to an extent makes journalists feel little concern for accountability in what they write" (Loo 2006, 67).

Historical Development

Political cartooning began in Cambodia shortly after the birth of the first Khmer-language newspaper, *Nagara Vatta*, launched in 1936 (Soth and Sin 1982). The appearance of the newspaper "correlated with an awakening of national consciousness" (Marston 2011, 32); actually, one of its editors, Son Ngoc Thanh, headed the independence movement. Cartoons were favored as a political tool because their messages could be interpreted in multiple ways—hopefully, befuddling to authorities, critical of government to the public. They, and satire generally, became prominent in the 1960s under the administration of Norodom Sihanouk, head of state and former king. Sensitive to both criticism of him by the press and criticism about his relations with the press, Sihanouk

alternated suspension of newspapers and other repressive actions with periods of wider latitude, even publishing three magazines himself, which contained political cartoons. John Marston (2011, 32–33), echoing the sentiments of Don Noel (1967), explains the strange logic of satire becoming important in publications owned by Sihanouk: "The fact that satire would appear under the imprimatur of royalty has its own kind of logic. . . . Who, after all, but the king dares commits lèse majesté?"

Noel reports that although the Sihanouk magazines carried political cartoons, only a Vietnamese-language newspaper in Phnom Penh, *Trung Lap*, had a regular political cartoonist (Noel 1967). One of Sihanouk's periodicals, the monthly satire magazine *Phseng-Phseng*, was very popular, with a circulation twice that of any other publication in Cambodia. *Phseng-Phseng's* popularity resulted from its use of photographs of personalities at public functions with "either wry subtitles or unlikely quotations put in the victims' mouths [and] . . . local cartoons and articles, ranging from humor and gossip to more frankly political material" (Noel 1967, 27–28). Most of the magazine was in Khmer. Sihanouk's other magazines, *Kambuja* (in English and French) and *Le Sangkum* (in French), appeared after Cambodia discontinued ties with the United States and were meant for foreign readership. As would be expected, the political cartoons of locals Huy Hem, Nhek Dim, and Khut Khun and those reprinted from abroad featured views similar to those of Sihanouk. The local cartoonists occasionally drew about domestic matters and individuals not favorable to Sihanouk (Marston 2011, 33).

Marston writes that a cartoon by Khut Khun (in *Le Sangkum*, June 1966) gives a clue to how Sihanouk thought of *Kambuja* and *Le Sangkum*. He says that the cartoon shows the magazines' staffs as a

jazz troop positioned on top of a globe, editors Chau Seng and Chea San serving as accompaniment to Sihanouk, who played a trumpet from which flowed copies of *Kambuja* and *Le Sangkum*. The overall caption in French was, "Our music begins to have some success." The cartoons, like the magazines as a whole, consciously strove to construct an

6.1. Cambodian political cartoonist Im Sokha. Courtesy of Im Sokha, via John Marston. Reprinted with permission from the *International Journal of Comic Art* 13, no. 1 (Spring 2011): 32–58. John A. Lent, publisher. Article by John Marston.

image of national identity to be presented to the world. (Marston 2011, 33)

Marston writes that Sihanouk's political cartoon use was a "logical extension of his personal style and the character traits he identified with, such as wit, sophistication and irreverence toward world powers" (2011, 33–34) and was intended to pass on the message that Cambodia and its leader possessed these characteristics comparable to other nations.

The period following Sihanouk's deposing in 1970 was rich in political cartooning, with more leeway given for cartoonists to attack state policy and more newspaper space, more prominently located, allocated for cartoons in more newspapers. Hol Sophon of *Koh Sântepheap* and Ung Bun Heang of *Nokor Thom* replaced Huy Hem and Nhek Dim as the country's top political cartoonists. The editor of *Nokor Thom*, Soth Polin, was partial to political cartoons, even publishing full front-page satirical cartoons in the Sunday edition of his newspaper (Ung Bun Heang, quoted in Marston 2011, 34).

After the defeat of the Pol Pot regime, during which political cartooning had ceased, the new People's Republic of Kampuchea government (1979–1989) rebuilt social institutions, including the press. The haven for cartoonists was *Kampuchea*, the first newspaper of the new government, distributed widely through the workplace.[2] It published the government's socialist line (except from 1987 to 1989). This is understandable because for its first five months, the paper was printed in Vietnam, Phnom Penh lacking adequate equipment; and for a while, its editorials were translated from Vietnamese, and when they were composed in Khmer, Vietnamese monitors screened them. Gradually, *Kampuchea* became more Cambodian and more open, and a training place for future generations of journalists.

One important cartoonist to emerge in the early 1980s was Im Sokha, first as an illustrator of fiction in *Kampuchea* and then as the daily's political cartoonist in 1987. As an illustrator, he often drew ordinary people reading *Kampuchea*; as a satirical cartoonist, throughout his career, he often illustrated ideas submitted by readers and editors. Marston writes that Im Sokha's cartoons most often represented "opposite political viewpoints drawn for different papers" (2011, 35); Im Sokha described himself, in Marston's words, as "an illustrator who gives form to other people's ideas for hire."

The cartoons drawn and sparked by readers, according to Marston, had

some claim to being the discourse of the mass readership, framed with reference to the elite discourse of the paper as a whole. These cartoons were never truly political and did not criticize specific political issues or state policy. . . . Im Sokha's cartoon style developed in this period from a somewhat stilted realism to light, uncluttered sketches serving their satirical points efficiently; part of the wit derived from the impression that the cartoons were drawn quickly and effortlessly. (Marston 2011, 37)

Writing in January 1990, the bureau chief of Thailand's the *Nation*, Kawi Chongkitthawon, said that "anything goes" with respect to *Kampuchea*'s cartoons,

6.2. A *Kampuchea* cartoon by Im Sokha, a panoramic depiction of the horrors of Pol Pot's reign of terror, December 20, 1990. Courtesy of Im Sokha, via John Marston. Reprinted with permission from the *International Journal of Comic Art* 13, no. 1 (Spring 2011): 32–58. John A. Lent, publisher. Article by John Marston.

but he qualified his comment, saying that none of Cambodia's six newspapers, including *Kampuchea*, ever ran cartoons critical "of the Cambodian leadership or their special relationship with Hanoi" and the Communist Party of Vietnam. He explained: "Observers said that there is a thin line dividing . . . what the authorities would tolerate and what they wouldn't. Each political cartoonist instinctively knows how far he and his cartoons can go. . . . They also refrain from attacking high-level officials suspected of involve[ment] in corruption. But they frequently hammer on corruption by low-ranking officials" (Chongkitthawon 1990). Chongkitthawon said that *Kampuchea*'s political cartoons in 1989–1990 "stressed the disparity of the haves and have-nots, the uneven development of the cities and the rural towns, the indifference of government officials toward public problems, and chronic red tape in government offices," as well as delayed payment to government employees. Modernity and its impact were a favorite topic of all six top newspapers, for instance cartoons depicting

> young couples in modern dresses and sometimes with dark sunglasses in front of high-rise buildings and expensive cars. One cartoon in *Pracheachon* newspaper—official mouthpiece of Phnom Penh—in December 1989, focused on a young couple in heavy petting inside a park. The girl wears a T-shirt with the word "Disco" on it. (Chongkitthawon 1990, 45)[3]

Modern Cambodian men were drawn as military dodgers owning luxurious cars or motorcycles, while those in rural areas were depicted as standing ready to defend their country. The most common cartoons, according to Chongkitthawon, lampooned Sihanouk and portrayed Pol Pot as the "most horrible and hated figure in Cambodia" (1990, 46).

Kampuchea's freedom, as well as that of other newspapers, was ebbing by May 1990. *Kampuchea* had a new editor, a nonjournalist and former ambassador to the Soviet Union, who followed the party line, dispensed with reader-inspired cartoons, and further politicized the paper's content. During the next couple of years, the newspaper was switched to the Ministry of Information, much of its staff was transferred to a broadcast station, its editor was intimidated and left Cambodia, and its circulation nosedived from a peak of fifty-five thousand to just three thousand.

A *Kampuchea* deputy editor who resigned during this chaos, Prum Nhean Vichit, started a weekly bulletin in 1992, *Sântepheap* (Peace), promoted as the country's first independent newspaper despite being glued to the policies of the Cambodian People's Party. Marston writes that *Sântepheap* consisted of mimeographed or photocopied pages stapled together, and the content was completely editorial, meaning opinionated (2011, 41). Cartoons by Im Sokha covered the entire front and back covers to attract readers, as *Sântepheap* was sold at newsstands. When Im Sokha left the newspaper, Marston (2011, 43) was told, he was replaced by a cartoonist who merely traced Im Sokha's drawings of heads onto his own pictures.

6.3. Im Sokha cartoon, *Sântepheap*, February 8, 1993. A takeoff on the story of the Trojan horse that uses Cambodian political figures. Courtesy of Im Sokha, via John Marston. Reprinted with permission from the *International Journal of Comic Art* 13, no. 1 (Spring 2011): 32–58. John A. Lent, publisher. Article by John Marston.

6.4. Im Sokha cartoon in the small newspaper *Sâmleng Polroddh Khmaer*, January 27–28, 1994, showing the editors of the successful dailies *Koh Sântepheap* (left) and *Reasmey Kampuchea* (right) in a vicious battle, with the editor of *Sâmleng Polroddh Khmaer* (center) pleading for peace. Courtesy of Im Sokha, via John Marston. Reprinted with permission from the *International Journal of Comic Art* 13, no. 1 (Spring 2011): 32–58. John A. Lent, publisher. Article by John Marston.

After a short stint in Thailand, Im Sokha became a cartoonist on *Reasmey Kampuchea* (Cambodian Rays of Light), a Khmer-language newspaper of high professional standards funded by a Thai media company and a wealthy businessman. The cartoons in *Reasmey Kampuchea* have been described as "skillful and sly, always discrete [*sic*], and never more than obliquely political" (Marston, 2011, 43).

At the birth of the 1990s, small (four-page) independent newspapers appeared, made up mostly of strong editorials, opinionated news, and excessive sensationalism. More than thirty newspapers dominated newsstand fare by 1993. Im Sokha's political cartoons regularly appeared often on the front pages of the mini-papers and one or two of his illustrations accompanying short fictional pieces on inside pages, making his impact on Cambodian graphic journalism significant. He drew by the instructions given by the editors, who themselves were often political pawns. Even his illustrations pushed to the limits of propriety and certainly would not have

6.5. A rare cartoon in 2010. *Kampuchea Thmey Daily*, June 2010.

been used in the socialist era (Marston 2011, 46). For a few years, cartoonists had a "field day—lampooning corrupt politicians, girl-crazy UN peacekeepers and even once-feared Khmer Rouge," Mark Dodd (1993) reports, adding that the country's co-presidents, opposition leaders, and former Vietnam-installed "corrupt and fat" ministers were unflatteringly caricaturized.

Rather quickly, the tide for political cartoons changed. By the mid-1990s, according to Marston, there were far fewer cartoons, virtually none on front pages, and newer cartoons "avoided the degree of stylized distortion which had been common in the past" (1997, 73). He concluded that political cartoons had ceased to be an "active strategy in the negotiation of public discourse." The government toughened its stance relative to the mass media overall. Although political cartoonists were not among the victims, an editor and former editor

of *Odom K'tek Khmer* (Khmer Ideal) were killed, the editor of *Tu Do* (Freedom) expelled, and two journalists imprisoned in 1996 (CPJ 1997).

The diminished status and cautionary nature of political cartooning continued into the twenty-first century. In 2006, political cartoonists Sen Samondara and Sam Sarath, both with the NGO Center for Social Development, talked about precautionary measures taken at the center. They said that they did not sketch the prime minister, who is angered by any drawing resembling him; that they avoid upsetting any political officials or criticizing anyone directly; and that they "control the meaning, because we don't want to irritate powerful people" (Sen Samondara, quoted in Barton 2006).

Finally, comic books over the years were rarely political, and when they were, the politicizing was done obliquely. For example, *Thoun Chey*, a folktale about a peasant boy who outwits the king, was reissued as a comic book several times, its anti-authoritarian plot appealing to common people during Cambodia's monarchy periods. Also, cartoonist Sin Yang Phirum offered mild criticism in her comics, especially on the topics of women and social issues. All of the comics were noncontroversial, even omitting mythic and religious imagery as proscribed by the government. Perhaps it was inevitable that some political topics found their way into comics, because two creators were also political cartoonists, Im Sokha and Em Satya, the latter drawing under the pen name Nono (Plaut 2004; Weeks 2010).

Notes

1. Not everyone was enamored by Bun Heang's efforts. John Weeks of Our Books, in 2010, labeled his work "opportunistic," "racist," and "chauvinist," calling Bun Heang "the most offensive political cartoonist you will see."

2. Marston (2011, 36) writes that work teams read aloud *Kampuchea* at consciousness-raising sessions.

3. The editor of *Kampuchea*, Khieu Kanharit, said that "disco" signified "modern people who are selfish and careless in Cambodian society" (Chongkitthawon 1990, 45).

Bibliography

Barton, Cat. 2006. "Power of the Pen: Political Cartoonists in Cambodia." *Phnom Penh Post*, December 29. https://www .phnompenhpost.com/national/power-pen-political-cartoon ists-cambodia.

Brouwer, Andy. 2006. "Bun Heang Ung: Surviving a Living Hell." http://andybrouwer.co.uk/bun.html.

Chongkitthawon, Kawi. 1990. "Editor Comments on Political Cartoonists." *The Nation* (Bangkok), January 2, 6.

Committee to Protect Journalists (CPJ). 1997. *Attacks on the Press in 1996: Cambodia*. February. https://www.refworld.org/ docid/47c564tb19.html.

Crothers, Lauren. 2014. "Ung Bun Heang, Popular Cartoonist, Dies at 61." *Cambodia Daily*, February 10.

Dodd, Mark. 1993. "Cambodia Cartoonists Celebrate New-Found Freedom." Reuters, July 19.

Loo, Eric. 2006. "Cambodian Journalism 'Flying Blind.'" *Media Development* 53, no. 3: 65–68.

Marston, John. 1997. "Em Sokha and Cambodian Satirical Cartoons." *Southeast Asian Journal of Social Science* 25, no. 1: 59–78.

Marston, John. 2011. "Im Sokha and Cambodian Satirical Cartoons." *International Journal of Comic Art* 13, no. 1 (Spring): 32–57.

Noel, Don O., Jr. 1967. *Cambodia: The Mass Media*. New York: Alicia Patterson Foundation.

Nou, Sotheavy. 2015. "Exiled Cartoonist Returns with a Smile." *Khmer Times*, July 27. https://www.khmertimeskh.com/ news/13743/exiled-cartoonist-returns-with-a-smile/.

Plaut, Ethan. 2004. "Reviewing a Forgotten Art." *Cambodia Daily*, October 30. https://www.cambodiadaily.com/news/reviewing -a-forgotten-art-927/.

Soth Polin and Sin Kimsuy. 1982. "Kampuchea." In *Newspapers in Asia: Contemporary Trends and Problems*, edited by John A. Lent, 219–39. Hong Kong: Heinemann Asia.

"Statement of Bun Heang and Phiny Ung to the Australian National University." n.d. Australian National University. https:// anulib.anu.edu.au/collections/rare-books-special-collections -manuscripts/drawings-bun-heang-ung-life-under-khmer -rou-0.

Stephens, Tony. 2014. "Bun Heang Un [*sic*]: Artist Endorsed the Worst of Pol Pot." *Sydney Morning Post*, February 15. https:// www.smh.com.au/national/bun-heang-un-artist-endured-the -worst-of-pol-pot-20140214-32r76.html.

Stuart-Fox, Martin, and Bunheang Ung. 1985. *The Murderous Revolution: Life and Death in Pol Pot's Kampuchea*. Bangkok: Orchid Press.

Weeks, John. 2010. Interview with John A. Lent and Xu Ying, Phnom Penh, June 19, 22.

Historical Perspectives

Wayang Influences

Linkages between traditional culture and art and modern satirical cartooning have been noted worldwide, and certainly in Asia as discussed throughout this book—for example, thousand-year-old Toba scrolls and, later, *ukiyo-e* paintings in Japan; nineteenth-century Kalighat temple paintings in India; and Song Dynasty "silent complaint," painted scrolls alluding to poetry in China. In Indonesia, the centuries-old wayang shadow-puppet performances have played a similar role of mocking upper-caste and upper-class dialects and improvising satirical, biting commentary.

Indonesian political cartoonists have given a nod to *wayang kulit* as a source of inspiration. Pramono R. Pramoedjo (1992), while political cartoonist of *Suara Pembaruan* and president of the Indonesian Cartoonists' Association, said: "All cartoonists know wayang and we take its stories, which have many messages for a better life." Cartoonist and animator Dwi Koendoro (1992), terming wayang a "philosophy, the story of mankind, of culture, rich with caricature," focused in on a part of wayang called *goro-goro*, in which, he said, "you can hear some caricature, satire—jokes about the government and its officials. It makes fools of the government. The parts of wayang I put in my strips are the two-dimensional aspects—style and philosophy." Indonesia's most prominent political cartoonist for decades, G. M. Sudarta (1992), even credited wayang with originating Indonesian cartooning. He showed how cartoonists used wayang clowns to depict traits for which they are famous—Semar, wisdom; Petruk, frankness; Gareng, spoken insults; and Bagong, stupidity. Sudarta used movements and nuances commonly identified with wayang, explaining: "Petruk, who speaks frankly, moves like a pointer with his finger extended, and Gareng shuffles. When I have a cartoon character point, it is indirectly saying it is speaking frankly" (1992).

Chapter 7

Indonesia

7.1. Petruk as a wayang figure.

109

Wayang has existed in Java for more than a millennium and is "regarded as the most important vehicle for teaching and preserving the complex treasure of local mystical beliefs through highly ritualistic performances from the great Hindu epics the *Mahabarata* [*sic*] and *Ramayana*" (Peacock 1968; quoted in Berman 2001, 23). The Javanese added clowns to wayang before 600 CE; they began to appear in cartoons about the early 1970s.

The Sukarno (1945–1967) and Suharto (1967–1998) Eras

The first president of Indonesia, Sukarno (born Koesno Sosrodihardjo), is also the country's first political cartoonist—more accurately, *possibly* the first *indigenous* political cartoonist. Colonial Dutch-language newspapers had published plenty of political and strip cartoons previously, but likely they were to serve the purpose Frantz Fanon (1965) gave for early media in colonized regions—to keep the colonists in touch with civilization, "their civilization." What Sukarno drew in 1935, in the opposition newspaper *Fikiran Rakyat*, had a completely opposite message: an Indonesian is pointing at Dutch colonialism and ordering it to leave.[1]

After decades of revolutionary struggle, imprisonment, in-country exile, broken alliances, and World War II collaboration with the Japanese, Sukarno led Indonesia to independence in 1945. Sukarno was not fond of comics (nor was his successor, Suharto), equating them with "garbage"; nor was he receptive to critical political cartoons. He obviously knew of their propaganda value, having seen them used throughout the Japanese occupation (1943–1945), the war for independence (1945–1948), and the immediate independence years. During those years, strip characters appeared in poster art and on walls alongside resistance slogans. Benedict Anderson found:

> Under the occupation, cartoons and posters were widely used, but they appeared exclusively under the aegis of the military authorities. The targets of the cartoons were typically outside society—the Dutch, the British, and the Americans. During the Revolution, posters and graffiti

7.2. Sketch of Augustin Sibarani. Artist unknown.

> were the most common and the most popular form. From forty newspapers and magazines I have checked from that period, only eight carried cartoons at all; even these cartoons appeared irregularly, and at rare intervals.
>
> Doubtless part of the explanation lies in the technical problems caused by shortages and disorders of those years. But the fact that the bulk of these cartoons were printed in papers published in Dutch-occupied Jakarta, not in towns held by the Republic, suggests that the full answer lies as much in the political-cultural as in the technical realm. (Anderson 1978, 292)

Once in power, Sukarno did not permit cartoonists to caricaturize him and banned cartoons that criticized the authorities or that took a political view different from those of the government. However, for some time, he tolerated the sharp barbs from the pen of Augustin Sibarani (1925–2014), who had been drawing controversial, frank political cartoons for the daily *Bintang Timur* since 1957. Sukarno even included Sibarani in cultural delegations and enlisted him in government projects. For example, when Sukarno needed a picture of deceased holy man Sisingamangaraja XII for his national

7.3. Sibarani cartoon portraying US Cold War–era diplomat John Foster Dulles's kite (resembling major Indonesian politician Syafruddin Prawiranegara) caught in the *rakjat* (people) tree.

heroes program, he asked Sibarani to create a sketch of the man, of whom no photograph existed, from the memories of his children (Philips 2014).[2]

In 1965, General Suharto wrestled power from Sukarno after an attempted coup supposedly backed by the Communist Party of Indonesia and a subsequent purge of communists that resulted in hundreds of thousands of killings. Although he was a communist, Sibarani escaped execution and jail but was detained for five days, after which he was blacklisted and banned from working. His workplace, *Bintang Timur*, quit publishing, and he tried to survive by "doing odd jobs, selling paintings and cartooning under a pseudonym for publications willing to risk affiliating with him" (Philips 2014). In 1985, political cartoonist G. M. Sudarta and the head of Lembaga Humor Indonesia, Arwah Setiawan, arranged for Sibarani to participate in an exhibition in Ancol, Jakarta, but when the minister of information heard of this, he threatened not to open the exhibition if Sibarani's works were included. Sibarani lived in France toward the end of Suharto's regime, where he regularly skewered the dictator on the pages

of *Le Monde*. He returned to Indonesia, where he continued to paint into his eighties. Other great political cartoonists since have heaped praise on Sibarani. Sudarta (1992) said that he used a "strong, direct, and sharp style"; Pramono (1992) said that he influenced virtually all Indonesian cartoonists. In 2008, he was declared "Indonesian Cartoon Maestro."[3]

To backtrack, the time of parliamentary democracy in Indonesia (1950–1959) was a "freedom to cartoon" decade when "freedom to express critics [criticism?] was uncontrolled" (P. Sunarto 2012, 214). Opinions expressed in political cartoons directed at opposing political parties were sometimes cynical, sarcastic, and limitless. Metaphorical political cartoons in this era were used to sharpen criticism, not just to soften messages. Overall, the balanced political situation "opened wide chances for cartoonists to express their opinion[s]," according to Priyanto Sunarto (2012, 214).

When I interviewed cartoonists in Jakarta in 1992, the Suharto government was being extremely restrictive, forcing political cartoonists to sidestep taboo topics, refrain from mentioning the vested interests of

Indonesia

7.4. Sibarani, "A Chess Game."

7.5. Dwi Koendoro (left) with John A. Lent, Jakarta, July 2013. Courtesy of Dwi Koendoro.

newspapers and government officials, and endure government and self-censorship. Dwi Koendoro (1992) gave as off-limits topics the monopoly of big business and the deep business involvement of Suharto's sons, the land business, and clashes between government ministers; Sudarta (1992) added criticism of the president's family, ethnic groups, and religions as well as the business interests of newspapers, almost all of which were appendages of conglomerates. In 1992, about ten large groups controlled Indonesia's media (Mahtum 1992)—for example, *Kompas* was part of a conglomerate that owned about seven newspapers and magazines throughout the country, while Gramedia owned film studios, magazines, bookstores, a bank, and five hotels (Sudarta 1992).

Additionally, cartoonists were often asked to change their ideas and drawings to satisfy editors. *Suara Pembaruan*'s political cartoonist, Pramono R. Pramoedjo, said: "Every morning, the editors and I meet to see if my sketch can be published. If it can be I then finish it. Every day, I make five sketches; three cannot be used. I put them in my files for possible other uses later on" (1992). Pramono said that he cannot deviate from the newspaper's views. Koendoro discusses a planned drawing with the editor beforehand, but even then, "sometimes the bargaining weight of the editor changes and the cartoon cannot be published" (1992). He added that *Kompas* editors "know what the government wants or does not want."

Sudarta (1992) said that he was expected to be at daily *Kompas* editorial meetings, one each in the morning

7.6. G. M. Sudarta (right) with John A. Lent, fronting some of the awards Sudarta has won for his cartooning, Jakarta, July 28, 1992. Photo by Ramli Badrudin. Courtesy of G. M. Sudarta.

and evening. He explained that at Indonesian newspapers, cartoonists had to be on the same "wavelength" as the editor and the newspaper. In his own case, if his viewpoint strongly differed from that of the editor, the two of them worked on a compromise. Sudarta said that the editor sometimes gave him the theme, "but I alone express it in cartoon form" (1992).

Self-censorship was one of the most severe problems faced by Indonesian cartoonists during this period, along with lack of training, a glutted pool of about three hundred cartoonists (most freelance), and low pay, according to Sudarta (1992). Koendoro, probably unintentionally, gave an example of self-censorship when he said: "We can do caricatures, but I stopped five years ago as I felt guilty of making fools of government ministers. I wanted to start a company in Indonesia, so I needed the government's help" (1992). He said that his weekly, sometimes sociopolitical strip *Pailul dan Panji Koming* had been cut on occasion when it was thought to have been too controversial. The strip was often satirical, based on news events and "anything of social or political significance."

Indonesian cartoonists, as with their colleagues nearly everywhere, knew how to sidestep the government through the use of subtleties and innuendoes, what Sudarta called the "Indonesian way." He explained:

We have a way. We want to make those in government whom we criticize, smile. And to make the common people smile to bring up their aspirations. Also, we have to make ourselves smile or we can be jailed. Today, cartoonists are more polite, indirect, smooth. It is the best way for us in Indonesia. As cartoonists, we only want to give the information. It is very important to deliver the cartoon safely to the government. (Sudarta 1992)

Pramono agreed, stating: "We can't hit government problems face to face. It's like *uedo* in Japan; we have to allow for saving of face. So, we caricature very carefully, not to make government people unhappy but to make them smile. We circle around the topic" (1992).

Difficult situations such as those with the Indonesian government can be breeding grounds for creativity, as exemplified by Sudarta: "The clove cigarette industry is monopolized by Suharto's son, who uses the business to profit himself. As a result, clove farmers are hurt by poor management at the top. I did a cartoon showing a man smoking. In the second panel, he is coughing violently. In the third panel, he says, 'Oh, the clove cigarettes are so smooth.' The message was subtle" (1992). Sudarta believed that this "Indonesian way" was effective because "we still have real political cartoons and many political cartoonists in the country." For him, political cartoons represented the "main menu of nearly all dailies," a view countered by Dominto Sudarno (1992), managing editor of *HumOr*, who said that only 13 or 14 of the 250 newspapers and magazines in Indonesia used cartoons.

HumOr, part of the Tempo group of publications, was started in 1980; its purpose, according to its president, Mahtum (1992), was to stimulate cartoon development throughout Indonesia and to entertain its forty thousand subscribers. About 40 percent of each eighty-four-page issue consisted of cartoons and illustrations. The twice-monthly magazine was a major venue for political cartoons until it folded in 1995.[4] In 1992, magazines such as *Tempo*, *Editor*, and *Prisma*, and newspapers such as *Suara Pembaruan* and *Suara Karya*, each had a regular special page for political cartoons.

113

7.7. Cover, *HumOr* magazine, June 10–23, 1992.

Indonesia had humor magazines before *HumOr*. From 1975 to 1976, Arwah Setiawan published twenty issues of *Astaga* (Good Lord) before he was forced to close, suffering from lack of funds and cartoonists. Because he believed that Indonesians did not understand or appreciate humor and cartoons, in 1979 Setiawan formed and headed the humor institute Lembaga Humor Indonesia. In our 1992 interview, he pointed out some of the traits of humor in Indonesia:

Indonesians are not familiar with subtle humor. Cartoonists have to show people where they have to laugh. They have to put punctuation marks where people should laugh. Like they are saying: "now laugh." Also, Indonesians are not irreverent enough for humor. If they criticize, they excuse themselves. The people can't laugh at God, can't laugh at the president, at ethnic groups. It is not a censorship problem only; this is inborn in them.

People are always strange to other people. Customs, accents are funny. People should be made to look ridiculous if they do wrong things in your thinking. If they are wrong by nature, I don't think they should be made fun of. Censorship is based on our inborn traits of not to laugh at God or at parents. (Setiawan 1992)

Contemporary Period

Protest Comics and Cartoons

Independent comic books were launched in the early 1990s, emanating from NGOs and art schools; they usually had a weirdness-for-its-own-sake tendency. An exception was the activist comic *Outran-Outran ing Muria* (Chaos in Muria) in 1993, drawn by art students and funded by an independent environmental group. Taking a stance against nuclear power, the book intended to give residents near the proposed site of Indonesia's first nuclear plant another side to the issue of nuclear energy from that of the government (Nugroho 2009). Others, particularly the comics community Apotik Komik (Comic Pharmacy) in Yogyakarta (started in 1997), used innovative production and distribution methods to make their social and political views known (Lent 2015, 139).[5] One member of Apotik Komik, Eko Nugroho, used his home surroundings as a gallery for evolving street exhibitions. Starting with his wall mural "Herk!," Nugroho daily added something to the work based on his direct interactions with passersby (Berman n.d., 113). In effect, this was an example of "participatory cartooning."

Hard-hitting independent cartoonists still take on sociopolitical problems. Aji Prasetyo closely monitors tensions between big businesses and foreign investors, and local people, in a comic strip reminiscent of *Doonesbury*; Dodi Irwandi protests how the McDonald's restaurant chain intrudes into and changes people's lives globally, and Sapto "Athonk" Raharjo, one of Indonesia's first independent cartoonists, beginning in 2003 has looked at Yogyakarta's seamier underside (Wirajuda 2015).

A lesson learned from the efforts of Apotik Komik and other activist independent cartoonists is that art "does not have to be permanent or sacred, as both are rather boring for the general public" (Berman n.d., 114). Berman concludes that Apotik Komik's work took on a sense of "the absurd with a touch of clever automation and a purpose to stretch their own neglect of, or at least their laughing at, the abuses imposed by the authoritarian regime of the recent past" (n.d., 115).

By the late 1990s, it became apparent that the link between politics and art needed repair and that something had to be done to shorten the intellectual distance between artists, their works, and the *rakyat* (public) (Berman n.d., 72).

Reformasi and Cartooning

When Suharto's Orde Baru (New Order) regime ended in May 1998, radical changes occurred in the cartoonist-government relationship. Political cartoonists criticized very openly and aimed their attacks directly at specific individuals and events.

This was very different from what transpired during the Orde Lama (Old Order) of Sukarno and the Orde Baru of Suharto. Wagiyono Sunarto (2008) finds that the myth and countermyth of Sukarno and his ideology was very much present in cartoons of media with political affiliations to Sukarno; the cartoon was used to attack the leader's opponents. Cartoonist Priyanto Sunarto (2005, 218–19),[6] in his research, discusses the use of metaphors and expressions of emotive stances used in cartoons during the Sukarno regime. Both authors make it clear that direct criticism was not sanctioned during these times. Taufan Hidayatullah (2007, 125–26) shows how leading political cartoonist Pramono worked during the Orde Baru. He used two types of cartoons—one that signified a compromise with any given situation, and one that was free of pressure and more straightforward. Instead of using indirect criticism against Suharto and other top officials, Pramono went after lesser figures around them.

The Reformasi (Reform) period likely has been the freest for cartooning in Indonesia. Beng Rahadian (2013), who was a political cartoonist in Yogyakarta, said that before 1998, "we could not say anything." He gave the example of Koendoro, who, in his strip *Pailul dan Panji Koming*, drew the government indirectly as a kingdom, but after Reformasi, he could draw even the faces of top officials and businesspeople. Actually, Rahadian (2013) thought that criticism had become "too direct" and perhaps not as much fun. As he explained, "Readers don't have to do anything now. Before, they had to participate in a guessing game of hidden meanings."

Some of the Indonesian political cartoons I have seen in recent years are scatological and explicitly sexual, to the extent that they would not be published in many of the world's most tolerant presses. Priyanto showed me a

115

Indonesia

7.8. "The Adventures of Two Dingo." *Rakyat Merdeka*, March 27, 2006. Controversial cartoon depicting Australian prime minister John Howard and his finance minister as dingoes fornicating.

7.9. "Siapa Peduli?" Priyanto Sunarto, July 28, 2001. Courtesy of Priyanto Sunarto.

cartoon he had drawn depicting a character "farting" out secret information, and two *Rakyat Merdeka* front-page cartoons in 2006 and 2013 severely soured Indonesia-Australia diplomatic relations. The 2006 cartoon depicted Australian prime minister John Howard in the guise of a dingo sexually mounting his foreign minister, while that of 2013 showed Prime Minister Tony Abbott as a peeping tom, cracking open a door marked "Indonesia" while masturbating and exclaiming, "Oh my God Indo . . . So Sexy" (Hale and Bachelard 2013).

Priyanto Sunarto, who has been a political cartoonist at *Tempo* magazine since 1978, agreed that the profession has much more freedom now and that "our only responsibility is to ourselves that we don't do cartoons that have bad effects on people" (2013). He said that after forty years, he knew *Tempo*'s policies well: which issues to tackle, which to avoid. Priyanto attends editorial meetings during which about four major issues are discussed. But if he thinks another issue is more important, he does not hesitate to draw it.

Tempo experienced rough times under Suharto. In the 1980s, it was banned for months because it had published interviews with demonstrators, and from 1993 to 1998 it could not publish after featuring a cover story about the corruption involved in the purchase of warships from Germany. During that interim, Priyanto drew short, animated political cartoons online. Since Reformasi, there have been complaints about *Tempo* stories, but not with the repercussions that existed under Suharto.

Priyanto talked about how he and other *Tempo* staff dealt with controversial material: "The policy at *Tempo* is that the chief editor is responsible for everything. We cartoonists are very careful. We hide some things, so the people know, but the government does not. We use indirect language. The exciting part is when we [the readers] figure out what the hidden meaning is and have a laugh" (2013).

As for the overall status of political cartoons in Indonesia, although more "freedom to cartoon" exists, other problems common worldwide have been debilitating. Chief among them are dwindling staff positions and space allocated to political cartoonists and the public's indifference to politics and political cartoons. Rahadian (2013) pointed out that freelance political cartoonists are very rare, as are newspapers with staff political cartoonists; he mentioned only *Kompas*, *Pos Kota*, *Media Indonesia*, the *Java Post*, and *Tempo*. Priyanto (2013) said that *Tempo* has a political cartoon only on Wednesday and Saturday, and as with other newspapers, it carries many spot illustrations. He added that some newspapers owned by conglomerates omit political cartoons, because they do not want disputes with politicians.

Professional Organizations

One characteristic of Indonesia's cartoons/comics world that stands out is how thoroughly it is organized. The overarching organization is the Indonesian Cartoonists' Association (PAKARTI), established on December 13, 1989. Pramono (1992), one of PAKARTI's organizers and a former president, said that the group is an amalgamation of smaller bodies that existed in Bali, West and East Java, and Sulawesi. He said that the purpose of combining them under one umbrella group was to have unification as a large union. PAKARTI has held competitions,

7.10. *Suara Pembaruan* political cartoonist Pramono R. Pramoedjo (right) at his caricature stand displaying his works, Jakarta, July 26, 1992. On the left is *HumOr* cartoonist Ramli Badrudin. Photo by John A. Lent. Courtesy of Pramono R. Pramoedjo.

exhibitions, and training workshops and has contributed members' cartoons to government campaigns on HIV/AIDS prevention, antismoking, adequate squatters' quarters, the environment, and pollution. Pramono listed at least fourteen regional affiliates of PAKARTI. There are likely more today.

In 2013, I was the guest of the cartoonists' groups Akademi Samali (AS) in Jakarta and Komikara in Bandung.[7] AS is one of the largest such communities in Indonesia; its members are both cartoonists and hobbyists. The group has quarters in the huge compound of the family of Beng Rahadian, a comic strip cartoonist who founded AS in 2005. Rahadian (2013) said that most meetings are discussions; among AS activities have been lending support to occasional comic art events, publishing eighteen issues of *Comicmao* in 2011–2012, holding workshops, and bringing out a comic book, *Jogja 5, 9 Sr*, after the 2006 earthquake in Yogyakarta, with all profits benefiting the victims.

Other groups formed in rural areas beginning in the mid-1990s, when some urban cartoonists went to *kampungs* (villages) in Semarang to show villagers how to

7.11. "Panji Koming," Dwi Koendoro, March 20, 2005. Dwi described this cartoon: "Many disasters were occurring in Indonesia; this one was of 'fool' parliamentarians fighting." Courtesy of Dwi Koendoro.

draw cartoons. A group, Kkang, was formed from among these farmers and other laborers that helped them get their cartoons published in local media or entered in competitions. Researcher Hikmat Darmawan (2013) said that Kkang acted as their brand name; with "Kkang" on their cartoons, some could be published in bigger newspapers. Similar groups appeared in other areas, but with decreased newspaper space available for cartoons, the drawers concentrated on drawing for competitions.

A Brief Conclusion

Indonesian political cartoonists often played cat-and-mouse games with authorities during the country's first fifty-three years of independence. Sometimes, they lost and paid the consequences; other times, they succeeded, getting their attacks on the government distributed through subterfuge and trickery. In 1998, they were free and expressed their opinions and stances directly with little interference. For much of the post-1998 years, Indonesian political cartoonists could be described as

among the freest in Asia. Considering the dire straits of most Asian political cartoonists relative to their degree of freedom, this may sound like a shallow accolade; however, it is a deserved and worthy compliment, taking into account the low point from which Indonesian cartoonists have elevated themselves. The unfortunate fact is that, now, they have more maneuverability to express themselves but fewer venues in which to do this.

Notes

1. In my view, it is not definitive that Sukarno's drawing was the first locally created political cartoon. It is known that a local newspaper comic strip, *Put On*, by Kho Wang Gie appeared in the Chinese-language daily *Sin Po* in 1931. Throughout the 1930s, the Dutch suspended some newspapers because of their political stands, and *Put On* was forced to move about because of the closures. It is possible that these suspended newspapers carried political cartoons.

2. Sibarani sued the Suharto government for copyright infringement in the 1980s when it planned to use his Sisinga-mangaraja image for the Rp 1,000 banknote. He lost the case, but authorities did not use the sketch.

3. Sibarani's early life reads like a movie script. During Indonesia's independence, Sibarani was stabbed in the chest by a soldier from his own side who was angry that Sibarani had been tasked with investigating corruption in the ranks. While he was hospitalized, Dutch troops entered his room, but a nurse stepped between them and said, "If you want to kill him, you have to kill me." A doctor told the soldiers that Sibarani was dying anyway, so advised them, "Don't waste your bullets." After the troops left, Sibarani escaped from the hospital. After the war, Sibarani dedicated his time to art (Philips 2014).

4. At least one humor magazine succeeded *HumOr*. On April 1, 2000, *Bog-Bog* (bullshit; in Balinese, lie) came out as a monthly, its most popular feature being cartoons, mostly gag.

5. In an earlier publication, I described Apotik Komik's distribution system:

The group used a wide range of materials and modes of expression to do comics, aiming to make art more accessible than just being on gallery walls. Its first work was a seven-hundred-meter by two-meter mural exhibited on the wall of a student residence; its most unusual wall comic was "Sakit Berlanjut" (Sickness Continues), made of corrugated paper that the students cut, pasted, and painted with India inks and then posted in various places around the city. Passersby were encouraged to take pieces of the artwork with them. Apotik Komik's non-wall, alternative comics included *Komik Seni* (Art Comic), *Komik Underground*, *Komik Ampyang* (Peanut Candy Comic), and *Komik Haram* (Forbidden Comic). The books employed metaphors and a playful style to discuss actual sociopolitical issues, giving a "broader, more disturbing view of some aspects of Indonesian society such as its reckless government, amoral bureaucrats, poverty, religious conflict and the rise and fall of its democratic life." (Lent 2015, 139, quoting Putranto and Purwanti [2010?])

6. Priyanto Sunarto and Wagiyono Sunarto are brothers; Priyanto is a political cartoonist for *Tempo*, while Wagiyono is the rector of Institut Kesenian Jakarta. Both wrote their doctoral dissertations on editorial cartoons and Sukarno (W. Sunarto 2013).

7. Komikara has been headed by Dr. Dwinita Larasati, an innovative and pioneering diary comics publishing house founder (Larasati 2011, 2013).

Bibliography

Anderson, Benedict R. O'G. 1978. "Cartoons and Monuments: The Evolution of Political Communication under the New Order." In *Political Power and Communications in Indonesia*, edited by Karl D. Jackson and Lucian W. Pye, 282–321. Berkeley: University of California Press.

Badrudin, Ramli. 1992. Interview with John A. Lent, Jakarta, July 25, 28.

Berman, Laine. 2001. "Comics as Social Commentary in Java, Indonesia." In *Illustrating Asia: Comics, Humor Magazines and Picture Books*, edited by John A. Lent, 13–36. Honolulu: University of Hawai'i Press.

Berman, Laine. n.d. "The Politics of Street Art: Authority, Compliance, and Resistance in the Public Realm; Indonesia from 1930." Unpublished manuscript.

Darmawan, Ferry, and Yasraf A. Piliang. 2015. "Cartoonist Visual Communication through Online Political Cartoon in the Era of the Government of President Susilo Bambang Yudhoyono." *Sosio Humanika: Jurnal Pendidikan Sains Sosial dan Kemanusiaan* 8, no. 2. https://journals.mindamas.com/index.php/sosiohumanika/article/view/604.

Darmawan, Hikmat. 2013. Interview with John A. Lent, Jakarta, July 11.

Fanon, Frantz. 1965. *A Dying Colonialism*. New York: Grove Press.

Gunawan, Iwan. 2013. Interview with John A. Lent, Jakarta, July 16.

Hale, Justin, and Michael Bachelard. 2013. "Abbott Cartoonist Recalled to Ridicule PM." *Sydney Morning Herald*, November 24. http://www.smh.com.au/federal-politics/abbott-cartoonist-recalled-to-ridicule-pm-20131124-2y3e9.html.

Hidayatullah, Taufan. 2007. "Makna kartun politek karya Pramono R. Pramoedjo periode 1980–1986." Master's thesis, Bandung Institute of Technology.

Koendoro, Dwi. 1992. Interview with John A. Lent, Jakarta, July 27.

Koendoro, Dwi. 2004. Interview with John A. Lent, Petaling Jaya, Malaysia, September 14.

Koendoro, Dwi. 2007. Interview with John A. Lent, Guiyang, China, September 7.

Larasati, Dwinita. 2011. Interview with John A. Lent, Singapore, February 23.

Larasati, Dwinita. 2013. Interview with John A. Lent, Bandung, Indonesia, July 13.

Lent, John A. 2015. *Asian Comics*. Jackson: University Press of Mississippi.

Mahtum. 1992. Interview with John A. Lent, Jakarta, July 28.

Masdiono, Toni. 2008. Interview with John A. Lent, Guiyang, China, July 13.

Molaei, Hamideh. 2018. "Justification and Knowledge: Prospecting the Modality of Indonesians' Informal Political Discussions on Facebook." *Journal of Asian Pacific Communication* 28, no. 2 (August): 323–44.

Nugroho, Id. 2009. "Comic Strip Campaigns against Nuclear Power." *Jakarta Post*, June 30. http://www.thejakartapost.com/news/2009/06/30/comic-strip-campaigns-against-nuclear-power.html.

Peacock, James L. 1968. *Rites of Modernization: Symbols and Social Aspects of Indonesian Proletarian Drama*. Chicago: University of Chicago Press.

Philips, Jake. 2014. "Radical Toons: The Lost Works of Indonesia's Top Political Caricaturist, Sibarani, Who Got Blacklisted and Pirated by Suharto." Coconuts Jakarta, October 14. https://coconuts.co/jakarta/features/radical-toons-incredible-true-story-indonesias-top-political-caricaturist-who-got/.

Pramono [Pramono R. Pramoedjo]. 1992. Interview with John A. Lent, Jakarta, July 26.

Putranto, Sugathi, and Nita Purwanti. 2010[?]. "Indonesian Alternative Comics from Yogyakarta, Indonesia." *SEAsite Indonesia*.

Putri, Edira. 2017. "These Cartoonists Are Revolting against Corruption in Indonesia." Culture Trip, September 26. https://theculturetrip.com/asia/indonesia/articles/ these-cartoonists-are-revolting-against-corruption-in-indonesia/.

Rahadian, Beng. 2013. Interview with John A. Lent, Jakarta, July 16.

Setiawan, Arwah. 1992. Interview with John A. Lent, Jakarta, July 29.

Sridharan, Anjana. 2017. "Post A: Political Cartoons in Indonesia." Indonesia Global Design Studio, February 17. https://indonesiadesignstudio.blog/2017/02/17/post-a-political-cartoons-in-indonesia/.

Sudarno, Dominto M. 1992. Interview with John A. Lent, Jakarta, July 28.

Sudarta, G. M. 1992. Interview with John A. Lent, Jakarta, July 28.

Sunarto, Priyanto. 2005. "Metafora visual kartun editorial pada surat kabar Jakarta 1950–1957." PhD diss., Bandung Institute of Technology.

Sunarto, Priyanto. 2012. "Editorial Cartoon Visual Metaphor in Jakarta Newspapers at 1950–1957." *Tawarikh: International Journal of Historical Studies* 3, no. 2 (April): 211–34.

Sunarto, Priyanto. 2013. Interview with John A. Lent, Jakarta, July 15.

Sunarto, Wagiyono. 2008. "Pemitasan dan perombakanmitos Soekarno dan ideologinya dalam karikatur politek di surat kabar Indonesia pada masa demokrasi terpimpin sampai akhir kekuaszan Presiden Soekarno 1959–1967." PhD diss., University of Indonesia, Jakarta.

Sunarto. Wagiyono. 2013. Interview with John A. Lent, Jakarta, July 9.

Talani, Noval Sufriyanto, Yasraf Amir Piliang, and Hafiz Aziz Ahmad. 2017 "The Power of the Visual Language of Editorial Cartoons as a Medium for Socio-Political Criticism in Indonesia." Proceedings of the International Seminar on Language, Education, and Culture. Faculty of Letters, Universitas Negeri Malang, October.

Wirajuda, Tunggul. 2015. "Indie Comic Artists Reaffirm Their Sense of Mission." *Jakarta Globe*, May 12. http://jakartaglobe.id/features/indie-comic-artists-reaffirm-sense-mission.

KELUARAN
PERTAMA
HARI INI

STRAITS
TIMES
112

Zunar and the Direct Way

For most of the 2010s, whenever Malaysian cartooning was mentioned, the name that came up immediately was Zunar (Zulkifli Anwar Ulhaque). He is known by cartoonists and defenders of freedom of expression worldwide for the many serious charges, arrests, book confiscations, and other harassments brought against him by the Najib Razak government, his highly publicized defiance and counterattacks, and his clever retorts and antics mocking Razak, his wife Rosmah Mansor, and the police.

Zunar was regularly in trouble and suffered many Razak reprisals for nearly a dozen years. He spent time in prison on several occasions; was charged with a record nine counts of sedition, punishable with forty-three years of imprisonment, and committing acts "detrimental to parliamentary democracy"; and was prohibited from leaving Malaysia. Printers of his books were harassed; his books were confiscated, damaged, and banned from bookstores; a gallery show of his works was ransacked by unknown assailants who also attacked him; and his office was raided by police multiple times.

With much bravado and what at times seemed like recklessness, Zunar reacted to these acts of harassment in cheerful, clown-like ways: posing for photographs while handcuffed; blacking out the printer's name on his books and turning the space into a "scratch-and-win" game for police to decipher (Zunar 2016); giving his books "ISPH" numbers rather than the universal ISBN (International Standard Book Number) label, because to him, ISBN meant, "I Support Barisan Nasional," the ruling coalition from independence to 2018; and using catchphrases such as "How can I be neutral . . . even my pen has a stand" and "Why pinch when you can punch?"

Zunar never ran out of symbols, metaphors, and ruses to keep the focus on the corruption of Najib and his wife, at the same time calling attention to his own plight. Among them: playing on popular culture icons in titling his books (e.g., *Pirates of the Carry-BN* [BN standing for Barisan Nasional] and *Supaman: Man of*

Chapter 8

Malaysia

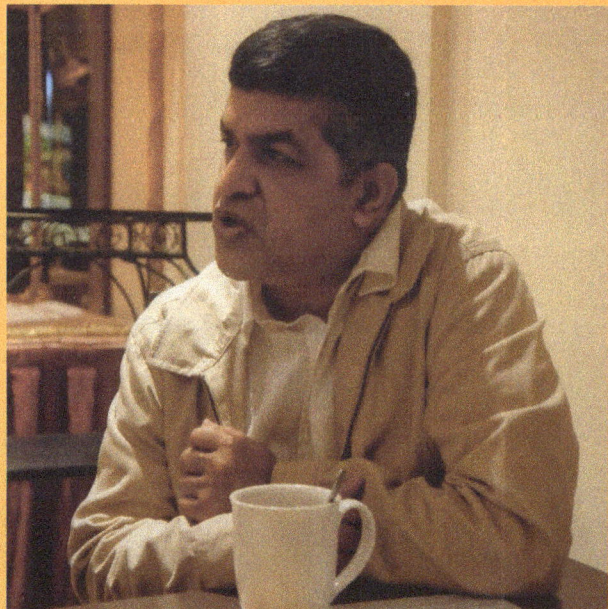

8.1. Zunar, Shah Alam, Malaysia, July 11, 2012. Photo by Xu Ying. Permission of Zunar.

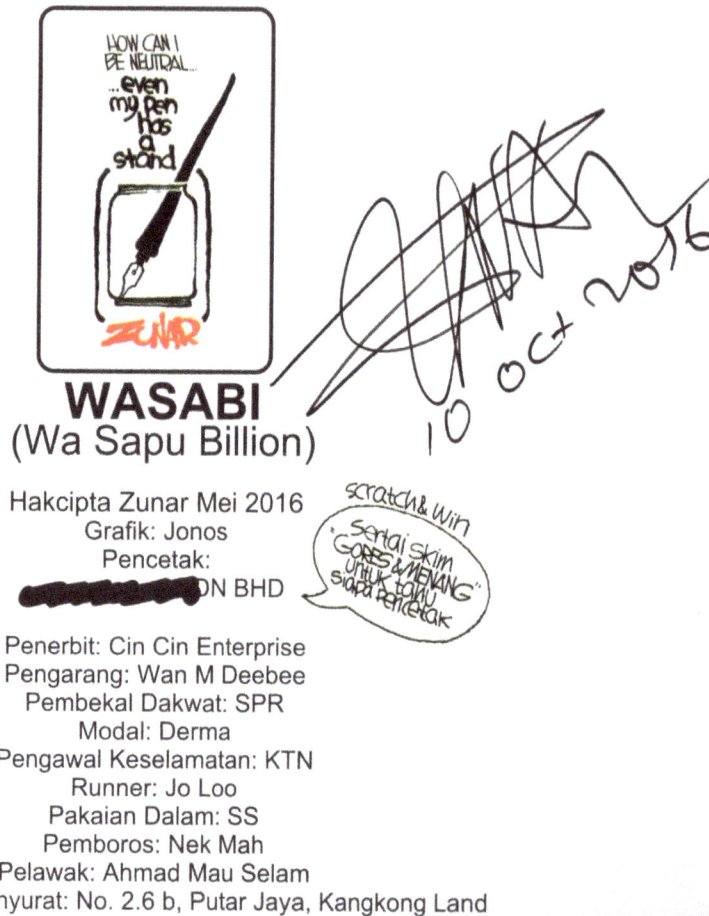

WASABI
(Wa Sapu Billion)

Hakcipta Zunar Mei 2016
Grafik: Jonos
Pencetak: ▬▬▬▬▬▬ON BHD

Penerbit: Cin Cin Enterprise
Pengarang: Wan M Deebee
Pembekal Dakwat: SPR
Modal: Derma
Pengawal Keselamatan: KTN
Runner: Jo Loo
Pakaian Dalam: SS
Pemboros: Nek Mah
Pelawak: Ahmad Mau Selam
Alamat surat menyurat: No. 2.6 b, Putar Jaya, Kangkong Land

8.2. Blacking out the printer's name and creating a scratch-and-win game to mock the censors. *Wasabi* (Wa Sapu Billion), Zunar, 2016. Permission of Zunar.

Steal [*supa* means corrupt]); turning the barcode on his books into prison bars for corrupt leaders; adorning Rosmah with huge gemstones and extravagant accessories and contrasting her with the typical threadbare housewife; including a tiny drawing of the police officer who arrested him in the bottom corner of nine hundred of his cartoons; and dressing as a pirate for the launching of *Pirates of the Carry-BN*—the list goes on (Zunar 2019).

Zunar had purpose behind his apparent showmanship. His goal was to get his messages out as widely as possible, and he succeeded in doing that by taking center stage and using his antics to attract the attention of the common people to Razak's corrupt government, and the international community to Malaysia's pitiful history of free expression. Zunar strove to relate political issues to Malaysians' everyday lives, "so they cannot say corruption is a political issue anymore. This is your issue. You're ultimately paying for the corruption" (quoted in Koshy 2019). His relentless barrage against

Razak's corruption and disdain for the law paid off; in a shock election outcome in 2018, opposition party coalition voters put Razak out of office, after which he stood trial for corruption. Zunar's lectures, speeches, and exhibitions abroad achieved his other purpose; as he said, "before my situation, the world did not know about the lack of press freedom in Malaysia" (Zunar 2016).[1] He acknowledged that he received much support from outside Malaysia: 250,000 letters of encouragement; testimonials by the likes of singer Harry Belafonte and Chinese writer Ai Weiwei; exhibitions; campaigns by Human Rights Watch, Cartoonists Rights Network International, Cartooning for Peace, and Reporters without Borders; and a number of prestigious awards honoring his courage.

The first time I interviewed Zunar, in August 1993, his cartoons had been appearing in the *New Straits Times* for a brief time; they were mainly political, he said, adding, "there is no 100 percent political cartoon in Malaysia." He hedged a bit on the degree to which

8.3. Zunar, *Cartoon-O-Phobia* cover featuring Prime Minister Najib Razak and his wife Rosmah Mansor. Zunar was arrested and charged with nine counts of sedition for publishing this book. Permission of Zunar.

Malaysian political cartoonists were free: "Compared to the US, we have less; compared to China and Singapore, we have more" (Zunar 1993). Zunar clarified that critical cartooning must be handled in Malaysia with caution and politeness, saying: "One must criticize obliquely and be prepared to respond to ministers and others who are criticized. If I am prepared to respond to the minister, then it is easier for him and for me. If you cannot do this, they can restrict you, stop your cartoons. You must be wise, know Malaysian politics, the insides and outsides of Malaysian politics" (Zunar 1993). A younger cartoonist, Deen (Nordin Misnan), who drew for *Gelihati* humor magazine at the time, said about the same thing—that even sensitive topics were possible fare for political cartoons, if handled "lightly" (Deen 1993).

Others who studied cartooning in the late 1980s and the 1990s felt that political cartoonists were given leeway by the authorities for a variety of reasons:

1. The Malay community's powerful political position in the country made it less likely that the government would censor Malay humor magazines.
2. The freedom was rooted in history in that cartooning was replacing dying traditional arts (*boria*, *wayang kulit*, and *bangsawan*), which allowed the public to vent grievances against the leadership through humor (Provencher and Jaafar Omar 1988; Jir 1989).
3. Many Malaysians considered cartoons a children's medium, and so the authorities did not treat them as a political threat (Provencher 1999, 18).
4. Cartoons and humor magazines were published in colloquial dialects that were almost illegible to many Malaysians (Provencher 1999, 18).
5. Cartoons were used and tolerated as a means to "cope with the stresses of multi-racial urban life,"

as Suhaini Aznam hypothesized: "If humor is the fine art of escape, Malaysians have unconsciously refined the art form. . . . Malaysians laugh so they will not punch each other. Humor allows Indians, Chinese and Malays to laugh at themselves, so they will feel less the sting of others' racial barbs. Here, humor is used to highlight stereotypes, and then to destroy them; to whittle away racial differences and reach a common, sympathetic cord" (Suhaini Aznam 1989, 42).

A sixth reason for a more relaxed relationship likely was that subjects of political cartoons were given the "light" touch, very different from the sledgehammer thump adopted by Zunar later.

The tenor of Zunar's cartoons and his outspokenness moved to a much higher pitch during the Najib Razak years, although it was beyond his normal range beginning with Reformasi in 1998, when people began questioning and criticizing the powers that be and the use and misuse of regulations with which they ruled.[2] Actually, Zunar had "retired" from political cartooning in the early 1990s, not being amenable to going "from one government newspaper to the next and the policy is the same" (Zunar 1993). Reformasi was the turning point for him, because it brought forward reformist ideas and alternative oppositionist tabloids as venues in which to disseminate them. It was also the awakening of the internet age. Zunar began drawing for the opposition *Harakah* in 1999 and the independent news site Malaysiakini in 2003. In 2009, he started a fortnightly political humor magazine, *Gedung Kartun* (Cartoon Warehouse), sixty-eight pages of "alternative news with a touch of humor and satire"; however, its inaugural issue was seized because the magazine did not have a publication permit, which Zunar disputed (IFEX 2016). Malaysiakini was also seriously harassed by authorities, who opened a criminal investigation concerning its financing; a government-linked group threatened to "tear down" its building (CPJ 2016).

With the 2018 change of governance, Zunar continued with his acerbic pen, tackling other issues such as

the raging racism and prejudice in Malaysia in *Kartun Anti-Racism*. To ensure that his messages were freely distributed, Zunar took the copyright off his cartoons, reasoning there was no point in holding those rights if no one could access his messages (Koshy 2019).

Zunar and others maintained a cautious wait-and-see attitude about the new government's campaign cries for a loosening of restrictions on freedom of expression.[3] They were old enough to be drawing when the leader of the new coalition, Mahathir Mohamad, was prime minister previously in 1981–2003, and remembered his authoritarian tendencies (Ramzy 2018, A4).

In fact, their wait was not long. In October 2019, the Home Ministry banned a comic book under the Sedition Act and the Communications and Multimedia Act on the grounds that its contents may "endanger public order and security" and "distort the mind of the public" (Kaos, Zolkepli, and Sivanandam 2019). At the same time, the ministry and police raided the Asia Comic Cultural Museum and an education office, both in Penang, and confiscated copies of the book. Entitled *Belt & Road Initiative for Win-Winism*, the 164-page comic book, published in Bahasa Malaysia, English, and Chinese, was charged with promoting communism and socialism and possibly disrupting the harmony and unity of Malaysia. Its producer was Hew Kuan Yau (with artist Chong Po Ling), curator of the Asia Comic Cultural Museum and a prominent former political party campaigner. With his political connections, Hew was able to get the country's finance minister to write the book's foreword, have copies sent to about 2,500 secondary schools, and have it included among "mementoes" that Prime Minister Mahathir presented to Chinese president Xi Jinping when they met in April 2019. Xi was actually photographed reading the comic in Mahathir's presence. The fallout was disastrous, not to mention farcical, as Hew resigned from his top business council position, the Dewan Rakyat (Parliament) experienced a chaotic session of jeering and name calling (leading to an opposition lawmaker being suspended), the prime minister's office distanced itself from the affair, the education ministry tried to retrieve the comic books sent to the schools, the police sought the assistance of historians to check the validity of the book's contents, and red-faced officials had to contend with the predicament that a comic book with government input was barred by the same government (Tan 2019; Lai 2019; *Star* 2019; Kaos, Zolkepli, and Sivanandam 2019).

Mahathir's government fell in February 2020, and within a half year of his successor Muhyiddin Yassin's rule, there was an alarming surge in violations of journalistic freedom. Zunar was among those investigated by authorities. On May 7, 2021, he was summoned by the police of the state of Kedah to be questioned about a cartoon he had drawn on the Malaysiakini website that lampooned the state's chief minister, Muhammad Sanusi Md. Nor. He was brought in under the Communications and Multimedia Act, Section 233, which bans "statements, rumors, or reports that could cause public mischief" (CPJ 2021).

The augmented authoritarianism of the Muhyiddin Yassin government was evident when it granted itself extraordinary powers in January 2021 by declaring a state of emergency and banning Parliament from holding sessions because of health (COVID-19) concerns. Two months later, authorities implemented an "anti–fake news" ordinance, banning any information about the pandemic or state of emergency not to their liking (Reporters without Borders 2021).

Lat and the Subtle Way

Malaysia's other cartoonist who has garnered international attention, for a longer period and for different reasons than Zunar, is Mohammad Nor Khalid, universally known as Lat. At the age of thirteen, Lat published his first comic strip and first comic book, and at seventeen he started his *Keluarga Si Mamat* (Mamat's family), which ran weekly in the *Sunday Berita Minggu* for twenty-six years. His full-time job was as a crime reporter for *Berita Harian* in Kuala Lumpur, which he accepted out of necessity, not choice; he was later transferred to the *News Straits Times*, the parent of

8.4. Lat, Ipoh, Malaysia, July 12, 2012. Photo by Xu Ying. Courtesy of Lat.

Berita. There, he became a column cartoonist assigned to portray Malaysian culture in a cartoon series called *Scenes of Malaysian Life*. After a four-month study stint in London, where he became familiar with British editorial cartoons, Lat turned *Scenes of Malaysian Life* into a series of popular editorial cartoons. From 1975 to 1978, he created enough editorial cartoons to compile into two anthologies, and in 1979 he brought out the autobiographical *Kampung Boy*, which defined the rest of his career. *The Kampung Boy* was published in sixteen editions by 2008 as well as a musical, a twenty-six-episode television series, and three animated vignettes to accompany the instruments of the Malaysian Philharmonic Orchestra. The strip's characters were displayed on both sides of an Air Asia plane, and the name "Kampung Boy" was applied to the private merchandising and book publishing company Lat set up after leaving the *New Straits Times* in 1984.[4] Although he became a freelance cartoonist, he continued "doing double duty" for the *New Straits Times*, turning out, every week for years, three *Scenes of Malaysian Life* and six front-page pocket cartoons (Lat 2000).

The range of Lat's social comments is wide, from "village life as seen through [a] young boy's eyes, to national politics, as observed by an irreverent bystander" (Suhaini Aznam 1989, 42). He insists that he is apolitical, although *Scenes of Malaysian Life* has pointed out alleged Israeli military excesses, caricatured Malaysian prime ministers at a time when this was disallowed,[5] and taken swipes at Lee Kuan Yew of Singapore (Dunfee 1989, 9; also Chandy 1980, 40–41;

8.5. *Kampong Boy*, Lat. Courtesy of Lat.

8.6. *Scenes of Malaysian Life*, Lat. Courtesy of Lat.

Lim Cheng Tju 1994, 59–60). However, as cartoonist-historian Muliyadi Mahamood (2003a, 68, 72) said, Lat puts politicians he is critical of in situations "unusual, abnormal, or unexpected" to their status and personality; this gets a laugh while making a point. He has a knack for caricaturing the different ethnic groups of Malaysia, and he strives to avoid being malicious, antagonistic, or insensitive (Chin 1998, 56). Lat values the judgment of his editors to determine what is socially acceptable, but he very rarely changes or drops a cartoon; he said that, although he had "pushed the line a little bit," he had avoided getting in trouble, and "only a handful of [his] cartoons were ever spiked" (Jayasankaran 1999, 36).

8.7. Abu Bakar Mohd. Nor, *Warta Jenaka*, September 14, 1936. The cartoon depicts the difficulties faced by the Malay (kneeling), who owes money to the Indian money lender (standing, left). Courtesy of Muliyadi Mahamood.

Historical Perspective

Similar to the Indian subcontinent, what are now known as Malaysia and Singapore were politically intertwined and hosted multiple languages under British colonialism. Such bifurcated countries whose boundaries sometimes defy logic make for perplexing decisions in determining the origins of cultural institutions. *Chong Shing Yit Pao* published its first political cartoon in 1907, *Warta Jenaka* and *Utusan Zaman* in the 1930s; all three newspapers were published in Singapore and all three are considered the first publishers of political cartoons—*Chong Shing Yit Pao* in Singapore and *Warta Jenaka* and *Utusan Zaman* in Malaysia. The determining factor relates to the dominant culture and language of the split country. This history concentrates on the cartoons in Bahasa Malaysia, the official language, and English, the colonial and international business language.

Warta Jenaka and *Utusan Zaman* (the Sunday edition of *Utusan Minggu*) were late in adopting cartoons, perhaps taking their cue from Arabic newspapers elsewhere, which generally shunned cartoons and other illustrated matter (Muliyadi 2004, 97). S. B. Ally and occasional readers provided *Warta Jenaka* with its roughly drawn editorial cartoons satirizing foreign and local issues such as colonialism, poverty, and immigration. Ally's cartoons incorporated *bangsawan* (traditional theater) hairstyles and costumes (Redza 1973). *Utusan Zaman* carried editorial cartoons from its beginning in 1939, created by

a journalist, Rahim Kajai, and drawn by Ali Sanat, who also did the first Malay comic strip, *Wak Ketok* (Uncle Knock), which also addressed social, political, and economic issues concerning Malaysia.

A third Malay-language newspaper, *Majlis*, published political cartoons in the 1940s; they were of three types: propaganda to unite Malays, critical commentary, and documentation of sociopolitical events. The cartoons were direct, supported by *pantuns* (folk ditties), proverbs, poems, and rhymed sentences; some looked like campaign posters for national unity (Muliyadi 2004, 71). As with *Warta Jenaka* in the 1930s, some *Majlis* cartoons criticized the bad behavior of certain Malays.[6]

Political-type cartoons continued during World War II; propagandistic drawing emanated from both sides. Anti-Japanese cartoons such as *Kerana Rakyat* (For the People) appeared in the first Malay-language film magazine, *Film Melayu*. Raja Hamzah and Senu Abdul Rahman drew nationalist comics (Provencher 1995, 183). Drawing pro-Japanese, anti–Allied forces cartoons was Abdullah Ariff, who, after the war, still managed to become a prominent politician despite his wartime collaboration with the enemy. In November 1942, forty-five of his strips in the Japanese newspaper *Penang Shimbun* were collected in a fifty-page book, *Perang Pada Pandangan Juru-Lukis Kita* (The War as Our Cartoonist Sees It). Captions were in Malay, English, and Chinese (Lim Cheng Tju 2009).

"Ah! Kamu chepat benar besar"

8.8. Peng, "Ah! Kamu Chepat Benar Besar" (Ah! You've Grown So Fast), *Berita Harian*, July 4, 1957. The *Straits Times* on its fast-growing sister paper, *Berita Harian*.

8.9. Early Malaysian cartoonist Rejabhad showing his first cartoon, Kuala Lumpur, July 21, 2000. Photo by John A. Lent. Courtesy of Rejabhad.

Describing the earliest Malay cartoons, Muliyadi Mahamood (2004, 67) said that they had long captions, often containing proverbs and "*pantuns* (folk ditties), rhyming elaborate sentences," and they used contrast in drawing style, animal imagery, and trademark characters, some based on figures in literature (Muliyadi 2004, 290–93).

After independence in 1957, Malay cartooning had new styles, themes, and individuals. It also had new media structures, policies, and regulations resulting from crises such as the Emergency (1948–1960), when Malaya faced a communist threat; the confrontation with Indonesia (1963–1966); and the May 13, 1969, communal rights incident. These and the creation of the Federation of Malaysia in 1963 led to government-instituted policies, a national ideology (Rukunegara), and new and amended regulations pertaining to mass media. Media and their content were strongly encouraged to be more patriotic, avoid sensitive issues, and promote national unity and racial harmony (Lent, 1977, 1978, 1979).

One-panel editorial cartoons existed in postindependence Malay dailies but not as frequently as later in the mid-1980s. In 1957 and 1958, Peng drew a weekly editorial cartoon column for the *Straits Times* that was translated into Malay for use in *Berita Harian*, under the title "*Berita Harian* Hidangan Hari Sabtu" (*Berita Harian*'s Saturday Column). Peng's cartoons documented rather than criticized or satirized subjects (Muliyadi 2004, 183). The column was halted after a year because it was difficult to communicate with Peng, who lived in Singapore and whose cartoons were not relevant to Malay life. For three months in 1963, *Utusan Zaman* used seven single-frame cartoons done by a reader named Rahim (real name not known) concerning the Malaysia-Indonesia confrontation. A group of career editorial cartoonists joined *Utusan Zaman* in 1966: Rejabhad and Mishar, who dealt with social subjects; and Razali MHO, Shukorlin, and Rizalman, domestic and international political topics.

Rejabhad published his first cartoon in 1958 just before serving fifteen years in the military. He compared drawing cartoons then with the situation in 2000:

When I drew then, everything was happy, happy, happy. The message in my head was ha, ha, ha. When my age grew up [I aged], the ha, ha, ha became small, the message big. The message is the current news. Not light issues. I now deal with heavy issues. But even though the message is heavy, the style is still cartoon-like. In the old days, I drew because of interest, for fun. Now, it is for my profession and will be until the end. (Rejabhad 2000)

Rejabhad continued to serve the military even after his discharge; he was dispatched to war zones in Bosnia, Somalia, and Congo to record activities through his cartoons later published in *Gila-Gila* humor magazine and elsewhere (Rejabhad 2000; also Provencher 1996). His military sketching (including combat) also contributed to his strip *Prebet Dabus* (Private Dabus) and the album *Dengan Rejabhad*.

Malay-language political cartooning really took off in the 1980s, following the lead taken by Lat in the English-language press. The works of Nan (Zainal Osman) and Rossem in *Utusan Malaysia* and Zoy, Abib, and Zunar of *Berita Harian* and *Berita Minggu* ushered in a new, looser phase with caricatures of the prime minister and other elements that before were disapproved. Lat and others acknowledged that cartoonists' freedom to express broadened considerably at that time. Ron Provencher and Jaafar Omar in their survey of humor magazines showed a number of examples of cartoons that lampooned the ruling political party's dilemma as it dealt with Malay nationalism, Islamic fundamentalism, and modernization. Provencher and Jaafar reported that political satire was very common, except in *Komedi*, and wrote that "UMNO [United Malays National Organisation] party politics is commented upon, as are corruption, the 'Look East' policy, prison conditions, and the military, as well as (in a very sly fashion) the powers of royalty, and the pressures to conform" (Provencher and Jaafar Omar 1988).

The abovementioned cartoonists of *Utusan Malaysia*, *Berita Harian*, and *Berita Minggu* touched on similar topics. Nan's *Malaysia Kita* (Our Malaysia) depicted

8.10. A detailed cartoon by Zoy, *Berita Minggu*, May 9, 1993.

social and political events in the same manner as Lat's *Scenes of Malaysian Life*; Rossem's single-frame series *Panorama* editorialized on Malaysian and international issues. Like others, he also drew a strip; his was about a policeman, which was Rossem's own occupation. Zoy's single-panel editorial series was *Ragam* (Whims), and Abib's column was *Tok Aki*, featuring a trademark character representing the public who followed local and global issues (Muliyadi 2004, 220–21). As has been the norm in Malaysia, these cartoonists had to be creative, symbolic, cultural, knowledgeable, careful, and self-censoring in getting their messages out.

One complaint heard throughout the history of political cartooning has been the lack of venues. In Malaysia, that issue was put aside when the humor magazine *Gila-Gila* (Crazy about Mad) appeared on April 1 (April Fools' Day) in 1978, followed by a run of similar magazines (as many as fifteen simultaneously, and total of fifty through 2003) throughout the latter part of the century. The founders of *Gila-Gila* were Mishar, Zuinal Buang Hussein, Azman Jusof, Rejabhad,[7] and Jaafar Taib. According to Jaafar, initially the public reacted as though "we were mad," but the first number of ten thousand copies quickly

8.11. Cover of *Gila-Gila*, April 2018. The progenitor of dozens of humor magazines after 1978.

sold out, and *Gila-Gila* eventually outpaced all types of magazines with a circulation of two hundred thousand.

By the 1990s, it had become obvious that the Malaysian humor magazine market was becoming saturated, and survival strategies were implemented, one of which was to cater to particular audiences with specific themes. Out of that strategy came the "exclusively for women" *Cabai*, started on April 1, 1997, by Sabariah Jais, who used her pen name for its title (Nik Naizi Husin and Hafez M. Soom 1993). Although these humor magazines were primarily entertainment oriented, *Gila-Gila* did include some sharp criticism.

Jaafar Taib, a founder of *Gila-Gila* and its head for decades, was not impressed with the large number of

humor magazines, believing that many were not suitable because of poor management. He pointed out that the magazines were in Bahasa Malaysia (with the exception of the short-lived *Flipside* in English), because it is the national language, most cartoonists were ethnic Malay, and rural people would not understand non-Malay magazines (Jaafar Taib 2000).

In 1991, another effort was made to better the profession with the establishment of Persatuan Kartunis Selangor dan Kuala Lumpur (PEKARTUN).[8] It hoped to promote cartooning by increasing outlets for cartoons and pushing for the gradual Malaysianization of comic strips and editorial cartoons. Started by Lat, Zunar, and Muliyadi, PEKARTUN was open to cartoonists working in Kuala Lumpur and the state of Selangor, which encompasses the capital city. Muliyadi, the first chair of PEKARTUN, explained that not many cartoonists worked elsewhere in Malaysia (Muliyadi 1993).

Helping to ensure that there is a future for political cartooning in Malaysia is the internet. Most of Zunar's cartoons that ruffled the feathers of government appeared on the Malaysiakini news website before being compiled into books. Increasingly, memes are used to post opinions in the form of illustrations and videos, creating "joke versions of real-life events, cultural symbols, and social ideas" (Pratama 2019). In Malaysia and Indonesia, much of the meme culture centers on the increasing Islam fanaticism. Dhany Putra Pratama of Universitas Muhammadiyah Yogyakarta studied Islamic fanaticism in these two countries through online comic and memes and argues that memes project freedom of expression, stating:

> To combat the strict control wielded by authorities over the Internet, the advocates of certain ideas attempt to attract public attention by devising new methods that are able to "slip" through government controls and restraints. Memes are currently the accepted form of expression of those designing to reach mass audiences. They are essentially sets of pictures that illustrate real events in a humorous manner. They are posted on social media and are shared by multiple users on the platform. Thus, they gain popularity at rapid speeds, and now thousands of users online are creating a flood of pictures branded as memes. (Pratama 2019)

Pratama's study categorized memes as "Islamic Memes: Forms of Positive Teachings," intended to spread the teachings of Islam; "Islamic Memes: Islam against the 'World,'" meant to relate rising Islamophobia globally; and "Islamic Memes: Islamic Fanaticism in Malaysia (and Indonesia)," primarily concerned with rejecting fanaticism in each country (Pratama 2019). Blogs also figure prominently in Malaysian political discourse (Lim Ming Kuok 2010).

A Brief Conclusion

The Malaysian cartoon field has witnessed many advances in its nearly century-old life, in numbers and kinds of venues and cartoonists, in the plethora of humor magazines (likely the largest or one of the largest in the world over a twenty-five-year period), and in professional development. The freedom to cartoon has also seen advances, but the situation is still shaky, acerbated by government/party ownership of newspapers, colonial-era regulations still on the books and even recently strengthened, a sensitive polity, and heavy doses of self-censorship. The cartooning community remains in an edgy predicament, waiting for the other shoe to drop.

Notes

1. I wrote a number of articles on the lack of press freedom in Malaysia after holding a lectureship at Universiti Sains Malaysia, 1972–1974. There was a reaction from two deputies in the Abdul Razak (father of Najib) administration, who labeled me a "know-it-all," as reported on the front page of the *New Straits Times*.

2. Carryovers from British colonialism, these laws were the Sedition Act, amended in 2015 to cover electronic media and to mete out harsher penalties, and the Printing Presses and Publications Act. The draconian Internal Security Act was abolished in the 2000s. Zunar also dreaded the Communications and Multimedia Act, which, he said, would be tougher on social media. He said that he was the first whose case was brought before the Multimedia Court (Zunar 2016).

3. For example, artist Fahmi Reza, who was charged under a law prohibiting offensive online comments (Ramzy 2018, A4; Griffiths 2019).

4. In my first of many interviews and chats with Lat (1986), he related the origins of the character:

> Suddenly, one day you start thinking about the place you come from, whether you like it or not. It just happens. In my case, it was during my first visit to the US in 1977. I was the guest of the State Department. I was in the big city and I was young, very young, and then suddenly, I remembered the place where I was born, which was Kota Bharu, Perak, a very small place. So, I said when I go back, I'm going to do a book about that place. I really missed life in the village. So, I came back and started it, I think, in 1978. . . . I just wanted the people to know about the village life. (Lent 1987, 28–29)

5. Lat told about drawing Prime Minister Tun Abdul Razak in 1974, a "very difficult time":

> I could not draw the back of [his] head. I did a story about the possibility in the future of all cars going to be banned from the city because it was too congested with traffic. So, everyone just comes in by motorcycle or bicycle. I did the prime minister riding a motorcycle with his outriders and all; I drew him from the back. In 1974, I was only twenty-three years old. So, the editor called me in and said, "This is Tun Razak." I said, "Oh no, this is a fiction." But still it looked like him. . . . The editor said, "but you have to change him, thicken the hair." (Lent 1987, 30)

6. For an excellent analysis of cartoons in *Warta Jenaka*, *Utusan Zaman*, and *Majlis* in the 1930s and 1940s, with images of the cartoons, Malay and English captions, and much explanatory text, see Muliyadi 2004, 19–96.

7. Rejabhad almost singlehandedly launched a humor magazine in 1973. *Ha Hu Hum* was published by Persatuan Pelukis Komik Kartun dan Illustrasi (PERPEPSI; the Association of Comic, Cartoon, and Illustration Artists), also started in 1973, to promote better wages and working conditions. *Ha Hu Hum* lasted four issues, halted when Rejabhad disagreed with the publisher over the magazine's potential audience and quit (Provencher 1995, 184). There may have been humor magazines in Malaysia before or shortly after *Ha Hu Hum*. Former minister of agriculture and secretary of the longtime dominant party United Malays National Organisation (UMNO) Tan Sri Sanusi Junid said that he published one called *Mat Jenin* before *Gila-Gila* (Sanusi Junid 2000).

8. This was in addition to the effort of PERPEPSI. In 2007, another organization was started for comics creators. Persatuan Penggiat Komik Malaysia (PeKomik), spearheaded by comics artist Muhamad Azhar Abdullah, added to the professional status of comics through an annual comics festival, the Anugerah PeKomik awards, and other events (Muhamad Azhar Abdullah 2009).

Bibliography

Chandy, G. 1980. "Lat: The Malaysian Folk Hero." In *New Straits Times Annuals*, 38–42. Kuala Lumpur: New Straits Times Press.

Chen, Mong Hock. 1967. *The Early Chinese Newspapers of Singapore, 1881–1912*. Singapore: University of Malaya Press.

Chin, Phoebe, ed. 1998. "The Kampung Boy." In *S-Files, Stories Behind Their Success: 20 True Life Malaysian Stories to Inspire, Challenge, and Guide You to Greater Success*. Petaling Jaya, Malaysia: Success Resources Slipguard.

Committee to Protect Journalists (CPJ). 2016. "Independent Malaysian News Website Faces Threats, Harassment." November 7. https://cpj.org/2016/11/independent-malaysian-news-website-faces-threats-h/.

Committee to Protect Journalists (CPJ). 2021. "Malaysian Cartoonist Zunar Investigated over Criticism of State Official." May 17. https://cpj.org/2021/05/Malaysian-cartoonist-zunar-investigated-over-criticism-of-state-official/.

Deen [Nordin Misnan]. 1993. Interview with John A. Lent, Kuala Lumpur, August 6.

Dunfee, E. J. 1989. "The Joker's Wild." *Asia*, March 19, 8–10, 12–13.

Gan, Sheuo Hui. 2011. "Manga in Malaysia: An Approach to Its Hybridity through the Career of the Shōjō Mangaku Kaoru." *International Journal of Comic Art* 13, no. 2 (Fall): 164–78.

Griffiths, James. 2019. "The Cartoonists Who Helped Take Down a Malaysian Prime Minister." CNN, May 29. https://www.cnn.com/style/article/malaysia-1mdb-najib-zunar-fahmi-reza-intl/index.html.

Hamedi Mohd. Adnan. 2003. *Penerbitan Majalah di Malaysia: Isu-isu dan Cabaran* [Magazine Publication in Malaysia: Issues and Challenges]. Shah Alam, Malaysia: Karisma Publications.

IFEX. 2016. "Zunar." IFEX, August 26; last updated February 9, 2021. https://ifex.org/faces/zunar/.

Jaafar Taib. 2000. Interview with John A. Lent, Kuala Lumpur, July 21.

Jayasankaran, S. 1999. "Going Global." *Far Eastern Economic Review*, July 22, 162.

Jir, Krishen. 1989. "Observations on the Social Function of Cartoons, Caricature and Comics." In *Karikatur Kartun dan Komik*. Kuala Lumpur: Balai Senilukis Negara.

Kaos, Joseph, Jr., Farik Zolkepli, and Hemananthani Sivanandam. 2019. "Belt & Road Comic Banned." *The Star* (Petaling Jaya, Malaysia), October 24. https://www.thestar.com.my/news/nation/2019/10/24/belt--road-comic-banned.

Koshy, Elena. 2019. "Zunar: The Unrepentant Cartoonist." *New Straits Times* (Kuala Lumpur), December 21.

Lai, Allison. 2019. "MCA Takes Several DAP to Task over Comic Book Fracas." *The Star* (Petaling Jaya, Malaysia), October 25. https://thestar.com.my/news/nation/2019/10/25/mca-takes-several-dap-to-task-over-comic-book-fracas.

Lat [Mohd. Nor Khalid]. 1986. Interview with John A. Lent, Shah Alam, Malaysia, November 17.

Lat [Mohd. Nor Khalid]. 2000. Interview with John A. Lent, Kuala Lumpur, July 22.

Lent, John A. 1977. "The Mass Media in Malaysia." In *Cultural Pluralism in Malaysia: Polity, Military, Mass Media, Education, Religion, and Social Class*, edited by John A. Lent, 32–42. DeKalb: Center for Southeast Asian Studies, Northern Illinois University.

Lent, John A., ed. 1978. "Malaysia's National Language Mass Media: History and Present Status." *South East Asian Studies* 15, no. 4 (March): 598–612.

Lent, John A., ed. 1979. *Malaysian Studies: Present Knowledge and Research Trends*. DeKalb: Center for Southeast Asian Studies, Northern Illinois University.

Lent, John A. 1987. "A Lot of Lat: An Interview with Malaysia's Premier Cartoonist." *WittyWorld International Cartoon Magazine*, Spring, 28–30.

Lim, Cheng Tju. 1994. "Just a Simple Man." *Big O*, January, 59–60.

Lim, Cheng Tju. 2009. "Forgotten Legacies: The Case of Abdullah Ariff's Pro-Japanese Cartoons during the Japanese Occupation of Penang." In *Drawing the Line: Using Cartoons as Historical Evidence*, edited by Richard Scully and Marian Quartly, 9.1–9.12. Melbourne: Monash University Press.

Lim, Ming Kuok. 2010. "Blogging and Democracy: Blogs in Malaysian Political Discourse." PhD diss., Pennsylvania State University.

Muhamad Azhar Abdullah. 2009. Interview with John A. Lent, Bangi, Malaysia, January 14.

Muliyadi Mahamood. 1993. Interview with John A. Lent, Kuala Lumpur, August 8.

Muliyadi Mahamood. 2000. Interview with John A. Lent, Kuala Lumpur, July 21.

Muliyadi Mahamood. 2003a. "Lat dalam Konteksnya" [Lat in Context]. In *Pameran Retrospektif Lat* [Retrospective Exhibition of Lat], 1964–2003, 48–82. Kuala Lumpur: National Art Gallery.

Muliyadi Mahamood. 2003b. "An Overview of Malaysian Contemporary Cartoons." *International Journal of Comic Art* 5, no. 1 (Spring): 292–304.

Muliyadi Mahamood. 2004. *The History of Malay Editorial Cartoons (1930s–1993)*. Kuala Lumpur: Utusan Publications.

Muliyadi Mahamood. 2012. Interview with John A. Lent and Xu Ying, Shah Alam, Malaysia, July 9.

Nik Naizi Husin and Hafez M. Soom. 1993. "Cabai: Kartunis Wanita Yang Gigih." *Sasaran*, July, 110–12.

Pratama, Dhany Putra. 2019. "Islamic Fanaticism in Indonesia and Malaysia as Seen through the Lens of Online Comics and Memes." *Advances in Social Science, Education and Humanities Research* 558: 1–17.

Provencher, Ronald. 1990. "Covering Malay Humor Magazines: Satire and Parody of Malaysian Political Dimensions." *Crossroads* 5, no. 2: 1–25.

Provencher, Ronald. 1995. "Modern Malay Folklore: The Humor Magazines." In *Asian Popular Culture*, edited by John A. Lent, 179–88. Boulder, CO: Westview Press.

Provencher, Ronald. 1996. "Travels with 'The Chief': Rejab Had, a Malaysian Cartoonist." *Journal of Asian Pacific Communication* 7, nos. 1–2: 55–75.

Provencher, Ronald. 1999. "An Overview of Malay Humor Magazines: Significance, Origins, Contents, Texts, and Audiences." In *Themes and Issues in Asian Cartooning: Cute, Cheap, Mad, and Sexy*, edited by John A. Lent, 11–36.

Bowling Green, OH: Bowling Green State University Popular Press.

Provencher, Ronald, and Jaafar Omar. 1988. "Malay Humor Magazines as a Resource for the Study of Modern Malay Culture." *Sari* 6: 87–99.

Ramzy, Austin. 2018. "Cautious Optimism for Freer Speech in Malaysia." *New York Times*, June 19, A4.

Redza. 1973. "Enlightening Cartoons Show." *Sunday Times* (Kuala Lumpur), October 28.

Rejabhad. 2000. Interview with John A. Lent, Kuala Lumpur, July 21.

Reporters without Borders. 2021. "Malaysia: New Malaysian Ordinance Threatens Very Concept of Truth." Press release, March 17. https://rsf.org/en/new-malaysian-ordinance-threatens-very-concept-truth.

Sanusi Junid, Tan Sri. 2000. Interview with John A. Lent, Kuala Lumpur, July 21.

Star, The. 2019. "Lawmaker Suspended over Comic Book Controversy." *The Star* (Petaling Jaya, Malaysia), October 24. https://www.thestar.com.my/news/nation/2019/10/24/lawmaker-suspended-over-comic-book-controversy.

Suhaini Aznam. 1989. "Quipping Away at Racism." *Far Eastern Economic Review*, December 14, 42, 46.

Tan, Joceline. 2019. "Worst Yet to Come?" *The Star* (Petaling Jaya, Malaysia), October 25. https://www.thestar.com.my/opinion/columnists/analysis/2019/10/25/worst-yet-to-come.

Toh, Terence. 2018. "Cartoonist Zunar on His Sedition Charges and Fight for Political Reform." *The Star* (Petaling Jaya, Malaysia), September 23. https://www.thestar.com.my/lifestyle/people/2018/09/23/zunar-cartoonist-sapuman-book.

Zunar [Zulkifli Anwar Ulhaque]. 1993. Interview with John A. Lent, Kuala Lumpur, August 7.

Zunar [Zulkifli Anwar Ulhaque]. 2016. Interview with John A. Lent, Shah Alam, Malaysia, October 9.

Zunar [Zulkifli Anwar Ulhaque]. 2019. *Fight through Cartoons: My Story of Harassment, Intimidation & Jail*. Singapore: Marshall Cavendish.

History

British colonialists were not in a hurry to introduce cartoons to Burma. The country's first newspapers appeared in 1836 (Hollstein 1971, 140; Blackburn 1982, 178), the first printed cartoon in 1912. Unlike other former British colonies of the region, Burma did not have its version of *Punch* in between those years. For example, the subcontinent (now India, Pakistan, and Bangladesh) had published at least seventy humor/cartoon magazines carrying the *Punch* moniker by 1900 (Scully 2013, 6–35; also Hasan 2007; Khanduri 2009).

The drawers of the first cartoons in Burma were not even individuals associated with newspapers and magazines; they were amateur colonial painters: the commissioner of Burma's railway, Martin Jones; physics professor Kenneth Ward; and high school principal E. G. N. Kinch, who together in 1913 formed the Burma Art Club. Jones published the country's first cartoon, which appeared in the *Rangoon Times* in 1912. Under the pen name Myauk (*myauk phyu* or "white monkey," the name the local people called Britishers), Jones humiliated a local woman who had attended a westerner's party (Aung Zaw 2003).

The Burma Art Club promoted Western painting and drawing, including cartooning, to Burmese students, the first among them Ba Gale (Shwe Ta Lay) (1893–1945) and Ba Gyan (1902–1953), both of whom went on to great prominence. Art historian Andrew Ranard writes that the club's students had "some affinity for this new genre because it possessed elements of exaggeration with which they were already familiar in Traditional painting. . . . Pagan painting and mural painting of Burma from the 17th to 19th centuries had a strong taste for caricature in its depictions of fairy-tale figures, demons, and beasts" (Ranard 2009, 92).

During their relatively short lives, Ba Gale and Ba Gyan made the political cartoon a fixture in Burmese journalism. Ba Gale's first cartoon appeared in 1915 in *Rangoon College Annual Magazine*; two years later, he became the first artist to draw a Burmese-language cartoon in *Thuriya* (Sun magazine). Although the editor

Chapter 9

Myanmar

9.1. "Sycophants of the Imperialists," Ba Gale, circa 1917. Anti-British parody of colonized Burmese, who carried the portly Britishers into the temple so as not to inconvenience them in removing their shoes.

137

9.2. "Tatmadaw" (Armed Forces), Ba Gyan, 1952. Caption: "The plan to not split the people and the Armed Forces."

9.3. Caricature of Ba Gyan at an exhibition of his drawings on the street where he lived, Yangon. Courtesy of Myat Kyi La Thein.

[W]hen Burma faced civil war and political turmoil in the 1950s [Prime Minister] U Nu asked Ba Gyan to come to see him. . . . The PM recognized Ba Gyan's influence and wanted him to draw cartoons that exhibited peace and unity. Ba Gyan replied that he was too busy to make the meeting. (Aung Zaw 2003)

Ba Gyan's work became "explicitly political and highly critical" after Burma received independence in 1948. Gallerist Aung Soe Min points to an example in a January 4, 1948, cartoon that shows British general Hubert Rance "departing Burma, waving goodbye to a local family as he tells them 'Take care of your children.' Behind the amicable scene are three children each symbolizing a damage caused by the Second World War: debt, destruction and economic crisis" (Aung Soe Min n.d.). Ba Gyan became increasingly adept at using metaphor and a cast of characters in his political and humor cartoons.

Ba Gale and Ba Gyan were talented in other dimensions of art and made important contributions to the advancement of Burmese cultural life. Ba Gale was a movie actor and director and Ba Gyan a commercial photographer, novelist under the pen name Thonnya (Zero), children's magazine illustrator, and animator. In fact, Ba Gyan produced Burma's first animated films, *Kye Taungwa* in 1934 and *Athuya* in 1935, and first comic book, *Ko Pyoo and Ma Pyone*, in 1937 (Myo Thant 2005).

Ba Gyan is memorialized by a street in Yangon named U Ba Gyan Street, where each year during the

of the *Rangoon Times* considered Ba Gale's cartoons "excellent" and stood him apart from other artists as a "political commentator on current affairs" (quoted in Aung Zaw 2003), parts of the reading public had difficulty interpreting his works, requiring long, explanatory captions written "poetically" by the editors (Aung Zaw 2003).

Both men were unsparing in their criticisms of the British as well as local politicians. Ba Gale made fun of political opportunists (Parliament "seatgrabbers," his term) and "sycophants of the imperialists." Aung Zaw exemplified the latter: "When some protested the British habit of wearing shoes inside temples, Ba Gale sketched a parody of those who helped carry the British masters on their backs to and from the temple" (2003; also Thaung 1995).

Ba Gyan, more popular in the 1930s as a supporter of the nationalists, was also unflinching in his attacks and backed down from no one. Aung Zaw claims:

Tazaung Daing festival, a cartoon exhibition is held. Ba Gyan began exhibiting cartoons on lanterns and paper outside his home prior to World War II, and this tradition was continued by others until 1997, nearly a half century after his death. It was revived in 2010 on the street named after him (Myat Kyi La Thein 2011).

Newspapers and magazines proliferated from forty-four in 1911 to more than two hundred by the close of the 1930s, and with them, cartoons did, too, as "low-cost sources of information," "avenues of public discourse, art, and entertainment," and "increasingly potent purveyors of role models, gender identity, ethical norms and values and other icons of identity" (Ikeya 2008, 1282).

The postindependence years saw a flourishing cartooning scene, plied by veterans such as Ba Gyan and Hein Sung but also newcomers who, according to Bertil Lintner, "often saw their role as the public's watchdog, armed with pen and wit, to ward against corruption and abuse of power" (1991, 32). It was the period when many of the cartoonists I interviewed in 1993 started their careers, not just with political cartoons and comic strips (*satirit kartun*) but with comic books and cartoon magazines (most, monthly) such as *Popular, Modern, Shwe Thway, Cartoon Nyung-Paung, OK*, and many others (Lent 2015, 177–78).

Using a schema developed by Myo Thant (2005), Myanmar experienced four distinct postindependence periods of cartooning. During the first stage of the 1950s and 1960s, numerous prominent cartoonists came on the scene, mainly drawing comic books and humor cartoons in which they created long-standing characters; newspapers, spurred by Pe Thein's *Pyidhu Kyemon* (People's Mirror) in 1951, in *Hathawaddy*, increased their cartoon input from weekly and monthly to daily, and any commentary became strictly controlled after the military seized power in 1962. The second phase, the 1970s to mid-1980s, marked a decline in the newspaper industry, forcing cartoonists to seek more work in cartoon magazines and comic books, which at the time began appealing also to an adult audience. The mid-1980s to about 2005, the third period, saw stagnation with growth, a brief loosening of government control, followed by

nearly total shutdown after the bloody coup of September 1988, and a miserable labor situation for cartoonists, who regularly freelanced for ten to fifteen periodicals while maintaining day jobs, in one case ferrying a riverboat. Maung Maung Aung described his work at that time as leaving him in poverty, while he lived with fear (Chastain 2016). Immediately following the 1988 coup, all periodicals except those of the government were closed, legislation and penalties were tightened, and some cartoonists were jailed or went into exile. Cartoons in government organs were very propaganda driven. In 1993 interviews, most Myanmar cartoonists claimed that the situation had changed for the better, despite saying that they were still hemmed in by lack of venues except those in government hands, close Home Ministry scrutiny, and multiple taboos such as caricaturing political leaders, sex, violence, and any political satire. A few cartoonists sought out novel ways to get their messages seen, as in this example from the early 2000s:

> They [cartoonists] joined writers and other artists who sipped tea at outdoor teashops, discussed politics and other topics in hushed tones, and created and shared their works. One cartoonist, Maung Sun Tan, who used teashops as a conduit for his forbidden work, sold his cartoons, loaded with metaphors, symbolism, hints, and innuendo, for two dollars each. (Mockenhaupt 2001, 73)

Maung Sun Tan said that he labored to get the message right: "If the message is too obvious, it will be censored; too obtuse and the reader won't understand" (Mockenhaupt 2001, 73). Myo Thant's fourth period as described above, contemporary times, carries the lingering issue of government control. Some cartoons were banned, particularly those of Aw Pi Kyeh, who in 2007 was declared persona non grata by the military government, after which all periodicals rejected his work. In 2011 and 2012, government pre-censorship was replaced by self-censorship, but shortly after, postpublication censorship was instituted, and private ownership of newspapers remained forbidden (see Lent 2015, 179–84, for a fuller discussion of these periods).

A fifth period is in order, encompassing most of the 2010s, with information I gleaned from interviews with eight cartoonists in Yangon in February 2018, observations, and the scant literature available. The cartoonists (with their birth names in parenthesis) are: Nay Myo Aye (Nay Zin Oo), Win Aung (Win Swe), Shwe Bo (Aung Bo Bo), Joker (Nyan Myint), Aw Pi Kyeh (APK,[1] Win Naing), Maung Maung Fountain (Saw Thar Htoo), Crab (Su Myat Htwe), and Kyaw Thu Yein (Kyaw Thu Yein Lwin).

Freedom to Cartoon

Most conversant about government/cartooning relationships among those interviewed in 2018 were Aw Pi Kyeh (APK) and Win Aung, probably because they were older than the others (APK was born in 1959; Win Aung, in 1962) and had lived during and suffered under varying degrees of harsh authoritarianism.

APK began his professional cartooning career in 1981, although he had published cartoons in university publications from 1976. A practicing engineer, he drew cartoons for magazines, since newspapers were scarce under the military socialist government (1962–1988), and their cartoon space was unofficially reserved for six or seven famous cartoonists. Drawing for monthly magazines, APK (2018) said that his cartoons were not on news but on "general truth" (not necessarily current), news being too old for a monthly. He soon began appearing in newspapers, the only young cartoonist given this opportunity.

APK described the military socialist authorities as very harsh on cartooning, stating:

We had to show our raw cartoons to the government office. They allowed some, banned others. For example, in a 200-page magazine, they might allow 100 pages and stop 100 pages, that space then being blank. Those pages had to be replaced and would be filled with different text and cartoons. Some pages would be banned again. Even after publication, the board would ban a few. In that case, if 1,000

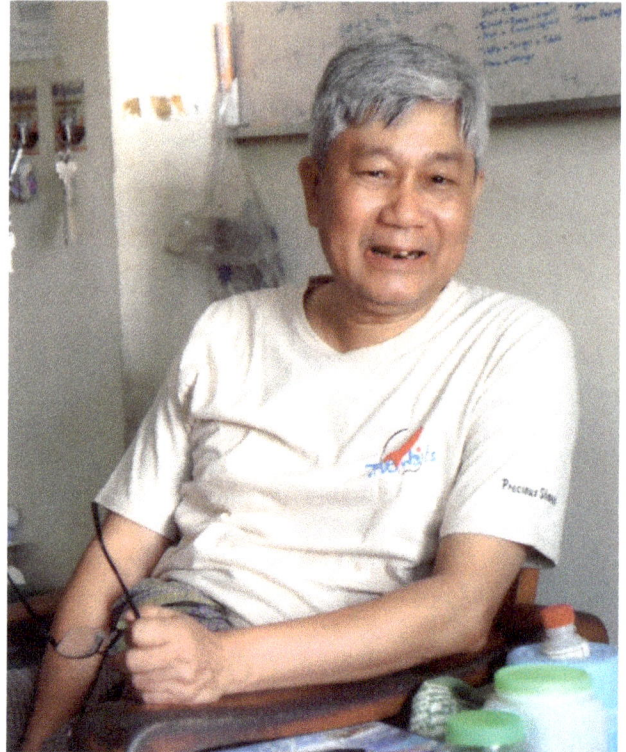

9.4. Aw Pi Kyeh in his home, Yangon, February 22, 2018. Photo by Xu Ying. Permission of Aw Pi Kyeh.

copies of the magazine were printed, those few pages had to be torn out of all 1,000 copies and given to the government board. Other cartoonists did not want their cartoons on the back of pages mine were on, because theirs did not appear too if mine were torn out. Like a trishaw with passengers back to back; if one wants to get off, the other also has to dismount to let that person out. (APK 2018)

More than three hundred of APK's cartoons were censored. He said that sometimes he changed the banned cartoons a bit and with subtlety resubmitted them later. APK is fond of using a football metaphor in describing his use of subtlety. As he told the Surreal McCoy and me later:

Under the previous military governments, cartoonists were limited to using a corner kick for their idea and the audience, using their heads, would knock it into the goal past the goalkeeper (censor). With the lifting of censorship cartoonists are now able to kick a penalty but the government still holds the red card, so they must be wary " . . . and not to kick too high otherwise the audience won't understand, or too low as the goalkeeper will stop it." (Surreal McCoy 2016, 294)

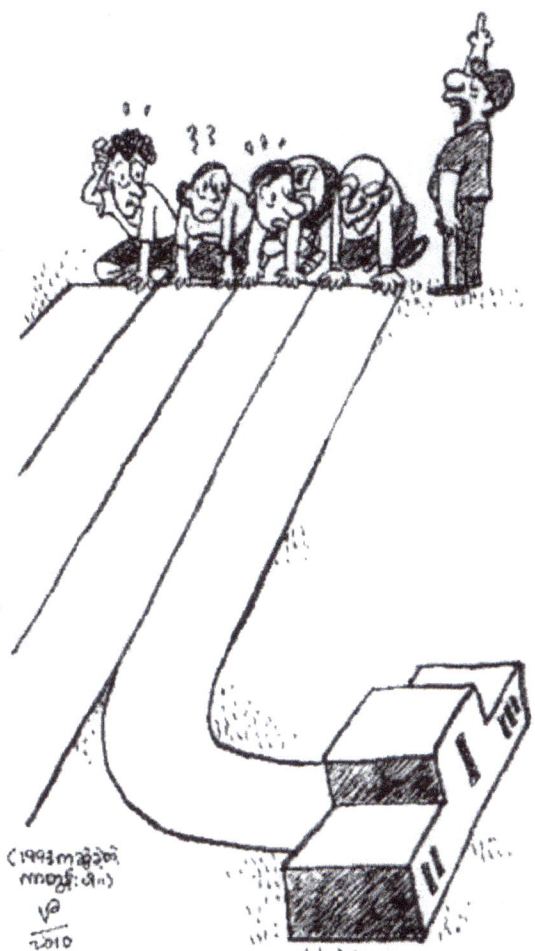

9.5. "A Foregone Conclusion," Aw Pi Kyeh. Foregone outcome of the 2010 election as rigged. Permission of Aw Pi Kyeh.

9.6. Drawings on a door in Aw Pi Kyeh's home, Yangon, February 22, 2018. Photo by Xu Ying. Permission of Aw Pi Kyeh.

At the time of the major crackdown in 1988, APK was an engineer in a jeep factory in the remote countryside. The workers were unaware of his sideline cartooning, but the secret police knew. When factory workers had a labor dispute, APK was questioned by the secret police for a full day, after which he moved to Mandalay and then to Yangon in 1993. APK said that after his arrival in Yangon, he was the only cartoonist the censor board wanted to question and the sole cartoonist among five hundred other artists, poets, writers, and filmmakers each given a full page in a green book the army published in 1995–1996.

APK agreed that the situation was better in 2018 and that he had drawn without censorship since 2012, but he added that cartoonists must be wary of the military's penchant to sue. He also felt that some cartoonists give editors much leeway in choosing cartoons, explaining:

"Some cartoonists draw many cartoons, allowing editors to choose one from perhaps ten. I draw one cartoon and the editors use it" (APK 2018). In some cases, cartoonists even seek others' input before submitting a cartoon to an editor; they draw cartoons with blank balloons and fill them in with dialogue suggested by teahouse patrons.

Win Aung suffered harsh treatment after the 1988 nationwide uprising when the dictator Ne Win was deposed and the military formed a ruling junta. He was imprisoned for six years, along with poets and others, for their political views. As he explained, the military "never says you are being imprisoned for political views; they find another excuse. Even today, the military can imprison us, even because I am talking with you" (Win Aung 2018).

9.7. Political cartoonist Win Aung, Yangon, February 20, 2018. Photo by Xu Ying. Permission of Win Aung.

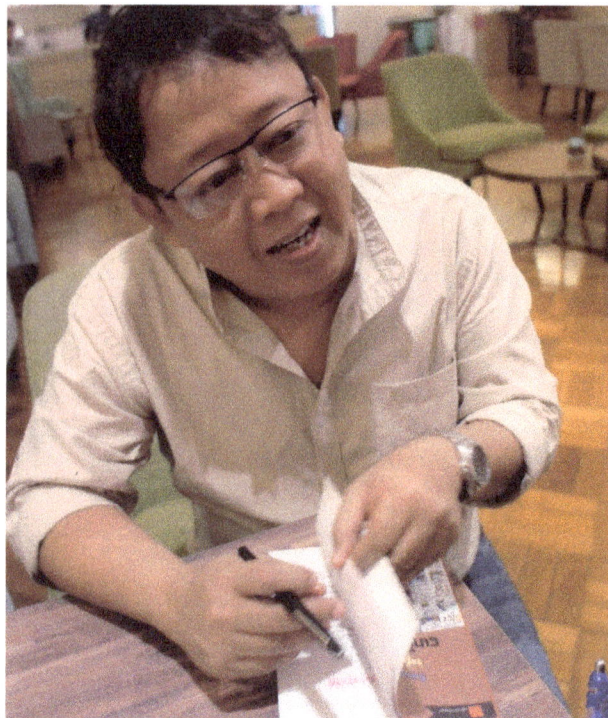

9.8. Political *and* editorial cartoonist Maung Maung Fountain, Yangon, February 23, 2018. Photo by Xu Ying. Permission of Maung Maung Fountain.

Although the overall climate is much more favorable for cartoonists, stumbling blocks remain, Win Aung said, mentioning a few: publishers and editors are fearful of the military authorities; colonial regulations on secrecy and other matters are still in place; and he and other cartoonists still feel it necessary to be subtle and careful. He cited the dual system of rule (both a military and a civilian government) as ineffective, saying: "The civilian government does not have complete power or authority, because it has no military; the military has no government" (Win Aung 2018).

Win Aung considers the harsh military regime after 1988 the best period for him to have drawn cartoons, because they had to be drawn secretly. "That was more pleasurable for me than saying what you wish more directly as now," he said.

Other cartoonists weighed in on the freedom issue. Then twenty-seven-year-old Nay Myo Aye said that because of the country's dual rule, cartoonists "must stand in the middle." As for himself, he said that he has no restrictions and can draw what he wishes; "if the media wishes to use it, they will; if the editor stops it, that's a type of self-censorship" (Nay Myo Aye 2018). Shwe Bo said that there are no restrictions, yet in the same sentence said: "If you draw a very strong cartoon about the military, the editor will not use it" (Shwe Bo 2018). More expansively, Joker (Nyan Myint) said that any hard-hitting cartoon is rejected by the editors and

that self-censorship exists. Still, he said, it is better than under the military junta, when beggars could not be drawn because of potential damage to the government's image (Joker 2018).

Distinguishing between an editorial and a political cartoonist, both of which he claims to be, Maung Maung Fountain said that when he "illustrates the editor's opinion, knows his taste, that is editorial cartooning. Drawing whatever he wants about politics is political cartooning" (Maung Maung Fountain 2018). He explained why he returned to political cartooning in 2012, after a sixteen-year lapse: "That year, a recently released political prisoner with a political group behind him began paying me 3,000 kyats [818 kyats to 1 US dollar in 2012] daily for one cartoon that he put on his Facebook page." Ridiculous as it may sound, Kyaw Thu Yein declared that "if you don't draw the government or military, you can draw anything." Self-censorship (which he called cartoonists' biggest problem) prevails out of respect for cultural values, he said; yet he added that editors have pulled his cartoons because they dealt with the military or government, seemingly beyond the realm of protecting cultural values.

9.9. Harn Lay's first political cartoon—a satire of Senior General Saw Maung, who, after assuming power after a bloody coup in 1988, claimed, "I saved Burma." The cartoon shows Saw Maung dragging Burma out of the water with a rope around her neck. Harn Lay's message was that Burma was saved but no longer was alive.

In Myanmar, as in other authoritarian countries, the line between abiding by ethical standards and cultural values and outright censorship is thin and flexible, and what is taboo or sensitive is determined more by the protective whims of the government or/and military rather than by cultural values and tradition. Avoiding, as practiced by Myanmar cartoonists, the critical depiction of pregnant women, disabled people, behavior in the mosque, or violence toward children does cut muster as sensitive topics, an issue of ethics. But not being permitted to draw about the country's civil war or any military organization, also labeled "sensitive," is more related to censorship than ethical standards.

The tenuousness of any degree of freedom in Myanmar came to light again in early February 2021, when the military staged a coup and declared a year-long emergency period, reacting to the previous November election when the National League for Democracy (NLD) won 83 percent of the available seats of the lower house of Parliament. The NLD leader, Aung San Suu Kyi, and other officials were arrested, and the mass media were severely curbed; both *7 Day News* and *Eleven* newspapers were shut down.

Cartoonists united in protest through the Myanmar Cartoonists Association and aligned with the

Professional Cartoonists' Organisation and Burma Campaign UK in a social media campaign to support local artists and bring awareness to the situation. Cartoonists drew themselves and others giving the three-finger salute of protest and posted the cartoons on a Three Fingers website. Proceeds from art sold was sent to help Mutual Aid Myanmar (Broken Frontier Staff 2021).

At least two cartoonists felt the need to flee Myanmar, fearing for their safety—Waiyan Taunggyi and Lagoon Eain, both pseudonyms. In a July 2021 interview with Carol (The Surreal McCoy) Isaacs, both said that they were in danger of being detained if they remained in Myanmar because of their antigovernment drawings. Taunggyi said that some media were afraid to use his cartoons, so he posted all of them on his Facebook page, while Lagoon Eain made fun of the military indirectly, substituting pictures of ancient Burmese commanders. During the protests, some demonstrators printed out Taunggyi's cartoons as "stickers and . . . quietly stick [them] to the army walls at night" (Marshall 2021).

These artists joined other Myanmar cartoonists who were exposing the oppression and absurdities of the military while in self-exile. Harn Lay, beginning in the early 2000s, used "humor as a weapon" in his regular cartoon attack published in *Irrawaddy*, while he resided in Thailand (Macan-Markar 2009).

Status of Cartoonists

Another major problem of the profession relates to cartoonists' labor. No Myanmar newspapers or other periodicals maintain staff positions; all cartoonists work as freelancers, earning the major portion of their money in unrelated jobs: tattoo artist (Nay Myo Aye), betel leaf merchant (Joker), engineer and motivational speaker (APK), physician (Kyaw Thu Yein), men's hairdresser (Shwe Bo), and a store employee (Crab).

In some cases, cartoonists consider drawing more of a hobby than a job; they draw to "make a better society," to fulfill a childhood dream, or to inform the public about the "situation." They all agree that it is difficult,

9.10. Kyaw Thu Yein's commentary on Myanmar's precarious electrical system. Permission of Kyaw Thu Yein.

and they cannot depend on the government or other entities for support. Besides their cartooning and day jobs, they take on other tasks such as drawing book covers, educational and consciousness-raising materials for NGOs and the government, illustrations, and advertisements. APK is a well-known motivational speaker who since 1992 has given more than one thousand talks all over Myanmar, for which he receives an honorarium and paid expenses. Maung Maung Fountain is the sole cartoonist who can live off his cartooning and illustrating, because, as he explained, he is single and living expense-free with his family of origin.

Payment for cartoons varies according to the status of the cartoonists.[2] APK lays claim to being the highest paid; he showed me a front-page, color cartoon in the *People's Daily* that was published while I was there that earned him US$40. He said that the average cartoon will fetch US$10. There is general agreement that cartoonists are underpaid; veteran Win Aung said that they are not paid

as well as civil servant street cleaners. When APK was invited to represent cartoonists at an artists/writers conference with national leader Aung San Suu Kyi in 2015, he told the group that Myanmar could lose many younger artists who cannot make a living from cartooning.

Working freelance, the cartoonists are at the mercy of editors, who often prefer the drawings of the seniors. Shwe Bo rated editors' selection of cartoons as a number one problem, because editors do not want to "take a chance on young cartoonists' drawings even if they are better" (Shwe Bo 2018). Joker (2018) and Maung Maung Fountain (2018) said similar things: "High reputation cartoonists' works are always used," and it is the editors' call, determined by the cartoonist's "reputation, seniority, and the quality of the work."

APK, Kyaw Thu Yein, Maung Maung Fountain, and Joker said that their cartoons had high acceptance rates by editors—100 percent, 90–95 percent, 90 percent, and 75 percent, respectively—some of this attributable to their senior status and likely the number of cartoons they dispatch daily. APK (2018) draws one cartoon daily, which is accepted; Joker (2018) does ten to fifteen daily and sends three or four to five different newspapers. Each newspaper normally publishes one of his drawings daily.

Women are absent from the rolls of political cartoonists. Su Myat Htwe (who goes by her childhood nickname, Crab) was mentioned as a political cartoonist by others; although she puts satirical works on her Facebook page, she does not consider herself a political cartoonist. Working full time in the business department of a Yangon company and caring for a young daughter, she draws when she can for exhibitions, competitions, an occasional NGO, and school and street caricature sittings. Like a few other female cartoonists, she has drawn a comic strip and a comic book.

Claiming that she would like to draw political cartoons, Crab regurgitated reasons given by male cartoonists for women's absence from the profession: it's too difficult, women are scared, expectations are too demanding for women, women have no sense of politics, it's too dangerous, it's not an expected female role in Myanmar (Crab 2018). Win Aung (2018) contributed another reason: that in a traditional Buddhist culture such as Myanmar, men are considered superior. APK (2018) breached the line, saying (perhaps in jest), "like driving, they don't know politics"; and Kyaw Thu Yein (2018) went even further: "Women are housewives; they love to cook. Some work outside. Life is simple and women depend on men in our culture. Women love to draw cute animals and comics. But, in political cartoons, it is difficult to draw cute things." Maung Maung Fountain (2018) attributed the lack of women cartoonists to their lifestyles, explaining: "Girls are more pressed down than boys. Much of society does not want girls to go higher; families don't want girls to be cartoonists."

Professionalization

Upgrading the professional status of political cartooning (actually, all cartooning) in Myanmar is sorely needed. Without an economic or morale-boosting support base, political cartoonists appear to be sputtering along, avoiding potholes whenever and however they can and hoping not to run out of energy.

Cartoonists have virtually no backing, sometimes not even from family members, who measure success merely on income earned. They lack a community mentality and a physical place for interaction, training, and exhibiting. The Myanmar Cartoonists Association (MCA), started in 2016, is a start in that direction, but after two years it had achieved "nothing" except an exhibition or two, according to its chairman, APK, who further said that, lacking a festival venue, the cartoonists exhibited cartoons on the side of a road. APK explained the MCA's quandary:

> We have no office. I asked my friend, the minister of information, to give us space in downtown Yangon. There have been meetings, meetings, meetings, but no decision. One problem would be, we cannot pay the rent of such a place. I am too busy to continually nag the ministry. Right now, we artists have discussions only on Facebook, but we need face-to-face contact. I asked the minister to help us

communicate with outside cartoonists. There is also concern among us that if the Ministry provides us space, it will expect us not to attack it. (APK 2018)

One of the MCA's activities, according to Nay Myo Aye (2018), is establishing a fund to help cartoonists when they are ill, jobless, or otherwise in need. Each of the two hundred members pays Ks.1,300/- to 1,600/- (one or two US dollars) monthly to keep the fund alive.

There have been a few other attempts to help establish the professionalization of cartoonists. Maung Maung Fountain was planning a private course on cartoon drawing in 2018. Cartoonists are quick to point out that they learned cartooning on their own, some because of childhood interest, imitating what came before them and dabbling in various forms of art. Their roads to success could be meandering, as related by Maung Maung Fountain:

> I started cartooning as a hobby while working at a railroad station where a poet taught me how to read cartoons. I had no cartoon or art drawing training. From 1988 to 1996, I became a political cartoonist drawing freelance mainly for magazines. I learned by myself. In 1996, it was difficult to get jobs, and the choices were to go to the forest with others (*taw ko*) or abroad. So, I left Myanmar to work on a cruise ship in their laundry. I started to do drawings on the side for the ship's stage settings. I returned to Myanmar in 2000, and from 2001 to 2012, I had a retail game shop. In 2015, I returned to political cartooning. (Maung Maung Fountain 2018)

Other attempts to encourage the profession included the publication of a humor magazine, *Yee Sa Yar* ("humor" or "funny"), which for a while published cartoons and articles concerning cartooning, and the establishment of the online Myanmar Silent Cartoon Group, where young cartoonist enthusiasts/aspirants post their wordless cartoons without going through an editor. Joker (2018) said that the group consists of 5,700 members, including senior cartoonists.

The internet offers a new venue for cartoonists, but it does not yet provide enough opportunities to fully sustain them. Nay Myo Aye (2018) supplements his other earnings with online political cartoons, for which he receives a higher rate than for those that are printed. He said that cartoonists use Facebook for "everything all the time," which others confirmed. In his case, political groups solicited the use of his Facebook-posted drawings, undoubtedly for a fee. Shwe Bo (2018) publishes his political cartoons in the online editions of *Irrawaddy* and *Moemakha* and posts them on both his Facebook page and that of a Facebook group in his hometown of Pyay. In some cases, cartoonists simultaneously send their drawings to print and online media, because print editors take time to respond, a practice frowned upon by APK as head of the cartoonists' association.

Concluding Remark

I wrote a few years ago that if the internet is not the salvation of Myanmar cartoonists, then they will have to survive as they always have, living by their wits (Lent 2015, 184). There is no reason to expect a different conclusion.

Notes

1. APK chose his nom de plume because it means "loud-speaker" in Burmese (Surreal McCoy 2016, 293). Pen names for cartoonists are very common in Myanmar, possibly to shield the individuals during the country's ongoing political turmoil, although other reasons were given for their use. Shwe Bo (2018) explained that it is a tradition and that some real names are too long or ugly; Kyaw Thu Yein (2018) said that it is part of the culture, a tradition, and necessary because many people have similar names, so pen names can separate and better identify them.

2. Other cartoonists gave rates they were paid: Nay Myo Aye: highest online, Ks.15,000/- (US$11–12), lowest online, Ks.5,000/- (US$3–4), highest newspaper print, Ks.10,000/- (US$7–8); Win Aung, highest, US$7–8, lowest, US$3–5; Joker, Ks.10,000/- to 15,000/-; Maung Maung Fountain, Ks.15,000/- for newspapers, Ks.25,000/- for magazines; Crab, US$5–10; and Kyaw Thu Yein, a range of Ks.10,000/- to 15,000/-.

Bibliography

Aung Soe Min. n.d. "Comic Culture in Myanmar: When Lines Shine a Light in the Darkness." Goethe Institute. http://www.goethe.de/ins/mm/en/kul/mag/20697882.html.

Aung Zaw. 2003. "Pioneers of Burmese Cartooning." *Irrawaddy*, August. https://www.irrawaddy.com/from-the-archive/pioneers-burmese-cartooning.html.

Aw Pi Kyeh [APK]. 2018. Interview with John A. Lent and Xu Ying, Yangon, February 22.

Blackburn, Paul P. 1982. "Burma." In *Newspapers in Asia: Contemporary Trends and Problems*, edited by John A. Lent, 177–92. Hong Kong: Heinemann Asia.

Broken Frontier Staff. 2021. "#threefingers for Myanmar: New Cartoonist Initiative Launches to Raise Awareness of Life in Myanmar after the Military Coup." Broken Frontier, March 24. https://www.brokenfrontier.com/three-fingers-for-myanmar-threefingers/.

Chastain, Mary. 2016. "Myanmar's Political Cartoonists Emboldened by Pro-Democracy Election Victory." *Breitbart Email Newsletter*, January 13.

Crab [Su Myat Htwe]. 2018. Interview with John A. Lent and Xu Ying, Yangon, February 24.

Hasan, Mushirul. 2007. *Wit and Humour in Colonial North India*. New Delhi: Niyogi.

Hollstein, Milton. 1971. "Burma." In *The Asian Newspapers' Reluctant Revolution*, edited by John A. Lent, 138–57. Ames: Iowa State University Press.

Ikeya, Chie. 2008. "The Modern Burmese Woman and the Politics of Fashion in Colonial Burma." *Journal of Asian Studies* 67, no. 4 (November): 1277–308.

Joker [Nyan Myint]. 2018. Interview with John A. Lent and Xu Ying, Yangon, February 21.

Khanduri, Ritu G. 2009. "Vernacular Punches: Cartoons and Politics in Colonial India." *History and Anthropology* 20, no. 4: 459–86.

Kyaw Thu Yein. 2018. Interview with John A. Lent and Xu Ying, Yangon, February 25.

Lent, John A. 2015. *Asian Comics*. Jackson: University Press of Mississippi.

Lintner, Bertil. 1991. "Avoiding the Draft." *Far Eastern Economic Review*, September 12, 32–33.

Macan-Markar, Marwaan. 2009. "Q&A: 'Cartoons Are My Way of Protesting against Burmese Junta.'" Inter Press Service News Agency, December 14. https://www.ipsnews.net/2009/12/qa-lsquocartoons-are-my-way-of-protesting-against-burmese-juntarsquo/.

Marshall, Glenn. 2021. "Interview with Myanmar Cartoonists." Professional Cartoonists' Organisation, July 1. https://procartoonists.org/interview-with-burmese-cartoonists/.

Maung Maung Fountain. 2018. Interview with John A. Lent and Xu Ying, Yangon, February 23.

Mockenhaupt, Brian. 2001. "Burma: Wordsmithery." *Far Eastern Economic Review*, September 20, 72–75.

Myat Kyi La Thein. 2011. "U Ba Gyan's Street: The Cartoon Street of Tazaung Daing." ASEAN-Korea Centre, November 22. http://blog.aseankorea.org/archives/1762.

Myo Thant. 2005. "Social Critics, Satirists and Humourists." Paper presented at the National Workshop on Copyright: Myanmar's Gateway to IP, Yangon, September 7.

Nay Myo Aye. 2018. Interview with John A. Lent and Xu Ying, Yangon, February 20.

Ranard, Andrew. 2009. *Burmese Painting: A Linear and Lateral History*. Chiang Mai, Thailand: Silkworm Books.

Scully, Richard. 2013. "A Comic Empire: The Global Expansion of *Punch* as a Model Publication, 1841–1936." *International Journal of Comic Art* 15, no. 2 (Fall): 6–35.

Shwe Bo [Aung Bo Bo]. 2018. Interview with John A. Lent and Xu Ying, Yangon, February 21.

Strangio, Sebastian. 2015. "Political Cartoonists Test Limits of Newfound Freedoms." *Nikkei Asian Review*, October 2. https://asia.nikkei.com/NAR/Articles/Political-cartoonists-test-limits-of-newfound-freedom.

Surreal McCoy. 2016. "Burma's Loudspeaker." *International Journal of Comic Art* 18, no. 1 (Spring–Summer): 293–96.

Thaung, U. 1995. *A Journalist, a General, and an Army in Burma*. Bangkok: White Lotus.

Win Aung. 2018. Interview with John A. Lent and Xu Ying. Yangon, February 20.

Chapter 10

The Philippines

Historical Overview[1]

The Philippines was endowed with illustrated periodicals as early as 1859–1860, with the appearance of *La Ilustracion Filipina*. Although its illustrations were highly exaggerated (the workhorse of editorial cartooning), they could hardly be called editorial cartoons, because they "always exaggerated and falsified the truth in an effort to picture the beauty of the Indios and particularly of the Indias [Filipinas]" (Retana 1895, quoted in Taylor 1927, 18).

Credited as the Philippines' first cartoonist, national hero José Rizal falls into the same category as other countries' founding fathers so labeled such as Sukarno in Indonesia, Benjamin Franklin in the United States, and Ho Chi Minh in Vietnam. Although such claims may have brought recognition and prestige to comic art, the verdict is still out concerning their veracity for want of substantiation in a new field such as comic art studies, the lack of a clear, stand-alone definition of "cartoon," and a number of other inhibiting factors. Sticking solely with Rizal, his thirty-four scene "The Monkey and the Tortoise" and other works he drew were not for publication, but were gifts for friends he visited in France and Germany (Lent 2009, 16; also Villarroel 1986, 16). Reportedly, Rizal did draw anti-Spanish propaganda, but, because these illustrated attacks have not turned up yet, there is no hard evidence that they existed or that they would meet the qualifications of being political cartoons.

More deserving of being termed editorial/political cartoons were the drawings in weekly satire magazines that appeared between 1884 and 1894, a period of relatively greater freedom, accompanied by Filipinos' awareness of their impoverished status, and higher-speed technology to disseminate information. The magazines, using personal allusions, sharp wit, and poignant sarcasm in their prose and drawings, attracted a welcoming readership. An early newspaper historian, Jesús Valenzuela, said of them: "They vulgarized the officials and other personages in Philippine history. . . . They contained clever allegories and allusions to the merits,

10.1. Cover of *Lipag-Kalabaw*, January 11, 1908. The vile Uncle Sam pays court to the maiden Filipina, who sells herself cheaply.

demerits of persons, things or institutions they wished to lampoon" (1933, 54).

First among the satire magazines were Don Pedro Groizard's *La Semana Elegante* (The Elegant Weekly) in 1894 and *Manila Alegre* (Merry Manila) a year later; the latter was noted for its caricatures of persons well known for their wealth, position, or rank. Groizard's magazines spearheaded a horde of followers, such as *La Puya* (Bovine Review) in 1895, the purpose of which was to promote a game called *toro*; *Manililla* (Miniature Manila) in 1887; *El Caneco*, 1890; *El Domingo* (Sunday), 1890; *El Pajaro Verde* (Green Bird), 1890; *Todo en Broma* (All a Joke), 1892; *La Moda Filipina* (Philippine Fashion), 1893; *Manililla-Sport*, 1894; *El Cinife*, 1894; *El Temblor* (Tremor), and *El Chiflado*.

Even after Spain's defeat in 1898 by the United States, the Spaniards continued to lampoon Filipinos and added Americans to the mockery. Their new satire magazines were *Te con Leche* (Tea with Milk), *El Cometa* (the Comet), *El Bejuco* (the Cane), and *La Restoracion*. *Te con Leche* was often brutal, depicting Filipinos as "barefoot rustics with matted hair and unkempt noses," placing General Emilio Aguinaldo (General Arthur MacArthur's foe in the largely forgotten, if ever recognized, Filipino-American War) in a monkey cage, and giving the United States a "few affectionate digs" (Esteban 1953, 7–8).

The proliferation of satire magazines did not ease up as the Filipinos did battle with the new American occupiers during the early years of the twentieth century.

Published in Spanish, *El Tío Verdades* (the Truthful Old Man, 1899) and *Biro-Biro* (1901) mocked Spaniards and Americans with two-toned, color cartoons and caricatures, as did *Miau* (a worldly cat that knew everything), whose content was 50 percent cartoons (Esteban 1953, 7–8; McCoy and Roces 1985, 7–18; Marcelo 1980, 18).

Notable during the early American occupation were the weekly illustrated magazines with articles and essays on current events and, of course, political cartoons. These magazines—*Lipag-Kalabaw, Telembang*, the *Philippines Free Press*, and the *Independent*—greatly boosted political cartooning. Inspired by the earlier illustrated magazines of the Spaniards, they differed in one major aspect, according to historian Alfred McCoy: "The older Spanish publications used graphics for illustration and individual caricature, while the new weeklies adopted the style of the Anglo-American political cartoon" (McCoy and Roces 1985, 15). The covers of these magazines carried a lead cartoon accompanied by an editorial that set the tone for the entire issue. Captions were written in both English and Spanish.

Lipag-Kalabaw had nearly as many lives as the hypothetical cat. Started in July 27, 1907, it caved in to political pressures after thirty-three issues on March 7, 1908, and restarted a month later, only to suffer closure again the following year. Thirteen years later, on July 22, 1922, it was revived as *Bagong Lipag-Kalabaw*, dropped out of existence in 1924, and restarted yet again in April 1949 as the Nacionalista Party organ critical of President Elpidio Quirino and the Liberal Party. It took its last gasps in September 1949, after twenty issues. Initially, *Lipag-Kalabaw* appeared on sixteen pages printed on inexpensive, thin, see-through paper, carrying "irrepressible cartoons" that lived up to the magazine's name, derived from a native plant that leaves a severe rash upon contact. The voice of independent radicals, it delighted in satirizing American do-goodism and Filipino parrotism, both in text and cartoon. Its highly skilled political cartoonists used many pen names likely to evade libel threats, the two most prominent being Taga Isorog and Makahiya (the latter possibly Jorge Pineda). *Lipag-Kalabaw*'s cartoons, as those of the other magazines,

often dealt with political corruption, nationalism, and the Philippine-American relationship.

Writing about pre-independence cartoonists generally, Alfred McCoy and Alfredo Roces describe them as

> above all else, passionate nationalists. But for them and their editors it was not enough that the Philippines should simply become independent. Not only should the nation be free of American domination, it should also be free of ignorance, injustice, inequality, and corruption. Although they might hold their fire over partisan politics, they were relentless advocates of what they saw as the interests of an emerging nation. As if judges sitting in the court of history the cartoonists summoned even the most powerful politicians for trial by caricature or sentence by satire when their failings threatened the nation's future. Insisting that public office was a public trust, the cartoonists condemned all—whether legislator, labor leader, senator, or civil servant—who let their hypocrisy or pride blind them to their true mission.
>
> [M]any artists had an implicit vision of the Philippines as a corporatist state that could accomodate [*sic*] all Filipinos as participating citizens regardless of race, gender, or culture. Such unity would, they felt, be impossible, unless everyone accepted a secular, nationalist ideology as their paramount loyalty. Cartoons insisted that mestizos and morenos (brown) should be equal, women should not vote until educated away from submission to Catholic clerics, and Igorots [indigenous peoples of northern Luzon] must accept national unification. (McCoy and Roces 1985, 312)

These cartoonists' works were exquisitely drawn, and their subjects (bureaucrats and politicians) were venomously caricatured as "spineless parasites," two-faced hypocrites, "traitors of the public interest and exploiters of the mass" (McCoy and Roces 1985, 312). They liked to depict the Philippines as a demure woman, "Filipinas," and Uncle Sam as a brash "troll-like old man using his cunning to pay court" to the virginal and coy Filipina who leads him on (McCoy and Roces 1985, 17).

Also started in 1907, the *Philippines Free Press*, at first the organ of the antivice Moral Progress League, had

151

Philippines Free Press

10 CENTAVOS · 10 CENTAVOS

Vol. XIV · Philippines Free Press, Manila, P. I., Saturday February 28, 1920. · No. 9

THE "REIGN OF TERROR" · EL "REINADO DEL TERROR"

10.2. "The Reign of Terror," *Philippines Free Press*, February 28, 1920. The danger of automobiles.

a more fluid journey than *Lipag-Kalabaw*. In the same year (1908) that it died for lack of circulation, a maverick Scotsman, Robert McCulloch Dick, bought what remained of the *Philippines Free Press*'s name, goodwill, and subscription lists for one peso. From the restart, the *Free Press* promoted a friendly feeling between Filipinos and Americans, campaigned for independence, fought courageously for its principles despite many libel suits and threats of deportation of Dick, and worked to advance literary endeavors. It was a newsmagazine years before *Time* in the United States (Lent 1971, 62). At first, its political cartoons were linear, but by the 1920s, the American style and form had been adopted. A fixture at the *Free Press* in the 1920s and 1930s was self-taught painter José Pereira, whose cartooning set the style for the profession with painstaking cross-hatching done in pen and ink.

The third and most militant of the nationalist magazines was the *Independent*, published from 1915 to 1931. Famous among its political cartoonists were painters

Jorge Pineda and Fernando Amorsolo. Credited with creating the character Juan de la Cruz, who replaced "Filipinas" as the national symbol, Pineda made himself economically independent by painting much commercial art. Amorsolo, later honored with the first National Artist Award,[2] drew some of the angriest cartoons of the period 1914–1919, depicting Spanish friars as "satanic monsters" and Chinese merchants as "crafty Orientals" (McCoy and Roces 1985, 17, 35).

During these early American times, political cartoonists heavily relied on jobs other than their chosen profession to put meals on their families' tables, since political cartooning was both personally risky and not financially lucrative.

Political cartooning was very evident in other early periodicals such as *Kikiriki* (Cock-a-doodle-doo), *Philippine Magazine*, *Liwayway* (Dawn), and other vernacular magazines that were part of the Ramon Roces chain. *Kikiriki*, begun in 1910, advertised itself as a "comic-satirical weekly, anti-pornographic, anti-libelous,

10.3. The *Independent*, May 26, 1917. The mayor declares that he *is* the municipal board, as board members fall into line.

(The Independent, 26 May 1917)

Goyo, the patriot... | **Too big for him**

10.4. "Goyo, the Patriot," by national artist Fernando Amorsolo, the *Independent*, September 16, 1916.

(The Independent, 16 September 1916)

(Dibujo de F. Amorsolo.)

anti-political and anti-tuberculosis" (Gleeck 1984, b). Its cartoons lashed out at local politicians, the trusts, US soldiers, and libel cases.

Philippine Magazine, started in 1904–1905, increased its political cartoons after A. V. H. Hartendorp became editor in 1925. The magazine was killed by World War II, and Hartendorp's attempt to resuscitate it after the war was squashed when he failed to receive a war damages payment that had been promised him (Hartendorp 1964). *Philippine Magazine*'s major cartoonist

was Ireneo L. Miranda, whose work was described as "of great beauty and occasional power" (Gleeck 1984, c). Miranda also drew daily political cartoons for the newspaper *El Debate*, doing them in between classes he taught at the University of the Philippines (McCoy and Roces 1985, 11).

In 1923, Don Ramon Roces started his magazine chain, eventually known for being heavily involved in editorial cartoons, publishing the first comic strip, and maintaining the country's largest *komiks* group. His first

The Philippines

10.5. "Pulling the Blind," Esmeraldo Z. Izon, *Philippines Free Press*. A comment on the declaration of martial law by President Ferdinand Marcos.

publication was *Foto News* (soon to be called *Liwayway*), followed by *Graphic* (1927), which, by the 1930s, featured two political cartoons per issue. A couple of points are worth mentioning about pre–World War II political cartoonists: (1) they started the pattern of political cartoonists also creating comic strips, a practice that continues to the present; and (2) they often were as free as their editors permitted them to be.

Esmeraldo Z. Izon, who began cartooning with the *Philippines Free Press* in 1938 and remained there for the rest of the century, talked about his political cartoon experiences at the *Free Press*, pointing out that the page one editorial was written by the associate editor:

> If he finished the editorial ahead, he gave it to the cartoonist to read and illustrate. If he was late, he sometimes drew stick figures and the spoken balloons to give an idea of what he wanted and gave this to the artist. It was up to the cartoonist to elaborate on this, or he drew other sketches of his own ideas on the subject and [the editor] chose the one to be used. Of course, both cartoon and editorial went to Mr. Dick [Robert McCulloch Dick, owner of the *Free Press*] for approval. (McCoy and Roces 1985, 11)

During the war, only the three TVT newspapers (the *Manila Tribune*, *La Vanguardia*, and *Taliba*), owned by the Roces family, and the largest of Ramon Roces's magazines, *Liwayway*, were permitted to publish under strict censorship. The Japanese added four newspapers of their own. In the hills were a number of guerrilla newspapers, hurriedly typed or mimeographed, lacking the time and equipment to include cartoons. An exception was the *Liberator*, which contained artwork by Izon. The *Liberator* was considered one of the top three underground periodicals of the war; Izon himself was later highly decorated for his patriotism. As with the many other guerrilla periodicals, the newsmagazine faced deadly circumstances during its production and distribution (Lent 1970, 260–74).

Cartoonists who spanned the World War II era included Izon and Gene Cabrera, both of the *Philippines Free Press*, and Gat (Liborio Gatbonton), long-time editorial cartoonist of the *Manila Chronicle* from its creation in the 1940s, and of *Taliba* before that. They established even more successful careers in the free-wheeling 1950s and 1960s, when the Philippines stood almost alone in Southeast Asia in maintaining a free and open atmosphere for political caricature, and when *komiks* as magazines and newspaper funnies flourished. Cynthia Roxas and Joaquin Arevalo Jr. write of postwar cartooning: "After the war, publications resumed operations. The editorial cartoonists, thrown into the huddle of new realities and wanting to find expression for their pent-up emotions that had been curbed during the Japanese occupation, soon became the focal point of interest in print media" (1985, 140).

10.6. Roni Santiago's portrayal of how Western media paint the Filipino, November 5, 1979. Courtesy of Roni Santiago.

Other prominent editorial cartoonists after the war were Demetrio Diego of the *Manila Times*; National Artist Carlos "Botong" Francisco, who had been editorial cartoonist of the *Evening News* for a short time; and Mauro "Malang" Santos, *Chronicle* editorial cartoonist and a contributor to the Philippines' first *komiks* magazine, *Halakhak Komiks*.

Many political cartoonists of the 1960s did double-duty work, also drawing newspaper comic strips. Topping the list was Larry Alcala, *Weekly Graphic* editorial cartoonist when he drew *Mang Ambo* in 1960, the first of twenty strip titles he created in his lifetime. Alcala was a human dynamo, at one time cranking out ten to twelve daily and weekly strips simultaneously, while also serving as a political cartoonist. He also is given credit for being among those who made the country's first animation.

In a 1988 interview I did with Alcala (simultaneously with Antonio Velasquez, a pioneer of strips and *komiks*, and Norman B. Isaac, *Manila Bulletin Today* political cartoonist), he explained his enormous productivity: "I can make more money with more strips. The more deadlines I have, the faster I become" (Alcala 1988).

The 1970s, despite being marred by martial law and the Ferdinand Marcos dictatorship, ushered in the careers of numerous editorial cartoonists. Again, a good proportion of them handled daily strips. Hugo Yonzon Jr. was among them, drawing *Philippines Daily Express* editorial cartoons and his strip *Sakay en Moy* after crossing over from the *Manila Times*. To make ends meet, he also painted on canvases in the *Daily Express* art room, which were often sold even while the paint was still wet (Yonzon 2008).

Boy Togonon started drawing strips after graduating from the University of Santo Tomas in 1972, and before the decade ended he had become the editorial cartoonist of the *Philippines Daily Express*, its sister paper the *Pilipino Express*, and the weekly magazine *Expressweek* at the same time, doing strips.

Roni Santiago, editorial cartoonist of the *Manila Bulletin Today* in the 1970s, received national recognition when his popular office-life strip, *Baltic & Company*, became one of the country's highest-rating television sitcoms. In his editorial cartoons, Santiago is apt to choose foreign topics, because they are "more open to humorous analogies" (Roxas and Arevalo 1985, 143). Simultaneously with his *Bulletin Today* work, he contributed two series to *Pilipino Funny Komiks*. Also of this period were works by Norman B. Isaac, editorial cartoonist of the *Bulletin Today*, whose early strips were *Laff-Drops* and

10.7. Political cartoonist Nonoy Marcelo at the *Manila Chronicle*, Manila, September 1988. Photo by John A. Lent. Courtesy of Nonoy Marcelo.

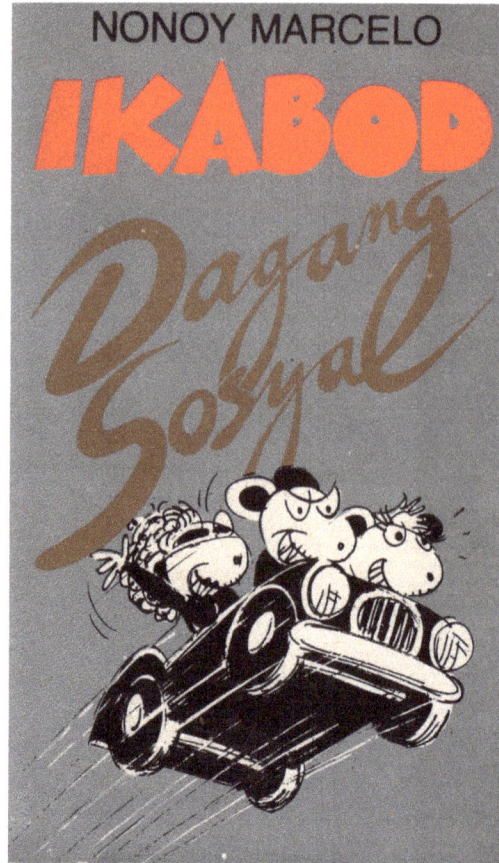

10.8. *Ikabod*, Nonoy Marcelo. Courtesy of Nonoy Marcelo.

Strip-Kolox; Tito Milambiling, *Balita* editorial cartoonist and author of that paper's *Bakok* and the *Bulletin Today*'s *Kusyo at Buyok*; and Nonoy Marcelo, longtime *Manila Chronicle* editorial cartoonist, known for his popular strips *Tisoy* and *Ikabod* and the Philippines' earliest animation shorts.

Marcelo's *Ikabod* stood out for its oblique ways of opposing the Marcos dictatorship. Situated in Dagalandia (Ratland), the strip's looney characters, according to Stefan Kanfer, "struggled under the dictatorship of swaggering, spendthrift rodents. Along the way, they tested the truth of old proverbs like 'In the valley of the blind, the one-eyed man is king'" (1984, 94). Marcelo was warned twice by the military for *Ikabod*'s critical stance, before being censored. From 1970 to 1977, Marcelo lived in Hong Kong and then New York City, from where he contributed political cartoons for which he was blacklisted by the Marcos forces. Later, he was told that it was safe to return to Manila with the conditions that he work at the government's National Media Production Center (NMPC) and not commit any punishable offenses. For two years, he produced animation for the NMPC while also surreptitiously drawing his *Ikabod* cartoons as a "balance to the big fat cats" and to "counter the opposition" (Marcelo 1988, 1992). In a 1992 interview, he said: "The security blanket that the NMPC promised me was saving my strips from being censored or abolished. No matter what I put in my cartoons, they

did not censor. I put in a lot of political. The authorities did not hit me because they thought it was coming from the NMPC" (Marcelo 1992).

The threat of censorship and other harassment severely subdued speaking about political matters, no matter how innocent. Larry Alcala recounted being told by the Marcos authorities to "tone down" his drawings; he went further, completely omitting political topics from his strips, using the rationale, "It's safer not to do them" (Alcala 1988).

One would have expected a boon time for political cartooning after the 1986 People Power Revolution, but the former vibrancy was gone, not to return. By the mid-1990s, about thirty cartoonists worked for the more than two dozen dailies and, according to *Manila Bulletin Today* cartoonist Norman Isaac (1992), all but a few of them suffered under large workloads and low pay. Deng Coy Miel (1992) concurred, and, before the end of the millennium, he joined at least six Philippine political cartoonists who had moved to Singapore, opting for its better wages and living conditions over the Philippines'

10.9. "Pork Barrel," Norman Isaac.
Courtesy of Norman Isaac.

relatively higher level of freedom. But that, too, was not a constant, as press freedom was significantly eroded by economic expediency practiced by government authorities and mammoth media conglomerates that joined forces to keep out "dreary" cartoons that might impede foreign investment opportunities or adversely affect vested interests. Cartoonists practiced self-censorship, as Miel (1992) said: "We have families to keep, and if we don't go along, we don't have jobs. I know the frame of mind of the powers-that-be . . . and know what they want."

Guidelines that political cartoonists were expected to follow were well understood: stick to illustrating the paper's editorial; play up positive aspects; refrain from dealing with the vested interests of the media owner; avoid unflattering caricature; "criticize the system, not the individual; the bureaucracy, not the bureaucrat"; and reflect society, not politics (Miel 1992). Rubbing out these elements left cartoonists with slim pickings; they could hardly be called "political cartoonists" or be kept as part of the vaunted fourth estate. They had become estate-less publicists.

Some cartoonists even wondered if the situation had not reverted to the restrictive Marcos times. Isaac (1992) called cartooning a "balancing act," saying: "It has gotten worse since 1989. Generally, the situation is not worse than Marcos times, but it is on our paper. I could do hard hitting cartoons then. I did not have to read the

editorial for my idea as I have to now. Now we are just illustrators of the editorial." Both Miel of the *Philippine Star* and Jess Abrera, political cartoonist for the *Philippine Daily Inquirer*, said that they also had to match their cartoons' views with those of the newspaper's management (Miel 1992; Allison et al. 1994, 12). Miel elaborated about his plight, complaining that he had not had a pay raise in the seven years he had been at the *Star* and that most issues he was assigned were

not challenging, so we do it as it is. It's like illustrating. You don't get to show what you've got. For example, businessmen will submit stuff that is printed as is in the *Star*, and then, the cartoonist is given the story to illustrate. We are spread out and don't focus on our work anymore. (Miel 1992)

Noel Avendano (1992), also of the *Manila Chronicle* along with Nonoy Marcelo, felt that cartoonists were not recognized as important by the public and especially not by editors. He said that editors "don't understand the situation or think of the stress or deadline we face; they just say, 'draw this.'" His colleague, Marcelo (1992), added: "Here, you can be called at 2 a.m. and be expected to do a cartoon."

Explaining the "thin skin" of newspaper owners, Isaac told of an incident he experienced the day before our 1992 interview. He had drawn a cartoon entitled "David and Goliath," with the newly installed president Fidel

Ramos as David and the "big ugly poverty" of Filipinos as Goliath. His publisher, shipping magnate Emilio Yap, demanded that the cartoon be pulled from the press and that Isaac draw a more positive one. Yap was also known to draw stick figures to guide *Bulletin* cartoonists in following his views. Veteran (since the 1960s) cartoonist Roni Santiago (2009) said that he quit drawing political cartoons for the *Bulletin* when Yap took over and required "tame, public relations political cartoons."

Marcelo (1992) thought that the cartoonist's role had deteriorated because "not many politicians worth hitting" existed; the "whole system was drifting here and there," not giving cartoonists a clear target; newspapers were simply businesses protecting their interests despite the high-sounding principles they shouted; the space in newspapers was not the artist's space but that of the paper's owner; increasingly, cartoons followed the day's editorial; and cartoonists shied from poking fun at top leaders.

Contemporary Perspective

The same continuing problems plagued Filipino political cartoonists in the 2000s, compounded by the global economic downturn and dwindling interest in newspapers with the shift to digitalization. Concerns and challenges political cartoonists faced were discussed at a 2008 workshop I helped organize at the University of Santo Tomas. The *Philippine Star*'s editorial cartoonist, Rene Aranda, said that he was apprehensive about threats he had received, relaying:

> I get paid for ridiculing people and I get threats. I told one person who threatened me over the phone that I was not afraid. He then told me my car license number. That scared me and I didn't drive my car for a while. . . . The newspapers have sacred cows, especially corporate ones. . . . Newspapering is not environment friendly; I foresee the death of print. (Aranda 2008)

Hugo Yonzon III thought that poor payment by newspapers, resulting in the loss of talented cartoonists, was a huge obstacle. He said that most members of Samahang Kartunista ng Pilipinas (the Cartoonists Association of the Philippines) had "day jobs"—seven were architects, others were in advertising, graphic arts, and other trades.

To gauge the Philippine political cartoon scene during a typical week in July 2008, I looked at six standard-sized and twelve tabloid Manila daily newspapers. Some observations:

- Except for two tabloids, all newspapers had an editorial cartoon.
- The space devoted to a cartoon varied from 7" x 8" in the *Manila Standard Today* to 1¾" x 3" in *Remate*.
- All of the cartoons dealt with local issues, except those of the *Manila Bulletin Today*.
- A number of the newspapers used the same topic on a given day.
- The majority of drawings illustrated the dailies' lead editorials.
- The cartoons shied away from the use of caricature and references to specific individuals or entities.
- In cases where several newspapers were owned by the same publisher, editorial cartoons were shared (e.g., the *Manila Bulletin Today* with its sisters *Balita* and *Tempo*; the *People's Journal* with *Taliba* and the *People's Journal Tonight*).
- Almost overwhelmingly, the editorial cartoons were cautious in tone, lacking the aggressiveness of old.
- Most of the works were simply drawn without details, artistic flourishes, or more than one character.

Generally, these points confirmed the views expressed by the cartoonists I interviewed.

The *Manila Bulletin Today* opted to use color drawings to illustrate its lead editorial cartoon, but what it chose for content was not just curious, but laughable as well. The lead cartoon in the sampled week was always celebratory, extending birthday wishes to the Sultan of Brunei, congratulating the head of a scholarly

10.10. *Manila Bulletin* publisher/ship mogul Emilio Yap's safe, but preposterous, concept of a political cartoon. Drawn by Norman Isaac. Courtesy of Norman Isaac.

10.11. Manila traffic, Hugo "Boboy" Yonzon III, 1995. Courtesy of Boboy Yonzon.

group meeting in Manila that week, commending the Philippine National Police for its community activities, celebrating Our Lady of Mount Carmel Feast Day and World Population Day, and praising the Christian apostle Saint Paul. For argument's sake, assume that an editorial cartoon should have a semblance of news value (that is, proximity, timeliness, prominence, consequence, or human interest); under those strictures, what the *Bulletin* produced was probably nothing more

than publisher Emilio Yap's scattered thoughts on whom or what he should curry favor with and what benefits would his many businesses accrue as a result.

Philippine political cartoonists continue to be flattened by the same weights they have long been familiar with: self-censorship and avoidance of offending the interests of media owners. These are closely intertwined. At a 2015 Cartooning for Peace event in Manila, *Philippine Star* cartoonist Rene Aranda bemoaned that as staff

The Philippines

cartoonists, he and some of his colleagues were "held hostage by our employment; so, you censor yourself." He added: "You can't hit sponsors; we can't do anything because they are our lifeblood; you have to tow the line" (Gotinga 2015). Freelance cartoonist Manix Abrera said that editors did not allow attacks on "certain institutions and people because they own the website or newspaper," while Steven Pabalinas of the *Manila Times* said that editors were "afraid of libel suits even if it [the cartoon] is not libelous" (Gotinga 2015).

Political cartoons increasingly abound on websites devoted to news as well as social media such as Facebook. A 2020 study of seventy editorial cartoons posted on Facebook regarding President Rodrigo Duterte's "enhanced community quarantine" during the COVID-19 pandemic found that they "continue to function as an opinion-oriented medium like their print predecessors" (Bantugan 2020). Findings such as this strengthen Marshall McLuhan's proposition that new media are extensions of those that preceded and should be welcomed, as they are in the Philippines and most of Asia.

A Brief Conclusion

What can be concluded about the status of Philippine political cartooning as it heads further into the 2020s? Well, at least there are still some places on Manila dailies for political cartoonists. Barring that, perhaps this answer given by Roni Santiago says it all. When I asked him about the differences between the 1960s, when he began his cartooning career, and 2009, the time of our interview, he simply said: "Not much changed. Only the characters changed. The issues are the same" (Santiago 2009).

Notes

1. A portion of this chapter is an updated, supplemented version of the "Philippine Editorial Cartoon" chapter I wrote for my 2009 book, *The First One Hundred Years of Philippine Komiks and Cartoons.*

2. Other painter/cartoonists have been bestowed this prestigious award, including Carlos "Botong" Francisco and Vincente S. Manansala.

Bibliography

Alcala, Larry. 1988. Interview with John A. Lent, Manila, September 26.

Allison, Tony, et al. 1994. "Figure It Out." *Asia*, January, 7–12.

Aranda, Rene. 2008. Untitled paper presented at the Cartooning and Comic Art: Catching Up in the Digital World workshop, University of Santo Tomas, Manila, July 12.

Avendano, Noel. 1992. Interview with John A. Lent, Manila, July 17.

Bantugan, Brian. 2020 "Public Opinion on the Duterte Administration's COVID-19 Period through Editorial Cartoons on Facebook." *Asian Journal for Public Opinion Research* 8, no. 4: 409–31.

Esteban, Cirilio. 1953. "They Managed to Laugh." *Deadline*, September, 7–8.

Gleeck, Lewis E., Jr. 1984. *General History of the Philippines.* Quezon City, Philippines: Historical Conservation Society.

Gotinga, J. C. 2015. "TV Feature: Iqbal Cartoon Featured in 'Europe Day' Celebration." CNN Philippines, May 11. https://www.cnnphilippines.com/lifestyle/2015/05/11/Iqbal-cartoon-featured-in-europe-day-celebration.html.

Hartendorp, A. V. H. 1964. Interview with John A. Lent, Manila, September 14.

Isaac, Norman B. 1992. Interview with John A. Lent, Manila, July 16.

Kanfer, Stefan. 1988. "Mighty Pens: Worldwide, Cartoonists Draw the Line." *Time*, September 12, 90–95.

Lent, John A. 1970. "Guerrilla Press of the Philippines, 1941–1945." *Asian Studies* 8, no. 2: 260–74.

Lent, John A. 1971. *Philippine Mass Communications: Before 1811, After 1966.* Manila: Philippine Press Institute.

Lent, John A. 2009. *The First One Hundred Years of Philippine Komiks and Cartoons.* Tagaytay City, Philippines: Yonzon Associates.

Marcelo, Nonoy. 1980. "Komiks: The Filipino National Literature?" *Asian Culture* 25 (January): 18–20.

Marcelo, Nonoy. 1988. Interview with John A. Lent, Manila, September 29.

Marcelo, Nonoy. 1992. Interview with John A. Lent, Manila, July 17.

McCoy, Alfred, and Alfredo Roces. 1985. *Philippine Cartoons: Political Caricature of the American Era, 1900–1941.* Quezon City, Philippines: Vera-Reyes.

Miel, Deng Coy. 1992. Interview with John A. Lent, Manila, July 16.

Retana, Wenceslao. 1895. *El Periodismo Filipino*. Madrid: Viuda de M. Minuesa de los Rios.

Roxas, Cynthia, and Joaquin Arevalo Jr. 1985. *A History of Komiks of the Philippines and Other Countries*. Quezon City, Philippines: Islas Filipinas Publishing.

Santiago, Roni. 2009. Interview with John A. Lent, Pasig City, Philippines, October 17.

Taylor, Carson. 1927. *History of the Philippine Press*. Manila: Manila Bulletin Publishing.

Valenzuela, Jesús Z. 1933. *History of Journalism in the Philippine Islands*. Manila: Self-published.

Villarroel, Fidel. 1986. "José Rizal: First Filipino Cartoonist?" *Life Today*, March, 16–17.

Yonzon, Hugo, III. 2008. Interview with John A. Lent, Manila, July 12.

It is tempting to join the chorus and declare that political cartoons do not exist in Singapore, nor does the freedom to cartoon, and leave it at that. Such a statement would likely elicit affirmative nods from compilers of press freedom indices and from cartoonists, even those in Singapore.

But such a hasty conclusion hurdles many important points, chief of which are that Singapore has had a long history of politically charged drawings dating to some of its earliest newspapers, and that the authoritarian governments of Lee Kuan Yew and his son, Lee Hsien Loong, pioneered a form of cartooning that since has swept much of Asia, what I call "guided cartooning." Under guided cartooning, the cartoonist is very aware of the red lines not to be crossed and the consequences if crossed, and strictly follows the guidance of the editor, who sometimes assigns the topics and stances, and screens the cartoons prepublication. The result: self-censorship with elements of pre-censorship carrying another name. A similar term, "oriented press" (or "cartoon"), goes back to 1938, under Francisco Franco's fascist regime in Spain (see a fuller discussion of "guided cartooning" in chapter 14 on Bangladesh).

Historical Overview

The first known cartoons in a Chinese newspaper in Singapore were used to take a side in the struggle between the revolutionary and reformist camps to change China. The organ of Dr. Sun Yat-sen's Tong Meng Hui (Chinese Revolutionary Alliance), *Chong Shing Yit Pao*, published a cartoon on its literary page, "Fei Fei," within three weeks after the paper's founding in 1907 (Chen 1967, 98–99). Lim Cheng Tju (2007, 183–84) found in his research that the paper published a total of forty-one cartoons between September 9, 1907, and March 21, 1908, when they ceased, possibly because of a change of editors, a lack of drawing talent, or threats from the ruling British authorities to charge the editors with seditious agitation against the Chinese monarchy. All but two of the cartoons were unsigned to avoid Qing

Chapter 11

Singapore

11.1. "Drawing His Claws," Liu Kang, 1946. A Japanese soldier torturously pulling out a prisoner's fingernails.

Dynasty persecution. The two signed cartoons were by Ma Xing-chi, who reportedly developed a drawing style that pieced together different Chinese characters to create hidden meanings (Lim Cheng Tju 2007, 184). Content was more important than form or style in these cartoons, which were often crudely drawn and "hardly funny"; all were anti–Qing Dynasty, related to political happenings in China, and "tools for agitation" (Lim Cheng Tju 2007, 186).

Other newspapers, such as the reformist *Union Times* and the conservative *Lat Pao*, followed *Chong Shing Yit Pao*'s lead, but without much enthusiasm. For example, the *Union Times* had published for nearly three years before it used its first cartoon, a foreign reprint, on July 29, 1909. Although *Chong Shing Yit Pao* and the *Union Times* fought a "battle of the pen" on their respective literary pages with "short comments, short stories, dramatic dialogues, Cantonese ballads, poetry and humor" (Chen 1967, 102), *Chong Shing Yit Pao*'s cartoon volleys on its "Fei Fei" page went unchallenged on the *Union Times* literary page. The cartoons in the next four or five Chinese newspapers were irregular in frequency, and often were reprinted from newspapers in China and Great Britain. Lim (2007, 188) attributed these shortcomings to a lack of cartooning talent in Singapore. When the Qing Dynasty was overthrown in 1911, cartoons in Singaporean Chinese newspapers continued to focus on happenings in China, rather than those in their resident country. For example, the first cartoon (May 20, 1914) in *Kuo Min Yit Poh*, the voice of the Singapore Guomindang Party, attacked Qing general Yuan Shi-kai, who hoped to revive dynasty rule in China with himself as emperor.

In the 1930s, Chinese intellectual Lu Xun's model that cartoons and woodcuts were artistic bedfellows, equally important in changing society, was brought to Singapore by Dai Yunlang, who had been studying at the Shanghai Art Academy. In Singapore, Dai was very active writing articles on culture and contributing cartoons to the *Nanyang Hong Weekly*. In May 1936, he started a Sunday art supplement for the leading Chinese daily *Nanyang Siang Pao*. Named *Wenman Gie* (World of Culture and Cartoons),[1] the supplement in its seven-month existence introduced China's creative woodblock movement to Singapore, and with it, a progressive intellectual and aesthetic discourse on the "roles that these two art forms could play in the social development of Nanyang" (Lim Cheng Tju 2004b, 267; also Lim Cheng Tju 2001). Besides Dai, the Nanyang Academy of Fine Arts in the late 1930s and 1940s also encouraged the study of woodcuts, and a number of its graduates built the radical reputation of woodblock print art in 1950s Singapore, a time when a "very strong sense of socialist euphoria" was brewing in the colony (Lim Cheng Tju

2004b, 272–73). As Lim pointed out, woodblock drawings are conducive to "social satire and the subversion of establishment views," and with cartoons were used by the very left-leaning People's Action Party (PAP), led by Lee Kuan Yew, in its goal to achieve independence (2004b, 274).

About the same time in the 1930s that Dai was strongly advocating the interconnectedness of woodcuts and cartoons for political consciousness-raising purposes, Singaporean cartoonists were rallying in support of China against the Japanese threat. Dai himself drew cartoons about Japanese imperialism, with allusions to British imperialism in Singapore (Lim Cheng Tju 2004a, 417). During the war with Japan, a number of artists and cartoonists were killed by the Japanese, and those who survived quit drawing from 1942 to 1945. One surviving artist, Liu Kang, documented the wartime Japanese actions that he and others experienced in a book of cartoons he drew, *Chop Suey*, published in 1946. These were the only cartoons he ever drew in his distinguished art career; he told Lim Cheng Tju that he chose cartoons because they were the "most direct and popular form of expression and medium" (quoted in Lim Cheng Tju 2004b, 419). *Chop Suey* has been reprinted multiple times and has been used in recent years by Singaporean state agencies to serve political and educational needs.

Chop Suey epitomized the postwar shift from cartoons about China to those emphasizing local issues, especially colonialism and the drive to independence. Other local societal and political upheavals that made it to the cartoonists' sketchpads were the economic recession, attacks on Chinese schools, the Malayan Emergency against communism, and social injustices and cruelties. Cartoonists emphasized values and morals, believing that cartoons had the capability to bring about social change. In 1953, high school teacher Qiu Gao Peng incorporated that mission in the weekly comic strip *Mr. Nonsense* he drew for *Nanyang Siang Pao*. The strip brought sensitive issues to the surface, sometimes in a brutal manner. *Mr. Nonsense* disappeared in 1955, when the strip depicted Singaporean politicians as pigs and as Adolf Hitler (Lim Cheng Tju 2014). Nevertheless, cartoons were an important vehicle in the drive to independence and the building of a new nation.

Political Cartoons and Heavy Guidance

Matters changed significantly in the ensuing years. Social realism gave way to modern abstract art, the socialist-leaning PAP and Lee Kuan Yew became more authoritarian, journalism including cartooning abandoned its revolutionary fervor and social change mission, and cartoonists began to steer clear of local issues. The main English-language daily, the *Straits Times*, dropped political cartoons in 1961. When they were resumed on an irregular basis in February 1979, they reflected on, rather than commented or opined about the day's issues. Cartoonists for both the English- and Chinese-language newspapers distanced themselves from local topics. The fate of cartooning in Singapore as previously known was sealed with Lee Kuan Yew's infamous purge of the Singaporean press in 1971, when publishers and editors were arrested and newspapers closed (Lent 1975). Thenceforth, the creed of Singaporean cartoonists has been to avoid local political issues and politicians, serve nation building as laid out by the powers that be, take guidance from the editors, and use self-restraint.

This mentality was much evident when I interviewed Singaporean cartoonists in 1992. *Lian He Zao Pao* cartoonist Heng Kim Song said that the bane of political cartooning was the tough government policies and self-censoring editors of the five dailies, all of them under the government fold. "Editors don't encourage local topics and the PAP government doesn't like anything it can't control," he said. Editors tell cartoonists what not to portray and that there is no need to criticize the government, because it rules well. The result, Heng said, was that the "cartoon scene is a cultural desert and cartoonists are lapdogs" (Heng 1992). Architect-cum-cartoonist Ken Lou said, "Almost anything imaginable can be banned," even the national airline and businesspeople who might be friends of government officials. Claiming

11.2. "The Next Lap," Heng Kim Song. Lee Kuan Yew handing over his title. Permission of Heng Kim Song.

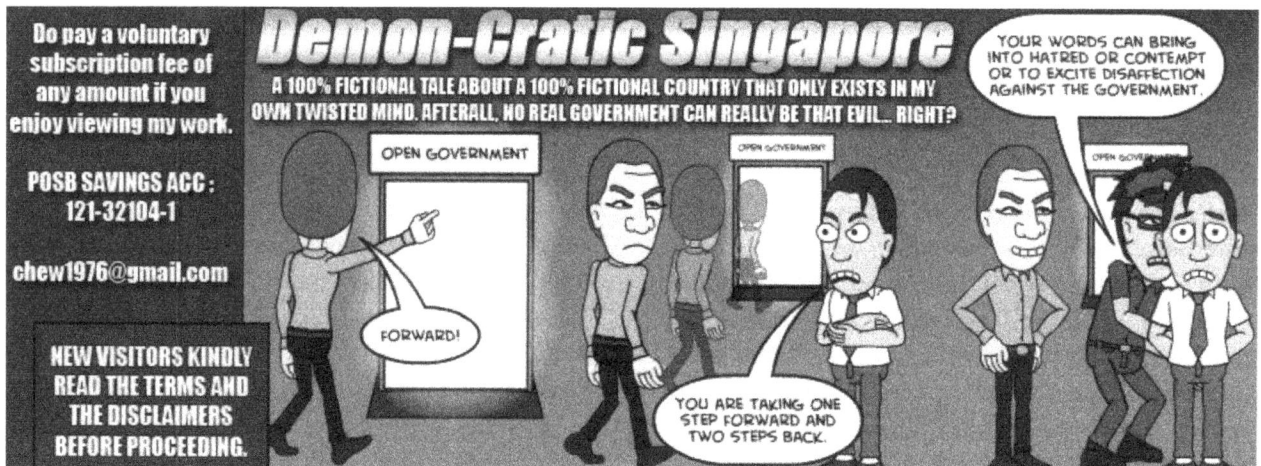

11.3. *Demon-cratic Singapore*, Leslie Chew.

there were many things to satirize, Lou said that editors did not tolerate mockery (Lou 1992). Cartoonists steered clear of caricatures and sensitive topics for fear of being blacklisted and for economic reasons. Most cartoonists were paid only if their cartoons were published, and seeing that two out of three submitted works were rejected, the situation put an oppressive burden on them (Heng 1992). In 1992, newspaper editors kept close check on their top staff, requiring daily morning and afternoon meetings, meant to tighten control, according to *Straits Times* political cartoonist José Ruiz (1992). *Straits Times* cartoonist Cheah Sin Ann (1992) described the meetings: in the morning, editors in a "monologue tell how it should have been done the day before; in the afternoon, they decide the next day's contents." Even cartoons

on international topics were vetted very carefully. The *Straits Times* used only syndicated cartoons on international issues, and they were "amusing, not hard-hitting," Heng (1992) said. Ruiz (1992) summed it all up: "Everything had to be nonconfrontational, from the editorials, to the fillers."

Lim Cheng Tju later placed the blame for this persistent type of thinking on "the middle level stagnation of narrow-minded bureaucrats and 'play safe' editors and publishers, with their over-zealous attitude of not rocking the boat, that limits the kind of material and potential possible for political cartoons" (2000b, 78–80). He went on to say that traditional definitions of political cartoons do not apply in Singapore, that political cartoons do exist in the country, but with different confines (the nonuse of caricatures) and purposes (serving development journalism).[2] Lim further explained: "They serve a consensus-shaping function in the political process that has evolved out of the negotiation between the needs of a new nation, requiring its mass media (in this case, political cartoons) to act as agents of social cohesion, and the political space, needed by political cartoonists to do their jobs creatively" (2000b, 80). This function fits snugly as an add-on in what I term "guided cartooning."

Singaporean authorities do not hesitate to take punitive actions against cartoonists they consider going against the grain. Two recent situations come to mind. In April 2013, Leslie Chew (Chew Pen Ee) was arrested for sedition over a cartoon he drew for his online satiric strip, *Demon-cratic Singapore*, started in 2011. The strip, with the subtitle "Evils Runs Foul in This 'Democratic' Country" and published almost daily on Facebook with about forty thousand followers, mocked a fictitious country, although "Singapore" originally was the title and the events satirized were Singaporean. The "subtlety" was rather transparent, blatant, and even taunting, as the strip made fun of "Emperor Lee," "Woody Goh," "Pink Loong," and "Marlboro Tan," all top leaders, and used double-entendre disclaimers such as "no (decent) politician had been harmed" and "any person claiming any resemblance is definitely insane and ought to be shot on sight for public safety." The cartoon for which Chew was charged dealt with the Malay population of Singapore. Chew was detained for forty-six hours, his residence raided, his passport impounded, and his computers and phones confiscated; he was required to post bond and report for bail renewal for three months. The sedition charge was dropped in July 2013, after which he was charged with contempt of court for four other cartoons. A month later, the attorney general's office agreed not to pursue the contempt proceedings if Chew removed the strips in question and posted an apology, which he did (Chun 2013; Jeanette Tan 2013).

In the second case, that of Sonny Liew, in 2015 the governmental National Arts Council (NAC) withdrew

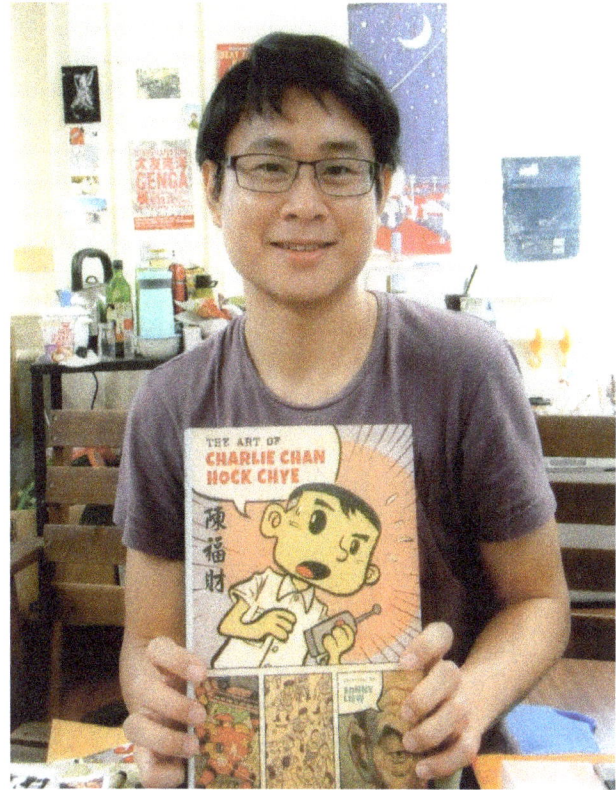

11.4. Sonny Liew in his Singapore studio with his award-winning book, December 1, 2016. Photo by John A. Lent. Permission of Sonny Liew.

a US$5,900 grant it had awarded Liew for his book *The Art of Charlie Chan Hock Chye* because it portrayed the nation's history from a different perspective than the official account; the book included roles played by Lee Kuan Yew's rivals, particularly left-wing trade union leader Lim Chin Siong. At that time, an official said that the book "potentially undermines the authority and legitimacy of the government and its public institutions"; but it was not banned (Cameron-Moore 2017). The NAC explained that they could not support the book, but they could support Liew by subsidizing his studio space (Liew 2016). When *The Art of Charlie Chan Hock Chye* won three prestigious Eisner awards in 2017, the NAC congratulated Liew. Liew ensured that his alternate story of Singapore was accurate, inclusive ("rather than championing a competing version"), and subtle (Johnson 2017, A4). Perhaps because of his international fame, Liew feels comfortable mocking specific politicians, normally an out-of-bounds subject in Singapore (McDougall 2020).

A. J. McDougall sums up very well the options a Singaporean political cartoonist has:

11.5. "Puppet Master," Morgan Chua, 1988. Lee Kuan Yew assesses his successor. Courtesy of Morgan Chua via Lim Cheng Tju.

You can leave Singapore, like Morgan Chua did when the government yanked the *Singapore Herald*'s publishing license in 1971 (due to Chua's pointed caricatures and illustrated criticism, legend says). You can hit the brakes on political criticism, and turn to light-hearted gag cartoons, like Tan Huay and Sam Liew did at the *Straits Times* in the 1950s and 1980s, respectively. You can continue to draw stinging political content, but focus your lens on every country except Singapore, as Heng Kim Song does for *Lianhe Zaobao*. You can riff off the subjects your editors give you to draw about, like Dengcoy Miel told C. T. Lim he does at the *Straits Times*. Or you can bypass the papers entirely and use Instagram and Facebook as a platform for your art. (McDougall 2020)

The Alternative Social Media

About the time that Leslie Chew ran afoul of the government because of his *Demon-cratic Singapore* online comics, the country's media regulators imposed new rules on ten Yahoo Singapore news sites and two domestic media companies, to ensure responsible news reporting but not to deter web freedoms, according to the minister of communications and information. Then, in 2015, the government's Media Development Authority, recognizing the growth of critical news websites, authorized what freelance online cartoonist Dan Wong

called a "very blatant [attempt] to put a collar on some people" (2016). The MDA required the posting of a US$50,000 performance bond to obtain a news website. Wong, who draws all of the cartoons for the Mothership website, for which he is paid, said that previously, "private investors" paid the site's fees before it turned to advertising sales for support. Other cartoonists agreed that some websites are sponsored, though anonymously, thus making it difficult to trace them. Cheah Sin Ann (2016) wondered where website funds emanated from, tossing out possible sponsors as "banks, opposition parties and even George Soros." He thought the sites were "elusive because if one is shut down by government, the sponsors will start another, and some are not even based in Singapore" (Cheah 2016). Illustrator-cartoonist James Tan (2016) mentioned a few news-oriented websites that are patron funded; the patrons are given an original cartoon in exchange for a few dollars' monthly donation. Facebook is also a place where social and political cartoons are posted. Wong's Facebook page, "A Good Citizen," attracted more than one hundred thousand views of a cartoon he drew depicting China acting as a child. He said that some social media sites lean far to the left or right, but his is "not anti-leftist nor anti-rightist, but anti-stupidity" (Wong 2016). Wong's take on current affairs has been labeled "irreverent," "occasionally gory," and "rebellious" (Lim Min Zhang 2018). Web/print designer-cartoonist Don Low uses Facebook for his cartoons when he has "something to say about a Singapore

11.6. "Space Not Enough," Don Low, October 2016. On the scarce living space in Singapore. Permission of Don Low.

issue," adding that his intent is "not to stir up people but rather to reflect on an issue." He admitted, "It's a tricky business to strike a balance. Cartoonists don't want to be direct on Singapore issues, but some cartoonists try to be more provocative to get attention. Not me" (Low 2016). Heng Kim Song looked at online political cartoons in a different light, stating that they "are drawn by amateurs with basic drawing skills to vent their frustration, and they are very bitter" (Heng 2016).

Although a few cartoonists thought that the authorities were rather slack in their monitoring of social media cartooning, officials as high as Prime Minister Lee Hsien Loong had voiced objections and taken action. In 2012, Lee ordered that a blogsite be removed and for the blogger to apologize for, among other things, questioning the sentencing of a man for a traffic offense. Earlier, in 2006, Lee lambasted the blogsite "mrbrown," complaining that the site's column had "hit out wildly at the government and in a mocking and dismissive sort of tone" (Alexander 2013).

Recent popular sites have been Choo Zheng Xi's "The Online Citizen," Alex Au's "Yawning Bread," Roy Ngerng's "The Heart Truths," Martin See Tong Ming's "Singapore Rebel," Gopalan Nair's "Singapore Dissident," "TR Emeritus," "Public House," "The Real Singapore,"

and Guay Chong Kian's "Semi Serious." These online artists probably have the same concern as Guay, of crossing the murky out-of-bounds markers (McDougall 2020). Cyberspace opened a place not only for alternative news perspectives but also for political satire (such as *Demoncratic Singapore*), readers' comments, and mainstream press criticism. For example, the "Real Singapore" website allowed anonymous user postings to overcome people's fear of criticizing the government, and "Sintercom's 'Not the *Straits Times*'" used to publish letters rejected by the *Straits Times* (Alexander 2013).

The government took action against social media by establishing the Protection from Online Falsehoods and Manipulation Act (POFMA) in October 2019. POFMA grants every member of the government the right to "correct, delete, or block access to any online content in order to prevent a diminution of confidence in the government" (Reporters without Borders 2020). In a review of the city-state's deteriorating press freedom performance, a Reporters without Borders official cited numerous government actions that hurt the media and, in turn, cartooning. Among them:

[The governing] People's Action Party has passed legislation that allows the government to oversee the appointment of those who run the leading media outlets, including their editors and the members of their boards of governors.

Under several laws, including the sedition law and criminal code articles, publishing information that for example, "promotes feelings of ill-will and hostility" within the population is punishable by imprisonment. The wordings of these laws gives judges considerable leeway and, as a result, fosters a great deal of self-censorship within the news media. (Reporters without Borders 2020)

The report states that the government rarely has to threaten or bring action against the media or journalists, because print, broadcast, and online outfits are either part of the Media Corp Group, owned by a state investment company, or Singapore Press Holdings, whose officials are government appointees (Reporters without Borders 2020).

Cartoonists' Views of Contemporary Political Cartoons

Two of the three individuals I interviewed both in 1991 and nearly a quarter of a century later in 2016 felt that there had been no improvement concerning the "freedom to cartoon," and the third described the current scene as "financially hard times for Singapore cartoonists" (Cheah 2016). Veteran political cartoonist Heng Kim Song situated Singaporean political cartooning in a "sad state," primarily because the profession is closely aligned to the mass media, which are closely scrutinized. He said that censorship of theater and film had been relaxed, because their audiences are more elitist or more infrequent (Heng 2016).

Not much of what cartoonists voiced in 2016 was encouraging enough to entice new entrants into the field. Besides being strapped in by what they are able to get through the screening process and have published, they also face challenges making a living from cartooning alone. Heng chooses to be a freelance cartoonist even though offered a contract, because he does not want to be under an editor's thumb and denied the

11.7. Philippines-born Deng Coy Miel, Singapore, November 26, 2016. Photo by John A. Lent. Permission of Deng Coy Miel.

opportunity to draw for other newspapers (Heng 2016). Others who are under contract with the monopoly-leaning Singapore Press Holdings (SPH) (with a total of eight newspapers in Chinese, English, Malay, and Tamil) are more like illustrators than cartoonists. It is difficult to fathom the rationale for the large art staffs that were retained at one time by the *Straits Times* and the *Sunday Times* (fifteen people, six of whom were cartoonists/ illustrators) or the *New Paper* (eight artists), when these newspapers are nearly devoid of political cartoons and local comic strips. Cheah Sin Ann, who earlier supervised the *Straits Times* art staff, attempted an explanation, saying that the artists also illustrated articles and were expected to be multitasked, fitting an "Asian mentality" that allowed publishers to "milk" cartoonists dry. For example, *New Paper* artists did charts, logos, graphics, and maps in addition to cartoons. Cheah said that it was necessary to have artists on duty twenty-four hours a day, because a cartoon must be vetted by a number of editors, each editor having the right to call for changes (Cheah 2000).

Deng Coy Miel, longtime staff member at the *Straits Times* and previously a political cartoonist in the Philippines, straight-out said, "We call ourselves illustrators, not cartoonists. Our function is to do illustrations, not political cartoons" (Miel 2016). Lim Cheng Tju agreed that most of newspapers' visual material is made up of illustrations, even what are classified as political cartoons are merely illustrations, missing caricature, a stance, or a viewpoint. Stating that not putting caricature in political cartoons is like "swimming with one hand," Lim thought that veteran cartoonists such as Dan Wong, James Tan, and Don Low do not even consider doing caricature; they do not think of themselves as political cartoonists, because they grew up in an era when there was an absence of political cartoons in Singapore (Lim Cheng Tju 2016b).

Both Tan (2016) and Lim (2016a, 2016b) equated political cartooning with anger, saying that that trait is missing in Singapore. Lim justified the absence of anger as he had done on other occasions: "Things are going well in Singapore, and cartoonists feel good about the status quo. Our cartoonists are not angry. Things are okay in Singapore society. If you wake up happy, you are not aware something is wrong" (Lim Cheng Tju 2016b). Perhaps some cartoonists release their frustration and anger in cartoons they do for the press in more tolerant countries. That is what Miel and Manny Francisco do. Miel and Francisco hail from the Philippines, as do a number of cartoonists and illustrators resident in Singapore since the late 1980s. Both send what Miel called their "attack cartoons" out of the country, mostly to Manila dailies. Heng's works had a steady run in the *New York Times* until the paper stopped using political cartoons in 2019.

The influx of established political cartoonists had a single purpose, "to keep the rice bowl intact," as Miel described it; these artists were forced or enticed to trade more freedom for more money. A third Philippines-born political cartoonist, Ludwig Ilio,[3] who had drawn for five Manila dailies before joining the *Straits Times* and then the *Business Times*, said that cartoonists came to Singapore "to make money, not political statements." Once in Singapore, he felt that they "became as 'neutral' as the newspapers for which they draw, just following the newspaper editors' advice" (Ilio 2016). Miel (2016) added, "For us foreigners, the *Straits Times* thinking is, adjust or go home." He thought that Philippine cartoonists were appealing to Singapore newspapers, because

they possessed English-language skills as well as a good sense of the visual familiar to Singaporeans (Miel 2016).

Ilio, Miel, and Francisco expanded on their getting used to the restrictive nature of Singapore cartooning. Ilio (2016) said that because nothing controversial is reported in the newspapers, there is nothing to attack, and if nothing is attacked, censorship is not necessary, while Miel said that although many topics are out of bounds, the term itself is vaguely spelled out. To learn what is not permitted, "you try to do something, and management says you cannot, and then, you fence yourself in," he explained (Miel 2016). Francisco found that what editors suggest and what they will permit to be confusing and contradictory. He said, "The *Straits Times* has tried to prevent us from making statements, even in illustrations. The paper is very cautious, conscious of how some readers will react. Yet, editors tell us to try something different, and when we do, they say, 'Well, I'm not sure . . . uh, we cannot do that'" (Francisco 2016).

As their colleagues everywhere, Singapore cartoonists want to be published and to earn a living; rejections hamper those needs and are to be avoided. To ensure that their work is published, cartoonists must "learn what editors want and don't want" and be guided by that formula, according to Heng (2016).

Overall, the future of Singapore print political cartooning looked bleak in the eyes of the cartoonists. Explanations for the jaundiced views they voiced are well known worldwide: audiences diverted by new media, drops in newspaper circulations and the number of newspapers, and severe infringements on the "right to cartoon." Francisco, with agreement from Miel, said that young artists' career aspirations now revolve principally around advertising, graphic design, and manga, areas that are more financially lucrative. Francisco thought that emerging artists had more options to make money and had no desire to work a job that is treated as a "labor of love." He went on to say, "Why did we get into cartooning? We wanted to change the world, provoke thought, be heard, and to have hundreds of people to share ideas with. We wanted to shake up the world. That passion is not there with newcomers" (Francisco 2016).

From Francisco's statement, an obvious question is: if artists did possess a "shaking-things-up" desire, where in Singapore could they safely fulfill that goal?

A Brief Conclusion

Gauging the overall political cartooning situation, journalist and comics historian Cherian George certainly kept the government squarely in the driver's seat without taking highly visible actions. As he said: "I suspect Singapore's authorities have hit a sweet spot where it's repressive enough to discourage critical work, but also rewarding enough such that people feel they have too much to lose and are therefore unwilling to take even small risks" (quoted in McDougall 2020).

Notes

1. Dai Yunlong also edited the *Nanyang Siang Pao* supplement, *Jinri Yishu* (Today's Art).

2. That is probably what *Straits Times* cartoonist José Ruiz meant when he told me in 1992, "I believe political cartooning in Singapore had no future; maybe no past."

3. When I interviewed Ilio, he had recently been dismissed by SPH after twenty years of service, and he and his family were returning to the Philippines the next day, jobless, to live on a small Philippine social security stipend (Ilio 2016). In the same interview session, Cheah Sin Ann said that SPH had also laid him off earlier, giving the reason "that they had bought a TV station, and it was not making money." Incredulously, Cheah said, "I did nothing to cause the TV station to lose money" (2016).

Bibliography

Alexander, Marlon. 2013. "Shaking Off the Fear of State Censorship in Singapore: Youth Hold Out Hope." IFEX, September 25. https://www.ifex.org/singapore/2013/09/25/state_censorship.

Cameron-Moore, Simon. 2017. "After Disapproval, Award-Winning Singapore Cartoonist Gets Official Congrats." Reuters, July 24. https://www.reuters.com/article/us-singapore-cartoonist-idUSKBN1A91JT.

Cheah, Sin Ann. 1992. Interview with John A. Lent, Singapore, July 23.

Cheah, Sin Ann. 2000. Interview with John A. Lent, Singapore, July 18.

Cheah, Sin Ann. 2016. Interview with John A. Lent, Singapore, November 25.

Chen, Mong Hock. 1967. *The Early Chinese Newspapers of Singapore, 1881–1912*. Singapore: University of Malaya Press.

Chun, Han Wong. 2013. "Singapore Won't Charge Cartoonists for Alleged Racial Insensitivity." Southeast Asia Real Time blog, July 29. https://blogs.wsj.com/searealtime/2013/07/29/singapore-wont-charge-cartoonist-for-alleged-racial-insensitivity/.

Francisco, Manny. 2016. Interview with John A. Lent, Singapore, November 26.

Heng, Kim Song. 1992. Interview with John A. Lent, Singapore, July 22.

Heng, Kim Song. 2016. Interview with John A. Lent, Singapore, November 30.

Ilio, Ludwig. 2016. Interview with John A. Lent, Singapore, November 25.

Johnson, Ian. 2017. "An Alternate History of Singapore, Told through a Comic Book." *New York Times*, July 15, A4.

Lent, John A. 1975. "Lee Kuan Yew and the Singapore Media: 'Protecting the People.'" *Index on Censorship* 4, no. 3 (Autumn): 7–16.

Liew, Sonny. 2016. Interview with John A. Lent, Singapore, December 1.

Lim, Cheng Tju. 1992. Interview with John A. Lent, Singapore, July 24.

Lim, Cheng Tju. 2000a. Interview with John A. Lent, Singapore, July 17.

Lim, Cheng Tju. 2000b. "Political Cartoons in Singapore: Misnomer or Redefinition Necessary?" *Journal of Popular Culture* 34, no. 1 (Summer): 77–83.

Lim, Cheng Tju. 2001. "'Sister Art': A Short History of Chinese Cartoons and Woodcuts in Singapore." *International Journal of Comic Art* 3, no. 1 (Spring): 59–76.

Lim, Cheng Tju. 2004a. "Chop Suey: Cartoons about the Japanese Occupation and National Education in Singapore." *International Journal of Comic Art* 6, no. 2 (Fall): 415–30.

Lim, Cheng Tju. 2004b. "Political Prints in Singapore." *Print Quarterly* 21, no. 3 (September): 266–81.

Lim, Cheng Tju. 2007. "Tong Meng Hui, Visual Self-Representations of the Chinese and the Birth of Chinese Cartoons in Early Twentieth Century Singapore." *Tangent* 6, no. 2: 180–94.

Lim, Cheng Tju. 2014. "Chinese Cartoonists in Singapore: Chauvinism, Confrontation and Compromise (1950–1980)." In *Southeast Asian Cartoon Art: History, Trends and Problems*, edited by John A. Lent, 142–77. Jefferson, NC: McFarland.

Lim, Cheng Tju. 2016a. Interview with John A. Lent, Shah Alam, Malaysia, October 9.

Lim, Cheng Tju. 2016b. Interview with John A. Lent, Singapore, December 3.

Lim, Min Zhang. 2018. "Comics Struggle to Find Space in Singapore." *New Paper*, August 6. https://tnp.straitstimes.com/news/singapore/comics-struggle-find-space-singapore.

Lou, Ken. 1992. Interview with John A. Lent, Singapore, July 23.

Low, Don. 2016. Interview with John A. Lent, Singapore, December 2.

McDougall, A. J. 2020. "Drawing the Line on Political Cartooning in Singapore." Coconuts Singapore, August 24. https://coconuts.co/singapore/features/drawing-the-line-on-political-cartooning-in-singapore/.

Miel, Deng Coy. 2016. Interview with John A. Lent, Singapore, November 26.

Reporters without Borders. 2020. "RSF's [*sic*] Denounces Singapore's Disregard of Press Freedom ahead of Its Universal Periodic Review." October 15. https://rsf.org/en/rsfs-denounces-singapores-disregard-press-freedom-ahead-its-universal-periodic-review.

Ruiz, José. 1992. Interview with John A. Lent, Singapore, July 23.

Tan, James. 2016. Interview with John A. Lent, Singapore, December 2.

Tan, Jeanette. 2013. "Singapore Drops Sedition Charges against Political Cartoonist Leslie Chew." Yahoo! Singapore News, July 29. https://sg.news.yahoo.com/singapore-drops-sedition-charges-against-political-cartoonist-leslie-chew-110257515.html.

Wong, Dan. 2016. Interview with John A. Lent, Singapore, November 30.

As with Indonesia, the Philippines, and Vietnam, Thailand credits an influential national leader as one of its earliest cartoonists. H. M. King Rama VI (ruled 1910–1925) drew satirical caricatures to embarrass corrupt officials that were published in the royal newspapers *Dusit Samit*, *Dusit Samai*, and *Dusit Sakkee*. The king made sure that his targets were easily identified, for example, drawing the director of royal railroads astride a locomotive (Lent 2015, 226, fig. 12.1; also Warat 2014; Sitthiporn and Chanansiri 2000). His interest in cartooning was not isolated just to exposing corrupt officials; he also coined the term *phap lo* (parodic image) to describe his drawings (Chulasak 1997, 6) and sponsored a couple of drawing competitions that included *phap lo*.

Pioneering Cartoonists

Rama VI was not the first cartoonist; that honor belongs to an unidentified artist who drew a cartoon that revolved around a riddle in the form of a poem. It was published in the magazine *Samran Wittaya* (Enjoyable Knowledge) in 1907. Apparently ignoring Rama VI's satirical drawings, which likely appeared before 1925, Karnjariya Sukrung (2000) claims that the cartoon of a European-educated artist, Pleng Tri-Pin, was the first; it appeared in the newspaper *Krungthep Daily Mail* in 1923. There was a royal connection in that Pleng had won a crown-endorsed competition. He was followed by a string of political cartoonists in the 1930s, such as Than Utthakanon (pen name, Thanya), known for his aggressive and penetrating caricature, and Chalerm Wuttikosit (Chalermwut), who, with Changchan Chankana (pen name Pranboon), did cartoons for the *Monday Morning Mail* (Gesmankit and Gesmankit 1980, 21). There were other pioneers more closely identified with comic strips, such as Sawas Jutharop, Chan Suwanakul, and Wit Suthisathien.

The late 1930s ushered in the career of Ramon Magsaysay Award winner Prayoon Chanyawongs, who

Chapter 12

Thailand

12.1. Cartoon by Pleng Tri-Pin, *Krungthep Daily Mail*. Courtesy of Warat Karuchit.

12.2. Prayoon Chanyawongs's verse editorial column, "Kabuan Karn Gae Jon." Courtesy of Warat Karuchit.

loomed large on the cartooning scene for years. Prayoon was a defiant protector of the "right to cartoon" and an ingenious innovator of unique cartoon forms. He began his career in 1938 when his works appeared sporadically in *Suphabboorut Weekly* and *Pachamit Weekly*. He received considerable notoriety for the long story folklore series *Chantha Korope* (Prince Korope), in which he used an indigenous genre, *cartoon likay. Likay* is a type of theater unique to Thailand, identified by its improvisation and sudden shifts in plots and characters. Prayoon, as did Sa-Ngob Jampat before him, adapted it to his story cartoons, making his readers part of the fictional audience (Verstappen 2017, 32–41). He used the character Sooklek (happy, good fellow) both in his cartoon *likay* strips and in his political cartoons to address political and social issues, especially poverty, corruption, and officials' abuse of power. Prayoon was a thorn in the

side of the government mostly because of his inventive mind, which came up with strategies to counter government censorship. When Field Marshal Thanom Kittikachorn's government censored him in 1968, Prayoon sewed his character Sooklek's mouth shut; after another warning, he abandoned the sewn lips and hid Sooklek's mouth behind a thick mustache until the end of Thanom's rule.

To have a respite from overt political cartoons, Prayoon created the verse editorial cartoon. The verse editorial was a montage of drawings within one large panel, which campaigned or instructed in verse on subjects such as plants, gardening, nutrition, and cooking. Verse editorials differed from conventional cartoons because of their poetic elements and the mixture of numerous drawings inside one frame, as well as their sometimes risqué nature (Lent 1997, 93).

12.3. Rated the top political cartoonist, Chai Rachawat, Bangkok, July 11, 2014. Photo by John A. Lent. Courtesy of Chai Rachawat.

Political Upheaval, the Mother of Scrappy Cartoons

Political turmoil often flushes out dormant cartoonists and stimulates others to take up the pen to do battle. The number of such ink warriors is exhaustive, a few of whom include painter Jacques-Louis David, who shined during the French Revolution; Thomas Nast, who battled New York City's corrupt political team; David Low, who became Hitler's bitter foe; and Liao Bingxiong and other Chinese cartoonists who did not let up on the Japanese invaders of the 1930s and 1940s.

In Thailand, a catharsis for lively political cartooning occurred in the early 1970s, achieved chiefly during and after the bloody May 17–19, 1972, disturbances that culminated in the people's victory over the government in the October 1973 demonstrations. It was then when some cartoonists took bold stands (Tansubhapol 1994, 1), new newspapers came onto the scene, and soon after, all dailies saw a need for at least one political cartoonist. This transformation of the press and political cartooning benefited greatly from the general liberalization of art and expression. Arun (1993) said that political cartoons

were everywhere, and a whole new generation of cartoonists became fixtures in Bangkok dailies then and throughout the 1970s, for example Chai (Chai Rachawat) of *Thai Rath*; Arun (Arun Watcharasawat) of *Nation's Review* and the *Bangkok Post*; Virachon, *Daily News*; Add (Annop Kitichaiwan), *Siang Puangshon Daily*; A-Ngoon, *Matichon Daily*; Muen (Chuchart Mueningul), *Prachachart Weekly* and *Matichon Daily*; and Yoot (Yoottachai Kaewdee), the *Bangkok Post*.

Chai Rachawat's Long, Eventful Career

Of those drawing cartoons at the time of the 1972–1973 domestic uprisings (e.g., Chai, Arun, Nop, et al.), Chai staged the most dramatic reaction. Chai quit drawing for a week, because of possible retribution to himself and *Thai Rath* and as a tribute to the hundreds of prodemocracy demonstrators killed or injured. He emphasized his point by vowing not to resume his popular strip *Poo Yai Ma Kap Tung Ma Muen*[1] until the government's dictatorial powers were replaced, and, in his last sequence before shutting down the strip, he depicted its once lively village turned into a wasteland. Chai's views were that if he could not say what he wanted, he would be silent, and that he censored himself so that his newspaper would not be closed (Chanjaroen 1992, C1). Chai already experienced the closure of the prodemocracy magazine *Maharahd* (Great People), for which he had drawn.

Chai's antigovernment cartoons in the *Daily News* (which he joined in 1973) earned him a place on the government's blacklist; he was accused of harboring communist sympathies. Fearing for his safety, he fled to Los Angeles, where he worked as a bartender, dining room busboy, studio darkroom worker, and cartoonist for a local Thai-language newspaper. Upon his return to Bangkok in 1973, Chai rejoined the *Daily News* but, three months later, switched to *Thai Rath* (Chai 1993; also Lent 1996).

At *Thai Rath*, he drew his political strip daily and a summary cartoon for the Sunday edition.[2] By the time of our first interview in 1993, he also drew business and political cartoons for two weeklies, another strip

12.4. Once lively fictional village of Chai's comic strip turned into a wasteland during the May 1992 political upheaval, *Thai Rath*. Courtesy of Chai Rachawat.

12.5. A summary cartoon by Yoot (Yoottachai Kaewdee), 1993. Courtesy of Yoot.

monthly for a bank,[3] and illustrations for other periodicals; presided over a TV production company; managed and wrote scripts for a one-hour weekly television talk show he hosted; taught courses at Silpakorn University; and was involved in investment projects. Chai seemed to have come full circle from his bookkeeping job; he said that cartooning was becoming "more and more of a hobby again" (Chai 1993).

In 1993, Chai saw as key problems for the profession: dismal payment, accounting for the low numbers of new

cartoonists; unappreciative editors; and an unstable political situation. He said that at times, he has had to leave cartooning for a while when there was a disruption or coup, such as for a week about the time of the 1992 riots. Chai felt that he was independent and free, and that compared to other Asian countries, so was Thai cartooning generally. He received indirect warnings from the government, but that was the extent of any interference; any harsher restrictions would arouse the people, which the authorities avoided (Chai 1993). Chai said that he sidestepped the publisher and editor (son of the publisher) of *Thai Rath* and attacked "rotten politicians" in league with them, reasoning that they "can't do anything about it as they can't get a better cartoonist," and that he didn't "have to depend on cartooning for [his] bowl of rice" (Chai 1993). He considered his cartoons "hard hitting," emphasizing that he depended on strong words more than the drawings; he pointed out that his colleagues at the *Bangkok Post* and the *Nation* used silent cartoons, because they were not sufficiently well versed in English to write captions.

Chai's acclaim escalated further, especially after he was chosen to draw the illustrations for two books authored by H. M. King Bhumibol Adulyadej (Rama IX): *Phra Mahajanaka* (The Great Father) in 1999, and *Rueang Tongdaeng* (The Story of Tongdaeng) in 2004. *Phra Mahajanaka* sold more than three million copies, becoming Thailand's best-selling book ever. The irony of the king's faith in a cartoonist is not lost, for it was also a king (Rama VI) nearly a century before who had helped launch Thai comic art. Chai designated the two books as his "proudest work" (Chai 2006).

Chai's work with the king served comic art well; after the huge success of *Phra Mahajanaka*, an abundance of Thai epic comic books hit the market (Chai 2006). In a 2006 interview, Chai talked about these experiences, explaining why he painted the king as a white silhouette: "That was my idea. If one paints the king's features realistically, there is no problem. But, if I draw him in cartoon style, there will be many problems. You cannot draw the king in cartoons. The people would complain it is disrespectful" (Chai 2006).

Chai was particularly proud to have been chosen to draw the story of King Bhumibol's dog, *Rueang Tongdaeng*, saying:

When the committee first asked me to do it, I hesitated, saying I was not familiar with drawing dogs. They said they had a second choice, but the palace said let Chai try to do it first. I drew up a sample of one chapter and the palace said for me to go ahead. After these works were done, I was in the presence of the king, and he gave me *krungrak*—like a

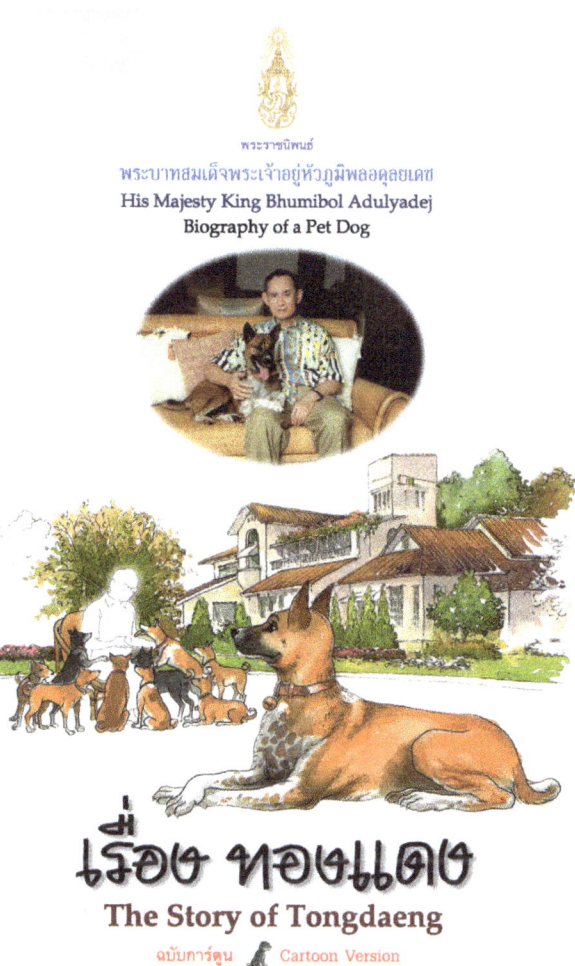

12.6. *The Story of Tongdaeng* by H. M. King Bhumibol Adulyadej, illustrated by Chai Rachawat, 2004. Courtesy of Chai Rachawat.

knighthood. It was like a medal called a fourth-class star. (Chai 2006)

A small drawback, according to Chai (2006), was that, out of respect for the crown, he had to be careful about other assignments he took at the time.

Chai reiterated problems of the profession he had mentioned earlier in 1993, but with slight twists. The political atmosphere continued to be off-balance with "too many coups; after each, cartoonists have to rethink and reorient their work" (Chai 2006). Editors remained a thorn, but this time, because they were "attached" to the older cartoonists, not giving newcomers a chance. Chai expounded on the point, stating: "Only I and a few others determine the cartoon work. We don't see new faces, and the editors don't care what we draw, just so they can use our names" (2006). Chai reserved

12.7. Left to right: John A. Lent, Arun Watcharasawat, Chuchart Mueningul, and Chai Rachawat, Bangkok, August 1, 1993. Photo by Oranuj Lertchanyarak.

some criticism for the cartoonists who, in his eyes, were "not flexible, don't know politics and other fields." He singled out political cartoonists of the Manager Group as exceptions.

On an individual level, Chai (2006) felt that he was "pretty much free," although he did receive anonymous threats, most of which he ignored, and politicians' bribery attempts, which he rejected. More generally, he said that "freedom to cartoon" depended on the liberalness of the administration in power, although it was also important to know which top politicians were tied to the newspapers' owners.

Chai continued drawing his daily strip and a political cartoon, despite successfully battling colon cancer and defending a 2013 defamation suit brought against him by then prime minister Yingluck Shinawatra. In a chat over lunch in 2014, Chai said that he reacted to a speech Yingluck had made in Mongolia defending her brother Thaksin Shinawatra, a former prime minister who had been ousted by a coup in 2006. Chai's comment about Yingluck's speech, posted only on his Facebook page, read: "Please understand . . . the female prostitute is not a bad person. The prostitute is merely selling her body. But that bad woman [meaning Yingluck] is selling out her country." Reactions to Chai's statement were swift with the setting up of a "We Hate Chai Rachawat Group"

and anti-Chai web boards, and the storming of *Thai Rath* by members of that political faction demanding Chai's dismissal. Outrage about Yingluck's comments criticizing Thailand's democracy and its constitution was widespread among the opposition, military, media, Senate, and the public. One result of the suit was a ruling that allows for the immediate shutting down of websites containing defamatory remarks about the prime minister.

Other Late Twentieth-Century Cartoonists

Besides Chai, the other major political cartoonists I interviewed in 1993 were Arun (Arun Watcharasawat), Muen (Chuchart Mueningul), and Yoot (Yoottachai Kaewdee).

Arun's career began while he was a university student in the early 1970s, as a part-timer on *Siam Rath*. Arun was fired from *Siam Rath* during the turbulence of the early 1970s, after which he became the art director of a science/nature magazine, *Wittaya Sarn*, while drawing for a second magazine and the *Nation* and establishing his own publishing house. In 1974, Arun quit *Wittaya Sarn* and devoted his time to his publishing company, drawing for the *Nation*, and handling the editorial section and political cartoons at a new newspaper he and fellow *Nation* staffers established, *Prachachart Daily* (Arun 1999). Initially, Arun's drawings imitated those of his mentor, Prayoon, but at *Prachachart*, he developed a "big head cartoon" style common in the United States, which he adjusted to Thai people's emotions and humor (Arun 1999).

In 1993, he was drawing one political cartoon daily for the *Nation* and its sister, the economics paper *Krung-thep*. Arun boasted of his "freedom to cartoon" using only his ideas, having no editorial policy to follow, and never having his work rejected. His formula for success, he said, was "working for twenty years and knowing how to be clever, and knowing what the editor, my friend, wants" (Arun 1993). Arun claimed to be anti–prime minister ("any prime minister"), saying, "Whatever statement the prime minister makes, I say it is not good" (Arun 1993). He and Muen, who joined our interview, agreed that Thai political cartooning was better than twenty years previously, with more freedom, higher salaries and better working conditions, a deeper appreciation of cartooning by the public, and recognition by newspaper proprietors of the importance of cartoonists. Both also said that they were "the property" of their newspapers, not permitted to draw political cartoons for other companies (Arun 1993; Muen 1993).

Muen drew for the Matichon (Voice of the People) newspapers (*Matichon*, *Kaosod* [Current News], and *Prachachart*) beginning in 1975. In 1993, each of these newspapers had its own staff cartoonist, indicating the importance Matichon proprietors gave to cartooning. Muen drew a daily political cartoon for *Matichon* and a strip for its Sunday edition. As a member of the paper's editorial board, which met twice daily, Muen (1993) said that he knew how the editors interpreted the news. His cartoons were screened by a subeditor; if he was dealing with a risky topic, the editors spiked the cartoon or asked him to make changes. He remembered one time when he drew a strong cartoon and left the newspaper building, making himself unavailable for modifications. The editor solved the problem by omitting the caption and letting the readers come up with their own interpretations. Muen (1993) quoted the editor as saying, "Erase

all the words, so no one can arrest us." One prohibited topic that was peculiar was calling a person a "black sheep," Muen explaining, "because all people should be white sheep. If you are a black sheep, you are not good. You can't use those words in a newspaper; they are insulting" (1993). Other subjects to sidestep are royalty, officials or their relatives when intoxicated, Buddhism, the military, and pornography, to avoid Thailand's lèse majesté law, libel suits, and closure of the newspaper (Muen 1993). The court system was also off-limits for many years.

The future of political cartooning looked good from Muen's vantage point. Most dailies had at least one staff cartoonist, the public liked the cartoons, and cartoonists' salaries were generous. Muen (1993) said that he was paid more than the editor, his salary split into three segments to make it less obvious.

The Twenty-First Century

In a second research trip in 2006, I concentrated my focus on the Kantana animation studio and the political cartoonist team at the Manager Group, although I also interviewed Pon at *Kaosod*, Sudjai Bhromkoed of the Cartoonthai Institute, Chai, and others.

The Manager Group was very visible on the cartoon scene in 2006, housing a team of five political cartoonists headed by Kamin (Chukiat Jaroensuk). *Manager* was started by businessman Sondhi Limthongkul, once an ally of Prime Minister Thaksin Shinawatra. After Sondhi clashed with Thaksin, he revealed what he knew as an insider about the prime minister's nefarious activities (Warat 2014).

Kamin (2006) traced his cartooning to his activist days when he drew protest cartoons that he posted on streetside walls. When the October 6, 1973, coup occurred, Kamin was jailed for a month, and a few years later he, like Chai, went to the United States to cool off—from 1976 to 1980. After his return to Bangkok, he joined the then monthly *Manager*, where he illustrated its covers. In 1986, the daily *Manager* started up

181

Thailand

with Kamin as its cartoonist. *Manager* owner Sondhi Limthongkul had a passion for cartoons, Kamin said, devoting a full page to them in a daily section called "Puchit Guan" (Mocking), made up of "satire on political news, a sense of humor on the news, fake news" (Kamin 2006)

The *Manager* cartoonist team had a different type of work pattern than other teams. Kamin explained that some team members were idea people, while others were visualizers. "If I have an idea, I call upon a visualizer to draw it up," he said, adding that this arrangement made for high-quality cartoons. His rationale was, "I read newspapers for three to four hours to get ideas, after which I don't have the energy to do a good drawing."

Team members indicated that they wavered from this division of labor. Bancha Sangthunchai (2006) said that he and his three fellow team members each did a cartoon daily; for example, Bancha an editorial cartoon for one of Manager's dailies, Yodpongsakul the strip *Rip Ginger* (meaning "spicy"). He said that Kamin held discussions with team members and gave them ideas, and also the group thought up ideas among themselves from which Kamin chose. At times, cartoon ideas came from readers, *Manager* employees, and owner Sondhi.

Kamin took credit for one political cartoon and the strip *Kon Koey Ruai* (The Person Who Used to Be Rich), both daily. He explained the strip:

It deals with what happened when the Thai economy collapsed. When the economy boomed about 1985, Thais bought name brands, expensive items. Then it collapsed. . . . Thais had to adapt. I would show how Thais could now use their brand name products; like use their brand name necktie to hang themselves. (Kamin 2006)

Overall, the "freedom to cartoon" (at least at Manager) in 2006 seemed relaxed, yet cautious. The Manager proprietor liked cartoons and supported his cartoonists, who, in turn, were well aware of the off-limits topics and were savvy about Thai politics. Kamin (2006), who had been sued twice by politicians, costing Manager financial loss, said that he gave the editors the right to

reject his work if they thought a legal problem would result. Rejection very seldom occurs, he said, because he controls himself "by not coming up with anything that can go to court" (Kamin 2006). "Once in a while, I get a call from the owner telling me 'to stay out of this case,' but not often, compared to the biggest Thai dailies that have rules to not hit certain things because their owners may have a close relationship with the prime minister" (Kamin 2006).

Manager cartoonists took necessary precautions to be fair and avoid legal or other setbacks. Team member Teerapongsack Sungkatip (2006) said, "If we think we are disparaging, we add a footnote to the cartoon saying it is just funny, not meant to offend." Apologies are given when thought to be merited. Teerapongsack (2006) gave the example of a cartoon of Jesus Christ talking with Mohammad about peace during the Iraqi War. An Islamic organization in Thailand complained, and an apology was printed in the newspaper. Bancha (2006) said that apologies to politicians are not given often, but "if we admit we are wrong, we issue an apology letter."

By 2006, the Manager Group and individual cartoonists had taken strong stands against Thaksin, helping remove him from office that year. Some of the prime minister's supporters held an anti–Manager Group rally outside the newspapers' offices, described by Bancha: "People were throwing stuff. Hundreds of motorcycles blocked the way out of the compound. They were against the whole company, not just the cartoonists. A bomb went off at night. No one was hurt. Some mysterious people threw a bag of shit. Some flowers got injured by the bomb [laughs]" (2006). Personally, Kamin received threatening "nasty letters and faxes," which he shrugged off with the flippant remark, "Let them put a bomb in my office; it's okay, because I am never there."

As for other problems cartoonists faced in 2006, Kamin (2006) singled out cartoonists who use their cartoon just to fill space, using only their hands and not their brains, and newspapers that "pick a guy who can draw, not the one who accumulates enough knowledge to do political cartoons." Bancha (2006) and Teerapongsack (2006) agreed that most Thai political cartoonists were not knowledgeable about politics, and both thought, from personal experience, that a Thai drawing for an English-language newspaper often was incapable of getting the gist of the cartoon across because of language deficiency.

The Matichon newspapers in 2006 were still the dailies *Matichon*, the business-related *Prachachart*, and *Kaosod*. Drawing political cartoons for *Kaosod* was Pon, a longtime illustrator and cartoonist of children's humor and folklore books and textbooks. He and four artist friends formed Thailand's first cartoonist team, the Benjarong Group, their mission to produce children's books. Pon (2006) said that he was asked to add political cartoons to his workload when *Kaosod* was started. His initial three-panel cartoon, *Kamnan Term* (a leader higher than the village head), did not succeed. He did much better with a strip mocking the newly installed prime minister, Banharn Silpa-archa, considered folksy and unsophisticated, his wife Jamsai, and his daughter who was a member of Parliament, nicknamed Na. Pon named his new strip using parts of their names, *Nuna Kubpa Jam* (Pon 2006). Pon said that the strip was a hit, even after Banharn left office.

Pon (2006) pointed out that whereas his children's cartoons were based on facts, sometimes with political cartoons, "the facts are not known, and you could be sued." He said that the strip had generated phone threats, not from politicians but perhaps from influential people or the Mafia. He took pride in a couple of popular characteristics of *Nuna Kubpa Jam*: that occasionally he had characters in the last panel jump out of the strip, and that he placed clues to lottery numbers in the frames. Pon (2006) said that some readers even turned his signature into lottery numbers.

Also unique about *Nuna Kubpa Jam*, according to Pon, is that it is a "contradictory counterbalance of soft comic characters with strong words comparable to the 'F' word" (2006). For example, he uses a giant lizard, "which is one of the worst insults here." He attributes the strip's success to his being "up to the minute with news events" (Pon 2006). Similar to views expressed by Manager cartoonists, Pon thought it very important that

political cartoonists know politics, as well as economics, the environment, and other topics. Other necessary traits, he added, were having a just mind and a dislike for politicians.

Political instability continued to be a defining mark of Thailand. Eight years after her brother was ousted and went into exile, Prime Minister Yingluck Shinawatra experienced the same fate after one of the world's largest and longest political protests, November 2013 to May 2014. The coup that toppled her was the result of rallies led by the pressure group the People's Democratic Reform Committee (PDRC); she was replaced by General Prayuth Chan-ocha.

Cartoonists joined the fray, but on opposite sides and with varying strengths of attack, according to a survey of the two top-selling English dailies, the *Bangkok Post* and the *Nation*, and the largest-circulation Thai dailies, *Thai Rath* and the *Daily News*. Aram Iamlaor and Savitri Gadavanij, in their analysis of eighty-seven political cartoons used in the four dailies during the six months of protests, concluded:

> It was found that the cartoons drawn by the cartoonists were totally different in terms of the political and public opinions. The cartoonists tend to draw cartoons that support their favorite politicians, political party, or political groups. It is obvious that Sia and Chai Ratchawat [*sic*] are completely different in terms of their opinion, even though they are working for the same newspaper, *Thai Rath*. Sia always draws cartoons that attack or criticize actions of the PDRC, while Chai Ratchawat always draws cartoons that criticize the government or Pheu Thai party, but his critics are more subtle and indirect like Sia's. For Khuaid from *Daily News*, his cartoons are quite neutral; however, he criticizes the PDRC a little more than the government or Pheu Thai party. For the three cartoonists from *Bangkok Post*—Dinhin, Mor, and Yoot—their cartoons seem to be the most neutral because they are not too aggressive, and they criticize both sides of the conflicts as well as the overall situations. In the case of Stephane Peray [Stephff] from *The Nation*, he seems to be a little on the PDRC's side, but his cartoons try to present the situations in the point

12.8. Widely shared political cartoon on social media when its creator, Sia Thai Rath (Sakda Sae-aew), was called in by the military for "attitude adjustment." Three countries urge Thailand to restore democracy, to which the junta responds: "Y'all don't understand . . . We're returning happiness to Thai people."

of view of a foreigner who lives in Thailand. (Iamlaor and Gadavanij 2017)

Like so many of its predecessors, the Prayuth government kept Thai political cartoonists on their toes, warning, detaining, and calling them in for attitude adjustment sessions. Prayuth's military junta quickly reshaped Thailand's government infrastructure by dissolving the legislative body, repealing most of the constitution, exerting control over the judiciary, and closing independent election monitoring stations (Williams 2016). He cracked down on dissent, limiting discussion on democracy and criticism of the government and increasing censorship of mass media and the internet. In 2015, Prayuth gave himself the authority to forcefully close media, while stating that he would no longer tolerate "irresponsible newspaper columnists." Earlier, the prime minister proscribed a list of "twelve values" he expected Thais to practice, a throwback to more than fifty years prior with Malaysia's Rukunegara and Indonesia's Pancasila.

Prayuth was elected prime minister in 2019 in a controversial election that questioned the legality and appropriateness of the king's sister standing for the office. Besides the prime ministership, Prayuth also assumed the posts of defense minister, head of the Royal Thai Police, and head of both the government's economic team and the Justice Ministry's Department of Special Investigation.

With Prayuth holding such vital positions dealing with investigation, arrest, and detention, cartoonists, as well as journalists as a whole, knew they were likely in for bad times. Some cartoonists had already felt his wrath when he was first appointed prime minister and they were summoned to explain their drawings to government commissions and the Royal Thai Army. Among the first questioned were veteran cartoonists Arun Watcharasawat of *Matichon Weekend* and Sakda Sae-aew (Sia Thai Rath) of *Thai Rath*; Arun, for a 2015 cartoon mocking an early draft of a new constitution; Sia Thai Rath, for a 2015 drawing making fun of Prayuth paying lip service to civil liberties at a United Nations event. Sia Thai Rath actually was called in for "attitude adjustment" and was diagnosed as biased. His "attitude" apparently was adjusted a bit as he admitted to self-censoring more after the session, and he agreed that he was biased—but only on the side of democracy and justice (Williams 2016; also Monruedee 2016). Sia Thai Rath had been on the military watchlist even before the 2014 coup; he has been called in for questioning at least twice and is told almost daily to "tone it down" by his editor, a warning relayed from government officials (CPJ 2015b).

Another political cartoonist who encountered difficulties under the Prayuth regime is Stephane Peray (Stephff), a French national who regularly drew freelance for the *Nation* beginning in 2003. In February 2016, he announced that renewal of his media visa, working permit, and press card were denied by the Foreign Ministry. The ministry told Stephff that it no longer considered his job as that of a journalist, eliciting this remark from the cartoonist: "This new rule was tailored-size for me" (Pravit 2016). Stephff immediately posted a barrage of exasperated messages on social media and in the press, sparking the ministry to call him and ask that he submit a letter of support from the *Nation*. For years, Stephff was self-syndicated, collaborating with a few newspapers in Kuwait, China, Korea, and France. In 2019, his work world as he had known it changed drastically. In June, the *Nation* ceased printing after forty-eight years, forcing Stephff to migrate to the paper's online version; Stephff abandoned his daily international self-syndication service, because fewer newspapers were willing to pay for cartoons and "censorship had become more and more unbearable" (Bado's blog 2019); and then, in October, he resigned from the *Bangkok Post*, where he had worked for a few months, when, in one week, three of his cartoons about Turkey and China were spiked. In an interview at the time, Stephff lamented: "When your hard work goes unpublished, you suddenly feel useless, and of course as a freelance employee, you are not getting paid either!" (Ajarn Street 2020). Stephff drew some cartoons for *Prachachart* after that. His next move was to create what he called "self-broadcast political cartoons . . . drawn directly for the readers to read" and supported by reader donations. In his plea for support, Stephff thanked donors in advance for enabling him "to piss off all the horrible people who rule us, control us, make us sick, slowly kill the future of our children" (Bado's blog 2019).

Prayuth's government also cracked down on the internet, ordering in 2015 the building of a firewall to

12.9. Kai Maew (Cat's Egg), a popular Thai satirical webcomic published from 2016 to 2018 before being taken down.

filter internet traffic into and out of Thailand. The order, signed by Prayuth, said that the single gateway would "serve as a tool to control access to inappropriate sites and the influx of information from abroad." The government denied that the initiative was designed to curb online freedoms and censor the internet, a charge made by the Committee to Protect Journalists (CPJ 2015a).

With fifty-two million regular users in Thailand in 2018, the eighth-highest number in the world, Facebook has provided Thai political satirists with an alternative venue. Two prominent pages by anonymous creators that tackled the injustices and denial of press freedom in recent years are Manee Mee Share[4] and Kai Meow ("cat's eggs," slang for cat's testicles). Manee Mee Share lasted from 2014 to 2016, pointing out political problems in a humorous way. The reason for its shutdown is not known, but likely it was because of the cartoonist's fear of continuing (Yoon 2018).

Kai Maew first appeared in 2016 but disappeared about January 2018, again for unknown reasons; it resumed shortly after on February 16, 2018, as Kai Maew X, with the same creator (Kaewta 2017). The first version of the page had four hundred thousand followers; the second, two hundred thousand. Prabda Yoon (2018) described Kai Maew as having simple, rough pen strokes and fewer aesthetic restrictions that Manee Mee Share, making it more adaptable to different punchlines

185

and material. It draws on popular culture topics and often uses wordless panels that caricature prominent Thais whose identities can be guessed.

Manee Mee Share had the feel of manga and often used characters who resembled newsworthy people. The main character was dressed in a military uniform and sported a Hitler-like moustache. Other satiric webcomics appeared from time to time but did not last long.

A Brief Conclusion

A couple of Thai political cartoonists have told me that they are the envy of colleagues in neighboring countries because of their relatively high level of "freedom to cartoon." (An aside: they say this after going into detail about their run-ins with authorities.) Nevertheless, I believe they *do* have more freedom, but how significant is such an accolade when you consider the situation in Vietnam, Myanmar, Laos, Singapore, Cambodia, and Malaysia?

Notes

1. Chai explained that the strip's headman, Poo Yai Ma, represented the Thai government and the villager Ah Joy, the Thai people, leaving little doubt that the strip was politically infused. Chai said that his cartoon was similar to *Doonesbury* and was the "oldest political strip" in Thailand at the time of our interview in 1993 (Chai 1993).

2. "Summary cartoons" are found in a few countries where I interviewed, namely Thailand, Sri Lanka, and Kenya. In Thailand, they were prominent in Sunday editions in the 1990s. Two cartoonists drawing them provided descriptions. Chai Rachawat termed the summary cartoon as thematic, "a batch of drawings within one panel on a theme in the news" (Chai 1993). Muen (Chuchart Mueningul) said that it was a "summary of the week's political news plus a news story," all encapsulated in one panel (Muen 1993). They were usually displayed in large, bold format in the opinion sections of newspapers.

3. Chai, who was a bookkeeping graduate, held such a position in a bank while fulfilling his hobby as a freelance cartoonist. He quit the bank work when he went to the United States in 1976.

4. The name has a somewhat convoluted origin story. Prabda Yoon said:

Manee is the name of a pigtailed girl character in a classic series of elementary-school textbooks, familiar to Thais who attended primary school between 1978 and 1994; "Share" is a play on the way Thai people pronounce the English word "chair"; and "Mee" is the Thai word for "have," so the page's name, in one sense, means "Manee has a chair" (its English handle is @maneehaschair). The chair is an allusion to the 1976 Thammasat University massacre, in which the government used violence to suppress student protests gathered at the university and the nearby Sanam Luang Square, leaving 46 dead. (The demonstrators were protesting the return of former dictator Thanom Kittikachorn, who had been driven into exile following an uprising three years earlier.) The far-right media at the time accused the students of lèse-majesté and, as a result, a considerable number of people said good riddance to the casualties. An American photographer from the Associated Press, Neal Ulevich, photographed a man with a metal chair raised above his head, ready to smash the corpse of a student hanging from a tree, a crowd looking on. The photograph became emblematic of that harrowing chapter in Thai history, a reminder of the impunity with which the far right inflicted violence that day. The reference to that chair in the name of Manee Mee Share connects the country's political problems with the forces that gave rise to the 1976 massacre. (Yoon 2018)

Bibliography

Ajarn Street. 2020. "Stephff the Cartoonist." April 18. https://www .ajarn.com/ajarn-street/hot-seat/stephff-cartoonist.

Arun [Arun Watcharasawat]. 1993. Interview with John A. Lent, Bangkok, August 1.

Arun [Arun Watcharasawat]. 1999. Interview with Monsinee Keeratikrainon, Bangkok, June 2.

Bado's blog. 2019. "Cartoonist Stephff Resigns from Bangkok Post." October 19. https://bado.bado'sblog.blogspot.com/2019/10/ cartoonist-stephff-resigns-from-bangkok.html.

Bancha Sangthunchai. 2006. Interview with John A. Lent, Bangkok, December 1.

Chai Rachawat [Somchai Katanyutanan]. 1993. Interview with John A. Lent, Bangkok, August 1.

Chai Rachawat [Somchai Katanyutanan]. 2006. Interview with John A. Lent, Bangkok, December 4.

Chai Rachawat [Somchai Katanyutanan]. 2014. Interview with John A. Lent, Bangkok, July 11.

Chanjaroen, Chanyaporn. 1992. "Cartoons Pack Potent Message." *The Nation* (Bangkok), May 27, C-1.

Chulasak Amornrej. 1997. "Rak Kaew Cartoon Than Utthakanon" [A Root of Thai Cartoons: Than Utthakanon]. *Krungthep Turakij*, June 6, 3.

Committee to Protect Journalists (CPJ). 2015a. "Internet Gateway Plan Threatens Online Freedoms in Thailand." September 29. https://cpj.org/2015/09/internet-gateway-plan-threatens-online-freedoms-in/.

Committee to Protect Journalists (CPJ). 2015b. "In Thailand, Cartoonist Detained and Warned He Could Be Prosecuted." October 5. https://cpj.org/2015/10/in-thailand-cartoonist-detained-and-warned-he-coul/.

Gesmankit, Pairote, and Kullasap Gesmankit. 1980. "Cartoon Techniques Widely Applied in Thailand." *Asian Culture* 25 (January): 21–23.

Iamlaor, Aram, and Savitri Gadavanij. 2017. "Humor in Thai Political Cartoons Published during the 2013–14 Thai Political Crisis." Paper presented at the Asian Conference on Media and Mass Communication, Kobe, Japan, October 27–29. https://papers.iafor.org/wp-content/uploads/papers/mediasia2017/MediAsia2017_38424.pdf.

Jitsiree Thongnoi. 2016. "Drawing and Crossing the Line." *Bangkok Post*, January 3.

Kaewta Ketbungkan. 2017. "Dangerously Funny Webcomic Satirizes Thai Politics." *Khaosod*, May 18. https://www.khaosodenglish.com/culture/net/2017/05/18/kai-maew-drops-rough-chuckles-thai-politics.

Kamin [Chukiat Jaroensuk]. 2006. Interview with John A. Lent, Bangkok, December 1.

Karnjariya, Sukrung. 2000. "Rebirth of Toons." *Bangkok Post*, July 1.

Kitichaiwan, Annop. 1990. *Political Cartoons by Add Daily News*. Bangkok: Bangkok Post.

Lent, John A. 1996. "Thai Cartoonist Chai: A Worker in Many Fields." *WittyWorld International Cartoon Bulletin*, no. 4, 3.

Lent, John A. 1997. "The Uphill Climb of Thai Cartooning." *Southeast Asian Journal of Social Science* 25, no. 1: 93–109.

Lent, John A. 2015. *Asian Comics*. Jackson: University Press of Mississippi.

Mastricolo, Patricia. 2018. "Thai Political Cartoon Goes Mysteriously Dark." Comic Book Legal Defense Fund, January 26. http://cbldf.org/2018/01/thai-political-cartoon-goes-mysteriously-dark/.

Monruedee Jansuttipan. 2016. "Thairath Cartoonist on the Pressures of Making Political Commentary in Thailand." BK, February 8. https://bk.asia-city.com/city-living/news/sakda-sae-aew-thairath-political-cartoonist.

Muen [Chuchart Mueningul]. 1993. Interview with John A. Lent, Bangkok, August 1.

Palatino, Mong. 2015. "Political Cartoons Defy Censorship to Expose Thai-Style 'Democracy.'" Global Voices, October 10. https://globalvoices.org/2015/10/10/political-cartoons-defy-censorship-to-expose-thai-style-democracy/.

Pon. 2006. Interview with John A. Lent, Bangkok, December 4.

Pravit Rojanaphruk. 2016. "Longtime Political Cartoonist 'Stephff' Loses Work Permit and Visa." *Khaosod English*, February 2. https://www.khaosodenglish.com/politics/2016/02/02/1454405787/.

Sitthiporn Gulawarottama and Chanansiri Maksampan. 2000. "Prawat Cartoon Thai" [The History of Thai Cartoons]. https://www.geocities.com/toonclick/history.html.

Sudjai Bhromkoed. 2006. Interview with John A. Lent, Bangkok, December 4.

Tansubhapol, Kulcharee. 1994. "Drawing on the Mind's Eye." *Bangkok Post*, February 1, 1.

Teerapongsack Sungkatip. 2006. Interview with John A. Lent, Bangkok, December 1.

Vatikiotis, Michael. 1995. "The Long Way Home." *Far Eastern Economic Review*, February 16, 62.

Verstappen, Nicolas. 2017. Thai Comics in the Twenty-First Century: Identity and Diversity of a New Generation of Thai Cartoonists." Research project, Chulalongkorn University.

Warat Karuchit. 2014. "The Uphill Climb to Reach a Plateau: Historical Analysis of the Development of Thai Cartooning." In *Southeast Asian Cartoon Art: History, Trends and Problems*, edited by John A. Lent, 75–104. Jefferson, NC: McFarland.

Williams, Maren. 2016. "Thai Cartoonist 'Invited' to Explain Himself to Government Commission." Comic Book Legal Defense Fund, June 28. http://cbldf.org/2016/06/thai-cartoonist-invited-to-explain-himself-to-government-commission/.

Yodpongsakul. 2006. Interview with John A. Lent, Bangkok, December 1.

Yoon, Prabda. 2018. "Peepholes in Happyland #3" *Art Review*, July 6. https://artreview.com/ara-summer-2018-opinion-prabda-yoon/.

Yoot [Yoottachai Kaewdee]. 1993. Interview with John A. Lent, Bangkok, August 4.

Defining political cartoons and their characteristics can be an onerous task because of linguistic and cultural differences; this applies to comic art generally (Lent 2004). Some traits of Vietnamese satire and political cartoons likewise may not be universal. Pham Thu Thuy indirectly made this point in her interpretations: first, humor is not required in Vietnamese satire, but criticism and attacks are; and second, *biem hoa* (cartoons) are similar to Western cartoons in that they expose social vices and follies through satiric devices, but dissimilar in that entertainment is secondary to political and social criticism and *biem hoa* usually do not generate laughter (Pham Thu Thuy 2003, 93). Cartoons that are for entertainment only are called *tranh vui*.

Pham Thu Thuy used Lawrence Streicher's (1967) categorization to further describe Vietnamese cartooning, paraphrasing that political cartoons debunk and expose those in authority, while social cartoons deal with nonpolitical affairs that confront those who don't have the ability or desire to change society. She seemed to contradict herself; political cartoons are to target authority, she said, but later she wrote that Vietnamese cartoonists must refrain from lampooning national leaders or criticizing state policies, and if they do, then not too realistically. The exceptions are government officials and company executives charged or convicted on corruption or other crimes (Pham Thu Thuy 2003, 93).

A key point to be made here is that mostly everywhere, political cartooning adapts to the political and economic milieu. Pham Thu Thuy was discussing Vietnamese political cartooning in the late 1990s, a less oppressive period and a time when a few cartoonists were willing to take chances.

Chapter 13

Vietnam

Changes, Constraints: 1993–2018

My interviewing of Vietnamese cartoonists spanned twenty-five years, first in Hanoi in 1993, then in Ho Chi Minh City in 2010, and the latest in Hanoi, 2018.

The conclusion I reached in 1993 was that Vietnam was the least developed in cartooning among Southeast

Asian countries. Comic books displayed in bookstores were translations (usually pirated) of those of the United States and Japan, falsely recredited to Vietnamese artists. Newspaper comic strips were nonexistent, and "political" cartoons invariably were miniature drawings, illustrating fiction or stories about HIV/AIDS, family planning, sports, bureaucracy, and the like.

The sparsity of newspaper political cartoons was not for lack of artists. Kong Ngoan, "cartoonist" head of the painting department of the party and major daily, *Nhan Dan*, said that his four-page daily had seven full-time artists, an incredibly large number for any daily in the world then or now. Their tasks, according to Kong Ngoan, were to illustrate two times weekly two short stories (called "black *Nhan Dan*") and brief funny accounts of societal problems (e.g., pollution, public use of roads, water safety) in a twice-weekly column, "Chuyen Lon Chuyen Nho" (Big Story, Small Story) (Kong Ngoan 1993). *Nhan Dan*'s international department editor, Phuong Ha, gave the artists' duties as designing pages, laying out advertising, and illustrating stories, explaining that the "cartoons" they drew two or three times weekly actually were illustrations, not funnies (nor political, I might add) (Phuong Ha 1993). In 1993, *Nhan Dan* occasionally ran one of these "cartoons" on its front page to promote a government campaign. The Sunday edition of *Nhan Dan* used illustration "cartoons" of a column or less on nearly every page. In a Sunday issue I looked at, there were twenty-one such images; the number depended on the articles' content (Kong Ngoan 1993) and was determined completely by the editor (Phuong Ha 1993). The decision concerning the size of an illustration used was based on the day's newsworthy issues.

In 1993, all three Hanoi dailies carried illustrations. The city's second-largest newspaper, the youth-oriented *Tienphong Chu Nhat*, used three or four cartoons in a typical week and some short story illustrations drawn by three full-time artists and occasional freelancers, the latter sometimes unpaid (Nguyen Thanh Chung 1993). The sister monthly, *Tienphong Cuoithang*, gave over its last page to joke cartoons submitted by freelancers.

13.1. An anti–Richard Nixon cartoon by Phan Kich, 1992.

Hanoi's third daily, *Hanoi Moi* (New Daily), carried a two-column illustration and a tiny story with "cartoons."

Paper shortages in 1993 played havoc with the number of stories and drawings used, the competition for the limited space being so keen (Kong Ngoan 1993; also Nguyen Thanh Chung 1993). *Nhan Dan* even discontinued publishing magazines. The most serious problem at the time was that of censorship, whether it emanated from the government, editors, or the cartoonists themselves. The editor gave "instructions" on all drawings, which had to be devoid of any criticism. In the past, Vietnamese cartoonists drew Richard Nixon, John Foster Dulles, and Henry Kissinger as part of anti-US campaigns, Kong Ngoan (1993) recalled, but this practice was discontinued when the country adopted a new policy of engaging more freely with other countries.

The political cartoon situation in Ho Chi Minh City in 2010 seemed to have deteriorated from conditions seventeen years earlier. Newspapers had many pages then, most filled with advertisements, but cartoons

![Cartoon](13.2)

13.2. Cartoon by DAD (Do Anh Dung).

13.3. The traffic flow by NOP (Ha Xuan Nong).

and illustrations were sorely missed. The city's two most popular dailies, *Thanh Nien* and *Tuoi Tre* (Youth), gave evidence to this scarcity. *Thanh Nien* on occasion published a cartoon by DAD (Do Anh Dung) to illustrate a story, and its weekly used an illustration on the children's page; *Tuoi Tre* did better, publishing a two-column color cartoon (*Biem Hoa* [Cartoon]) by Sate, a two-column color sports cartoon, and cartoons by NOP (Ha Xuan Nong), all spaced over a few days. Seldom did *Tuoi Tre* contain more than one cartoon on a given day.

What struck me as different and strange in 2018 was the difficulty finding newspapers on Hanoi streets sold by vendors or at newsstands. Veteran cartoonist Ly Truc Dung, called "the living encyclopedia of Vietnam cartooning" by cartoonist Le Phuong, explained: "The people ignore the newspapers because many are government organs, a lot of the news is not reported in the newspapers, and the newspapers are bought by organizations." He gave an example: "A factory will have a newspaper, and all the workers might buy

copies, but whether they read them is another matter" (Ly Truc Dung 2018).

In 2018, about eight hundred newspapers and magazines were published in Vietnam, of which fifteen to twenty used political cartoons, and only a short handful of cartoonists had full-time positions, namely Do Anh Dung or DAD with *Lang Cuoi* magazine, Ha Xuan Nong or NOP with *Lang Cuoi*, and Le Anh Phong or LAP with *Tuoi Tre* and *An Ninh The Gioi* (Le Anh Phong was also senior editor of *Tuoi Tre Cuoi* [Laughing Youth]) (Le Phuong 2018). Ly Truc Dung had been full-time earlier but had too many other responsibilities in 2018 to continue, editing a page of four cartoons for the monthly *My Thuat*, organizing and chairing the Vietnam Press Caricature Contest, Bamboo Dragon Cup, working for an NGO to protect bears in Vietnam, helping produce a series of television shows, and drawing occasional cartoons for *Van Nghe* magazine and to post on Facebook (Ly Truc Dung 2018). Le Phuong (Leo) said that at one time half of his income came from cartooning; now, it is 25 percent. He is paid handsomely for drawing two color covers monthly for *Tuoi Tre Cuoi* magazine and eight cartoons monthly for a police security magazine,

13.4. Political cartoonist Le Phuong showing his work, Hanoi, March 1, 2018. Photo by Xu Ying. Permission of Le Phuong.

An Ninh The Gioi. He cut back on his cartoon output, which had been more than twenty monthly, because he lost some of his passion for cartooning as the impact on the public had diminished (Le Phuong 2018). The average payment for a cartoon in Vietnam is equivalent to US$10 to US$15 (Le Phuong 2018; Ly Truc Dung 2018). There are also approximately thirty cartoonists who work freelance.

As in Myanmar, most drawers of cartoons consider what they do as a hobby, a chance to appear in print. Le Phuong (2018) said that very few of them have good techniques or professional backgrounds. Job security is at a minimum, as there is no guarantee an editor will select their work. One seventy-year-old cartoonist complained to Le Phuong that if he submits ten cartoons, only one might be used (Le Phuong 2018).

With these unstable conditions and the strict censorship they must endure, some artists find other means to supplement their cartoon payments, or move to other endeavors, or simply shy away from entering the profession in the first place. For example, Le Phuong does graphic design, illustrations, logo designing, branding, book covers, and caricatures. He said that the latter are commissioned as company celebratory gifts for officials upon retirement, for which Le Phuong is paid a hefty US$300. In Nguyen Thanh Phong's (2018) case, he left political cartooning to write his own comics/graphic novels and, with his lifelong friend Nguyen Khanh Duong, eventually start their own comics publishing

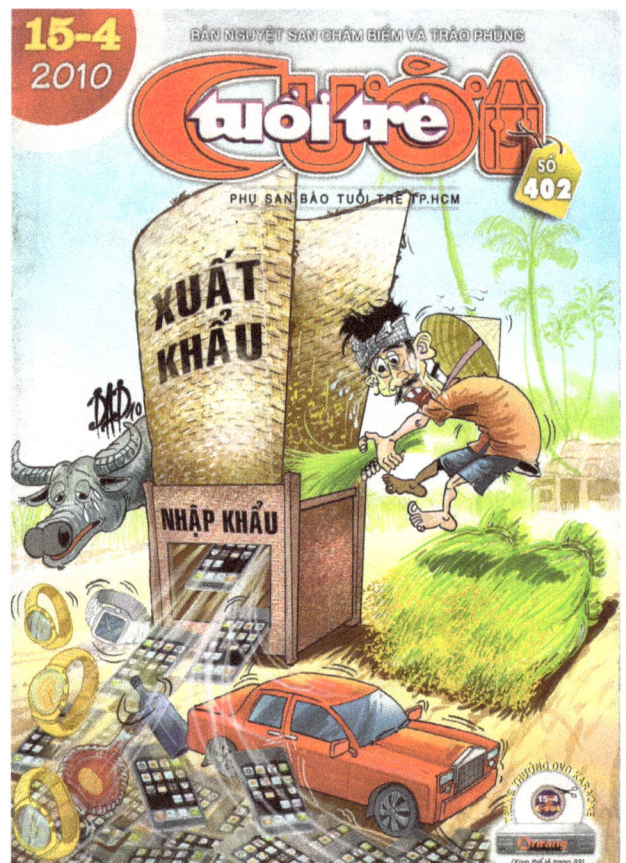

13.5. Humor magazine *Tuoi Tre Cuoi*, April 15, 2010.

company, Comicola (Comic Online Alliance). Ly Truc Dung (2018) remarked it was a pity that new political cartoonists are few in Vietnam.

An important venue for cartoons and satire in Vietnam is the twice-monthly humor magazine *Tuoi Tre Cuoi*, founded in 1975 as the voice of the Ho Chi Minh branch of the Communist Youth Union. *Tuoi Tre Cuoi*, part of Vietnam's largest-circulation (four hundred thousand plus) daily *Tuoi Tre*, uses caricatures, satire, and illustrated jokes on nearly every page. Although claiming to be nonpolitical, there have been, over the years, cartoons that bordered on criticism of the government, one example being a drawing by NOP showing an office with a bottomless opinion box placed over a garbage pail (Keenan 1997, 45). The magazine was important enough in the late 1990s to inspire a popular stage show in Ho Chi Minh City. In 2015, *Tuoi Tre Cuoi* started its Facebook page and soon had 550,000 followers.

The Wronging of the Right to Cartoon

Vietnam has a long history of media suppression rampant during long periods of colonialism, war, national fragmentation, and the communist ideology.

With government and party ownership, a number of outright taboos, tough legislation, and self-censorship, the press and by extension cartoonists walk a tightrope. Political cartoonists admit to playing it safe, distancing themselves from criticizing certain policies and individuals, or attempting to get messages across by visual cues recognizable to readers but hopefully not to authorities. Of course, the use of verbal cues depends on the intellectual awareness of audiences; for example, *Tuoi Tre Cuoi* caters to the widest possible audience, many of whom require visual cues.

Forbidden or sensitive topics for cartoonists, according to Le Phuong (2018), include negative images of Ho Chi Minh or contemporary high officials, religions, the so-called saints (honorable Vietnamese leaders who protected and helped people), and the military. Nguyen Thanh Phong (2018) added violence, sex, political views,

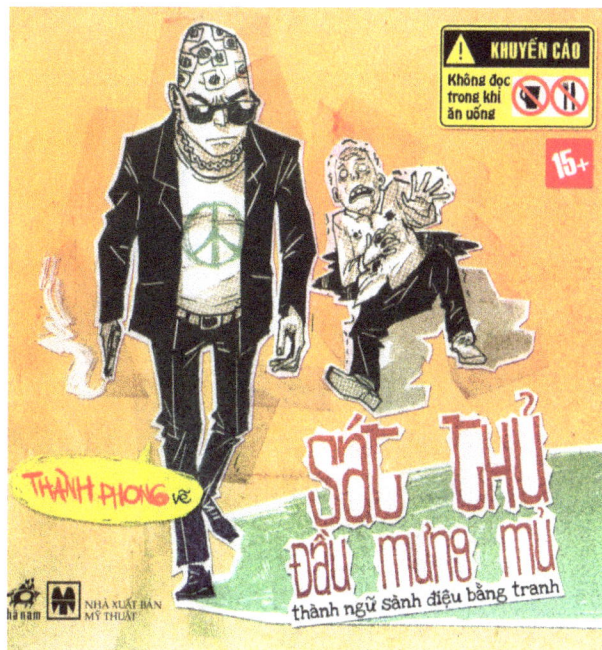

13.6. Cover of Nguyen Thanh Phong's controversial *Sat Thu Dou Mung Mu*. Permission of Nguyen Thanh Phong.

wrong depictions of historical figures, and portrayals that make the Communist Party, police, and military look bad. He said that the big issue with bringing out comic books and graphic novels was obtaining a permit from the government-owned publishing houses. Without the permit, printers will not attempt to produce a book. Phong said that the government publishing houses "scrutinize, question, and cut material," sometimes in less than logical or reasonable ways, citing these examples:

Before publication, my book, *Long Than Tuong* [Holy Dragon Imperator], was censored a lot. On page 135, a man is being slashed by an axe. "Too much blood," the publishing house said. We were told to reduce the size of the text of onomatopoeia, but we did not have to reduce the amount of blood shown. On another page, they thought there were Chinese characters, maybe with hidden messages. But, actually, it was a boy's face that looked like Chinese characters to the censor. There were many funny things like this with the censor. (Nguyen Thanh Phong 2018)

A side remark is in order here. Some comic books and graphic novels play similar roles as cartoons and strips, disseminating political views, propaganda, and social

13.7. Political cartoonist/comic art historian and organizer Ly Truc Dung in his home, Hanoi, March 2, 2018. Photo by Xu Ying. Permission of Ly Truc Dung.

awareness messages while also being subject to government and public censure. Phong was made aware of this possibility upon publication of his satirical book *Sat Thu Dou Mung Mu* (The Killer with a Head of Festering Sores) in 2011. The book is made up of about 120 individual drawings, each captioned with a twisted version of a Vietnamese idiom. Nguyen Hong Phuc gives the example: "'When a horse is sick, the whole stable refuses grass,' which means 'love people like loving oneself,' was revised to 'when a horse is sick, the whole stable can eat more grass,' which implies a degree of selfishness and uncaring for others" (2017). Reacting to public criticism that the book could be a bad influence on language usage, the director of the overriding Vietnamese Publishing House asked the book's publisher to explain why it was published; rather than answer that question, the publisher stopped publication and attempted to retrieve all of the already printed copies. This decision was reversed when the publisher heard young people defend the book at a public assembly and republished it with a new title (Nguyen Hong Phuc 2017).

Self-censorship and that by editors forestall the need for the government or military to take repressive action. Le Phuong (2018) said this in essence: "Because political cartoonists are censored by the editors and self-censorship exists, . . . no one is having trouble with the authorities." He admitted being careful about his cartoons, because his family members (including his wife) worked for the government, and he did not want to affect their jobs. Ly Truc Dung had a similar dilemma; for a number of years, he was employed by the Ministry of Planning, during which time he discontinued cartoon drawing. If the government must directly get involved in the vetting, it is "very harsh," Dung (2018) emphasized, pointing out that two censorship groups exist, one in the Ministry of Culture and the other in the Communist Party Department of Character and Ideology.

If drawing political cartoons cannot support one financially, lacks public and government respect and support, and is beset by obstacles such as censorship and scarcity of venues, why do it? I asked Dung. His altruistic reply was:

I hope I will help to better the Vietnamese people. Two hundred and fifty thousand Vietnamese died in the land reform period. Two to three million Vietnamese have left the country for the United States. People have been hungry, very poor. There has been a lot of fighting, fighting, fighting. Now, a lot of poverty. Before, Vietnam's level of living was even with China and Singapore. Now, China and

13.8. Ly Truc Dung cartoon posted on Facebook for select friends. Permission of Ly Truc Dung.

Singapore are much higher. My mission is to help Vietnamese society. (Ly Truc Dung 2018)

Dung's tenacity perhaps was captured in his response to a patron at an exhibition who asked if he was afraid of potential government harassment. He answered, "I work from early morning to night. If I have to go to prison, I just want to know which one has pen and paper" (Ly Truc Dung 2018).

As already evident, Ly Truc Dung is a very important and respected cartoonist who has contributed much to contemporary cartooning in Vietnam. Born in 1946, he graduated from Weimar University of Architecture in 1973. Altogether, he lived in East Germany for eleven years—1966–1973 as a student and 1982–1987 working at *Die Welt* and a worker's union. Dung (2018) said that he has drawn well over a thousand political cartoons since 1979, many in *Van Nghe* magazine; this was in addition to his other professional work. He has been described as having an international laugh language inspired by a Vietnamese folklore tradition (Hoa Si Biem n.d.). Dung is well aware that cartooning has changed dramatically in this age of speedy information by social media, stating, "The information itself is no longer as important as the public comments about that information" (Mi Ly 2012).

He laments young people's hesitancy to enter the profession and encourages them through his lectures and interviews and by providing them with a platform on which to be recognized. In 2007, Ly Truc Dung started the biannual Vietnam Press Caricature Contest, Bamboo Dragon Cup. For some time sponsored by the government magazine *The Thao Van Hoa* (Culture and Sport), the competition awarded substantial cash prizes (e.g., US$1,500 for first prize) to winners who drew on assigned themes that were safe in the context of Vietnam's politics. After the fourth competition in 2014, the Bamboo Dragon Cup ran out of funds and lapsed until its revival in 2018 (for more on Ly Truc Dung, see Mi Ly 2012).

Historical Overview

Political satire predated the arrival of colonists in Vietnam, as it had in other parts of Asia. Oppression nurtures satire, and the Vietnamese people have had their share of authoritarianism and its ill effects. They have found ways to laugh at authorities going back to the feudal period, when humorous folklore such as *Trang Quynh* or *Ba Giag Tu Xuat* told satirical stories about "smart ordinary characters who often troll and humiliate the rich and the authorities, even the kings" (Chi Do Huu 2022).

The Frenchmen Lelan in the 1890s and André Joyeux and Alfred Cézard a decade or two later were early drawers of cartoons about Vietnam, usually mocking the Vietnamese and Chinese people and skewering the racial order of the colonists. Indigenous artists took their cue from these cartoonists, some even studying under Joyeux while he was the inaugural director of the country's first art school. Joyeux and Cézard eventually published books of cartoons about their stays in Vietnam, *La vie large des colonies* (The Colonial Good Life) in 1912 and *Album* in 1909, respectively.

Michael Vann writes that, strangely, the colonists' cartoons even found their way in the "anti-colonial, nationalist, and communist movements" (2010, 83, 108). He says:

> However, when the colonized adopted the colonizer's art of caricature, the medium became a method for critiquing the empire without using racial stereotypes. This art form also served as a way to communicate social and political criticism to a population with a relatively low level of education and literacy. . . . In this way, the earlier phase of colonial cartoons, despite their obvious racism, paradoxically contributed to the rise of a Vietnamese tradition. During the various phases of Vietnamese revolutionary upheaval from the 1920s to the 1970s, there was a clear connection between the propaganda of the nationalist and the communist movements and the earlier development of cartoon and caricature in the colonial era. (Vann 2010, 108)

Cartoons by local artists came a bit later. In fact, nationalist leader Ho Chi Minh (Nguyen Ai Quoc) drew the first political cartoon (against French colonial rule) in *Le Pariah* in 1922 (Pham Thu Thuy 2003). The first ongoing comics characters, Ly Toet, created by Nhat Linh (pen name Dong Son), and Xa Xe, by foremost painter Nguyen Gia Tri, comically portrayed the difficulties of colonial life and created a "safe space for subtle political commentary" (Vann 2010, 108). *Ly Toet* first appeared in 1930 in the weekly *Phu Nu Thoi Dam* (Woman Today)

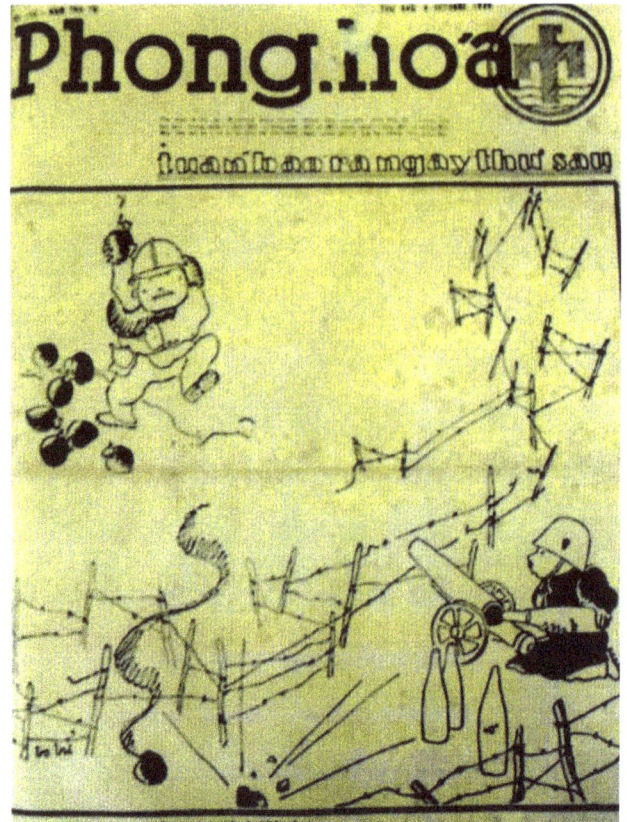

13.9. Cartoon cover of *Phong Hoa*. Permission of Ly Truc Dung.

and was relocated in 1932 until 1936 to *Phong Hoa* (Culture and Customs), the chief editor of which was Nhat Linh himself. When the government closed *Phong Hoa*, *Xa Xe* was published in the weekly *Ngay Nay* (Today) from 1936 to 1941. Except for these separations, these two characters mostly appeared together, portrayed as members of the "uneducated 'official class'" and used to "strongly criticize the backward lifestyle and to reflect the conflicts between undated values and Western culture. In addition, they were also used to point out many wicked aspects of the colonial government and the local puppet-headed Vietnamese offices: corruption, exploitation, authoritarianism" (Chi Do Huu 2011, 66–67).

As noted above, distinctions between cartoons and illustrations in Vietnamese newspapers and magazines have been blurry. This was particularly evident during the long periods of war, but it is still a trait today. Such drawings were/are propagandistic, depicting military life or government campaigns and lacking humor. Famous painters drew illustrations for magazines and books, including Si Ngoc (Nguyen Si Ngoc), Bui Xuan Phai, Duong Bich Lien, Dang Duc Sinh, Van Da (Nguyen Van

Da), and Huy Toan (Le Huy Toan), the latter a military illustrator of *Arts and Literature of the People's Army* known for his realistic battle scenes. More active as cartoonists were artists Mai Van Hien and Phan Ke An. Using the pen name Phan Kich, Phan Ke An drew satirical drawings during the war with France, serving as a cultural militant in the Press and Propaganda Service (Tran Van Can, Huu Ngoc, and Vu Huyen 1987, 73–74).

When the country was split in 1954, with a communist ideology in the north and capitalism in the south, the purposes of comic art significantly changed, those in North Vietnam predominantly propagandistic, those in South Vietnam largely entertainment oriented. The cartoonist who made the biggest impact in South Vietnam was Nguyen Hai Chi, who drew under the pseudonyms Tran Ai and Cap, but more often as Choé.

Born in 1943, Choé dropped out of school after the third grade to help support his family. He began doing satirical drawings while in the military and continued as a cartoonist (as well as an oil, silk, and watercolor painter, writer, poet, and music composer) until his death in the United States in 2003 (Liberty Art Viet Nam 2014). He was the scourge of the South Vietnamese authorities for his "sharp and often grotesque depictions of those he deemed responsible for the state of his country" (Thuc-sinh 1984, 9). He spared no one and nothing, striking out most often against the North and South Vietnamese authorities, as well as foreign leaders such as Nixon and Kissinger. David Shipler, in a special to the *New York Times*, gave a few examples of Choé's acid humor:

> President Nixon, dressed as a fiendish doctor, prepares a wicked-looking hypodermic needle filled with a serum of dollars. Cambodia's President, Lon Nol, in diapers, lies on the floor clutching a baby body in the form of a bomb. . . . President Nixon and Mao Tse Tung, their arms extended for an embrace, walk toward each other on a bridge of suffering Vietnamese peasants. (Shipler 1973, 14)

Choé told the *New York Times* that he drew out of sadness, anger being of no help, and that in the polarized atmosphere he found himself in, he spoke up only for the "victimized peasant who is at the mercy of the powerful." He admitted to being responsible for the confiscation of a number of newspapers and the trials of some publishers because of his unwillingness to alter his cartoons to suit censors. Sometimes the censors themselves deleted parts of his cartoons or banned them outright. An example he gave referred to his drawing after the North Vietnamese negotiator at the Paris talks, Le Duc Tho, rejected the Nobel Peace Prize. Choé drew Tho hurling a bucket labeled with a skull and crossbones into the faces of the Nobel committee. The censor erased Tho from the cartoon, because dramatizing the act would add to his importance (Shipler 1973, 14).

Choé paid a price for his outspokenness; he was arrested at different times by both the Saigon-based Nguyen Van Thieu government and the Communist forces and imprisoned. During Thieu's last months in power, on February 4, 1975, Choé was arrested as a Communist agent; the police denied the arrest, although the *Saigon Post* wrote in the space normally reserved for Choé's cartoon: "Following the arrest of our cartoonist Choé by the national police, his column is left vacant beginning Thursday. We hope he will be freed soon to resume his work for our readers' service" (Thuc-sinh 1984, 9).

After South Vietnam's fall in 1975, Choé drew as "Ta" in *Tin Sang*, one of two remaining dailies. In April 1976, he was detained in a reeducation camp without charges or trial as a "dangerous reactionary and counterreactionary." He was released after eleven years in 1987, when he continued drawing cartoons for the dailies *Lao Dong* (Labor) and *Cong An* (Public Security) and pursuing his painting career. Choé was credited with drawing more than fifteen thousand cartoons, some of which appeared in foreign periodicals such as the *New York Times*, *Asahi Shimbun*, *Newsweek*, and others; his main targets were corruption, social vices, violence against women, and war (*Nhan Dan* 2009).

By the waning years of Choé's career, the late 1990s, the situation relative to political cartoons and humor/cartoon periodicals had improved a bit. For example, *Lao Dong*, which carried Choé's cartoons in its Saturday

13.10. "The Victory of Guns over Butter," Choé.

edition, devoted an entire section called "Xa Xu Bap" (Letting Off Steam) to humorous illustrations, satirical verses, and modern parodies of proverbs and old sayings. Three magazines specialized in humor and satirical cartoons in this period, namely the already mentioned *Youth Humor*, *Relaxation*, and *Humor*, brought out by the Fine Arts Association of Vietnam (Pham Thu Thuy 2003, 98).

Political cartoons commonly perceived as drawings critical of the political and societal situation of a country are nearly nonexistent or cleverly hidden in today's Vietnam. One veteran cartoonist proudly showed me some of his drawings that were hard-hitting, well-executed pieces of satire—truly political cartoons—but he dampened the spirit of the moment by saying that they were posted on Facebook solely for his friends.

A number of cartoonists see Facebook, and the internet more generally, as alternative venues. Chi Do Huu (2022) said that whereas *Tuoi Tre Cuoi* cartoons are mediocre and compromising, those on the internet are sharp. Depending on how severely the government regulates the internet, it is a potentially significant carrier of political cartoons. One-half of Vietnam's population are active users of Facebook.

A Brief Conclusion

Vietnam is encrusted in a group of Asian countries (e.g., China, Laos, North Korea, and Myanmar) where political cartooning has been anathema to government, party,

and/or military ideologies and practices for decades. Any change in this scenario will likely be small and short-lived, as history has shown thus far.

Bibliography

Brown, Marianne. 2014. "Can Vietnamese Comics Win Readers' Hearts?" BBC News, June 22. http://www.bbc.com/news/world-asia-27338112.

Chi Do Huu. 2011. "Comic Art in Vietnam: A Brief History." *International Journal of Comic Art* 13, no. 1 (Spring): 62–86.

Chi Do Huu. 2022. "Nationally, Much Less; Transnationally, A Struggle to Grow: Comic Art in Vietnam." In *Transnationalism in East and Southeast Asian Comics Art*, edited by John A. Lent, Wendy Siuyi Wong, and Benjamin Wai-ming Ng. Cham, Switzerland: Palgrave Macmillan.

Hoa Si Biem. n.d. "Cartoonist Ly Truc Dung." https://hoasibiem.com/1365/hoa-si-biem-ly-truc-dung.html&prev=search.

Hung Nguyen Long. 2018. Interview with John A. Lent and Xu Ying, Hanoi, March 1.

Keenan, Faith. 1997. "License to Laugh." *Far Eastern Economic Review*, September 4, 44–45.

Kong Ngoan. 1993. Interview with John A. Lent, Hanoi, August 11.

Lent, John A. 2000. "Political Adversaries and Agents of Social Change: Editorial Cartoonists in Southeast Asia." Paper presented at the Popular Culture Association conference, New Orleans, April 22.

Lent, John A. 2004. "Defining Comic Art: An Onerous Task." *Journal of Communication Studies* (April–June): 1–11.

Le Phuong [Leo]. 2018. Interview with John A. Lent and Xu Ying, Hanoi, March 1.

Liberty Art Viet Nam. 2014. "Choé (Nguyen Hai Chi)." February 26. http://libertyartvietnam.blogspot.com/2014/02/choe-nguyen-hai-chi-1943-born-in-giang.html.

Ly Truc Dung. 2018. Interview with John A. Lent and Xu Ying, Hanoi, March 2.

Mi Ly. 2012. "Painter Ly Truc Dung: Making a Politician Grow Old Quickly, Draw Caricatures for a Long Time." *The Thao Van Hoa*, June 22. https://thethaovanhoa.vn/van-hoa-giai-tri/hoa-si-ly-truc-dung-lam-chinh-khach-gia-nhanh-ve-bie.

Nguyen Hong Phuc. 2017. "Comics in Vietnam: A Newly Emerging Form of Storytelling." *Kyoto Review of Southeast Asia*, no. 32. http://kyotoreview.org/issue-16/comics-in-vietnam-a-newly-emerging.

Nguyen Thanh Chung. 1993. Interview with John A. Lent, Hanoi, August 10.

Nguyen Thanh Phong. 2018. Interview with John A. Lent and Xu Ying, Hanoi, February 27.

Nhan Dan. 2009. "Cartoonists' Works Light Up City." November 10.

Pham Thu Thuy. 2003. "Speaking Pictures: *Biem Hoa* or Satirical Cartoons on Government Corruption and Popular Political Thought in Contemporary Vietnam." In *Consuming Urban Culture in Contemporary Vietnam*," edited by Lisa B. W. Drummond and Mandy Thomas, 89–109. London: Routledge Curzon.

Phuong Ha. 1993. Interview with John A. Lent, Hanoi, August 11.

Shipler, David K. 1973. "A Sad Young Saigon Cartoonist Wields an Angry Pen." *New York Times*, November 20, 14.

Streicher, Lawrence H. 1967. "On a Theory of Political Caricature." *Comparative Studies in Society and History* 9, no. 4 (July): 427–45.

Thuc-sinh. 1984. "Choe: Detained Cartoonist." *Index on Censorship* 13, no. 6 (December): 8–9. https://journals.sagepub.com/doi/abs/10.1080/03064228408533803.

Tran Van Can, Huu Ngoc, and Vu Huyen. 1987. *Vietnamese Contemporary Painters*. Hanoi: Red River.

Vann, Michael G. 2010. "Caricaturing 'the Colonial Good Life' in French Indochina." *European Comic Art* 2, no. 1: 83–108.

South Asia

Birth of a Cartoon Community

Pride, enthusiasm, and a strong feeling of camaraderie encircled the nearly twenty major cartoonists I interviewed and chatted with in Dhaka, in October 2016, this despite the governmental and religious intolerance under which they worked. They took pride in having the longest-lasting humor/cartoon magazine, as well as one of the oldest and most popular comic strips, in all of South Asia; they enthused about the recent launching of a local comic book presence with two producers and an outlet, and they displayed a fused purpose to advance their profession.

Unlike in other parts of Asia, Bangladesh's cartooning community consists of a number of up-and-coming and middle-aged practitioners who, at one time or another, were either a staff member on and/or a contributor to *Unmad* (Mad), a cartoon/humor magazine founded in 1978. These cartoonists sparked an explosion of activity while adding a professional flair, leading to the organization of the Bangladesh Cartoonist Association (BANCARAS) in 2010–2011; the Bangladesh Cartoon Fest with an exhibition in 2012; and Cartoon People, a community of comic art enthusiasts learning drawing skills and posting work on YouTube, and the Akantis Comic Art School, both in 2016. Three professional political/humor cartoonists sparked most of this burst of innovation: Ahsan Habib, longtime head of *Unmad*; Mehedi Haque, the unifying force of Bangladeshi cartooning, executive editor of *Unmad*, and founder of BANCARAS, Dhaka Comics, and Akantis; and Tanmoy (Syed Rashad Imam), political cartoonist, graphic novelist, and organizer of Cartoon People.

Since its founding in 1978 by college student friends Ishtiaq Hossain and Kazi Khalid Ashraf, *Unmad* not only provided established humor writers and artists with a stable platform but served as a mentoring station and launching pad for the careers of at least two generations of amateur cartoonists. The first issue of *Unmad* sold an unexpectedly whopping three thousand copies (Habib 2016), eventually peaking at twenty-five thousand copies. Because it took two to three months to produce,

Chapter 14

Bangladesh

14.1. Mehedi Haque, Dhaka, October 14, 2016. Photo by John A. Lent. Permission of Mehedi Haque.

14.2. Cover of *Unmad*'s anniversary issue featuring longtime publisher/editor Ahsan Habib pulling the strings, 2015. Permission of Ahsan Habib.

Unmad started out as a triquarterly and later became a monthly. Ahsan Habib, with six others, joined the team with the second issue, but by the ninth issue, *Unmad* was falling apart. At that point, Habib quit his bank job and assumed responsibility for the magazine, which resumed in 1985 as a monthly. He recalled his mother's concern: "You cannot tell the father of your wife, you do cartoons," she said (Habib 2016). Because cartoonists and humor writers were scarce as well as "moody and irresponsible," there were times when Habib and a few staff members had to fill in parts of the fifty-six-page issues themselves (Shahid 2018). Until the 1990s, *Unmad* was often filled with political cartoons that directly criticized the government, until it faced three defamation cases. Since then, *Unmad* has focused on social commentary rather than direct politics (Shahid 2018; also Siddiqua 2016; Roy 2014). From 1980 to 1993, *Unmad* competed with *Cartoon* humor magazine, founded by Mohammad Harun-Or-Rashid (Lent 2015, 261–62; Harun-Or-Rashid 1990, 1993).

BANCARAS was an idea floated by a gathering of some junior cartoonists with Ahsan Habib in the *Unmad* office in June 2010. Swiftly, the suggestion turned into reality, and the group was established with Mehedi Haque as president and veteran political cartoonists Rafiqun Nabi, Ahsan Habib, Shishir Bhattacharjee, and Sharier Khan as advisers. The purposes of BANCARAS were to connect cartoonists with one another; promote cartoonists to the public as well as publishers and editors; work jointly on issues of copyright, payment, rights, and syndication; and collect, in an online gallery and published book, the best cartoons annually. Founder Mehedi Haque (2016) said that a specific reason for setting up BANCARAS was because of the arrest, jailing, and exiling of cartoonist Arifur Rahman, saying that there was "no voice for matters like this" (A. Hossain 2011). In early January 2011, BANCARAS held a three-day exhibition, and in November 2012 it inaugurated its first Bangladesh Cartoon Fest. The five-day program, featuring an exhibition of the works of thirty-five local cartoonists and animation screenings of three Bangladeshi studios, was meant to showcase and promote creativity (Hasan 2012).

Cartoon People was the brainchild of Tanmoy, a young and energetic *Dhaka Tribune* political cartoonist who felt a huge need for a media platform for art lovers. He started Cartoon People as a sort of interactive, friendly, and easy-to-approach tutorial for individuals of all ages interested in art, cartooning, drawing, sketching, or doodling. He came up with the concept because, as he said, "Think about the reaction from your parents when you have the 'I want to become a full-time painter/cartoonist' discussion with them.[1] In Bangladesh, we don't have an institutional backup for cartooning" (*Daily Star* 2016).

The online tutorial Cartoon Show Dhaka, started on October 27, 2016, and channeling on YouTube, is a place where cartoon buffs meet, interact, and learn from local cartoonists and handouts with detailed instructions. Cartoon People also offers Sketchbook Saturday, a mobile cartooning school where every Saturday, anyone interested can join a sketch walk in different areas of

Dhaka, sketch what they see, come in direct contact with established cartoonists, and then "sit in a circle and share tricks and tips while giving constructive criticism to each other, without hurting anyone of course," Tanmoy said (*Daily Star* 2016).

Before Cartoon Show Dhaka, instructional workshops existed, at least seven led by Ahsan Habib and *Unmad*. Tanmoy (2016) said that they stopped when they became too large to handle. Cartooning was part of the instruction in Khondokar Abu Sayeed's in-home art school started in 1988. Assisted by his artistic wife, Gemy, Sayeed taught thirty to forty students per session sketching, painting, cartooning, strip cartooning, and clay sculpting (Sayeed 1993).

In 2016, when so much was being implemented in the cartoon world, Mehedi Haque established Akantis, a school divided into sections on basic cartoons, drawing, character design, and comic book design. Maximum enrollment per course is sixteen. Students meet every Friday and Saturday, have lunch and take five hours of instruction for four weeks (Haque 2016). Akantis offers video tutorials gratis and two open sessions monthly with guest speakers, and plans to start other courses in anatomy drawing, 2-D animation, and traditional media painting (Zaman 2019; also Hammadi 2016).[2]

History

To determine when cartooning began in Bangladesh, the time of establishment of "Bangladesh" must first be determined. Officially, Bangladesh was born after the 1971 War of Liberation. Previously, the territory was British India, and then East Pakistan. Some cartoons existed in that part of British India in 1930; however, it was the cartooning from the beginning of the Language Movement in the 1940s to 1971, dealing with widespread discontent over political dominance and linguistic, ethnic, and religious differences, that opened the pages of Bangladesh's cartoon history.

One of the cartoonists whose career spanned the three distinct geopolitical systems was Kazi Abul Kasem

(pen name Dopiaza), who started out in Calcutta in 1930, drawing political and social cartoons and a strip and illustrating literary verses as cartoons. Much of his work appeared in the *Daily Azad* (1936–1992), both while that paper was located in Calcutta and after its transferal to Dhaka in 1948. Kasem (1993) said that many opportunities came to him in his new homeland. Others who drew vitriolic cartoons of the politics of the 1950s and 1960s and the subsequent independence period, in magazines, posters, banners, placards, and leaflets, included Quamrul Hassan, Zainul Abedin, Qayyum Chowdhury (Qa-Chow), Rashid Chowdhury, Murtoza Bashir, Debdas Chakravarty, Mizanur Rahim, Mostafa Aziz, Mahmud Zamir, Subhash Dutta (Mita), Kalam Mahmud (pen names, Birbal and Titu), Hasheem Khan (Chabi Khan), Nazrul Islam (Nazrul), Rafiqun Nabi (Ranabi), Serajul Huq (Sarda), and Banizul Huq (Bamiz). Their periodical outlets were the newspapers *Daily Azad*, *Purbadesh*, *Morning News*, and *Dainik Bangla*, and general magazines such as the weekly *Bichitra* and *Weekly Forum* and the monthly *Sacitra Sandhani*. *Bichitra* and the *Weekly Forum* have been singled out for their political cartoons: *Bichitra* because of the role it played in "mixing a few objective chuckles with the solemn business of nation building" (Qureshi 1980, 27); the *Weekly Forum* for being the "only publication to start using political cartoons in Bangladesh by Bangladeshi cartoonists" (Ranabi 1993).

Ranabi (1993) thought that the country's cartooning tradition was strengthened during the two years before the war between West and East Pakistan, when cartoons ("some crude") pointed out the "political figures of [West] Pakistanis, their mismanagement, their hatred of Bengali people." Some cartoonists actively participated in political movements both before and after 1971. For instance, self-labeled "freedom fighter" and cartoonist Saiful Alam was jailed from 1975 to 1978 for his political beliefs aligned with the socialist party, the Chhara League.[3] His cartoons were fiercely combative, one example of which is a magazine drawing created on President Hussain Muhammad Ershad's departure from power in 1990, showing him, former Pakistani president

14.3. Veteran political cartoonist Shishir Bhattacharjee, Dhaka, July 27, 1993. Photo by John A. Lent. Permission of Shishir Bhattacharjee.

Yahya Khan, and Adolf Hitler, all with garlands of skulls around their necks.

As would be expected, independence spawned a boom in political cartoons, but it was short-lived with the arrival of autocratic rule. Powerful daily newspaper cartoons vanished; the few cartoons that remained came out in the recently launched *Unmad* and weeklies such as *Bichitra*, which carried Ranabi's *Tokai*, a social commentary strip.

This trend of mainstream dailies staying relatively idle and weeklies filling in with satires and cartoons continued through the 1980s, during the repressive Ershad government. *Daily Star* political cartoonist Sharier Khan described the satires and cartoons:

> The satires were written in the same spirit of political cartoons; they intended to send an antigovernment message through humor and fictitious characters resembling the powerful ones. The advantage of such satires was that we all knew what it was about, but the government could not take a legal action as these were legally works of fiction.

However, satires have to be properly read and understood. The readers must have a certain level of maturity to understand the real meanings of the satire. (Khan 2007)

With the return of democracy in the 1990s, and tied to it more freedom of expression, newspapers expanded in number with more features, including political cartoons, some even making the front page. Sharier Khan (2007) gave special credit to Shishir Bhattacharjee of *Vorer Kagoj* for redefining the "proper use of cartoons as a tool for editorial positions of a newspaper" with his front-page political cartoons in the late 1980s and early 1990s.

Bhattacharjee saw patches of brightness in Bangladeshi political cartooning when I interviewed him in 1993, referring to new newspapers popping up and "witty ideas coming out," primarily from newcomers. He hoped that someday, skilled artists would draw the clever ideas. Bhattacharjee thought of himself as a serious artist who had a hobby of cartooning (Bhattacharjee 1993). His artistic skills showed in the striking caricatures he drew in his front-page cartoons, both innovative at the time. During the 1980s, he drew anti-Ershad political caricature cartoons for magazines, usually *Desh Bandhu* (Friend), before it was banned in 1987, and then the Communist Party newspaper *Ekota* (Unity). By 1993, Bhattacharjee drew political cartoons solely for *Vorer Kagoj*; they were published on alternate days. He explained the front-page positioning:

> *Vorer Kagoj* is a new paper and it wants a high circulation. They put my political cartoons on the front page for prestige purposes. Cartoons are a big attraction. The people like front-page caricature cartoons very much. Most of the cartoons relate to political issues; some deal with social.
>
> Quamrul Hassan used caricature in his cartoons during the revolution, and he inspired me a lot. There were front-page political cartoons during the Language Movement of the 1950s and 1960s, but they were on the bottom half, not the top as in *Vorer Kagoj*. (Bhattacharjee 1993)

During the Ershad regime, Bhattacharjee's cartoons brought some reprisals from the government, usually directed to the editor; they included shrinkage of government advertising to, and noncooperation with, *Vorer Kagoj* as well as threatened litigation. Bhattacharjee (1993) said that he was careful in his caricatures of top officials, but he did not spare them.

Bhattacharjee's paintings were also critical of the political system and its leaders, always done in a satirical manner. Art critic Abul Mansur said of his paintings: "Shisher's macabre interpretations of the social condition in which he lives, his agonized criticism directed towards the godfathers of the society and his keen sense of wit and jest have given his paintings a distinct artistic vocabulary of his own. It is also true his cartoons draw heavily from his paintings, which are very natural. They compliment [*sic?*] each other" (Rosan 2005).

Other political cartoonists at the time wielded a strong pen against the government and political parties, varying the pressure they applied to fit the circumstances and to be able to keep drawing. Saiful Alam (1993) said that religious groups and political parties gave him grief, even threatening to kill him, but regional and national leaders left him alone. He explained that he did not directly strike out against the government, because the owner of *Shandwig Magazine*, for which he drew regularly, was friendly with the government; he added: "Usually, we do subtle cartoons and criticize the whole organization, but not individual leaders." The exceptions were Ershad and accused collaborator, Golom Azad. He showed me a cartoon that portrayed Azad sitting on a turtle holding the Pakistani flag and a sword, the implication being that like a turtle, he could change by putting his head in a shell (Alam 1993).

Alam drew politically charged covers and the lead cartoon for *Shandwig* from 1989 to the end of 1992. At the top of the list of problems he saw in 1993 was that no staff cartoonist positions existed; all cartoonists worked as freelancers, paid per cartoon. "If I work freelance, I can earn enough for my smoking," he said in jest (Alam 1993). Much of his income came from drawing commercial cartoons. The other political cartoonists leaned on outside support: Bhattacharjee, Nazrul Islam, and

14.4. Political cartoonist Nazrul Islam, Dhaka, July 25, 1993. Photo by John A. Lent. Courtesy of Nazrul Islam.

Ranabi, college teaching; Asiful Huda, commercial designing, acting, and writing plays.

Cartoonists complained about other problems of political cartooning: low and late payments, riskiness, lack of training, and professional neglect. Nazrul Islam, who began drawing political cartoons in 1972, which were published in the daily *Ganokantho*, experienced all of these shortcomings but thought the main difficulty was that newspapers did not encourage cartoonists. He said: "When the editor cannot write on a topic, he tries to have a cartoon drawn on it." Only *Bichitra*, for which he was drawing, consistently favored cartoons, because its editor was an art school graduate, Islam (1993) said. Although he thought that the early 1990s were better years for political cartooning than even the immediate postindependence period, he deplored the then current practice of the "editor having the idea, the cartoonist, the hands." Instead of drawing only what the editor suggested, Islam gave him two or three cartoons from which to choose (Islam 1993). Editors were reluctant to pay the average five- to ten-dollar equivalent in takas,

14.5. Caricature of Kazi Abul Kasem. Courtesy of Kazi Abul Kasem.

sometimes holding up payment for months; they rationalized that because cartoons did not require coloring or shading, they should not fetch high prices, Islam (1993) lamented.

Speaking as a political cartoonist who began his career in 1930, eighty-one-year-old Kazi Abul Kasem said that he lived by a philosophy of standing with his compatriots. "When the masses of Bangladesh are enraged on a subject, then I am with them, on the same line. What my countrymen want, I have done," Kasem (1993) emphasized. He said that the ideas for his political cartoons were his own, but he had used editors' suggestions when they were good. Kasem believed that only the upper sector of society truly understood the "inner meanings" of cartoons, and they alone respected the profession. He saw religious mullahs as hindrances to cartooning and drawing in general, but they were not as strong as previously. He wondered whether, had his own parents not died when he was young, he would have been directed away from cartooning as a career (Kasem 1993).

Although known primarily for his strip cartoon *Tokai*, highlighting social issues with occasional political overtones, Ranabi (Rafiqun Nabi) drew straight-up political and pocket cartoons during the movements that led to the 1971 revolution, particularly for the

tabloid *Weekly Forum*. He began drawing cartoons in 1961 while an art student at the University of Dhaka, mainly for literary magazines, posters, leaflets, and the like. As Ranabi remembered, "As an art student, I was just practicing drawing, and slowly, slowly, I started putting captions on them, witty things on the drawings" (Ranabi 1993). Ranabi's political cartooning continued in the weekly *Bichitra* and its sister daily, *Dainik Bangla*, through the 1970s, as well as in the *Express* and *Kalyan Forum* (R. Hossain 2019).

He began musing about doing a comic strip in the late 1960s but put the idea aside as war engulfed the country, taking time off to study in Greece and then fretting for two more years on how to conceptualize his character (see Ranabi's sketch of *Tokai* in Lent 2015, 257, fig. 14.2). He decided that Tokai was to be a poor street boy, later described by a *Daily Star* reporter as "always cheerful making fun and uttering witty scathing reflections, in his usual Dhakaite language, on things around him, which constitute contemporary society" (Rashid 2004). The strip began in *Bichitra*, where it stayed from 1978 until 1999, when it moved to *Weekly 2000* magazine. Bangladeshis accepted *Tokai* immediately, sending in suggestions for the strip, scolding Ranabi for not taking proper care of the character (for example, not clothing him warmly), questioning why he did not deal with certain social and political issues, and imploring him not to terminate *Tokai* when he considered doing this in 1993 (Ranabi 1993). Ranabi said that his intention was not to insert politics into *Tokai*, but readers expected political and social messages and often read unintended meanings into the strip, making Tokai a "social character." Eventually, because of public demand, Ranabi began to place messages in *Tokai*—not "direct political" ones but those with social and current themes (Ranabi 1993). A few examples:

[A]sked if he knows what a family is, the homeless Tokai reflects, "I know mine—footpath, dustbin, the crows etc." . . . Often he makes fun of the society's hypocrisy. Asked what his vow is on the Children's day, a grave Tokai says, "To grow up soon." . . . Tokai's world is full of fantasies where he talks to crows, cows, and other animals. . . . To the

14.6. Cartoon by Nasif Ahmed, the *Daily Jankantha*, Dhaka. An accusation that the prime minister was adding to the widespread destruction occurring in Bangladesh.

fantasy of a crow wondering what would happen if it could exchange life with Tokai, the puzzled boy answers, "What else! We would have [our] meal at this same dustbin!" . . . Often, Tokai's satire is rather direct. In answer to what he prefers as a daily meal, rice or bread, Tokai says, "Nothing special! Whatever people throw away!" (Rashid 2004, quoted in Lent 2012)

The word *tokai* had no original meaning, but over time, it came to describe poverty and unalleviated frustration and was added to the Bengali dictionary in 1990 (for more on *Tokai*, see Lent 2015, 257–59).

Ranabi reiterated the same litany of difficulties as others: low payment, lack of interest by editors, self-censorship, no training, lack of respect and sense of importance, few people entering cartooning, and fewer still women. Ranabi could recall only one female cartoonist, Samira Sayed, who drew for *Unmad* and *Cartoon* humor magazines in the early 1980s. He ventured reasons for the drought of female cartoonists: women become housewives and their professional work is not accepted in their husbands' houses; they don't have an outside world to draw about; they don't take cartooning very seriously and give up too easily (Ranabi 1993).

The Bangladeshi cartoon scene took a turn for the better at the beginning of the twenty-first century. During the first decade of the new century, newspapers used cartoons more often than before; some published weekly satire and humor sections; most had their own cartoonist as a permanent contributor or staff member; and other instances of progress were noticeable such as a few exhibitions and competitions (Khan 2007). Prominent among the latter was the annual Anti-Corruption Cartoon Competition, organized beginning in 2006 by Transparency International Bangladesh. Additionally, a crop of new cartoonists appeared beginning in the mid-1990s through 2010; they became the generation that added a large dose of professionalism to comic art. They included Mehedi Haque, Tanmoy (Syed Rashad Imam), Khalil Rahman, Nasreen Sultana Mitu, M. A. Kuddus, Biplob Kumar Chakoborty, Nasif Ahmed, Sadatuddin Ahmed Amil (Sadat), twin brothers Md. Humaun Kabir Manik and Md. Kamruzzaman Ratan (who cooperatively go by Cartoonist Manik-Ratan),[4] Asifur Rahman (Rats Asif, not to be confused with Arifur Rahman), and Morshed Mishu. Some commonalities among them, besides being relatively young and energetic, are that nearly all had been affiliated with *Unmad* and mentored

14.7. Poignant cartoon by Nasreen Sultana Mitu on the 2013 collapse of a garment industry building that cost 1,134 lives. Permission of Mitu.

by Ahsan Habib, most are college graduates (at least six in fine arts at the University of Dhaka), and all benefited from the opening of new dailies, some with weekly humor supplements, as outlets. For example, *Prothom Alo*, a daily founded in 1998, has regularly carried eleven supplements on topics such as psychology, sports, science, happiness, health, and information technology. Its supplement *Rôsh + Alo* (Humor and Light), a humor magazine published on Mondays, is an attractive venue for cartoonists. Other dailies that carry humor supplements are *Kaler Kantho* with *Magaz Dholai* (Brainwash); *Samakal*, *Pachal* (Gossip); *Daily Jugantor*, *Bicchu* (Woodpecker); and *Daily Inquilab*, *Upohaar*. These supplements invite theme-oriented works, organize competitions, and encourage amateur cartoonists. The sixteen-page supplements have popularized the new dailies, which the corporate sector launched as an investment in mass media at the start of the twenty-first century (Sahid Ullah 2012).

Even during the 2010s, when political cartoons sometimes were shelved to allow space for advertising or dropped for fear of government reaction, labeling oneself a cartoonist was a source of pride; cartooning had become a serious profession (Manjabeen 2015).

During interviews in 2016, political cartoonists had serious complaints about restrictions and self-censorship, but overall they were content that about a dozen of them were salaried as staff cartoonists, that a professional infrastructure was in place, and that younger individuals, including a few women, were attracted to cartooning.

The most prominent woman cartoonist in Bangladesh is Nasreen Sultana Mitu, who signs as Mitu. Like others, she got her start at *Unmad* under the tutelage

of Habib. She said that she drew four political cartoons weekly for the *Daily New Age*, the number depending on the "political situation and type of government we have" (Mitu 2016). Mitu believes that political cartoons play a very strong role in Bangladesh, citing her own cartoon about the May 2013 collapse of a garment manufacturer's building that claimed 1,134 lives and injured more than double that number. Mitu described a drawing of a pair of blue jeans with a blood-splotched price tag attached as "almost a symbol of oppression in [the] readymade garments sector and labor rights" (Direz 2018). The cartoon was widely used; its internet posting received more than 100,000 hits. Personally, Mitu received threats and complaints that she was ruining Bangladesh's garment industry (Mitu 2016).

Mitu weighed in on the lack of women cartoonists in Bangladesh, saying:

We are told to obtain a more secure and respected career. So, few take cartoon jobs. The reason for the scarcity is complex. The root is religion, Islam. But, Islam is different here. Also, we have not recovered from a colonial mentality. Girls are brought up differently here. The vision of life for them is that after marriage, they give their lives to their family. Their vision is narrower. Most girls cannot go out freely; it is difficult for them to come out of the box. As girls, they lack courage, can't move freely. Cartoonists need to know public thinking, but if a girl cannot go out, she can't find that out. (Mitu 2016)

Mitu considered that the major problem of Bangladeshi political cartooning concerned newspaper policy, stating: "You cannot choose a newspaper to draw for to match your beliefs; cartoonists are not synchronized with the policies of the paper they work for" (Mitu 2016).

Guided Cartooning

At least fifty years ago, I (and others) wrote about what we termed a "guided press," common throughout the so-called less-developed countries. A "guided press" is one that strictly follows government dictums, suggestions, and policies and nurtures devastating self-censorship. I don't hear the term now; perhaps guided presses are so common (even in formerly free societies) that the term is not needed; it is redundant. Obviously, cartooning can be, and is being, guided throughout the world at an alarming pace—by governments, religion, corporatism, and media themselves.

What Bangladeshi cartoonists discussed with me can be termed "guided cartooning." A couple of hard-hitting political cartoonists said that they have been pressured to relinquish cartooning in favor of animation and painting, others regularly face the frustration of seeing their cartoons spiked for various reasons, and most of them have been concerned about proposed legislation that will seriously hamper online cartooning. The cartoonists know their limits and the penalties they face if they cross the line, although the line is not always clearly marked. In some instances, they find subtle means to get their messages across.

Guided cartooning has a long tradition in Bangladesh, probably for the entire fifty-year existence of the country. This is understandable in the context of Bangladesh's infrastructure of quasi-authoritarian governments, a strong, conservative Muslim religion, and ministerial and big corporation ownership of mass media.

Guided cartooning existed when I first visited Bangladesh in July 1993, a time when government retaliation against cartoonists already had a history. In 1993, cartoonists such as Shishir Bhattacharjee, Saiful Alam, and Asiful Huda told me that the government and religious fundamentalists censored or otherwise threatened them.

All agreed that what criticism cartoonists did dish out was "cautious and muted."

In my interviews nearly a quarter of a century later (October 2016), traits of guided cartooning were frequently mentioned, among them: self-censorship, vaguely stated regulations, a government/politician/corporate-owned press, a preference for foreign over local issues, fewer and milder political cartoons, cartoonists expected to join government campaigns, and the limited use of caricatures of top officials.

At first glance, what appears strange is that the daily newspapers (especially English-language ones) most of the time do not carry political cartoons, yet nearly all of them employ at least one staff cartoonist. *Kaler Kantho* has three staff cartoonists; one of them, Biplob Kumar Chakoborty (2016), explained that it's because the daily's publisher is wealthy. Chakoborty said that he draws seven or eight cartoons and illustrations weekly for *Kaler Kantho*, but they are not political, or, at least, not directly political. Although Bangla-language newspapers are more prone to cover local issues than English-language dailies, Chakoborty pointed out that the issues often are violence, traffic, battered women, and the like. He said that many of his cartoons deal with the sport of cricket, adding: "In Bangladesh, it is caricature that is considered political and we cannot draw caricatures of the prime minister" (2016).

Others agreed that the number of political cartoons printed has dwindled significantly. Sadatuddin Ahmed Amil (Sadat), staff political cartoonist for the *Daily Star* since 2010, like others, said that the number of political cartoons depends on current issues and the political situation. Calling the present a boring time, he said: "There are a number of issues to say something about, but we can't." He and others saw a freer atmosphere in the early 2010s, during Prime Minister Sheikh Hasina's first term (Amil 2016). Cartoonists such as Nasreen Sultana Mitu (2016) of the *Daily New Age* and Zahid Hasan Benu (2016) of *Naya Diganta* (New Horizon) blame the present situation on the lack of a strong political opposition.

Sadat gave another reason for the drop in usage of political cartoons: fear of reprisals. He said that, as the leading English-language daily, "we [the *Daily Star*] are under pressure. The paper has had about seventy lawsuits against it, the result of an issue we wrote about criticizing the prime minister. There has been a 60 percent reduction in our political cartoon output. In two years, I have not drawn the prime minister" (Amil 2016). Sadat's predecessor at the *Daily Star*, Sharier Khan, who joined the newspaper shortly after its 1991 beginning and worked in various capacities, quit drawing political cartoons in 2013, when "all the militant forces and Prime Minister Sheikh Hasina took aim at the *Daily Star*." Claiming that his decision was based on his love of independence, Khan said, "I can't do cartoons that someone tells me what to think. I never want to be a staff cartoonist, because I don't want anyone to tell me what to draw. If I don't feel I own the cartoon, I don't do it. When you make creativity a factory, you get factory products. Cartoonists need passion; you draw what your heart feels" (Khan 2016).

Shishir Bhattacharjee, of the nation's largest circulation daily, *Prothom Alo*, supported the premise that the "freedom to cartoon" in Bangladesh has taken a severe hit in recent years. Since the late 1980s, Bhattacharjee has joined newspapers run by an editor, Motiur Rahman, he admires for his editorial independence—first *Ekota* (Unity), followed by *Azker Kagoj* (Daily Newspaper), *Vorer Kagoj*, and *Prothom Alo*, the latter founded by Rahman. Bhattacharjee said that he and Rahman had met with a financier who pledged a large sum of money to support *Prothom Alo* with no expectation of returns as long as the paper remained free. "I started doing cartoons as I felt they should be done," Bhattacharjee said; "it is very difficult now, but no one will admit it is difficult." In his view, if a cartoonist supports the opposition, limited as it is, troubles will ensue. "Before, if a minister did something funny [weird, illogical], I drew it, but not now," he added, "because now I will be sued and the minister's supporters will post the case in a distant town inconvenient for me to reach." Although he had been sued for what he called a "ridiculous" amount of money by a businessman criticized for his corruption, Bhattacharjee does not have much trouble doing

14.8. Tanmoy (Syed Rashad Imam), political cartoonist/graphic novelist and organizer of Cartoon People, Dhaka, October 19, 2016. Photo by John A. Lent. Permission of Tanmoy.

political cartoons today, but he admits that he does just one or two per month (Bhattacharjee 2016).

The repressive political atmosphere has forced some cartoonists into other areas of comic art such as animation, comic books, and humorous drawing. In a backhanded manner, this has benefited comic art more generally. For instance, Mehedi Haque, staff cartoonist for the *Daily New Age*, for which he draws three or four cartoons weekly (some of which are not published), in 2012 started Dhaka Comics, a comic book company publishing high-quality titles, some authored and drawn by Haque. After two years, the company broke even financially and has been growing ever since. Five of Dhaka Comics' first thirty-four titles were commissioned by the government, according to Haque (2016). A second comic book company, Mighty Punch, came onto the scene in September 2013, publishing four titles, all in English—*Shabash*, a jackfruit superhero who fights people who genetically modify food (Anis Rahman 2019); *Legend of Zooey*, the country's first female superhero; *Ms. Shabash*, a female journalist bent on writing

14.9. Censored political cartoonist, actor, and animator Asiful Huda, Dhaka, October 18, 2016. Photo by John A. Lent. Permission of Asiful Huda.

serious stories but assigned to interview the head of a skin-whitening lotion company; and *Lathial*, a bamboo-stick-wielding woman warrior. Mighty Punch founder Samir Asran Rahman, who creates and writes all the stories, said that fantasies of Bangladesh are used as topics to avoid "getting into political and cultural issues that will cause us problems" (S. A. Rahman 2016).

Tanmoy (Syed Rashad Imam) also aided the Bangladeshi cartooning environment after he found that the types of political cartoons he had been submitting to the *Dhaka Tribune* in 2013 were no longer welcome; the newspaper was not keen on publishing political cartoons and taking risks (Tanmoy 2016). Besides pioneering in graphic novels in Bangladesh with *Majib*, a twelve-part visual biography of the nation's founding father, Sheikh Mujibur Rahman (assassinated father of Sheikh Hasina, the present prime minister), Tanmoy also started the aforementioned Cartoon People community.

Animation benefited from the lull in political cartooning as well. As an example, one of Bangladesh's most forceful political cartoonists, Asiful Huda,

formerly of *Amar Desh* (My Country), turned to animation when *Amar Desh* was closed by the government, its editor imprisoned, and Huda made jobless with no prospects of getting a newspaper appointment in a very cautious atmosphere (Huda 2016). Huda has completed three animation shorts and has started to outfit a small studio in his home, from which he hopes to earn enough to support his family for the time being. Unfortunate for Huda is that much of the nation's animation is commissioned or purchased by government agencies, and, as he said, when the authorities "know the cartoons were made by Mr. Huda, they will push away" (Huda 2016).

As seen above, even in producing comic books and animation, cartoonists must be careful not to offend the government, a major source of their funding. Such self-censorship permeates all aspects of mass media in Bangladesh. Cartoonists relate many instances in which newspaper editors and they themselves must pull their punches. Nasreen Sultana Mitu said that cartoonists don't draw prominent people directly and have been known to avoid caricaturing the prime minister on issues pertinent to her; instead, they replace her in the cartoon with a "lesser minister." She said, "You can draw as long as you self-censor" (Mitu 2016). Haque told about a cartoon he drew for the *Daily New Age* depicting the prime minister in a positive, friendly pose while holding a bloody stick behind her back: "The editor told me I should remove the stick, which I did, and the cartoon lost all of its meaning, made no sense without the stick" (2016). Before putting any of his cartoons online, Haque must first receive approval from his editor. Tanmoy turned to social media because his newspaper editor censored regularly, which, he said, "really pissed me off." Bhattacharjee (2016), stating that there is "too much self-censorship," listed topics a cartoonist must avoid or treat very gingerly: religion, social taboos, freedom fighters of the 1971 War of Liberation, and women's rights. A former political cartoonist for the daily *Alokito Bangladesh*, Md. Zonayed Azim Chowdhury, said that the paper's editor pressured him with "guidelines—you cannot criticize the court, the flag, etc." (2016).

14.10. Senior cartoonist M. A. Kuddus of the *Daily Ittefaq*, Dhaka, October 15, 2016. Photo by John A. Lent. Permission of M. A. Kuddus.

Newspaper ownership determines much self-censorship. In Bangladesh, a large proportion of the mass media is owned by politicians or top businesspeople who are both tied to government and dedicated to protecting their vested interests and those of two or three dying political parties. Senior cartoonist M. A. Kuddus of the *Daily Ittefaq* said that the paper's owner, the minister of forestry and environment, gives a "little bit of direction," but all staff know that "this is his house and they have to follow him" (Kuddus 2016). He pointed out that when there were protests against building a power plant that would threaten the Sundarbans (an ecologically significant mangrove forest), he was not permitted to draw about the incident. *Kaler Kantho* is owned by Ahmed Akbar Sobhan, a housing tycoon, mall owner, and the country's "biggest businessman," according to cartoonist Chakoborty, who said that staff cartoonists are free unless they draw against Sobhan's business interests. "I can do some cartoons that others can't," Chakoborty said, qualifying his assertion: "If, for example, one of his buildings collapses, we cannot write or draw about the disaster. I can draw about it—and then quit" (Chakoborty 2016). The interests of *Prothom Alo*'s owner are also off-limits, according to Bhattacharjee.

Naya Diganta was owned by political party leader Mir Quasem Ali, who was hanged in 2016, accused of being a collaborator during the 1971 War of Liberation. *Naya Diganta* political cartoonist Zahid Hasan Benu said that the government confiscated Quasem's properties, including Diganta Media House, which it closed except for the daily newspaper (Benu 2016). And as another example, *Vorer Kagoj* is owned by a businessman/member of Parliament on the side of the ruling party.

Kuddus summed up the problem of ownership well, stating: "The biggest problem here for political cartoonists is that people we should caricature are newspaper owners, as government officials are buying daily newspapers. These people are well connected, so you cannot satirize or criticize many others who are family or friends of these owners" (Kuddus 2016).

Another characteristic of "guided cartooning" is the prevalence of vaguely stated regulations, to be interpreted by the authorities to suit their purposes and to keep cartoonists off-balance and generally cautious. Some Bangladeshi cartoonists cited this as a problem, mentioning Act 57 of 2016. Mitu described Act 57 as "not precise" and a "risk as a tool" (2016). Primarily designed to hinder online criticism, the regulation is a danger to freedom of expression and, by extension, "freedom to cartoon,"[5] in a country where a number of bloggers have been killed or forced out of Bangladesh by Islamic extremists. Mitu (2016) said that Act 57 so far has only been used against some vulgar online cartoons about the prime minister. Huda (2016) interpreted the law as an effort to stop all criticism of the government.

As a less conspicuous means of control, "guided cartooning" avoids worldwide media splashes such as that of cartoonist Arifur Rahman, whose jailing and exiling resounded for years, leaving a blight on Bangladeshi society. In September 2007, Arifur Rahman was arrested and jailed for a cartoon he drew for *Alpin*, then the weekly satire magazine of *Prothom Alo*, the charge being, "hurting the religious sentiment of the people." The cartoon, called "Naam" (Name), set off a firestorm across Bangladesh, landing Rahman in prison for six

14.11. The cartoon that led to the jailing, beating, torturing, and exiling of Arifur Rahman.

months, listing him on a website with a fatwa directed against him and other death threats, and subjecting him to brutal beatings and disgusting harassment such as having human feces thrown in his face and mouth. Killing Rahman was a ticket to heaven, he was told. The offending four-panel cartoon seemed harmless: A mullah asks a boy his name and the boy tells him. The mullah scolds the boy and tells him to always put Mohamad in front of his name. The mullah then asks the name of the cat the boy is holding, and he answers, "Mohamad Cat." In 2010, Rahman relocated to a Norwegian city that serves as a haven for exiled cartoonists. There, he also faced problems when a man tore down some of his works from an exhibition, calling them "blasphemous" (Sen 2017; Aishwarya and Harikumar 2017; Pial 2008; Roostami 2017). There was speculation at the time of Rahman's arrest that a gang of Islamic fundamentalists used the cartoon as a pretense to attack and bring down the activities of militant Islamists (Ahmed 2007).

The second case that drew the attention of international press freedom monitors was that of Ahmed Kabir Kishore, jailed in May 2020 under the Digital Security Act of 2018. Kishore was accused of using his satirical cartoons on social media to spread "rumours about Father of the Nation Bangabandhu Sheikh Mujibur Rahman, the War of Independence of Bangladesh and the coronavirus pandemic, and using slander, confusion and discord in order to create chaos" (Kabir 2021). Also accused with Kishore was writer Mushtaq Ahmed, who died in prison. Kishore was granted bail in March 2021 after ten months of imprisonment, before and during which he was brutally tortured, according to a case he filed under the Torture and Custodial Death (Prevention) Act of 2013 (*Daily Star* 2021).

A Brief Conclusion

"Guided cartooning" lies somewhere between libertarianism and authoritarianism, definitely leaning much closer to the latter. It differs slightly because quasi-private ownership of media exists in Bangladesh,

215

and control is maintained through a mixture of guidance and strong-arm tactics, if necessary, rather than total state ownership, strong, oppressive regulations, and the sledgehammer repercussions of authoritarianism. But, because "guided cartooning" is not absolute, cartoonists often don't know exactly where the red line they cannot cross is located, and thus they are wary about maneuvering across or around it through subtlety and hidden messages. As stated at the outset, this is a dilemma cartoonists increasingly face, even in so-called democracies.

Notes

1. There were exceptions. Mehedi Haque was encouraged by his father, a political columnist, who, upon seeing the fourteen-year-old's renderings of Tarzan and Asiful Huda's cartoons, asked him to illustrate his columns. At sixteen, Haque became acquainted with Ahsan Habib and *Unmad*, which he described as a "dream place for cartoonists" (Haque 2016). Ahsan Habib himself benefited from his own father's antics to acquaint his children with culture. Habib said that his father held weekly writing competitions with small prizes, staged musical programs, and supported the handmade magazines the children created, all carried out in the home. All family members became writers, brothers Humayun Ahmed and Muhammed Zafer Iqbal of national acclaim (Roy 2014).

2. Haque has also played a role in introducing the concept of graphic novels to Bangladesh; his tentatively titled *Identity* was near completion in 2016. Preceding him as graphic novelists were Sharier Khan and Tanmoy.

3. Saiful Alam was second in command of a military sector during the war with Pakistan (Alam 1993).

4. Manik-Ratan work as a team; as they said, "We can make more; we always did things together; we like the same cartoons." They began drawing cartoons for *Unmad* in 1998, while in high school. They recalled initially not receiving acknowledgment from Ahsan Habib for the cartoons they submitted. They said: "Then Ahsan Habib called us. He was not sure we both could draw cartoons so he put us in separate rooms to demonstrate that we could draw. He wanted to make sure we didn't copy from each other. We passed" (Manik 2016; Ratan 2016).

Since then, they have studied animation and set up their own studio, Nerd Rabbit Animation Studio. Manik-Ratan have also been active in *chika* (wall art), which has thrived for generations as a form of aesthetically drawn protest art. Street art gives them an opportunity to give messages on "burning issues,

like politics, poverty, and the Liberation War" (Auer 2012). The brothers pointed out advantages of graffiti: "It belongs to no one and everyone," anyone can enhance a message by adding to it, and one does not have to go through formal channels to be exhibited (Auer 2012). This type of political and social messaging had been a handy alternative during times when media were suppressed. In many cases, street artists are now reposting their work on social networks.

In addition to *chika*, other platforms of the cities are adorned by nonformal types of art, such as the thousands of brightly colored trishaws and the street surfaces themselves. Twice a year (International Mother Language Day, February 21, and Bangla New Year, April 14), Baishakh is celebrated, when roads are closed to allow street painting, usually on a theme (e.g., the abolishment of religious intolerance) (Chakoborty 2016).

5. Social media were increasingly scrutinized as the 2010s closed. In May 2020, cartoonist Ahmed Kabir Kishore was among eleven individuals charged with posting antigovernment information on social media. Kishore was detained under the Digital Security Act, passed in 2018, which journalists and activists fear will be misused to further limit freedom of expression. The antigovernment information Kishore was accused of spreading criticized the authorities' handling of the coronavirus outbreak (Al Jazeera 2020).

Bibliography

Ahmed, Jahed. 2007. "Cartoon Row in Bangladesh: Sentiment That Dies Hard." Islam Watch, September 22. https://www.islam-watch.org/JahedAhmed/Bangladesh-cartoon-sentiments-dies-hard.htm.

Aishwarya, A., and Nirupama Harikumar. 2017. "A Fight Armed with Humor." *Times of India*, May 6.

Alam, Saiful. 1993. Interview with John A. Lent, Dhaka, July 25.

Al Jazeera. 2020. "Bangladesh Cartoonist, Writer Charged for Anti-Government Posts." May 7. https://www.aljazeera.com/news/2020/5/7/bangladesh-cartoonist-writer-charged-for-anti-government-posts.

Amil, Sadatuddin Ahmed [Sadat]. 2016. Interview with John A. Lent, Dhaka, October 20.

Auer, Soraya. 2012. "Painting the Streets." *The Star* (*Daily Star*), May 4. https://archive.thedailystar.net/magazine/2012/05/01/art.htm.

Benu, Zahid Hasan. 2016. Interviews with John A. Lent, Dhaka, October 15, 20.

Bhattacharjee, Shishir. 1993. Interview with John A. Lent, Dhaka, July 27.

Bhattacharjee, Shishir. 2016. Interview with John A. Lent, Dhaka, October 19.

Chakoborty, Biplob Kumar. 2016. Interview with John A. Lent, Dhaka, October 15.

Chowdhury, Md. Zonayed Azim. 2016. Interview with John A. Lent, Dhaka, October 20.

Daily Star. 2016. "A Platform for Cartoon Lovers," December 9. https://www.thedailystar.net/star-weekend/spotlight/platform-cartoon-lovers-1327117.

Daily Star. 2021. "DMCH Medical Board Examines Kishore's Health, Suggests Few Tests." March 18. https://www.thedailystar.net/bangladesh/news/dmch-medical-board-examines-kishores-health-suggests-few-tests-2062833.

Direz, Valérie. 2018. "Free Speech: Draw to Move the Rows! Meet Mitu, the Cartoonist from Bangladesh!" Le Crayon, February 3. http://www.lecrayon.net/Le-blog/Libres-Paroles/Free-speech-Draw-to-move-the-rows!-Meet-Mitu-the-cartoonist-from-Bangladesh.

Habib, Ahsan. 1993. Interview with John A. Lent, Dhaka, July 25.

Habib, Ahsan. 2016. Interview with John A. Lent, Dhaka, October 17.

Hammadi, Saan. 2016. "School for Cartoons and Comics." *New Age Youth*, August 21. http://www.newagebd.net/3188/school-for-cartoons-and-comics/.

Haque, Mehedi. 2016. Interview with John A. Lent, Dhaka, October 14, 20.

Harun-Or-Rashid, Mohammad. 1990. Interview with John A. Lent, Budapest, August 22.

Harun-Or-Rashid, Mohammad. 1993. Interviews with John A. Lent, Dhaka, July 24, 25.

Hasan, Rakibul. 2012. "Innovation at Its Best." *Daily Star*, November 25. http://www.thedailystar.net/campus/2012/11/04/festival.htm.

Hossain, Anika. 2011. "Here's to a Bright and Funny Future." *Daily Star*, January 14. http://www.thedailystar.net/magazine/2011/01/02/exhibition.htm.

Hossain, Rafi. 2019. "Crosstalk: Of Arts and Culture." *Daily Star*, September 14. https://www.thedailystar.net/showbiz/interview/crosstalk-arts-and-culture-of-Bangladesh-1799554.

Huda, Asiful. 1993. Interview with John A. Lent, Dhaka, July 27.

Huda, Asiful. 2016. Interview with John A. Lent, Dhaka, October 18.

Islam, Nazrul. 1993. Interview with John A. Lent, Dhaka, July 25.

Kabir, Ahsan. 2021. "Reflections of Life: Mushtaq Is My Brother." *Daily Star*, March 11. https://www.thedailystar.net/opinion/online-exclusive/news/mushtaq-my-brother-2058969.

Kasem, Kazi Abul. 1993. Interview with John A. Lent, Dhaka, July 26.

Khan, Sharier. 2007. "Cartoons as a Medium to Create Public Opinion." Transparency International Bangladesh, August 22. https://www.ti-bangladesh.org/oldweb/cartoon_image/Writeup_ShahrierKhan.pdf.

Khan, Sharier. 2016. Interview with John A. Lent, Dhaka, October 17.

Kuddus, M. A. 2016. Interview with John A. Lent, Dhaka, October 15.

Lent, John A. 2012. "Sanmao and Tokai: Popular Street Urchins of Asian Comic Strips." *International Journal of Comic Art* 14, no. 1 (Spring): 35–50.

Lent, John A. 2015. *Asian Comics*. Jackson: University Press of Mississippi.

Manik, Md. Humaun Kabir. 2016. Interview with John A. Lent, Dhaka, October 20.

Manjabeen, Nashid. 2015. "Silent Boom in Bangladesh Cartoon Industry." *Financial Express*, April 16. http://www.thefinancialexpress-bd.com/2015/04/16/88916.

Mitu, Nasreen Sultana. 2016. Interview with John A. Lent, Dhaka, October 14.

Pial, Omi Rahman. 2008. "Arif Is Free, Is He?" Cartoonist Arif, May 27. https://www.cartoonistarif.com/2008/05/arif-is-free-is-he.html.

Qureshi, Mahmud Shah. 1980. "Cartoons: Mirror of Bangladesh Society." *Asian Culture* 25 (January): 26–28.

Rahman, Anis. 2019. "Shabash, the First Ever Bangladeshi Superhero: Transnational, Transcultural, and Transcreated." *Popular Culture Studies Journal* 7, no. 2: 107–21.

Rahman, Asifur [Rats Asif]. 2016. Interview with John A. Lent, Dhaka, October 17.

Rahman, Samir Asran. 2016. Interview with John A. Lent, Dhaka, October 20.

Ranabi [Rafiqun Nabi]. 1993. Interview with John A. Lent, Dhaka, July 26.

Rashid, Harun ur. 2004. "The Myth of Tokaii." *Daily Star*, May 30. http://archive.thedailystar.net/2004/05/30/d40530140189.htm.

Ratan, Md. Kamruzzaman. 2016. Interview with John A. Lent, Dhaka, October 20.

Roostami, Fardin. 2017. "Arifur fortalte at han opplevde situasjonen som svaert truende." https://www.amta.no/debatt/avistegnere/ytringsfrihet/arifur-fortaite-at-han-opplevde.

Rosan, Robab. 2005. "The Arts: Shishir Bhattacharjee." *Daily New Age*, April 8. http://www.newagebd.com/2005/apr/08/arts.html.

Roy, Taposh. 2014. "Humayun Ahmed Did Not Die from Cancer: Ahsan Habib." Risingbd, September 15. http://www.risingbd.com/english/Humayun_Ahmed_did_not_die_from_cancer_Ahsan_Habib/17860.

Sahid Ullah, Mohammad. 2012. Correspondence with John A. Lent, July 25.

Sayeed, Khondokar Abu. 1993. Interview with John A. Lent, Dhaka, July 26.

Sen, Jaideep. 2017. "Toons Shall Overcome: The Fight for Freedom of Expression." *Indian Express Indulge*, May 12. https://www.indulgexpress.com/culture/cover-story/2017/may/12/toons-shall-overcome-fight-for-freedom-of-expression-1469.html.

Shahid, Sarah Nafisa. 2018. "A Mad, Mad World." *Daily Star*, July 13. http://www.thedailystar.net/star-weekend/longform/mad-mad-world-1604560.

217

Siddiqua, Fayeka Zabeen. 2016. "Happily Humorous." *Daily Star*,
April 8. http://www.thedailystar.net/star-weekend/star-people/
happily-humorous-1205722.

Tanmoy [Syed Rashad Imam]. 2016. Interviews with John A. Lent,
Dhaka, October 17, 19.

Zaman, Nasir Uz. 2019. "Akantis School: A Platform for Cartoonists." *New Age Youth*, December 8. https://www.newagebd.net/
article/92941/akantis-school-a-platform-for-cartoonists.

218

Historical Overview

As with China, Japan, and Indonesia, India had a rich tradition of satire and caricature long before the arrival of Western colonists. Temple sculpture using caricature has been found in India dating to at least 200 CE; satirical drawings abounded from at least the mid-eighteenth century sold at the Kalighat market around the Kali Temple of Kolkata (formerly Calcutta). These colorful prints became souvenirs of pilgrims to the temple and mocked priests gone astray as well as Bengali "dandies" (Indian men who became westernized).

India was well ahead of all Asian countries in the speed and quantity with which it produced cartoon periodicals. The first was the *Delhi Sketch Book* (1850–1857), and by 1900 at least seventy cartoon magazines, a large number of them called *Punch*, had appeared across India (Hasan 2007, 12). Many were independently minded nationalist magazines; some were pro-British, possessing "professions of loyalty" (Mitter 1994, 156); others were radically pro-independence (e.g., *Awadh Punch*, 1877–1936). *Awadh Punch* (aka *Oudh Punch*) was the most influential and longest lived. Published in Lucknow in the Urdu language, it pushed for the "supremacy of the Muslim cultural elite" (Hasan 2007, 91), advocated for the extension of rights for Indians, and commented critically on the British establishment's corruption (Scully 2013, 23–25).

Intense rivalries developed among the different *Punch* versions and other vernacular newspapers within a language group, for instance between *Oudh Punch* and *Oudh Akhbar* or between comic newspapers in Gujarat such as *Gujarati Punch*, *Gup Shup*, and *Hindi Punch*. Plagiarism, particularly of Britain's *Punch*, was not unheard of among the vernacular *Punch* magazines of India. The inaugural number of the *Delhi Sketch Book* already considered this eventuality, humbly (or facetiously) stating that it was not "arrogant enough" to imitate London's *Punch*. Its stated purpose was to be "simply a vehicle for drawings and caricatures," and, according to Chattopadhyay (1992), it hardly had "any

Chapter 15

India

15.1. The hypocrisy of Brahmans indulging in women, alcohol, and meat. Gaganendranath Tagore, 1917.

obnoxious" work directly criticizing the political, religious, or social beliefs of India.

Parsee Punch appeared in 1854 as India's second cartoon magazine, followed by *Indian Punch* in 1859 and the *Indian Charivari* in 1872. The latter, a fortnightly published in Kolkata by Colonel Percy Wyndham, at the time was secretly edited and written, possibly because of its overt racism. The second-longest-lived of the cartoon magazines was *Hindi Punch* (1878–1930), which had as its personification Punchoba, an Indian version of Mr. Punch in England. Others continued to appear (and disappear) throughout the remainder of the century and into the next: *Parsee Punch* (Mumbai), *Delhi Punch*, *Punjabi Punch*, *Urdu Punch*, *Puneath Punch* (in a remote Bengali town), *Panjab Punch* (Lahore), *Punch Bahadur* (Mumbai), *Rewari Punch* (Gurgaon), *Sar Punch* (Gorakhpur), *Rafiq Punch*, and *Basantak* (Kolkata), among others. *Basantak* was different in name and drawing style; the editor's nephew drew satire in a style reminiscent of the mocking Kalighat prints sold at

Kolkata's Kali Temple from the mid-eighteenth through the nineteenth centuries (Lent 2015, 15–16).

Cartoon/humor magazines have been a valuable staple in India's mass media fabric, although there has not been a successful one for a while. Scattered throughout the twentieth century were attempts to start and sustain viable cartoon/humor magazines, but most were short-lived (Varghese 1992). More successful and longer lasting were *Shankar's Weekly* (1948–1975) and *Tom's Magazine* (est. 1990). As India's most famous satirical magazine, *Shankar's Weekly* aimed to make people laugh (Malhotra 1990), but while meeting this goal, it launched the careers of some of India's top political cartoonists. Its founder, K. Shankar Pillai, began his own cartooning in 1932 (Bhogwekar 1990; also Lal 1987). *Tom's Magazine* was self-published twice monthly by cartoonist Toms (V. T. Thomas) (Gopalakrishnan 2009). Toms had been the cartoonist for *Malayala Manorama* and for years drew a strip underlaid with political satire. Although not identified strictly as a cartoon magazine, *Ananda Vikatan* (Happy Jester) of Chennai published much humor and many cartoons from its beginnings in 1926. Movie mogul S. S. Vasan initiated the Tamil-language weekly (Madhan 1993), which in its lifetime did much to train and provide an outlet for top Tamil cartoonists.

A number of important artists filled the annals of Indian political cartooning in the first half of the twentieth century. The nephew of literary giant Rabindranath Tagore, Gaganendranath Tagore drew sharp social and political satire for *Virup Vajra* (Play of Opposites), *Adbhut Lok* (Realm of the Absurd), and *Naba Hullod* (Reform Screams). In hundreds of humorous cartoons, Tagore depicted "various phases of modern life in Bengal with its many foibles and imperfections, many inconsistencies and moral turpitudes" (Gangoly n.d., iii). He reveled in making fun of westernized Indians trying to be more English than the English, and in the hypocrisy of Brahmans indulging in women, alcohol, and meat rather than pious activities. These caricatures paralleled the earlier Kalighat paintings just as drawings in *Basantak* had done. In South India, the Tamil poet C. Subramania Bharati, as editor of the fiery weekly *Indian* in

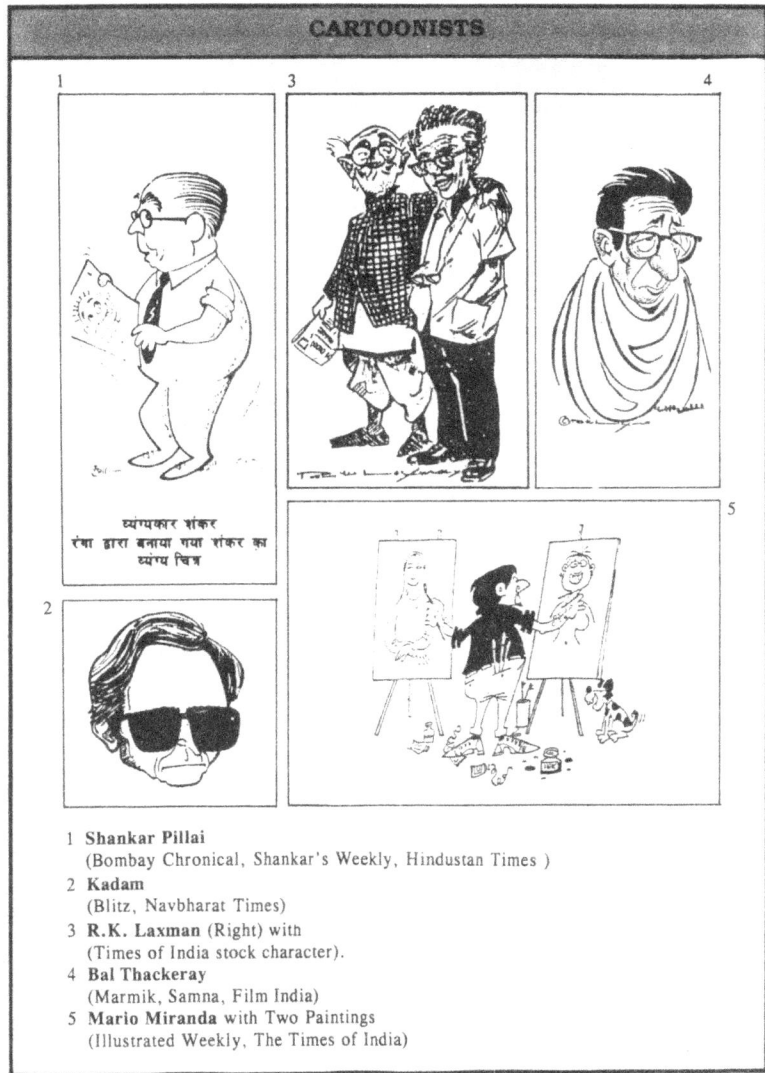

व्यंग्यकार शंकर
रंगा द्वारा बनाया गया शंकर का
व्यंग्य चित्र

1 **Shankar Pillai**
   (Bombay Chronical, Shankar's Weekly, Hindustan Times)
2 **Kadam**
   (Blitz, Navbharat Times)
3 **R.K. Laxman** (Right) with
   (Times of India stock character).
4 **Bal Thackeray**
   (Marmik, Samna, Film India)
5 **Mario Miranda** with Two Paintings
   (Illustrated Weekly, The Times of India)

15.2. Caricatures of twentieth-century giants among Indian cartoonists. Courtesy of K. N. Sahay.

Chennai[1] and then Puducherry, used many cartoons beginning in 1906; the entire front page almost always was a cartoon blasting the British or moderates. Bharati worked hand in hand with the artist/engraver in the very laborious process of engraving cartoon blocks (R. A. Padmanabhan 1991, 51). In 1910, he planned to start *Chitravali*, a monthly made up solely of Tamil and English cartoons, but had to back off when the British imposed restrictions on all local nationalist newspapers. Also, in Chennai, the *Hindu* printed its first political cartoon in 1925, a drawing that attacked the Justice Party, and the weekly edition of *Tamil Nadu* was regularly using the cartoons of K. R. Sharma by the 1920s.

Other pioneering political cartoonists were Jatin Sen, whose cartoons graced the pages of the monthlies *Manasio Marmabani* and *Bharat Barsha* beginning in 1917; Chandi Lahiri, who started the use of pocket

cartoons with his *Third Eye View* in Kolkata's *Amar Bazar Patrika*; and Rudolf von Leyden (Denley). Von Leyden was an interesting character. Raised and educated (culminating in a PhD in geology) in Germany, he moved to Mumbai in 1933, where he set up a commercial art studio and traipsed through the remotest parts of the subcontinent, painting what he saw. He also became the main art critic of the *Times of India* and regularly contributed political cartoons to the daily. During World War II, his cartoons were "jingoistically anti-German" (Arbuthnot 2018); during the drive to independence, they concentrated on the divides in Indian society.

The state of Kerala has had a rich harvest of political cartoonists, producing the highest number of any state in India. Numerous reasons have been given for this phenomenon: "the mercurial, binary and combustive

HE HAS SWALLOWED IT

CAN YOU DIGEST IT?

SHANKAR

The Simla Conference has ended.

15.3. "He Has Swallowed It," Shankar (Kesava Shankar Pillai), *Illustrated Weekly of India*, January 8, 1971. Courtesy of the *Ranchi Express* and K. N. Sahay.

nature of politics in Kerala" (M. Nair 2018), very high literacy and newspaper readership, and an "ancient and deep-rooted" propensity for satire among Malayali people. Keralite maestro Abu Abraham (1995) has added his take on the issue; he writes that Malayali literature, beginning with primary school readers, was "humorously sardonic" and that sarcasm is a "well-known trait" of the Malayali. Abu gives acute poverty as a possible reason also, because, as he notes, "[s]atire is an expression of discontent, a form of protest against the condition of life around" (Abraham 1995). Abu's nephew, Ajit Ninan, *Times of India* political cartoonist after R. K. Laxman, attributes it to Kerala being a "matriarchal society where the only way to get back at women is humor, while in the North, men beat the women" (Ninan 2009). Longtime cartoonist E. P. Unny, also from Kerala, attributes it to the prevalence of tea shops in the state, which for manty years contributed to political discourse (Unny 2019a; C. Padmanabhan 2015).

Likely the first political cartoon in Kerala appeared in the humor monthly *Vidooshakan* (Jester), published in Kollam in October 1919. In the 1930s and 1940s, a number of humor magazines came onto the scene, such as *Sarasan* in Changanacherry, *Narmada* in Kottayam, *Vikadakesari*, and *Naradan*. Celebrated humorist Sanjayan (M. R. Nair) edited two satire weeklies in the coastal town of Kozhikode between 1935 and 1942: *Sanjayan* and *Viswaroopam*. Another Keralite political cartoonist was K. Shankar Pillai (pen name Shankar), who mentored talents from the state such as Abu

Abraham, O. V. Vijayan, P. K. S. Kutty (Puthukodi Kottuthody Shankaran Kutty), T. Samuel, Kerala Varma, and C. J. Yesudasan. Kutty, whose career spanned well over fifty years beginning in 1940, worked on English dailies until switching to the Bengali newspaper *Aaj Kaal* in 1987. Kutty said that he was one of only eight cartoonists in all of India when he joined the *National Herald* in 1941 (Kutty 1995). Yesudasan edited at least three humor magazines; created the first Malayalam pocket cartoon, *Kittuvammavan*, and the first pocket cartoon in Malayalam to feature a female character; and was staff cartoonist for the daily *Malayala Manorama* for years. Yesudasan (1993) said that the purpose of his cartoons was simply to give readers "the freedom to laugh for a few minutes at the expense of politicians."

Shankar must be considered one of the undisputed masters of Indian political cartooning because of his excellent draftsmanship, meticulous research, and critical political acumen. He made it a point to meet politicians but did not hesitate to fiercely criticize them if he thought it necessary. Nationalist leader Jawaharlal Nehru, during his frequent imprisonments by the British during the 1930s, closely followed Shankar's cartoons in the *Hindustan Times*, and after he became independent India's first prime minister, Nehru told the cartoonist, "Don't spare me, Shankar."[2] Despite Nehru often being the butt of Shankar's drawings, the two had a close camaraderie, sparking one observer to quip, "A true friend can only draw such cartoons about his beloved and best friend" (Khanduri 2014, 114). One of Shankar's

15.4. R. K. Laxman, *Times of India* office, Mumbai, July 10, 1993. Photo by John A. Lent. Courtesy of R. K. Laxman.

15.5. Sudhir Tailang, New Delhi, July 9, 2009. Photo by John A. Lent. Courtesy of Sudhir Tailang.

proteges, R. K. Laxman (1998, 76), credited him with elevating the editorial cartoon from "mere decoration" in newspapers to the status of editorial commentator and political analyst.

Laxman described post–World War II governments as full of eccentrics who owed their positions to having been imprisoned under the British. Their priorities were trivial in light of India's myriad problems, making Laxman's job a "paradise," as he explained: "These individuals came up with ideas that seemed to be purely for the benefit of the cartoonist" (Laxman 1998, 78).

Nevertheless, the period especially after independence spawned a number of distinguished political cartoonists who were able and willing to get to the gist of the social and political reality. At the top of the list were Laxman and Abraham. Others were Harishchandra Lachke, recognized as the first Indian cartoonist on the *Times of India*'s front page (in 1945) and the most popular in the Marathi language; C. J. Yesudasan; Sudhir Dar, mainly working for the *Indian Express* as a freelancer after leaving the *Hindustan Times* in "disgust" in 1989 (Dar 1993); P. K. S. Kutty; O. V. Vijayan, a satirical cartoonist, novelist, and short story writer (Vijayan 2002); K. Shankar Pillai and P.K. Manthri, prominent Kerala cartoonists in the 1950s–1960s (R. Nair 1993a); B. V. Tamamurthy (Murthy), with the *Deccan Herald*

beginning in 1955; Bal Thackeray, a staunch Hindu nationalist, full-time right-wing politician, and founder of *Marmik* (1960) cartoon magazine and the Shiv Sena party; and the combative Rajinder Puri.

These and other stalwart cartoonists of the latter third of the twentieth century made up a body of distinguished political cartoonists never seen in India (or any other Asian country for that matter) before and not likely to be seen again. They included those not afraid to speak up against power, such as Shankar, who satisfied Nehru's request not to be spared by attacking him at least four thousand times in his cartoons; or Abu, who retorted at a press conference in 1975 when officials declared the Emergency, "But why stop the spread of humour?"; or those who used a deep-thrust attack on politicians, such as Rajinder Puri; or those who "neither screamed nor lost poise" (Unny 2019b), but got their message across in a suave manner, such as Sudhir Dar.

Strange as it sounds, the Emergency (1975–1977) led to a revolution in journalism and political cartooning with a flood of new newspapers and a sudden awareness of them and their cartoons by the public. Sudhir Tailang (1993) explained: "Everyone wanted to know about the Emergency. There were many new papers, circulations went up, and regional newspapers made fortunes. Much money came into newspapers, and with money, many new cartoonists appeared. By the 1980s, newspapers were no longer a mission, but a business concern." E. P. Unny (1993) of the *Economic Times* had similar views, stating: "Certainly, cartooning changed since the Emergency, more focused, more issue-based, bolder." He said that before the Emergency, cartoons were "just jokes on the country, allegorical, circumlocating." Ravi Shankar Etteth (no relation to K. Shankar Pillai), cartoonist for *India Today*, said that the "political parameters of criticism and response" were very different before and after the Emergency. Before, he explained, the symbol for politicians was of "gentlemen who never did anything evil" (Etteth 1993).

From the Political Cartoonists' Mouths

To capture the essence of Indian political cartooning in the latter part of the twentieth and early twenty-first centuries, I rely here on interviews I did with sixteen political cartoonists in Chennai, New Delhi, Mumbai, Trivandrum, and Kottayam in 1993, and six nearly a generation later, in 2009, in Thrissur and New Delhi. While in Trivandrum and Chennai in 1993, I participated in a workshop and symposium, respectively, where I heard the views of and intermingled with eight cartoonists and editors.

How and under what circumstances cartoonists became interested in drawing elicited the common answers, that a number drew on walls, in the sand, or on any flat surface even before entering primary school, or that they were influenced by a teacher or by the works of a cartoonist.

Wildly different was the reason given by Pran Kumar Sharma, a very popular creator of comic strips and books, most with messages on antiterrorism, harmony, and other platitudes. Pran traced his motivation to become a cartoonist to India's Partition in 1947, when his family escaped from Pakistan to India, experiencing unimaginable savagery on both sides of the border. Pran (2009) remembered seeing Muslims killing Hindus and Sikhs and burning their houses in Pakistan before he and his family were evacuated in cramped trucks to

15.6. Pran and his character Sabu in his home office/studio, New Delhi, July 5, 1993. Photo by John A. Lent. Courtesy of Pran.

India. There, he expected the "nightmare" to end, but "[i]t was not over. Hindus were killing Muslims. There were bodies of Muslims lying on both sides of the tracks. This affected a nine-year-old boy like me. From that day on, I thought when I grow up, I will try to put a smile on the face of man. I became a cartoonist at the age of nine" (Pran 2009).

Escaping Pakistan about the same time as Pran, chief artist/cartoonist for the Gujarati-language Janmabhoomi newspaper group, Rupam (Ramesh Chande) also had a rough start. In Pakistan, his father was a newspaper hawker, and the family was extremely poor. Rupam said that there was no money for studying or paper, and he resorted to drawing with charcoal on footpath tiles. He began freelancing for the *Karachi Daily Gazette* in 1946. After Partition, he became a refugee in Mumbai, where

15.7. Cartoon by Rajinder Puri. Courtesy of Rajinder Puri.

15.8. Cartoon by Sudhir Tailang. Courtesy of Sudhir Tailang.

he slept on pathways until he managed to find a shack with no electricity, where he drew his cartoons. He joined *Janmabhoomi* in 1948 (Rupam 1993).

Political cartoonist/activist Rajinder Puri's early career can be summed up with the words, "I quit" and "unemployed." His "very checkered career" (his words) resulted from his feeling of not being free initially on the *Hindustan Times* (1959–1968) and the *Statesman* (1969–1970). He left the *Statesman* twice and quit two

editor jobs (the *Evening News* and *Motherland*) before he even started them, the first because the proprietors "did not like my concept of the job," the second because of "government interferences" (Puri 1993). Puri was unemployed again in the early 1970s, saying that no proprietor or editor would "touch me"; he decided to start his own magazine, *Stir*, where he was "proprietor, editor, tea boy, cartoonist, everything." *Stir* lasted two years, filled with his "violently anti-Congress,

15.9. Abu Abraham and John A. Lent, Abu's home, Trivandrum, July 12, 1993. Photo by John Vilanilam. Courtesy of Abu Abraham.

'What are you going to be when you grow up—illiterate, or unemployed?'

15.10. Cartoon by Abu Abraham. Courtesy of Abu Abraham.

anti-Nehru, anti–Indira Gandhi" diatribes, but it folded in 1974 when the advertisers in concert withdrew all ads (Puri 1993). Puri dipped in and out of cartooning and column writing throughout the 1980s and 1990s, at the same time he was trying to implement political and social change by organizing demonstrations and cofounding and leading three different opposition parties. At the time of our 1993 interview, he was doing political cartoons yet again with the *Statesman*. Just before that in 1990, he had a regular political cartoon, *News Hound*, in the *Indian Express*, but quit when a new editor started changing his work (Puri 1993). When I interviewed Puri in 2009, he had just retired from a five-year stint as a *Tribune* cartoonist; he said he was finished with all cartooning and writing, because it was "futile." "Even when you write the most damaging

charges, they are simply ignored. Total silence. So, forget it," he said (Puri 2009).

Hindustan Times political cartoonist Sudhir Tailang had his first cartoons published in a Hindi daily when he was ten years old. Many others of his cartoons were published in all the major newspapers and magazines throughout his school years, making him a "celebrity" in his town, as well as a "rich man." He avoided visiting the newspapers for fear that the editors would notice his youth and quit using his cartoons. Tailang (1993) said that he received letters while in primary school addressed to "Dear Respected Mr. Tailang."

R. K. Laxman, a giant among Indian cartoonists, was already entranced by political cartoons (particularly those of Britain's David Low) when he was two or three years old. He remembered:

Low's work came by slow boat around the Cape of Good Hope, one month late. The cartoons had no relevance at all when they got here. Low's cartoons came ten in a bundle in a cardboard tube. They were wrapped in tissue paper. I was fascinated by them. But I never copied his or any other cartoonist's works in my life. I'd be ashamed if I did. I would pose in front of a mirror and sketch myself. When I was allowed to go out later in my youth, I'd go to the marketplace to sketch. (Laxman 1993)

Another cartooning maestro, Abu Abraham, also started early, doing funny drawings in the sand of the family's courtyard when he was three. Abu even remembered his first cartoon; it was about a Malayalam saying that a dog about to moan gets a coconut on his head (Abu 1993a). He did not draw many cartoons while in college and, upon graduation, became a reporter for the *Bombay Chronicle*, where he also drew cartoons. In 1950, Shankar asked him to draw for *Shankar's Weekly*, which he did, until he went to London in 1953 for a three-month holiday and stayed for sixteen years, during which he was staff cartoonist first for the *Observer* and then the *Guardian*.

Freelance cartoonist Suresh Sawant also started out drawing on the floors of the family house, but no one dared to step on his art or erase it. His preservation secret? Sawant drew theological figures he had seen in the movies, and as he told it: "People had to jump over my drawings, because they were afraid to step on the gods" (Sawant 1993).

Sudhir Dar (1993) had a jarring experience early in his career when his pocket cartoon, *Out of My Mind*, was advanced to the vaunted front page of the *Statesman*. He said that his bubble was burst a day later when the editor handed him a reader's letter, simply inquiring, "Dear Sir, Who is out of his mind, you or Sudhir Dar?" Letters poured into the *Statesman* for three months about this very question, until the editor called for a halt.

What inspired Ajit Ninan (2009) to take up cartooning were the "Italian nuns" who schooled him. "They were very strict," Ninan said, and he began to draw "to bring humor to this atmosphere."

Characteristics and Problems of Pre-Modern-Age Cartooning (1990s)

In the early 1990s, there was an abundance of newspapers and magazines that regularly used political cartoons. Most dailies had a staff cartoonist, considered the "personality of the paper," according to Sudhir Tailang; he added in jest, "not more because two cartoonists can't sit together" (Tailang 1993). Usually, the newspapers carried a political cartoon on the front page. A content analysis conducted at the University of Madras in April 1993 found that the five surveyed national dailies[3] all had political cartoons prominently displayed on the front page. Magazines were also receptive to cartooning; for example, a city the size of Chennai supported two decades-old, humor-type periodicals: *Ananda Vikatan*, circulation 250,000; and *Thuglak*,[4] 140,000.

Political cartoonists in Delhi had no difficulty finding subject matter in 1993 (or now), according to Sudhir Tailang, who elaborated:

> When you leave your house in Delhi, every few meters, you are inspired to do a cartoon. Because life in Delhi is

that way. The abusive language of the driver who cuts you off, the bus that almost runs you over, the taxi driver who refuses or overcharges you, the banker who makes you feel you're begging for your own money. Every moment of life in Delhi inspires. No water in taps, power cuts, load shedding, leaders not working for you. When you use these ideas, the people feel you are in touch with them. (Tailang 1993)

He said that politicians were very obliging in providing material, most of whom he thought "worked full time for the cartoonists, not the people" (Tailang 1993).

Indian political cartoonists have been no different from colleagues worldwide in regularly using metaphors and symbols, the workhorses of the profession. In times of strict government scrutiny of the press, such as during the Emergency, they were used as subtle messages. In India, symbols also have been thought of as markers of ethnicity, helping cartoonists to relate more closely with readers.

Perhaps the most visible symbol in South Asia is the Everyman, a character always present, usually with his mouth shut, an unobtrusive bystander who cannot be ignored. The most popular of these characters was R. K. Laxman's "Common Man." Laxman began his lifelong career on the *Times of India* in Mumbai in 1947. He told me that Common Man just developed in 1947, 1948, and 1949. As he remembered:

> I was drawing bureaucrats, the people, etc., and I'd have to put twenty people in to represent the masses. It took time and I had deadlines. So, I dropped the number to ten, then to five, then two, and finally one day, this fellow in stripes was staring back at me from the drawing board. So, he represents the clerks, the workers, etc. It saves time drawing many people. Other cartoonists say to me, you have symbolized the masses; there is nothing left for us as he is the common man. (Laxman 1987; see a full account of the author's day with Laxman in Lent 1993)

To my query, how can Common Man be common when he hobnobs with prime ministers and other celebrities?, Laxman answered: "Common Man is a mythical figure.

15.11. Laxman's ever-present "Common Man" (left). Courtesy of R. K. Laxman.

He never talks. He represents the silent majority. The whole world revolves around him. He is everywhere. To think he is real is wrong. From the first day, he never opened his mouth. In cabinet meetings and the like, they think of the Common Man" (1993). For ten years, Laxman only did one *Times of India* political cartoon daily, fending off the paper's request for him to also draw a pocket cartoon. He said: "The editor tempted me; I said no. He tempted me with money; I said yes. Didn't bat a lash" (Laxman 1993).

Problems that Indian political cartoonists encountered in the 1990s were similar to those that other countries' artists faced: lack of training, technical issues, no encouragement for entering the profession by parents and society,[5] low pay, unknowing and noncaring editors, insufficient professionalism, and the absence of a marketing concept among cartoonists (Shetty 1993). Abu Abraham (1993a) felt that the problems in India did not differ from those anywhere else, stating: "You can be

a hack and make a lot of money or stand up for what you believe in. No one is going to give you liberty on a platter. If you have no consistency, you have no credibility."

Many of the problems related to the regional press's handling of cartoons. Rupam, who drew for a Gujarati-language group, saw a dismal future for non-English-language cartooning, as there was no new generation coming up. "The Gujarati people are business oriented; the young cartoonists study English to get jobs on the English-language papers. Why would they come here?" he asked (Rupam 1993). Speaking about Tamil-language cartooning, A. Ma Swamy (1993), editor of *Rani Weekly*, claimed that these newspapers did not have the "financial strength to withstand politics and are afraid of the political parties," so they avoided cartoons and did illustrations instead. The cartoonist for *Dinakaran*, Dinakaran Raghu (1993), agreed that Tamil-language cartooning was dying and that "for the sake of security, do not attack the government." Longtime staff political cartoonist for *Deepika Daily* in Kottayam, Raju Nair (1993b), lamented that "no one knows about regional cartoonists," and because of that, breaking into the English-language press was difficult. He failed to understand how more than thirty million Indians spoke Malayalam, yet its press and cartoonists remained unknown. Although he drew for the English-language *Hindu*, Keshav (Venkata Raghavan P. Keshav) clearly summarized the status of Tamil dailies:

> The language press cartooning is very, very weak only doing illustrations which they call cartoons. Only illustrators who double as cartoonists. There's not a serious comment in these drawings. Very rarely do Tamil papers and magazines have a full-time cartoonist. They can't afford a good cartoonist. The ideas of the "cartoons" by illustrators come from the editor. (Keshav 1993)

Speaking generally about the cartoons of the non-English press, Sudhir Tailang tagged them as "crude," traveling "the wrong road from the beginning." He added, "They have played to the galleries. [The cartoonists'] drawings are not cartooning; they are just simply an abuse. They just draw a picture and then put an abusive, very rough caption over it" (Tailang 1993).

The Twenty-First Century

Political cartoonists I interviewed on two separate occasions in 2009 did not give their profession much chance of surviving. They said that with the departure of the old-timers about ten years earlier, political cartooning was dying. Sudhir Tailang, then with *Asian Age*, described his generation of cartoonists as "running on the runway at high speed, but just before takeoff, the tires are punctured. My generation was starting to have an impact before the bubble burst" (Tailang 2009). He used another analogy to make his point: "My generation is like the tiger that is nearly extinct, but unlike the tiger, there is no law to protect cartoonists."

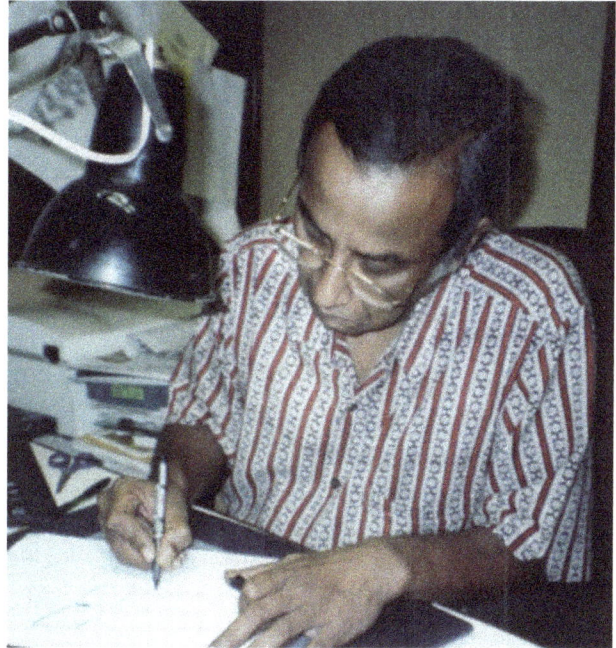

15.12. *Times of India* political cartoonist Ajit Ninan, New Delhi, July 7, 2009. Photo by John A. Lent. Courtesy of Ajit Ninan.

E. P. Unny (2009) remembered that fifteen years earlier, all New Delhi dailies had front-page pocket cartoons; in 2009, out of twelve dailies, only the *Times of India*, *Asian Age*, and the *Indian Express* had a pocket cartoon on page 1, and the *Hindustan Times*, *Pioneer*, and *Mail Today* used one on an inside page. Troubling to Ajit Ninan (2009), staff cartoonist at the *Times of India*, was the huge disparity between the daily's writers and cartoonists. He said that while the *Times* spent lavishly on its approximately 150 writers, its two or three artists were expected to do everything, and "not even be given an allowance for a long-distance call." Perhaps the biggest issues dealt with the nature of the cartoons and reader response. Rajinder Puri (2009), Unny (2009), Gokul Gopalakrishnan (2009), and Tailang (2009) decried the lack of comment in political cartoons; their feeling was that so-called cartoons were illustrations devoid of opinion and designed not to offend the powers that be. Puri (2009) felt that "stand-alone comment was rare," and, along with Gopalakrishnan (2009) and Tailang (2009), thought that the cartoons were "silly," full of "hype trivia," and a tool of "dumbing down." Puri (2009) and Tailang (2009) laid much of the blame for the deterioration of political cartooning on the editors, who treat cartoons as filler, not art; do not know the difference between a cartoon and an illustration; and are focused on the beautification of the pages with visuals. Sify.com cartoonist Satish Achary said that editors see cartoons as simply a "funny visual" (D'Mello 2013). Political cartooning has been derailed by other distractions; as Tailang (2009) alliteratively put it: "The three 'Cs' (crime, cricket, cinema) replaced the one 'C' (cartoons)."

Also, blame for the decreased prominence of political cartooning in India must be shared by those who champion the worldwide thinking that newspapers should function solely as businesses, owned by conglomerates with interlinks to politicians and political parties, all protecting their common vested interests, not those of the public. Keshav (1993) said that the result of such corporate/political interlinks is that newspapers "can't afford to rub those in power the wrong way" (D'Mello 2013).

Another indication that political cartooning was stagnating was the lessened reader response. As mentioned elsewhere, even the most controversial cartoons usually brought silence. Tailang said that in the late 1990s, he received about ten calls and three letters daily, compared to the five reactions he had had in the three years prior to our 2009 interview.

Freedom to Cartoon

Indian "freedom to cartoon" took some hard knocks in the 2010s. Although the conditions were not as dire as in neighboring countries, they had deviated enough from the norm in India to grab the attention of cartoonists and the mass media more generally. In September 2012, political cartoonist Aseem Trivedi was served with three charges, including sedition, for his online "Cartoons against Corruption," which Mumbai police had banned the year before. Trivedi's rudimentary drawings mocked the "corrupt elites" ruling under then prime minister Manmohan Singh, as well as India's national symbols (ABC's The World 2017). Although the Mumbai High Court dropped the charges against him in 2015, Trivedi continued to warn that speech freedom was "not in good condition" under the succeeding government of Narendra Modi, which he accused of attempting to shut down any criticism of the authorities (Kleinfeld 2016). In a 2016 interview, Trivedi explained: "The government is trying to use nationalism like it used to use religion. It is trying to silence dissidents and divide people. Anyone who criticizes Modi is labelled as anti-national or somebody who supports Pakistan" (Kleinfeld 2016; also Human Rights Watch 2012). Trivedi, fearing a shutdown of social media, also mounted an online "Save Your Voice" campaign and an online "magazine of resistance" called *Black and White*, to support speech freedom globally (Kappal 2016).

There have been other incidents that have not boded well for political cartoonists. On August 5, 2019, a lockdown began in Kashmir that lasted for months, shutting all communication lines, including the internet. The internet blockade disrupted the routines of online cartoonists such as Suhail Naqshbandi, as well as others such as S. Tariq of the daily *Kashmir Images*, who had no means to send his cartoons to the paper. Legendary Kashmir cartoonist Bashir Ahmad Ashir was able to publish his cartoons in the Urdu daily *Srinagar Times*, but not to share his work online. Naqshbandi said that he hesitated even to draw about Kashmir's political situation in the "environment of shock and fear felt by every Kashmiri." He had quit his political cartoonist position on the daily *Greater Kashmir* months earlier because of "persistent censorship" (Maqbool 2019). Assam cartoonist Nituparma Rajbongshi faced considerable backlash in early 2019, including a warning from Twitter, because of his cartoons opposing a bill that sought to grant citizenship to non-Muslim minority communities from Afghanistan, Bangladesh, and Pakistan. There also were attempts to have him arrested (Agarwala 2019).

Major political cartoonists have expressed their fears about what has been happening in India. Vishwajyoti Ghosh thought that Indians had lost their sense of humor, declaring:

> Over time, we have forgotten to laugh at ourselves and mastered the art of getting hurt! Too many times, the political cartoons have been taken off, and even banned. A lot

of good humor in our times happened during the period of Emergency, where a repressive regime was imposing censorship. Humor was an act of rebellion then. That unfortunately is on the decline now. (McCabe 2015)

Judges on the Indian Supreme Court would have agreed, saying in 2015 that political cartooning was not a safe profession, with growing intolerance among the public and authorities who no longer took cartoons in good humor (*Times of India* 2015).

The mind-boggling diversity of India, with fourteen major languages, hundreds of secondary languages and dialects, ethnic groups of every hue, a full range of major and minor religions, and tightly delineated class and caste systems, is a challenge to unification. It does not take much to bring tensions to the point of eruption under these conditions. An example was a political cartoon that K. Shankar Pillai drew in 1948 that was included in the nation's political science textbook for Class XI in 2006, which caused an uproar in Parliament in 2012. The cartoon depicts Nehru about to whip the snail on which Dr. B. R. Ambedkar is seated. Dr. Ambedkar rose from being born a Dalit (India's lowest caste) to being called the father of the Indian constitution. The intent of the cartoon was to humorously show the "helplessness" of Dr. Ambedkar and the frustration of Nehru in getting a constitution drafted for the new nation.

Sixty-four years later, a member of Parliament strongly objected to the use of the cartoon in a textbook, equating its message to the "master-slave paradigm" and with "perpetuating the caste stereotypes." Before tempers cooled, the concerned textbook was withdrawn, an examining committee was formed, the snail cartoon and twenty-one others were expunged from future printings of the textbook, and a minister offered his government's apologies, in effect overruling the cartoonist's freedom of speech (manifested as humor) in order to uphold the Dalit's freedom of speech (manifested as anger). The minister did not want to be responsible for the cartoon's circulation for fear that his government would be culpable of complicity in the "alleged" attempt to denigrate Ambedkar. He also feared the possible interpretation of

caste discrimination receiving official recognition (Balakrishnan, Venkat, and Manickam 2019, 138–40).

This convoluted case study exemplifies the thin-skinned sensitivities cartoonists face in multicultural and multilingual India, and politicians' close scrutiny of cartoons when it suits or offends their interests.

Alternative Cartooning Forms

In light of the fragility of the "freedom to cartoon," with business conglomerates enclosing newspapers, government clamping down on cartooning as in Kashmir, and other infringements, cyberspace is increasingly becoming a preferred venue, especially for amateur cartoonists. Some of these practitioners are mentioned in the section on women below, notably Kanika Mishra. Among others are Mir Suhail and Rachita Taneja. Mir posted his fierce cartoons on Facebook and in *Kashmir Reader* and is known for not considering any topic taboo, whether women's rights, the Iraq War, petrol prices, or the presence of the army in Kashmir. Taneja, with her Facebook strip *Sanitary Panel*, described as "feminist, political and hilarious," attempted to be confrontational with simple doodles about contemporary issues. Besides gender inequality and sexism, she also concentrated on free speech after hearing that people were being arrested for posting their opinions about politicians on Facebook (Sharma, Ratnam, and Bag 2015).

An anonymous cartoonist duo from Kolkata launched a web strip *Crocodile in Water, Tiger on Land* (*CWTL*) in September 2010 that "lampoon[ed] everybody . . . [but did not] abuse anybody." The weekly strip employed the television set as representing the government and big media in its wide-ranging spoofs, which favored "researched and grounded intellectual satire" over slapstick. *CWTL* was popular and lasted through the decade (Sharma, Ratnam, and Bag 2015). Webcomics were used extensively in India and the Indian diaspora in late 2019 and 2020 to explain issues related to the contentious Citizenship Amendment Act (Raghav 2020).

15.13. Kanika Mishra's character Karnika Kahen fending off attacks by followers of a guru charged with rape. Courtesy of Cartoonists Rights Network International.

Another new venue allowing Indian cartoonists to express themselves politically on old and recent issues is the graphic novel, the first published in India in 1994, not followed by a second until a decade later. Despite the jerky start, many graphic novels have been released since then: some on controversial historical events, examples being *Amar Bari Tomar Naxalbari*, about India's Maoist uprising, and *Delhi Calm* (Gravett 2010), concerning Emergency-era India; and others on present-day issues such as *The Believers*, about religious intolerance in Kerala, *All Quiet in Vikaspuri*, on the water wars of present-day Delhi, and *Munnu: A Boy from Kashmir*, the story of a boy growing up in a volatile militarized state.

Women Cartoonists

At various places in this book, there are a few paragraphs about the rarity of female political cartoonists in Asia. Women comic book artists and graphic novelists are plentiful in countries such as Japan and South Korea, and to a lesser but still important degree in Malaysia, Indonesia, and China. In every country globally where I have interviewed, I ask the question, "Why very few women cartoonists?" And the answers are the same: women do not have social mobility; women do not have the aggressive temperament necessary to draw critical drawings. Women are expected to marry and tend to a family, which prevents them from holding a political cartoonist position. Women are not up to the dangers and threats that come with the job.[6]

India is a bit of an exception. There is a handful of women cartoonists tackling important topics in hard-hitting fashion, fending off death threats and other harassment while doing so. The topic they invariably deal with today is the outlandish number of rapes in India—more than thirty-two thousand reported incidents in 2017. Foremost among these female pen-wielding warriors is Kanika Mishra, a cartoonist and web animator residing in Mumbai. Upon hearing that a popular religious leader of millions of devoted worldwide, Asaram Bapu, was accused of raping the teenager daughter of two of his followers, Mishra posted a cartoon on her Facebook page "putting the soon-to-be-charged holy man squarely in the crosshairs of her cartoon everywoman, Karnika Kahen" (CRNI 2014). Once *India Today* magazine and the most watched news channel, Aaj Tak, published her cartoons, "abusive comments and threats . . . started coming in hordes and the intensity and severity of abuses became beyond tolerance," Mishra said (CRNI 2014). Her email account and Facebook page were hacked; her cell phone number was widely distributed by Bapu's followers; threats were made to post her phone number and picture on prostitution websites; and she received multiple death threats. Mishra did not cower and continued to take on Bapu through her cartoons, widening her attack to include the guru's son, also arrested on rape charges. After four months of such brutal harassment, and as her ordeal was publicized worldwide, the abuse finally subsided, and she continued to take on other issues through her drawings. Her determination earned her the 2014

Cartoonists Rights Network International Award for Courage in Editorial Cartooning.

In 2018, another female journalist/cartoonist, Swathi Vadlamudi, received online death threats and calls for her arrest because of a cartoon she had posted on social media. Her intention was to condemn two recent gruesome rapes by drawing the Hindu god Ram and his wife Sita, and having Sita say how grateful she was not to have been kidnapped by Ram's zealous followers (Raj 2018), a reference to right-wing support for the accused rapists. Rachita Taneja, creator of the online *Sanitary Panel* strip, also faced "scary" comments of "abuse and humiliation" because of her cartoons (Chatterjee 2018).

Other women have broached serious societal and political issues through forms of comic art such as strips, comic books, and graphic novels. Beginning in 2014, Bangalore-based Aarthi Parthasarathy did a weekly webcomic, *Royal Existentials*, parodying the royalty of old to discuss current happenings in India. She also helped create a "collective of women, non-binary, queer artists" called Kadak, which deals with a gamut of social issues, particularly gender and sexuality, through storytelling (Jooha 2019). Other comic/graphic novel collectives including women exist in India. In 2015, an anthology of amateur cartoons, *Drawing the Line: Indian Women Fight Back*, was published by Zubaan, filled with short cartoon sketches by a group of young women about what it was like to be a woman in India. The impulse for the reactions they expressed came from a highly publicized rape in 2012.

The known history of Indian political cartooning by women barely reaches back to the latter part of the twentieth century. Among the pioneers were Mita Roy, Maya Kamath, and Nalini Reddy. Mita began her career as a teenager in 1985, when, on her own initiative, she went to an inundated area near Lucknow during flood time, drew six cartoons of the scene, and submitted them unsolicited to *Pioneer*. All six were published. She continued to draw political cartoons and a strip for *Pioneer* and its Hindi edition, *Swatantra Barat*, and then for *Amar Ujala*, until, constrained by family responsibilities,

15.14. Political cartoonist Maya Kamath (1951–2001). Courtesy of the Indian Institute of Cartoonists.

she had to quit (Khanduri 2014, 176). Kamath's career was cut short in 2001 when she died at fifty years of age. Her early years as a political cartoonist were with the *Deccan Herald*; she worked from home, giving her "flexibility" in managing family matters (Khanduri 2014, 179). Kamath also drew political cartoons for the *Times of India*, the *Indian Express*, and *Asian Age*, as well as a family strip, *Gita*, in the *Evening Herald*, and a syndicated current affairs series, *The World of Maya*.[7] Reddy was leaving her political cartooning position at a "well-rated small-size newspaper" when Ritu Gairola Khanduri (2014, 178) interviewed her in 2003, because "she found herself mired in innuendos and criticism" and suffered humiliation. Another prominent female comic strip cartoonist, as well as writer, illustrator, and playwright, was Manjula (Manjula Padmanabhan), who drew light political cartoons and a strip, *Suki*.

A Few Parting Words

The future of Indian political cartoons gets mixed reviews. Those sharing Unny's forecast believe that the internet is the salvation of the form. Others do not envision a renaissance, as they recount the rapidly decaying "indispensables" of Indian cartoons—the stand-alone political cartoon, front-page pocket cartoon, fixed cartoon space, and plentiful newspaper staff cartoonists (Jha 2013). Indian political cartooning has been crippled by a series of setbacks—distractions and attractions that have stolen its show; smothering levels of commercialism that elevate advertisements over cartoons in vying for favored space; corporate/political/governmental interlinks that demand flattering rather than criticizing cartoons—but it is still hobbling along, determined to stay afoot until a prosthetic is made to help it regain its strength and move forward.

Notes

1. In this chapter, I use the new names for major cities, even in the historical context, for instance Mumbai for Bombay, Chennai for Madras, and Kolkata for Calcutta.

2. Nehru's frankness concerning caricatures done of him was related by Madhan (1993), who told about a Chennai cartoonist's encounter with the prime minister. He said that when "Nehru came to Madras, a local cartoonist drew him but thought he had made his nose too big. So, he did another version and asked Nehru to autograph it. Nehru flipped the page and saw the other cartoon. 'Why not this one? This is what caricature is all about—the longer nose,' he said."

3. The sample included the *Times of India*, *Hindustan Times*, *Hindu*, *Indian Express*, and *Pioneer*.

4. Muhammad bin Tughlaq was a fourteenth-century Delhi sultan known for "screwing up" (Ramaswamy 1993).

5. Madhan (1993) said his parents "trembled" that he would not fit in being a cartoonist; his grandmother in her dying hours admonished him: "For God's sake, do something worthwhile."

6. Sudhir Tailang suggested reasons for India's shortage of women cartoonists:

Perhaps they have not been given a chance to express themselves. And, for women to make fun of others is the last thing they'd do. Traditionally, girls are not allowed to giggle or laugh. Their grandmothers would say if you giggle, you won't get married. As women go out of the home, a time will come when there will be women cartoonists. They have more freedom in the big cities, and it is seeping down day by day. (Tailang 1993)

7. In addition to these women, there may have been a few others who did political cartoons, such as Shugufta Khalidi, who was political cartoonist-cum-correspondent with the *Kashmir Times* in the 2000s.

Bibliography

ABC's The World. 2017. "Indian Cartoonist Aseem Trivedi Once Arrested for Sedition, Says Free Speech 'Not in Good Condition.'" Australian Broadcasting Corporation, October 21. http://www.abc.net.au/news//2017/10/22/indian-cartoonist-arrested-sedition-free-speech-under-threat/9069294.

Abraham, Abu. 1993a. Interview with John A. Lent, Trivandrum, July 12.

Abraham, Abu. 1993b. Untitled presentation at the Workshop on Cartooning, Trivandrum, July 12.

Abraham, Abu. 1995. "Why Does Kerala Produce So Many Cartoonists?" *Indian International Centre Quarterly* 22, nos. 2–3 (Summer–Monsoon): 60–64.

Agarwala, Tora. 2019. "Assam Cartoonist Faces Backlash for Anti-Citizenship Bill Cartoons." *Indian Express*, January 10. https://indianexpress.com/article/north-east-india/assam/assam-cartoonist-nituparna-rajbongshi-anti-citizenship-bill-protests-in-north-east-5530827/.

Arbuthnot, Mollie. 2018. "Bombay Satire: Rudolf von Leyden's Political Cartoons in India in the 1930s and 40s." British Library, Asian and African Studies Blog, December 12. https://blogs.bl.uk/asian-and-african/2018/12/bombay-satire-rudolf-von-leydens-political-cartoons-in-india-in-the-1930s-and-40s-.html.

Athavale, Sanika. 2020. "Satish Acharya: 'Cartoonist Must Be Critical of Government in Power.'" The Logical Indian, February 29. https://thelogicalindian.com/exclusive/satish/acharya-cartoonist-19938?infinitescroll=1.

Balakrishnan, Vinod, and Vishaka Venkat, eds. 2019. *Politickle Lines: Conversations with Indian Cartoonists.* Newcastle upon Tyne, England: Cambridge Scholars Publishing.

Balakrishnan, Vinod, Vishaka Venkat, and Muthukumar Manickam. 2019. "Virality in the Environment of Political Cartoons: When History Intersects with Representations." *European Journal of Humour Research* 7, no. 2: 137–52.

Bhogwekar, Shankar. 1990. "The Pioneer of Indian Cartooning." *Independent* (Mumbai), January 3.

Cartoonists Rights Network International (CRNI). 2014. "Kanika Mishra Creates Karnika Kahen, India's First Cartoon Everywoman." https://cartoonistsrights.org/2412-2/.

Chatterjee, Rituparna. 2018. "Why We Need More Women in Editorial Cartooning." She the People, May 21. https://www.shethepeople.tv/blog/gender-gulf-editorial-cartooning-kshitij-bajpai.

Chattopadhyay, Devasis. 1992. "Drawing on Humorous Lines." *Statesman*, June 20.

Dar, Sudhir. 1993. Interview with John A. Lent, New Delhi, July 7, 1993.

D'Mello, Yolande. 2013. "Who Killed the Political Cartoon?" DNA India, September 15. https://www.dnaindia.com/lifestyle/report-who-killed-the-political-cartoon-1888969.

Etteth, Ravi Shankar. 1993. Interview with John A. Lent, New Delhi, July 7.

Gangoly, O. C. n.d. Introduction to *The Humorous Art of G. T. (Gogonendranath Tagore)*. Calcutta: Birla Academy of Art and Culture.

Gokul, T. G. 2009. "G. Aravindan's 'Small Men and the Big World': Re-Defining the 'Comic' in the Strip." *International Journal of Comic Art* 11, no. 2 (Fall): 44–55.

Gopalakrishnan, Gokul. 2009. Interviews with John A. Lent, Thrissur, India, March 19, 20, 23.

Gravett, Paul. 2010. "Indian Comics: A Visual Renaissance." October 18. www.paulgravett.com/articles/article/indian_comics.

Hasan, Mushirul. 2007. *Wit and Humour in Colonial North India*. New Delhi: Niyogi.

Hindu, The. 2010. "Gems from Veteran Cartoonists." June 8.

Human Rights Watch. 2012. "India: Drop Sedition Charges against Cartoonist." October 12. https://www.hrw.org/news/2012/10/12/india-drop-sedition-charges-against-cartoonist.

Jha, Prashant. 2013. "Stand-Along [*sic*] Political Cartoon Is on the Brink of Extinction." *The Hindu*, June 17. https://www.thehindu.com/news/cities/Delhi/standalong-political-cartoon-is-on-the-brink-of-extinction/article4822366.ece.

Jooha, Kim. 2019. "'What Should One Do?' Is the Pertinent Question Now: An Interview with Aarthi Parthasarathy." *Comics Journal*, June 13. http://www.tcj.com/an-interview-with-aarthi-parthasarathy.

Kappal, Bhanuj. 2016. "The Indian Political Cartoonist the Government Doesn't Want You to Know About." *New Statesman*, November 17. https://www.newstatesman.com/world/2016/11/indian-political-cartoonist-government-doesnt-want-you-know-about.

Keshav, Venkata Raghavan P. 1993. Interview with John A. Lent, Chennai, July 21.

Khanduri, Ritu Gairola. 2014. *Caricaturing Culture in India: Cartoons and History in the Modern World*. Cambridge: Cambridge University Press.

Kleinfeld, Philip. 2016. "An Interview with India's Most Wanted Cartoonist." Vice, November 24. https://www.vice.com/sv/article/zn8y94/aseem-trivedi.

Kumar, Rajeesh. 2009. Interview with John A. Lent, New Delhi, July 8.

Kutty, P. K. S. 1995. Correspondence with John A. Lent, January 6.

Lal, Anupa. 1987. "The Pied Piper of Delhi." *Reader's Digest* (India), October, 83–92.

Laxman, R. K. 1987. Interview with John A. Lent, Philadelphia, June 26.

Laxman, R. K. 1993. Interview with John A. Lent, Mumbai, July 10.

Laxman, R. K. 1998. *The Tunnel of Time: An Autobiography*. New Delhi: Viking.

Lent, John A. 1993. "R. K. Laxman and India's Common Man." *Philippines Communication Journal* (March): 63–69.

Lent, John A. 2009. "An Illustrated History of Indian Political Cartooning." *International Journal of Comic Art* 11, no. 2 (Fall):3–25.

Lent, John A. 2015. *Asian Comics*. Jackson: University Press of Mississippi.

Madhan. 1993. Interview with John A. Lent, Chennai, July 21.

Malhotra, Jyoti. 1990. "The Pioneer of Indian Cartooning." *Independent* (Mumbai), January 3.

Maqbool, Majid. 2019. "How the Clampdown Has Silenced the Cartoonists of Kashmir." *The Wire*, October 29. https://thewire.in/rights/how-the-clampdown-has-silenced-the-cartoonists-of-kashmir.

Mari. 1993. Untitled presentation at the Symposium on Cartoons, Chennai, July 22.

McCabe, Caitlin. 2015. "Indian Cartoonist Talks about the Increase in Self-Censorship." Comic Book Legal Defense Fund, February 18. http://cbldf.org/2015/02/indian-cartoonist-talks-about-the-increase-in-self-censorship/.

Mitter, Partha. 1994. *Art and Nationalism in Colonial India, 1850–1922: Occidental Orientations*. Cambridge: Cambridge University Press.

Mitter, Partha. 1997. "Cartoons of the Raj." *History Today* 47, no. 9 (September): 16–21. https://www.historytoday.com/archive/cartoons-raj.

Muthiah, S. 1993. Interview with John A. Lent, Chennai, July 22.

Nair, Malini. 2018. "Satire and the Malayali: Why India's Best Cartoonists Almost Always Come from Kerala." Scroll.in, December 10. https://scroll.in/magazine/903768/the-best-indian-cartoonists-usually-come-from-kerala-but-why.

Nair, Raju. 1993a. Correspondence with John A. Lent, August 28.

Nair, Raju. 1993b. Interview with John A. Lent, Trivandrum, July 13.

Ninan, Ajit. 2009. Interview with John A. Lent, New Delhi, July 7.

Padmanabhan, Chitra. 2015. "The Growing Shrillness of Politics Is a Problem for the Cartoonist." *The Wire*, August 12. https://thewire.in/media/the-growing-shrillness-of-politics-is-a-problem-for-the-cartoonist.

Padmanabhan, R. A. 1991. "Earliest Cartoons in South Asia." *Vidura*, July–October, 51.

Pran [Pran Kumar Sharma]. 1993. Interview with John A. Lent, New Delhi, July 5.

Pran [Pran Kumar Sharma]. 2006. Interview with John A. Lent, Drexel Hill, Pennsylvania, June 5–6.

Pran [Pran Kumar Sharma]. 2009. Interviews with John A. Lent, New Delhi, July 7, 10, 11.

Puri, Rajinder. 1993. Interview with John A. Lent, New Delhi, July 5.

Puri, Rajinder. 2009. Interview with John A. Lent, New Delhi, July 7.

Raghav, Krish. 2020. "In India, a Wave of Political Webcomics Are Chronicling Huge Nationwide Protests." Hyperallergic, January 15. https://hyperallergic.com/537472/in-india-a-wave-of-politi cal-webcomics-are-chronicling-huge-nationwide-protests/.

Raghu, Dinakaran. 1993. Untitled presentation at the Symposium on Cartoons, Chennai, July 22.

Raj, Prithvi. 2018. "Indian Journalist Threatened over Anti-Rape Cartoon." BBC News, April 18. https://www.bbc.com/news/ world-asia-india-43806970.

Ramaswamy, Cho. 1993. Interview with John A. Lent, Chennai, July 21.

Rupam [Ramesh Chande]. 1993. Interview with John A. Lent, Mumbai, July 10.

Sawant, Suresh. 1993. Interview with John A. Lent, Mumbai, July 10.

Scully, Richard. 2013. "A Comic Empire: The Global Expansion of Punch as a Model Publication, 1841–1936." International Journal of Comic Art 15, no. 2 (Fall): 6–35.

Sharma, Sanjukta, Dhamini Ratnam, and Shamik Bag. 2015. "The Future of Political Cartoons." Mint, June 12. https:// www.livemint.com/Leisure/HsrB67kr3GXa8inroCy4DN/ The-future-of-political-cartoons.html.

Shetty, Prakash. 1993. Interview with John A. Lent, Kottayam, July 12.

Swamy, A. Ma. 1993. "Cartoons and the Tamil Press." Paper presented at the Symposium on Cartoons, Chennai, July 22.

Tailang, Sudhir. 1993. Interview with John A. Lent, New Delhi, July 6.

Tailang, Sudhir. 2009. Interview with John A. Lent, New Delhi, July 9.

Times of India. 2015. "Growing Intolerance Making Cartooning Unsafe Job: SC." February 5. https://timesofindia.indiatimes .com/india/growing-intolerance-making-cartooning-unsafe -job-sc/articleshow/46125757.cms.

Unny, E. P. 1993. Interview with John A. Lent, New Delhi, July 7.

Unny, E. P. 2009. Interview with John A. Lent, New Delhi, July 7.

Unny, E. P. 2019a. "The Kerala Connection: E. P. Unny Decodes the State's Strong Bond with Political Cartoons." Indian Express, October 20. https://indianexpress.com/article/ express-sunday-eye/truth-be-told-malayalam-cartoon -shankar-cartoonists-boban-molly-toms-mahakshamad evata-100-years-6073271/.

Unny, E. P. 2019b. "The Sudhir Cartoon Neither Screamed nor Lost Poise." Indian Express, November 27. https://indianex press.com/article/opinion/columns/sudhir-dar-cartoonist -dead-this-is-it-6138386/.

Varghese, A. V. 1992. "Funny Business in a Spin." Deccan Herald, May 31.

Vijayan, O. V. 2002. Vijayan: A Cartoonist Remembers. New Delhi: Rupa Publications.

Vins [Vijay Narain Seth]. 1993. Interview with John A. Lent, Mumbai, July 8.

Yesudasan, C. J. 1993. Correspondence with John A. Lent, October 4.

238

Iran is steeped with a rich and robust cartoon presence. The history of Iranian cartooning and caricature stretches back to the Mughal Empire to Persia's east five hundred years ago. The Mughal court used the Persian language extensively, and the emperors Akbar (1542–1605) and his son Jahangir kept groups of court painters, including caricaturists, to draw psychological portraiture. At the beginning of the nineteenth century, decades before comic strips, itinerant Persian artists told romantic, heroic, and religious stories in comics formats as they decorated coffee and tea houses to attract customers, their only payment being food and lodging. These muralists employed techniques of sequencing and a series of scenes squared in numbered divisions as in comics. Also, in the nineteenth century, humor magazines appeared, more than four hundred different titles by 1900. They continued to thrive in the twentieth century; one of the longest lived and most prominent was *Tofigh*, a weekly killed by Shah Moham-mad Reza Pahlavi's government in 1971, after many years of publishing.

According to cartoonists I interviewed, the 1979 Islamic revolution and its aftermath were turning points for cartoons, as they were popularized to be under-standable to common people; there were more venues for them with the proliferation of newspapers and maga-zines; the times were politicized with the formation of a new type of government and the onset of the Iran-Iraq War; and cartoonists were itching to create a new international language to identify with fellow cartoon-ists around the world (Tabatabei 1999; Niroumand 1999; Baniasadi, 1999; Mehrabi 1999). To accomplish the latter, a small group of cartoonists from the University of Fine Arts in Tehran formed Kasni (the name of an herbal medicine with a bitter taste, known as an effective cura-tive), which organized cartoon exhibitions throughout Iran, opened up international connections, absorbed isolated Iranian cartoonists from outside Tehran, and published *Kayhan Caricature* in 1991.

In more contemporary times, the richly government-supported cartooning community has benefited from a sturdy infrastructure consisting of a museum, many

Vignette: Iran

I.1. Left to right: Beynaz Neyistani, Touka Neyistani, Mohammad Ali Baniasadi, John A. Lent, Mana Neyistani, and Mrs. Baniasadi. Later, brothers Touka and Mana and their families fled Iran for political reasons. Tehran, October 8, 1999.

I.2a and I.2b. Atena Farghadani and the cartoon that sent her to prison.

exhibitions, an elaborate biennial, humor magazines (as many as six at a time), and organizations. Binding many of these professional entities is the House of Cartoons, started in the mid-1990s by Massoud Shojai Tabatabei. Primarily a training center, the House of Cartoons for years offered daily courses at both the beginning and advanced levels (Tabatabei 1999). In a class to whom I lectured in 1999, more than half of the twenty or more students were women.

Iran is teeming with professional and amateur cartoonists, evident when viewing the list of winners and participants in international competitions worldwide. A large number of them are young to middle age, make their living in other professions (architecture, teaching, graphic designing, illustrating), and take to cartooning to express themselves, to be "spiritually fulfilled," or to while away time (Lent 2001, 47). Cartooning has also fostered a sense of camaraderie and social purpose among artists who, in the 1990s and early 2000s, organized themselves into about ten small clubs (e.g., White Crow, Zangooleh, Talkhak, Koktus, Meeshatpa, Famous) for professional linkage and advancement. Among their activities were teaching young people to draw, holding exhibitions, publishing a weekly cartoon newspaper, and selling their cartoons, the profits from which they donated to charities (Alidoosti 1999).

Unique for an Islamic country such as Iran is the growing number of women cartoonists. The most renowned is Marjane Satrapi, who created the graphic novel *Persepolis*, later turned into an animation feature after she left Iran. Best known to global press freedom advocates is Atena Farghadani, who in 2014–2015 was arrested and jailed twice, the first time for insulting parliamentarians by drawing them as imitating monkeys and stupid cows, in protest of their vote to restrict contraception and ban certain birth control methods, and the second time for publicly discussing her mistreatment by the guards while imprisoned. The feisty, then-twenty-eight-year-old defied the authorities while incarcerated, going on hunger strikes and flattening paper cups into a canvas on which to draw. Farghadani was forced to undergo humiliating virginity and pregnancy tests and was charged with "illegitimate sexual relations," because she shook hands with her visiting lawyer, who also was jailed. After an international outcry, she was released (Lent 2015, 441–43).

Red lines not to be crossed are prevalent for all Iranians; however, restrictions on women generally "splinter the red lines" (Lent 2015, 443). The difference is subtle, but it is there, as female cartoonist Elham Ataeiazar said: "In the workplace, there is no discrimination in wages or opportunities, but there is a limitation on the concept of women, on how women are portrayed" (2013). After two years as a newspaper political cartoonist, Ataeiazar quit, saying that "it was impossible" because of publishers' and editors' censorship (2013).

I.3. Iran's first female cartoonist, Parvin Kermani, Tehran, December 22, 2013. Photo by John A. Lent. Courtesy of Parvin Kermani.

Nearly all of the seven women I interviewed in 2013 were able to eke out a living by cartooning, supplemented by earnings from teaching, entering and winning competitions, selling exhibited work, illustrating children's books, sculpting, and painting.[1] Iran's first female cartoonist, Parvin Kermani, recalled that when she started drawing cartoons in 1969, there were "no women and only a few men cartoonists" (2013). Kermani was trained in cartooning by Hassan Tofigh, one of the brothers who had founded *Tofigh Weekly*.

The restrictions cartoonists must work under almost always relate to religion, because in an Islamic state such as Iran, almost everything relates to religion. Defying the norm can lead to serious consequences, as Atena Farghadani and others have found out. At least three of my key interviewees in 1999 (Mana and Touka Neyistani and Nikahang [Nik] Kowsar) left the country after being arrested, harassed, and jailed, and there have been others who have fled for fear of serious repercussions, such as Kianoush Ramezani in 2009, after criticizing elections with his online cartoons. By 2012, a dozen of Iran's cartoonists had chosen to live abroad. Kowsar (2012, 142) reported that by 2009, many newspapers had stopped using political cartoons, except for those that are conservative and pawns of the government. Other periodicals have been closed, their journalists arrested.

Echoing the "exchange of the forbidden cassette recordings and printed copies of speeches by Ayatollah

241

I.4. The cartoon that led to Mana Neyistani's arrest, imprisonment, and self-exile. Courtesy of Mana Neyistani.

Ruhollah Khomeini in the 1970s," exiled activists use the internet to get information into Iran, which is then passed around secretly (Bahrampour 2013).

Exiled cartoonist Kianoush Ramezani categorized Iranian cartoonists as those who are exiled, whose major themes are the Islamic Republic and Iranian human rights; those in government, who work for the government media or operate as government watchdogs of other cartoonists and prefer topics such as favorable Islamic propaganda, attacks on Israel and imperialism, and mockery of the West; and those who are neutral, who find ways to publish and exhibit their cartoons, favoring visual and nonpolitical themes (Stransky 2013).

This is likely a fair assessment. If change occurs, it probably will occur among neutral cartoonists who will be forced to kowtow to the government in order to publish. The moral fortitude of these artists, and their level of dependence on cartooning for their very survival, will determine the path they will take.

Note

1. Five of the women I interviewed were Farzane Vaziritabar, twenty-six years old in 2013, also an accomplished sculptor; Parvin Kermani, a teacher for twenty years and cartoonist for *Gol Agha* (Flower Man) and other magazines and newspapers since 1969; Shiva Zamanfar (born 1982), a caricaturist, drawing faces on large tableaus in oil and selling them to the public; Elham Ataeiazar, educated as a physicist, a prolific cartoonist and illustrator on at

I.5. A cartoon by Nik Kowsar with symbols for censorship. Courtesy of Nik Kowsar.

I.6. Farzane Vaziritabar. The cook as artist. Courtesy of Farzane Vaziritabar.

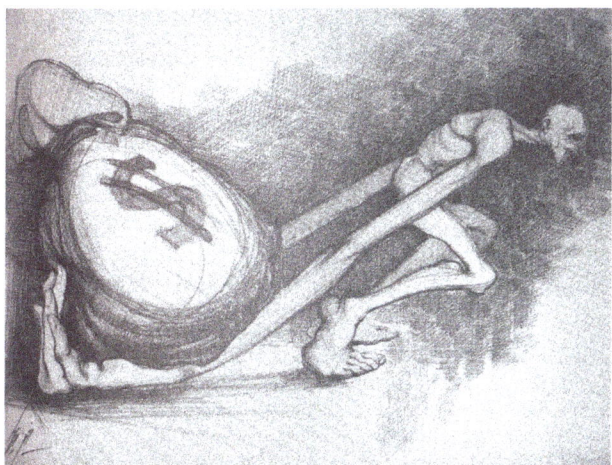

I.7. Zeynab Nikche. The Sisyphean wage earner. Courtesy of Zeynab Nikche.

least four magazines and *Etemad Meli Daily*, as well as an illustrator of many children's and adult books; and Zeynab Nikche (born 1984), a painter, cartoonist, animator, children's book designer, and television logo designer. Ataeiazar and Vaziritabar feature women and their issues in their cartoons. All were interviewed in Tehran on December 22, 2013.

Bibliography

Alidoosti, Fa'ez. 1999. Interview with John A. Lent, Tehran, October 2.

Ataeiazar, Elham. 2013. Interview with John A. Lent, Tehran, December 22.

Bahrampour, Tara. 2013. "Striking Back, Even from a Half World Away." *Washington Post*, June 1. https://www.washingtonpost.com/local/striking-back-even-from-half-a-world-away/2013/06/01/5d3dc182-ca27-11e2-8da7-d274bc611a47_story.html.

Baniasadi, Mohammad Ali. 1999. Interview with John A. Lent, Tehran, October 3.

Kermani, Parvin. 2013. Interview with John A. Lent, Tehran, December 22.

Kowsar, Nikahang. 1999. Interview with John A. Lent, Tehran, October 7.

Kowsar, Nikahang. 2012. "Being Funny Is Not That Funny: Contemporary Editorial Cartooning in Iran." *Social Research* 79, no. 1 (Spring): 117–44.

Lent, John A. 2001. "Iran: A Country Teeming with Cartoonists." *Comics Journal*, no. 233 (May): 46–48.

Lent, John A. 2015. "A Brief Introduction to Some Iranian Women Cartoonists and Their Works." *International Journal of Comic Art* 17, no. 2 (Fall–Winter): 441–56.

Mehrabi, Massoud. 1999. Interview with John A. Lent, Tehran, October 3.

Neyistani, Touka. 1999. Interview with John A. Lent, Tehran, October 6.

Nikche, Zeynab. 2013. Interview with John A. Lent, Tehran, December 22.

Niroumand, Mohammad-Hossein. 1999. Interview with John A. Lent, Tehran, October 2.

Stransky, Olivia. 2013. "Iranian Cartoonist Kianoush Ramezani on Three Kinds of Cartoons." Sampsonia Way, May 24. http//www.sampsoniaway.org/interviews2013/05/24/Iranian-cartoonist-kianoush-ramezanion-three-kinds-of-cartoons/.

Tabatabei, Massoud Shojai. 1999. Interview with John A. Lent, Tehran, October 1, 2.

Vaziritabar, Farzane. 2013. Interview with John A. Lent, Tehran, December 22.

Zamanfar, Shiva. 2013. Interview with John A. Lent, Tehran, December 22.

243

Introduction

Satire and political humor have permeated Nepalese culture for many centuries, found in folk stories such as those of religious and mythological figures (e.g., Ganesh, Unmutta Bhairab, and Neparsing Devta), and stories based on ethnic proverbs and satirical poetry, an example of the latter being famous poet Bhanubhakta's anti-government verses penned while serving prison time in the mid-nineteenth century (R. K. Panday 2000). Witty and satirical frescoes centuries old depict husbands on all fours led on leashes by their wives, a monkey shaking the columns of a palace, and humans performing contortionist sex acts, often with humorous elements.

This rich heritage of challenging and mocking tradition and authority continues, having survived political dictatorships, repressive monarchial rule, and natural disasters. It thrives through humor clubs, comedy shows, and festivals; the most prominent and longest-lasting festival is Gaijatra (the Cow Festival), which has lent itself well to cartooning.

Dating to about five hundred years ago, Gaijatra came about when a Malla king attempted to console his wife after the death of their child, ordering representatives from each family similarly stricken to come to the palace to show the queen that she was not alone in her grief. Some afflicted families came with cows, honoring a religious belief that only a cow's horn opens heaven's gates. Urban dwellers wore cow masks. The gathering made for a festive and carnivalesque atmosphere, which became apparent to the queen.

Renowned Nepali humor researcher Ram Kumar Panday (2000) said that the annual one-week-in-August Gaijatra draws hundreds of groups demonstrating different things through various guises, costumes, jokes, and other forms of levity. Even in the most authoritarian periods, this public frolicking and lampooning the authorities is permitted. As Panday remarked: "It was the freedom day for humorous criticism" (2000).

Cartoons found a place in Gaijatra, especially in the 1960s and 1970s, with the emergence of new humor magazines and humor editions of other periodicals,

Chapter 16

Nepal

16.1. The guiding figure of Nepali humor and cartoons, Ram Kumar Panday, Kathmandu, October 27, 2016. Photo by John A. Lent. Courtesy of Ram Kumar Panday.

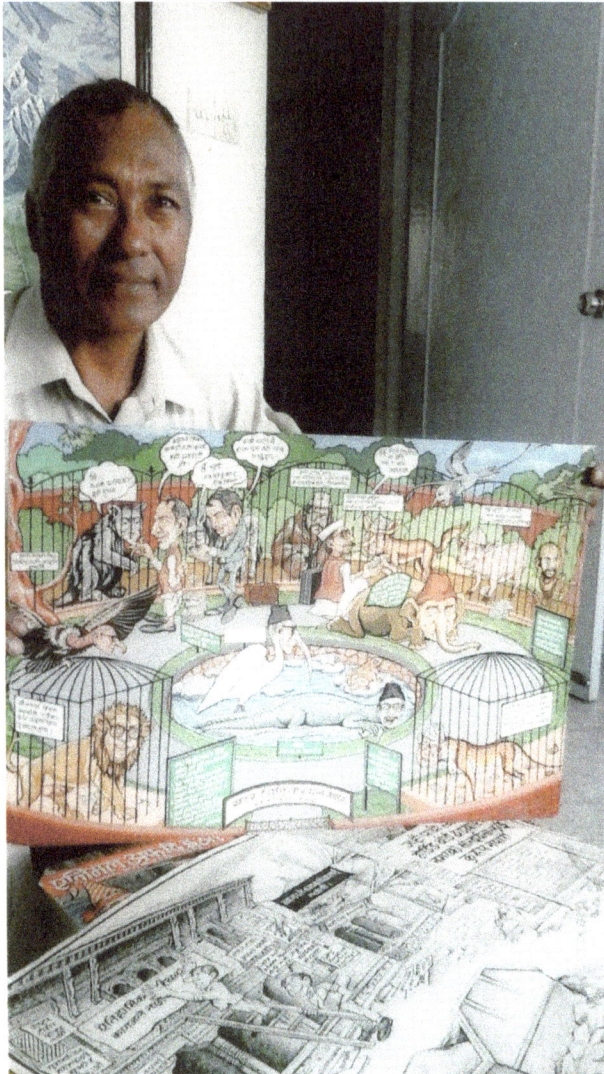

16.2. Ashok Man Singh with one of his cartoons, Kathmandu, October 24, 2016. Photo by John A. Lent. Permission of Ashok Man Singh.

published just for the festival. In 1962,[1] the *Naya Samaj* newspaper brought out a humor issue during Gaijatra, which sparked other periodicals to follow suit. The country's top film magazine, the monthly *Kamana* (Wish), started a tradition of filling an entire issue with cartoons for Gaijatra, a number of which were criticized as pornographic or scatological. Suman Manandhar (2002), responsible for selecting and laying out the cartoons, defended the practice of portraying women sexually and using much adult content as meeting "public demand," and as a means to reach the goal of selling twice the number of copies as the previous year.

Kamana's cofounder, famous painter and cartoonist Ashok (Ashok Man Singh), explained further: "The

16.3. Humor magazines *Muskan* (left) and *Bhandbhailo* (right). Courtesy of Ram Kumar Panday.

younger generation is into modernization, and sex content is okay by them," at the same time qualifying this remark with: "Usually the cartoonists dealt with the environment and politics" (2016). On one occasion in the 1990s, according to Ashok, *Kamana* used its centerspread to caricature the prime minister as a "no-brain police officer," the result of which was: "The government wanted to take me into jail and I hid out for four days" (Ashok 2016).

For a number of years beginning in 1984, a cartoon magazine, *Bhandbhailo* (Anyone Can Do Anything), made its once yearly appearance during Gaijatra. At its peak, *Bhandbhailo* had a print run of fifty thousand to sixty thousand copies. Panday (2000) said that its design and cartoons were of high quality, and the annual played a key role of unifying cartoonists: "Just before Cow's Festival [they] gather, work late at night, do some drinking, invite humor writers in, and come up with themes. Any theme can come up. Then they divide the themes among the cartoonists to draw." He went on to say that most cartoonists contributed with senior artists and writers acting as advisers, and that *Bhandbhailo* showed them the importance of working together (R. K. Panday 2000).

Aside from Gaijatra, other stimulants to the professionalism of cartooning are the humor association HaSaNe (Hasya Byanga Samaj Nepal) and the Cartoonists' Club of Nepal. Ram Kumar Panday started HaSaNe in 1991, with divisions for cartooning, writing, and stage performance and branches in seven places throughout Nepal. Former secretary Dharma Raj Baral (2000) listed the group's missions as gathering cartoonists "to show

16.4. Humor performers at a Nepali potato party, Ram Kumar Panday's home, Kathmandu, October 2016. Photo by John A. Lent. Courtesy of Ram Kumar Panday.

them how to improve their cartoons, how to develop relations with cartoonists outside of Nepal, to find out what is done outside the country, . . . to critique Nepali cartoons," and to provide training. HaSaNe and its president, Ram Kumar Panday, also organize an annual "potato party," an ongoing fun fest held during Tihar (Festival of Lights) since 1978. I was an honor guest at the 2016 potato party, which my notes describe as follows:

An annual potato party at Panday's Paradise [home and rental guesthouse of R. K. Panday and his family]. Was supposed to start much earlier but began at 2:10 and ended 5:20 p.m. Made up of stand-up comedians, poets, humor writers, and cartoonists. About 60 [humor-related writers, artists, musicians, and stage performers] present, 16 of whom performed. Some humorous music performed live. At end of performances, an all-potato meal is served to all, and participants are presented certificates. Much laughter. Recorded for YouTube, TV coverage, and *Annapurna* daily. Called "potato" because it is a common vegetable in curries and also a flunk [school flunky] is called a "potato" [a zero is shaped like a potato].

Panday (2016) hopes that this type of intermingling leads to learning from and cooperating with one another: for instance, a cartoonist not skilled at writing learning from a writer.

The Cartoonists' Club of Nepal, founded in 2001, has attempted to advance Nepalese cartooning through exhibitions, competitions, seminars, meetings of cartoonists, its website (Cartcon), and the publication of a book on cartooning. Its president, Abin Shrestha, gave as his goals for the club, to "extend the club's activities, bring the skills of thirty-plus members to international standards and encourage them to compete globally, and have an international exhibition in Nepal" (A. Shrestha 2016). The club also was successful in getting the Nepal Academy of Fine Arts to recognize cartooning and illustrating as academic fields.

History

It is remarkable that cartooning has endured, and even made advancements, given the topsy-turvy world of Nepalese government and politics. Barring from this discussion the earlier periods of colonialism and the 105-year autocratic rule of the Rana family starting in the mid-nineteenth century, and looking only at the first five years of the twenty-first century, the country witnessed the palace massacre of King Birendra and his entire immediate family (ten in all) on June 1, 2001; the on-and-off armed conflict/ceasefire between the Maoists and state security forces; the state of national emergency declared in November 2001 by King Gyanendra; his semicoup in October 2002 when he dismissed the prime minister; and, finally, Gyanendra's coup of February 1, 2005, when he took all executive powers to himself and reinstated emergency restrictions (Hutt 2006, 362–64, 366, 373).

Semblances of political cartoons were visible in the late 1930s and early 1940 through illustrated posters resembling cartoons that were plastered on Kathmandu streetside walls by the revolutionary artist Chandraman Maskey, who in 1940 was sentenced to eighteen

247

years imprisonment with hard labor for his anti–Rana regime activity. Of course, his drawings attacked the Rana dynasty. Tangible proof of the posters does not exist as Maskey destroyed his works as he was about to be arrested. Early periodical cartoons, all anonymously drawn, were published in six issues of *Udaya* in 1943 and 1944 (Biwash 2002). *Aawaaj* (Voice) supposedly used cartoons in 1951, but this has not been authenticated.

What is documented is that the Shah brothers (first, Gobardhan using the name Gobardhan Bikram, and a year or two later, Sashi) drew political cartoons in *Samyukta Prayas* in 1957 (Gobardhan's recollection; 1956, according to Sashi) (Shah 2002). Gobardhan's first published pictorial commentary dealt with concern that King Mahendra would make a mistake in his choice of a new prime minister in 1957. He sent it unsolicited to *Samyukta Prayas* as a reader, not a cartoonist. The weekly newspaper printed a few other Gobardhan cartoons until it was suspended; then, its editorial board launched *Janaprayas*, which carried on the practice of using cartoons. Gobardhan Shah was inspired by cartoons in foreign magazines he saw regularly while working in the Nepalese foreign service (Shah 2002). The pioneer cartoonists of Nepal also were often exposed to imported, cartoon-laden copies of *Blitz* and *Current* from India and imitated the styles of their cartoonists.

Sashi Shah drew political cartoons beginning in 1958, under the instruction of the editor of *Samyukta Prayas* and *Janaprayas*. For whatever reasons, his cartoons did not carry his name. He talked about the early days of Nepali cartooning in a 2002 interview with my graduate student and assistant Fungma Fudong:

> There were no proper tools to make cartoons in those days. There weren't many newspapers in Nepal. There wasn't any trend of printing cartoons in papers. They were considered a waste of money. . . . We didn't have offset presses like we do nowadays. We didn't even have zinc blocks. We had to make use of wooden blocks to make cartoons, which obviously did not print nicely. . . . Newspapers sometimes used to pay and sometimes, they didn't. . . . Things weren't done

16.5. Longtime freelance political cartoonist Khokana (Mohan Shyam Maharjan), Kathmandu, October 27, 2016. Photo by John A. Lent. Permission of Mohan Shyam Maharjan.

in a professional manner back then. Cartoons were just for making's sake. (Shah 2002)

Those who submitted cartoons to periodicals in the late 1950s into the early 1970s did so at the request of editors, who often had to guide them even about the basics of cartooning.[2] Nepal's top political cartoonist,[3] Batsyayana (Durga Baral), admitted:

> A friend introduced me to the publisher of *Naya Sandesh* [New Message]. I took a job of a cartoonist not out of interest, but much like a profession, and simply as a job. I had no idea or knowledge about cartoons. The editor explained to me what and how I was supposed to make cartoons. I made whatever he told me to do and I did it for four years. (Batsyayana 2002)

Veteran cartoonist/animator Ujjwol Kundan Jyapoo (2002) extended the time frame up to the twenty-first century, stating that Nepali cartoonists "did not really understand what a cartoon is about. For them, they look at some magazines and newspapers, then, they start off their careers as a cartoonist in this manner."

16.6. "Democracy," Batsyayana (Durga Baral). Courtesy of Ram Kumar Panday.

Starting as a cartoonist in the 1960s and 1970s was not a joyride. Khokana (Mohan Shyam Maharjan)[4] (2016), who began his career with *Naya Sandesh* in 1971, concurred with Sashi Shah and Panday (2000) in remembering the lack of proper tools and the need to use woodblock prints; he said that by the time the blocks were cut, "other news surpassed the event I drew about three or four days earlier." Khokana added the unavailability of resource materials as a problem, recalling, "In the beginning, it was very difficult to find pictures of ministers and other people we wanted to satire. The editor had seen these people, but we hadn't. So, he would describe the person to me: he has a moustache, wears a cap, etc. I would draw sketches from his descriptions until he said, this is the closest to what he looks like" (2016). As indicated above, government officials were quick to react; within three or four hours after a cartoon appeared, editors could expect a government phone call with the query "why did you make this?," Khokana said. Taking a stand on an issue usually was not the prerogative of cartoonists; they were essentially hired visual "hitmen." Khokana (2016) said that he had drawn for both a Communist and a National Democratic newspaper simultaneously, explaining that, working as a freelancer, he drew what was assigned to him, and that he made more money than if he were one publisher's permanent staff artist.

Similar issues plagued Batsyayana when he started doing cartoons in *Naya Sandesh* in 1966, particularly being assigned topics by the editor and having to

put up with time-consuming, imperfect woodblock printing. He added that there were not many newspapers and magazines at the time, and he was alone as a cartoonist (Batsyayana 2002). Three other cartoonists joined the ranks shortly thereafter: Tek Bir Mukhiya, Balram Thapa (*Samikccha*), and Khokana. A common perception of the 1960s, and to some extent today, is that any artist can make cartoons; this is bothersome to Batsyayana, who prefers to be called an artist, but he believes that not any artist can be a cartoonist. He explained: "There is a distinct difference between the two. Making cartoons requires hard mental practice or mind workouts, but an art requires one to pour out emotions or sentiments on it. A cartoon needs to be humorous and satirical at the same time conveying a message" (Batsyayana 2002).

As with other early cartoonists (e.g., the Shah brothers, Mukhiya, and Panday), Batsyayana left cartooning for five or six years, returning to his hometown and establishing an art studio. However, he resumed cartooning about 1978, when his friends launched a literary magazine, *Prangan*, and requested his services (Batsyayana 2002). Until he signed a contract with Kantipur Publications in 1996, he had worked on a freelance basis. While with Kantipur, he ran afoul of the authorities for a cartoon implying that King Gyanendra was tossing the constitutional monarchy into the garbage. For that drawing, articles in the official press called for confiscation of his property and even his death. The editors of sister dailies *Kantipur* and the *Kathmandu Post*

16.7. *Kaliyug* (Ironies), humor magazine founded by Ram Kumar Panday, 1971. Courtesy of Ram Kumar Panday.

were immediately arrested; and the next day, *Kantipur* "affirmed its commitment to the constitutional monarchy and democracy" (Wikipedia 2019).

The few cartoonists of the 1960s and 1970s did not produce much work because doing cartoons was not a family-sustaining job, media were not thrilled about using them, and censorship was tough. The known cartoon output of Gobardhan Shah during this period was a total of four cartoons; Batsyayana completed about twenty in three years (Haviland 2006).

Responsible to a large extent for the increased publication of cartoons was the setting up of the Gaijatra festive issues of *Naya Samaj* newspaper and *Kamana* magazine, already discussed, and the appearance of other magazines, including some devoted entirely to humor, from the 1970s to the 1990s. As with so many aspects of Nepalese humor and cartooning, geography teacher Ram Kumar Panday brought out the first regularly published magazine fully devoted to humor, *Kaliyug* (Ironies), in 1971. It was banned for political reasons after two years.

Other humor magazines that started in the 1980s and 1990s nourished political cartooning. A popular one was the bimonthly *Muskan* (Smile), started in the 1980s and lasting more than twenty years. At its peak in the late 1990s, its circulation was thirty-five thousand copies, but that number dwindled to one-third by 2000. The reasons for the plunge, according to editor-in-chief Dharma Raj Baral (2000), were a change of distribution managers and a "politically changed situation." "The public loses interest in humor magazines when politics is not at fever pitch," he said. Ten cartoonists regularly submitted cartoons to *Muskan*, usually when "we ask and if they have time," according to Baral (2000).

Phoo Mantar came out for a while in the mid-1990s, and there were other humor magazines such as *Jhyaikuti, Fumantar, Bhundipuran,* and *Hasyauli Thattauli. Hasyauli Thattauli*, issued six times between 1991 and 1994, was started by Devendra Panday soon after he left the tenth grade. He and three friends collected some money and printed three thousand copies of the first issue. Panday admitted to using a ruse to sell more copies of the second issue, explaining: "For the second issue, I made some cover designs for both the back and front sides. People mistakenly bought two copies. People loved it" (D. Panday 2002). When *Bhandbhailo* assumed the marketing of *Hasyauli Thattauli*, its circulation shot to fifteen thousand, a success that lasted for a short time before the periodical was forced to close because of stiff competition from a flood of new magazines and newspapers. Devendra Panday (2002) said that the surge in humor magazines resulted because of the government's relaxation of restrictions and that under previous, more stringent regulations, humor magazines only came out during Gaijatra; but the "situation is such nowadays that every day is Gaijatra." He added: "Before, people had to wait for a year to see cartoons, but now, they get them every day. Too much overdose of politics; people don't have to wait anymore. This was one of the factors why our magazine stopped" (D. Panday 2002).

The New Millennium

Cartoonists faced some harrowing situations in the closing years of the millennium, when there were many changes of political administration, a Maoist military movement, and emergency periods. In 1991, a case was filed against the publisher and two editors of *Drishthi* weekly for a cartoon called *Lakdi Chor Nyayadhis* by Rabin Sayami, and the following year, the editor of *Bimarsha* weekly was jailed for a week and fined Rs. 500 for a cartoon by Khokana mocking the supreme judge and the Supreme Court. Threats to cartoonists came from the government and other political factions. Devendra Panday (2002), who drew unfavorable cartoons of the Maoists, quit drawing them for fear of losing his life, stating: "I think one day they'll come and kidnap me and kill me eventually."

At the dawn of the twenty-first century, some factors related to Nepali political cartooning changed for the better while others no less important either remained fixed or deteriorated. The number of venues for cartoonists increased beyond Gaijatra and an occasional newspaper, to 1,620 (230 daily) regularly published papers. More people began to draw, and the number of "very popular and prominent" cartoonists rose to fifty (R. K. Panday 2000). Some were even able to survive by cartooning.[5] At the time, a few women entered the profession, and the organization of a comic art community was on its way.

Sashi Shah, there at the very beginning, said in 2002 that he saw a "good" future for cartooning with the advancement of education and more opportunities as the number of periodicals and their circulation increased. Cartoonist animator Rajendra Rana, Devendra Panday, teacher/cartoonist Sushma Rajbhandari, and Durga Baral all agreed that advancements had been made, each singling out a particular accomplishment and mentioning obstacles still in the way. They hesitantly felt that one could make a living by full-time drawing, "if one gets chances . . . but chances are rare" (R. Rana 2002), if one can endure the "hectic" work and stress (D. Panday 2002), and if one has exposure in the field (Batsyayana 2002; Rajbhandari 2002).

Two female cartoonists, Sangee Shrestha and Sushma Rajbhandari, both freelancers, felt that they were treated equally with their male colleagues in terms of opportunities and payment; both said the issue that damns them is the before- and after-marriage decision. Shrestha explained, "A woman has to get married in our society, and she has to make a crucial decision. It's either your work or your family" (2002). Rajbhandari echoed similar sentiments: "Women in most parts of our country are suffering from many social obstructions. . . . The problem here is not about surviving in a male world but of sociocultural traditions" (2002).

Other improvements were made to comic art by 2002, such as competitions and exhibitions, the humor society HaSaNe, the Cartoonists' Club of Nepal, and technology that helped cartoonists to better network, to spread their work beyond Kathmandu, and to upgrade their works using better reproduction techniques. But side by side were persistent shortcomings: the lack of support for the arts and cartooning specifically; very few newspapers powerful enough to sustain a cartoonist's living wage; inadequate workplace supplies; the need for higher standards of professionalism concerning training, imitation/plagiarism, and a sense of overall ethics; and an often unstable, turbulent government/political system that kept editors and cartoonists in a constant state of flux. For example, cartoonists for years hid behind nicknames, in some cases using two or three monikers, switching as their identities were about to be revealed. Later, they retained the pen names, because they had become known and popular by them. A few examples of unethical behavior were revealed by cartoonists in 2002. Rajendra Rana (2002) was irked by cartoonists who "poison the ears" of publishers by putting down other cartoonists to "steal" their jobs; others showed concern for an inordinate amount of imitating, often of R. K. Laxman of India (R. Rana 2002; Jyapoo 2002; Shah 2002; Batsyayana 2002; D. Panday 2002). Another lingering problem was the feeling of jealousy

16.8. Cartoon by Rabin Sayami. Courtesy of Ram Kumar Panday.

and guardedness endemic to a small, tightly condensed community such as that of comic art.

The biggest issue for Nepali cartoonists in 2002, as it has been for most of the field's history, is their relationship with the government and politicians. Censorship existed, as well as self-restraint by editors and cartoonists who knew how far they could go. Although he said that his political cartoons had not been censored, Rajendra Rana (2002) said that Nepal had two types of government, Shree Paanch Sarkaar or monarchy and Shree Paanch ko Sarkaar or His Majesty's government. He expanded: "We cannot touch the royal family, but we can draw anything about employees of His Majesty's government." Ujjwol Kundan Jyapoo (2002) agreed that the royal palace "cannot be touched," nor the high court of justice. Otherwise, the feeling of cartoonists at the beginning of the 2000s was that they had much freedom. Batsyayana talked about a risk of having such freedom:

> Nowadays, we are totally free to do anything and say anything we want through our cartoons. This has kind of created another risk. A risk of not having anything to say at all. It's Gaijatra every day. It does not create the same kind of effect it used to in the Panchayat system. It has become more challenging to come up with something that'll attract our readers' attention. Something new and original and different. They read about general things every day. I guess it's something that was evident to happen from a closed world to an open world. (Batsyayana 2002)

Whatever freedom the cartoonists had likely disappeared during the turbulent times that followed when

uncertainty ruled, as already mentioned. The media and their artists faced stringent state control at times, as well as periods when the red lines not to be crossed wavered, forcing cartoonists to skirt issues and self-censor. Keeping cartoonists and other media personnel guessing what is allowed and not allowed and what to do and not to do has proven to be a strong and less noticeable control strategy.

Despite this situation in 2005 and thereafter, when King Gyanendra seized power, declared an emergency, and imposed strict censorship, people depended on a handful of political cartoonists, especially Rajesh K. C. and Batsyayana of the Kantipur dailies, to push the envelope of what was allowed and keep them informed. K. C. (he uses initials for his last name) said that he and a few other cartoonists did "what journalists have been barred from doing," adding that he had to draw a line that he could not cross, but with every cartoon, he got "bolder." Boldness on the part of a few cartoonists was evident in their caricaturing of King Gyanendra and the monarchy, previously off-limits but fair game in their minds when he decided to run the government (Pudasaini and Mallapaty 2008). As Rabin Sayami said, "If the king had remained a constitutional monarch, I guess we wouldn't be drawing him." One example of a cartoon from the Kathmandu paper *Rajdhani* that defied government directives in an ingenious manner "showed a politician giving a speech inside his bedroom because public speeches are now banned"; another "showed a journalist faxing his story and a government censor hiding under the table, reading the story as it is fed through the machine" (Cartcon 2005b). This type of visual commentary continued in the succeeding years of uncertainty, with cartoonists taking on issues such as political party power struggles, shortages of essential products, and ineffective law-and-order mechanisms.

Contemporary Times

The picture that cartoon historian Ram Kumar Panday painted of humor and political cartoons in 2016 was

16.9. Abin Shrestha and his character, Kathmandu, October 25, 2016. Photo by Ram Kumar Panday. Permission of Abin Shrestha.

dismal, with a few bright touches. He said that although many newspapers exist, only five each of the Nepalese-language and English-language dailies are popular, and only a few use political cartoons of high quality. He also said that humor magazines have disappeared, and most newspapers are politically one-sided, being organs of political parties. On the positive side, Panday felt that cartoonists were paid well and had more freedom of expression, but their cartoons had virtually no visible effect on government (R. K. Panday 2016). Khokana (2016) thought that the authorities' inattention to political cartoons resulted because "they had finally digested them." Ashok Man Singh, now head of the Read and Write Publishing House, agreed with his

colleagues' assessments, saying that when he began in the 1970s, drawing people in the news was scorned upon, necessitating that he use a pseudonym, Manasing. He said: "People took the cartoons seriously," adding with a bit of remorse, "not now." Ashok lamented that many aspects of political cartooning are stalemated, not differing much over the years: only about ten cartoonists can live off newspaper payments, few dailies have their own staff cartoonists, and training is nearly nonexistent, as are chances to learn from sources outside of Nepal (Ashok 2016). Another problem alluded to in interviews is what I have been calling "guided cartooning," whereby cartoonists are coached by editors on what to draw and how (Y. Ghimire 2016; R. K. Panday 2016; Ashok 2016; Khokana 2016).

Prominent staff cartoonists in the 2010s were Batsyayana and Abin Shrestha of the sister dailies *Kantipur* and the *Kathmandu Post*, Rajesh K. C. and Basu Chhetij of the *Annapurna Post*, and Rabin Sayami. Abin, who is senior cartoonist and chief subeditor of the Kantipur newspapers, on a daily basis draws a front-page pocket cartoon for the *Kathmandu Post* and a front-page, color political cartoon for *Kantipur*. He also does a weekly strip in the company's children's magazine and published one issue of a comic book he created in 2009, called *Ko Bhanda ko Kam*. He began his career on the *Nepali Times Daily* in 1993 and joined *Kantipur* in 2008 as the sole staff cartoonist. He described Kantipur Publications as a rich media house consisting of one weekly and two daily newspapers, and one magazine, one TV channel, and one radio station. Because it pays well, the company is able to keep its staff. Abin said that he receives no pressure from *Kantipur*'s administration (or from the government), because a major condition of his accepting the position was that he would have total freedom (A. Shrestha 2016). He added, "Sometimes, I meet with the editor, and it is hard to convince him to let my cartoon be printed, but I usually convince him. But, rarely, sometimes I can't" (A. Shrestha 2016).

Rajesh K. C. first drew cartoons for the government-owned *Rising Nepal*, the country's first English-language daily, where he was heavily censored. In 1993, K. C.,

253

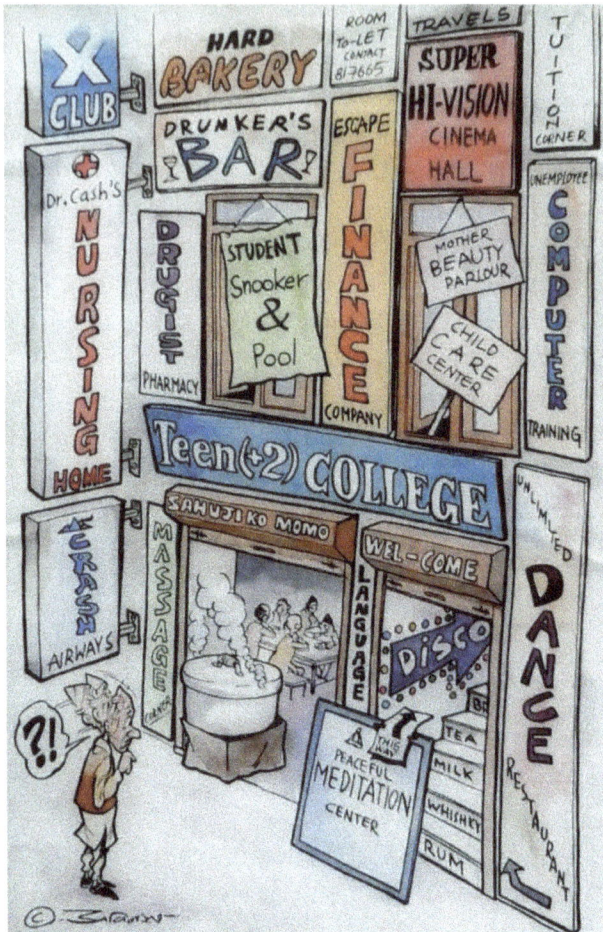

16.10. Cartoon by Abin. Permission of Abin Shrestha.

inspired by the work of R. K. Laxman of India, was able to convince the editor of *Kantipur* to allow him to introduce the pocket cartoon concept to Nepal with his own nameless common man character (eventually named Phalano) in 1998. K. C. said that Phalano is an Everyman, a silent listener who wears clothing that is an "amalgam of the different attires of the hills, mountains, and the Tarai" (Bana 2016), and observes the "social and political absurdities" in Nepal (Kaphle 2018). In an interview with Anup Kaphle, K. C. talked about his cat-and-mouse-game with the authorities and their censors. He remembered the day after King Gyanendra took over the government; with about one hundred heavily armed soldiers occupying his newspaper offices, he drew a cartoon "illustrating a man running for an ambulance for his pregnant wife because the telephone line was dead" (Kaphle 2018). He drew other metaphorical cartoons at the time. K. C. keeps a keen eye on corrupt politicians and other nefarious figures, while "drawing a line of

self-censorship" to avoid disrupting communal harmony by not attacking religion, ethnic groups, or cultural artifacts. In recent years, he has also focused on two business ventures—the café Phalano Coffee Ghar and a clothing store, Phalano Luga. K. C.'s creativity has served him well; he has made more than two hundred designs for Phalano Luga's clothing, employing colloquialisms, witty catchphrases, and a Nepali flavor that often draws on the country's latest happenings.

Rabin Sayami and Basu Chhetij also have championed the causes of the public, taking on those in power in the process. Rabin was honored in 2016 with the prestigious Parijat Kala Puraskar award for spreading awareness through his satirical cartoons, published by Nepal Republica Media. Some of his cartoons have elicited legal action and strong denouncements. In 2013, Rabin (along with the publisher and editor of Himal Media) was hit with a contempt of court charge for a cartoon that portrayed the chief justice as a monkey. The case was quashed when the bench ruled that contempt of court could not be exercised "if the person [has] spoken or publicized truth or commented in a fair manner" and "on personal matters of any judges or their administrative decisions" (Legal News from Nepal 2007). At times, Rabin's cartoons can be savage, as reported in the August 31, 2018, edition of the *Nepali Times*:

> Last week, Rabin Sayami drew a savage cartoon that tore the government to shreds over its callousness in not investigating the Kanchanpur rape case and killing a protestor. It depicted a smiling Pushpa Kamal Dahal and a smug Prime Minister Oli with a smoking gun in his hand. The rapist holds a bloody knife, and has his back turned. Sayami was warned by his friends to be careful and that he might be sent to jail. He says the cartoon was a test: "To see if we are still a democracy." (Bhattarai 2018)

That cartoon has been on the minds of journalists, photographers, and cartoonists since the promulgation of a new penal code in 2018 that "criminalized photography . . . , slapped heavy fines and jail terms for recording conversations . . . , and announced strict punishments

16.11. *Himalayan Times* front-page cartoon by Khapang.

for sending, receiving, or using online data" (Bhattarai 2018). Another bill would prohibit publishing personal information about public officials. These actions made the media community anxious and apprehensive, especially because, within two weeks after the laws were enacted, the editors of three prominent dailies were summoned to meet with authorities, a photojournalist was warned, and a top official used the age-old rationale that because the media failed to self-regulate, the government had to step in. As in moves toward authoritarianism elsewhere, the Nepal laws are broadly defined and open to different interpretations. Editors and other journalists pointed to "increased censorship in a planned way"; the curtailment of all forms of expression, especially investigative journalism; the conversion of the Press Council from a watchdog on unethical journalism to an arm of government; and a general sense of intolerance (*Nepali Times* 2018).

In an informal survey of seventeen Sunday editions of predominantly national newspapers on October 23, 2016, I found that the interviewees' statements were for the most part valid.[6] There were a total of seven drawings that could be called political cartoons—three front-page pocket cartoons and four full-size political cartoons. Three were prominently placed on front pages in full color (*Rajdhani*, *Himalayan Times*, and *Nepal Samacharpatra*). They all were Sunday editions, which normally carry more cartoons than the dailies. As is increasingly common, the newspapers carried nonopinionated illustrations.

A Brief Conclusion

Satire thrives best in authoritarian times, and for some cartoonists, these are the most fun times as they try to outwit the censors, provide the public with different opinions, and stay out of jail or worse. Cartooning in Nepal has a long history of ups and downs, of on-and-off relationships with the authorities, and the situation is not likely to stabilize in the near future.

Notes

1. Rochak Ghimire (2000) gives the date of 1961. Confusion results occasionally when converting from Nepal's dating system, Bikram Sambat, to that of the West. BS is fifty-six years ahead of CE.

2. Among the earliest political cartoonists were the painter Kulman Singh Bhandari (Gwange), who drew political cartoons for *Hal Khabar* (Biwash 2002) in 1959, and others who began in the 1960s and early 1970s such as Durga Baral (Batsyayana), Tek Bir Mukhiya, Balram Thapa (Baratha), Mohan Shyam Maharjan (Khokana), Narasiingha Bhakta Tulachan (Kaushik), Rama Kamara, and Ram Kumar Panday. Balram Thapa drew for the government daily *Gorkhapatra* early on, contributing a regular cartoon feature called *Rameko Chartikala* and social cartoons such as *Rangabiranga*.

3. Baral chose the pen name of a Hindu sage named Batsyayana, said to have had knowledge of every art, because as a college teacher in the 1960s, Baral could have been fired and arrested for publicly commenting on politics.

4. Khokana (2016) said that his pen name is the name of his birthplace, which he hoped to popularize. Originally, his pseudonym was Mohan.

5. Ram Kumar Panday (2000) reported that those who made a living from cartooning were Rabin Sayami, Abin Shrestha, and Basu Chhetij. Tek Bir Mukhiya worked as an artist and book designer, Mohan Shyam Maharjan in a government office, Dhiresh Kumar Dahal in a bank, Rajesh K. C. in a tourism office, Durga Baral as an artist, Balram Thapa as a designer for the government daily *Gorkhapatra*, and Ashhok Man Singh as a book publisher.

6. The newspapers were: *Kantipur*, the *Kathmandu Post*, *Karobar Daily*, *Gorkhapatra Daily*, the *Himalayan Times*, *Nagarik News*, *Nepal Samacharpatra*, *Rajdhani Nepali National Daily*, the *Annapurna Post*, *Naya Patrika National Daily*, the *Himalayan*, *Aarthik Abhiyan*, *Commander Post*, *Sourya National Daily*, *Janasawal National Daily*, *Madhyanha National Daily*, and *Aarthik National Economic Daily*.

Bibliography

Ashok [Ashok Man Singh]. 2016. Interviews with John A. Lent, Kathmandu, October 24, 27.

Bana, Binit. 2016. "A Man of the People." *M&S VMag*, March 25. http://mnsvmag.com/news/2016-03-25/a-man-of-the-people-20160815154358.html.

Baral, Ajit. 2006. "Batsyayana and His Cartoons: Now in a Book." United We Blog: For a Peaceful and Democratic Nepal, June 26. http://www.blog.com.np/united-we-blog/2006/06/26/batsyayana-and-his-cartoons-now-in-a-book/.

Baral, Dharma Raj. 2000. Interview with John A. Lent, Osaka, July 26.

Batsyayana [Durga Baral]. 2002. Telephone interview with Fungma Fudong, Summer.

Bhattarai, Sewa. 2018. "Gagging the Press in Installments." *Nepali Times*, August 31. https://www.nepalitimes.com/banner/gagging-the-press-in-installments/.

Biwash, Gyanendra. 2002. "Chitra Bichitra ko Byangachitra" [Artistic and Fantastic Cartoons]. *Rajdhani*, September 3, 1.

Cartcon. 2005a. "Journalists Face Arrest over Cartoon about Monarchy." Cartoonists' Club of Nepal, August 26. https://cartoonistsclubofnepal.wordpress.com/2005/08/25/six-journalists-face-arrest.

Cartcon. 2005b. "Nepalese Press Use Cartoons to Get Around Censorship." Cartoonists' Club of Nepal, March 10. https://cartoonistsclubofnepal.wordpress.com/2005/03/10/nepalese-press-use-cartoons-to-get-around-censorship/.

Cartcon. 2008. "Nepali Toons in Trying Times." Cartoonists' Club of Nepal, December 6. https://cartoonistsclubofnepal.wordpress.com/2008/12/06/nepali-toons-in-trying-times.

Corporal, Lynette Lee. 2009. "Media-Asia: Editorial Cartoonists Turn to Pens and Mice." Inter Press Service News Agency, July 21. https://www.globalissues.org/news/2009/07/31/2369.

Ghimire, Rochak. 2000. "Hasyabyanga ko Bikasma Nepali Patrakarita ko Yogadaan" [Role of Nepali Media in the Development of Humor and Satire]. *Madhuparka* 33, no. 4: 27–29.

Ghimire, Yubaraj. 2016. Interview with John A. Lent, Kathmandu, October 27.

Gurubacharya, Binaj. 2005. "Nepalese Press Use Cartoons to Get Around Censorship." Associated Press, March 10. http://cartoonistsclubofnepal.wordpress.com/2005/03/10.

Haviland, Charles. 2006. "Drawing Laughter amid Nepal's Woes." BBC News, August 1. http://news.bbc.co.uk/2/hi/south_asia/5153716.stm.

Hutt, Michael. 2006. "Things That Should Not Be Said: Censorship and Self-Censorship in the Nepali Press Media, 2001–02." *Journal of Asian Studies* 65, no. 2: 361–92.

Jigyashu, Bhim Rana. 1999–2000. "Byangyachitra ko Itihaas Ra Nepali Byangyachitra" [History of Cartoons and Nepali Cartoons]. *Madhuparka* 33, no. 8: 5–9.

Jyapoo, Ujjwol Kundan. 2002. Interview with Fungma Fudong, Kathmandu, Summer.

Kaphle, Anup. 2018. "Story of the Common Man: Q&A with Rajesh K. C." Roads and Kingdoms, June 4. https://roadsandkingdoms.com/2018/qa-with-rajesh-k-c-common-man/.

Kauba, Pat. 2011. "A Thousand Words." *ECS Nepal*, no. 121 (November). http://ecs.com.np/features/a-thousand-words.

Khokana [Mohan Shyam Maharjan]. 2016. Interview with John A. Lent, Kathmandu, October 27.

Kundan, Aryal. 2001. *Nepali Press Ma Cartoon* [Cartoons in the Nepalese Press]. Kathmandu: Nepali Press Institute.

Legal News from Nepal. 2007. "SC Game for Healthy Criticism of Judges." November 9. https://nepallaw.blogspot.com/search?q=SC+Game+for+Healthy+Criticism+of+Judges.

Lent, John A. 2002. "Cartooning on the Top of the World." *Comics Journal*, no. 242 (April): 107–8.

Manandhar, Suman. 2002. Interview with Fungma Fudong, Kathmandu, Summer.

Mishra, Sanjive. 2003. "A Cartoon Is Worth a Thousand Words." *Nepali Times*, July 3. https://www.archive.nepalitimes.com/news.php?id=2894#.XnEkvahKiUK.

Nepali Times. 2018. "Cartoonists Hit at Restrictions." August 24. https://www.nepalitimes.com/from-the-nepali-press/cartoonists-hit-at-restrictions/.

Panday, Devendra. 2002. Interview with Fungma Fudong, Kathmandu, Summer.

Panday, Ram Kumar. 1997. *Nepalese Cartoons: A Portfolio of Cartoons of Nepal by Representative Cartoonists*. Kathmandu: Ratna Pustak Bhandar.

Panday, Ram Kumar. 2000. Interview with John A. Lent, Osaka, July 27.

Panday, Ram Kumar. 2016. Interviews with John A. Lent, Kathmandu, October 23, 27.

Pokhrel, Peshal. 2005. "Toon Time." *Nepali Times*, June 24–30. https://cartoonistsclubofnepal.wordpress.com/2005/06/24/toon-time/.

Pudasaini, Surabhi, and Smriti Mallapaty. 2008. "Beyond Words." *Himal*, May. http://old.himalmag.com/component/content/article/10489-beyond-words.

Rajbhandari, Sushma. 2002. Interview with Fungma Fudong, Kathmandu, Summer.

Rana, Bhola B. 1982. "Nepal." In *Newspapers in Asia: Contemporary Trends and Problems*, edited by John A. Lent, 462–79. Hong Kong: Heinemann Asia.

Rana, Rajendra. 2002. Interview with Fungma Fudong, Kathmandu, Summer.

Shah, Sashi. 2002. Interview with Fungma Fudong, Kathmandu, Summer.

Shrestha, Abin. 2016. Interviews with John A. Lent, Kathmandu, October 25, 27.

Shrestha, Sangee. 2002. Interview with Fungma Fudong, Kathmandu, Summer.

Wikipedia. 2019. "Batsyayana." https://en.wikipedia.org/wiki/Batsyayana.

Brief History

All over Asia (and likely, the world), prominent cartoonists have shattered their parents' dreams and plans for their futures. In Sri Lanka, the same. The country's pioneer political cartoonist, Gamvasi Senarth Fernando (G. S. F.) (1904–1990), was groomed to be an Ayurvedic physician. At the age of twelve, G. S. F. was taken by his father to Colombo to study medicine under a famous Ayurvedic doctor who was his father's friend (Art by Ceylonese Artists 2017). In more recent times, well-known political cartoonist Awantha Artigala gave up a scholarship and a nearly finished science degree—the privilege of higher education denied his siblings, who had to work to help support the family (Daniel 2015).

The reasons parents are adamant or at a minimum hesitant about political cartooning as a career are nearly universal—low pay, lack of respect for the profession, and the inherent dangers, the latter so obvious in Sri Lanka. Those who became political cartoonists give altruistic reasons for their choice—make the world a better place (Artigala), provide "cognition of reality" (Udaya Prema), speak the truth (S. C. Opatha), or "give political knowledge and get people on one side" (Winnie Hettigoda).

Relatively speaking, political cartooning is a newcomer to Sri Lanka, primarily dating to the 1940s, although Bevis Vawa contributed cartoon humor in story format to the *Daily News* and the *Ceylon Observer* in the 1930s. Pioneering political cartooning in the 1940s were Aubrey Collette (1920–1992), who drew for the *Times of Ceylon* and then the *Ceylon Observer*, 1947–1964, and G. S. Fernando, who was first a commercial artist and then was made main artist of the Times Group Newspapers in 1933;[1] he later succeeded Collette as the group's chief cartoonist.

Collette, a member of the '43 Group (Ceylon's modern art movement) and an accomplished artist, was an art master initially at Royal College in Colombo. In a left-handed way, his abrupt dismissal from the college led to his cartooning. The story (actually, Collette's) goes that one day, in an attempt to enliven his history class, Collette drew caricatures of government officials on

Chapter 17

Sri Lanka

17.1. W. R. Wijesoma's cartoon of Sri Lankan politicians. Prime Minister S. W. R. D. Bandaranaike wields a rolling pin. Courtesy of W. R. Wijesoma.

the blackboard, and as he was completing an unflattering caricature of the education minister, that minister dropped in on the class (Collette 1970). The mishap was fortuitous for the island's comic art and the *Times of Ceylon*, whose editor called Collette's cartoons the paper's "most popular feature" (Siriwardena 2016). After he moved to the Lake House Group, his witty and biting cartoons fit well with the satirical column penned by Tarzie Vittachi, editor of the group's *Ceylon Observer* (Siriwardena 2016). As with so many Sri Lanka political cartoonists, Collette also drew a newspaper comic strip, *Sun Tan, the Asian Sensation*.

Longtime journalist/author S. Muthiah talked about Collette and his collaboration with Vittachi from first-hand observation:

Collette was one of the most brilliant cartoonists. He was a burgher, went to the best schools, grew up as a

Western-oriented journalist. At Lake House, he teamed with Tarzie Vittachi as editor. Tarzie was as brilliant and vicious in words as Collette was in drawings. As a team for five years, they created brilliant satire and cartoons together. It had to end. It ended in the most tragic circumstances. At the height of the 1960 election when the UNP [United National Party] seemed a shoo-in, they produced a cartoon with Mrs. [Sirimavo] Bandaranaike [of the Freedom Party] in bed with a big stomach. On either side of her were the leaders of the Trotsky and Communist parties, also in bed. It was called "Strange Bedfellows." It also appeared in Sinhalese newspapers. That one cartoon lost the UNP the election. Both Collette and Vittachi left Ceylon. (Muthiah 1993; for a theoretical analysis of Collette's cartoons, see Singhal 2016)

G. S. Fernando is considered one of Sri Lanka's finest watercolorists, adept at depicting rural country life

17.2. "Societal Nonsense," *Lankadipa*, July 18, 1993.

and "giving life to women on canvas." Fernando's work captured "[t]he village damsel sporting local village attire (cloth and jacket) which revealed several inches of bare midriff carrying a pot of water tucked to her belly, [a] woman bathing in the river semi dressed, a tantalizing figure of a woman dancer, bring[ing] splendor visuals from his brush" (Art by Ceylonese Artists 2017). His political cartoons tackled social evils, charged after politicians, and generally satirized social and political issues. G. S. F. is reputed to have created the first newspaper picture story, called "Neela" and published in the *Sunday Lankadipa*, and was the art director of

Sri Lanka's first Sinhalese film, *Rajakiya Wickramaya*, released in 1925 (Art by Ceylonese Artists 2017).

Close on the heels of Collette and G. S. F. were W. (Wijerpage) R. Wijesoma (1925–2006) and Mark Gerreyn (1931–1989). Wijesoma's career spanned more than a half century spread over a range of newspapers and encompassing several features new to Sri Lankan political cartooning. He took credit for introducing the first pocket cartoons, *What a Life* (1953) in both the *Times of Ceylon* and the Sinhalese *Lankadipa*, and *Tikiri-Tokka* (Tiny Nook) in the *Sunday Lankadipa*; and a new-style strip of four panels on four separate news

17.3. Heavy-hitting S. C. Opatha, Colombo, July 17, 1993. Photo by John A. Lent. Courtesy of S. C. Opatha.

events, called *Sittarapati*, which he described as having a "cinema effect with perforated edges" (Wijesoma 1993).

Wijesoma started his newspaper career as a proofreader at the *Times* in 1947, and by 1952 he was drawing a series, *Politicians of Lanka*, for the *Sunday Times*, followed by *What a Life*, *Wijesomage Siththara*, and *Tikiri-Tokka*. Because of differences with the editor and payment difficulties, he left the Times newspapers and succeeded Collette at the Lake House Group in 1968; there, he drew cartoons for the dailies *Ceylon Observer*, *Daily News*, and *Janatha*, and the Sunday *Silumina*. He continued through the government takeover of Lake House and renaming of the group as Associated Newspapers in 1973, even though he found it "very difficult to plug the government line" (Wijesoma 1993). "I gave the newspapers cartoons that could go through [be accepted] because there was no other place to work," he said. At Associated, he drew the four-panel strip called *Drawn and Quartered by Wijesoma*.

When the United National Party (UNP) gained power in 1977, political interference with the newspapers intensified under the group's new chairman, described by Wijesoma as having "nothing up here" (pointing to his head), taking orders from the government daily

(Wijesoma 1993). In 1981, Upali Wijewardena, while in the midst of starting his own newspaper group, Upali (the *Sunday Divaina* and *Sunday Island* in October 1981 and the dailies the *Island* and *Divaina*, February 1982), invited Wijesoma and thirteen other Associated journalists to join him. Wijesoma (1993) said that he had complete freedom at Upali, and his cartoons were appreciated to the extent that the owner even stopped the press on one occasion to include one of his drawings (Seneviratne n.d.). As with Collette before him with his *Citizen Perera*, and those who came later, Wijesoma had a "common man" character, the downtrodden, barely and shabbily clothed Punchisingho (Samaranayake 2006). Cartoons by Wijesoma were described by one writer as perceptive, brief, precise, pregnant with several layers of meaning, and bubbling with wit (Seneviratne n.d.).

Mark Gerreyn started with the Lake House Group in 1953, drawing political cartoons initially for *Dinamina* and then the *Daily News* as well as the strip *Simple Simon*. After long service with Lake House, he drew for the *Sun* and the *Island*. He continued to draw cartoons until his premature death in 1989, aged fifty-eight (Gerreyn 2019).

Another cartoon feature of Sri Lanka that emanated in the 1950s was a peculiar, one-panel social satire cartoon in which a number of people answer a question or comment on a current topic. For example, one person in the panel might ask, "Have you heard . . .?," to which the other half dozen or so each respond in a humorous way while making a point. Henry Tennekoon started this cartoon type in the 1950s with his *Samaja Samayan* (Societal Nonsense) in *Lankadipa*. This type of cartoon repeatedly used the same setting and locale, only changing the topic and responses to it. For example, Winnie Hettigoda's *Halt* in the 1990s was built around a bus stand (halt) where seven individuals commented on a current issue.

Other political cartoonists who advanced the profession beginning in the 1960s were S. C. Opatha, Camillus Perera, and Jiffry Yoonoos.

Opatha began as a political cartoonist on the *Ceylon Daily Mirror* in the early 1960s, wielding a savage pen

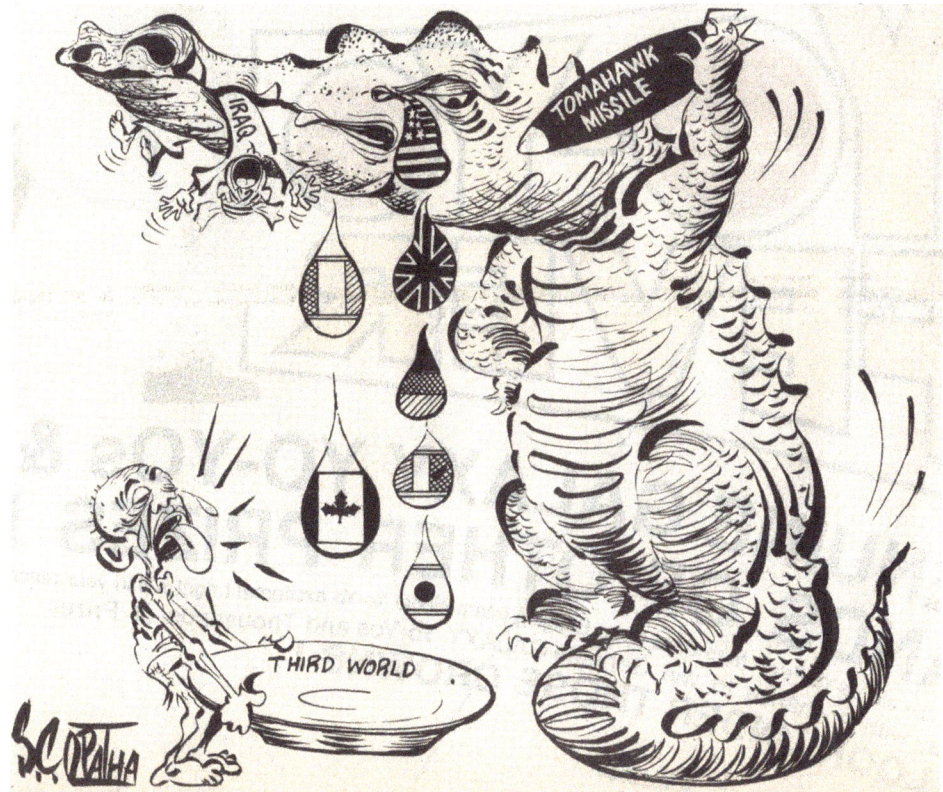

17.4. S. C. Opatha cartoon, the *Sunday Observer*, July 18, 1993. Courtesy of S. C. Opatha.

in the relatively free atmosphere of the time. His cartoons attacked issues such as national and international politics, poverty, terrorism, population growth, and the environment and usually included his bystander character, Silva. Opatha said that he had a free hand in the 1960s and could criticize "anything, anyone," but everything changed in the 1970s under the Sirimavo Bandaranaike government and steadily worsened thereafter (Opatha 1993). His life was often threatened through phone calls and letters during the decade, he said, but he never changed his route or hid, relying on his predestination philosophy: "If you come into the world with a certain program, and it is to die by a bullet, nothing can stop that" (Opatha 1993). Opatha's stock as an oppositionist force was bolstered in 1977 when he and another cartoonist, Chanrandran, drew a booklet of cartoons denigrating the Bandaranaike government. Published by the opposition in time for the national elections that year, the thirty-page booklet, which sold one hundred thousand copies, was credited by other cartoonists, and by Opatha, as damaging Bandaranaike's campaign (Wickramanayake 1993; Hettigoda 1993; Opatha 1993). Wijesoma (1993) did not think that the booklet affected the national election and called it a "horrible thing."

Bandaranaike tried to have Opatha and Chanrandran arrested, but, according to Opatha, "the Gods saved us" (Opatha 1993).

At the time of our interview in 1993, Opatha daily drew a political cartoon for the *Observer* and a humorous front-page pocket cartoon for the *Daily News*. To beef up his income, he also drew regularly for the Singapore *Straits Times* and was owner, art director, and chief artist of Pack Ads, an agency of ten artists he had started in 1990.

Camillus Perera (1939–) best described himself by saying that he is not a political cartoonist, but neither is he not. Known for founding and editing a long line of comics papers under his Camillus Publications, Camillus injects politics into his stories, because it is part of people's (his characters') everyday life. His characters are the downtrodden, poor working class; his objectives through them is "to focus public attention on inequities, injustices, and absurdities in society and to prompt readers to question why things continue the way they do" (Camillus, quoted in Union of Catholic Asia News 2002). The exception to the abject characters he has created and nurtured is Megodis Thuma, a gentle but crafty parliamentarian featured in the *Sathuta* comics paper. Columnist Nalaka Gunawardene (2010), an avid fan, wrote that Camillus draws nearly everything: pocket cartoons, political cartoons, satirical comic strips, and comics papers. He exemplified Camillus characters by describing his own favorite, Siribiris, who, he said, portrayed "Everyman personified: long-suffering, taken for granted by politicians, exploited by businessmen, hoodwinked by corrupt officials, and always struggling to simply stay alive. He is down but not out" (Gunawardene 2010). Siribiris's comeback, Gunawardene said, is "to puncture their inflated egos and ridicule them at every turn" (2010). Famed journalist Ajith Samaranayake called Camillus "one of the most lovable institutions in Sinhala journalism," whose cartoons graced practically every newspaper, offering a "wryly witty commentary of not only politicians . . . but also ordinary people both as the individual as well as the mass" (quoted in Seneviratne n.d.).

After an impressive semiprofessional football stint, Camillus began his cartooning career in 1965, first drawing for the newspaper *Dawasa*, followed by a stay at the afternoon *Janatha*. He participated in the birthing of the sixteen-page comics paper; his most popular character, Gajaman, appeared in the first issue of *Sathuta*, launched in August 1972. Within a short time, Camillus Publications dominated this industry. In 2006, Camillus returned to newspaper cartooning, contributing *Davase Tokka* and *Sathiye Tokka* to *Rivera Weekly* (for more on Camillus as a publisher, see Lent 2001).

Yoonoos and His Travails

Jiffry Yoonoos (1932–2003) remembered there being only three or four "pro-government" political cartoonists in Sri Lanka when he joined the Tamil-language daily *Thinakaran* of the Lake House Group in 1964. After sixteen years, he left Lake House/Associated Newspapers because of its sycophantic relationship with United National Front (UNF) authorities and moved to the Communist Party daily, *Aththa*. Yoonoos said of his years at Lake House/Associated:

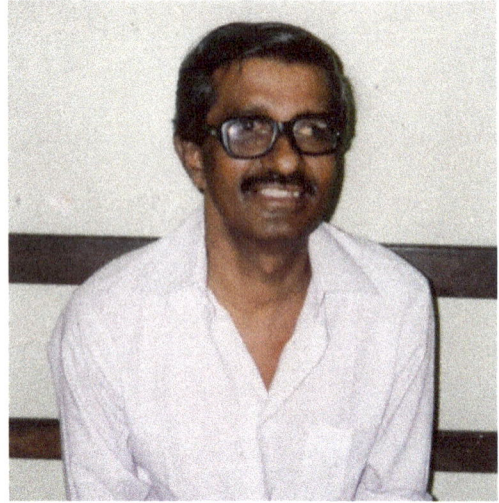

17.5. Jiffry Yoonoos while a hospital patient, Colombo, July 19, 1993. Photo by John A. Lent. Courtesy of Jiffry Yoonoos.

I did not like working there as the work was boring, always supportive of government. I was put on the market research desk. I drew maps of the various electorates, putting in police stations, hospitals, and bridges. I realized the government wanted that information so they could blow up bridges, etc. to keep people from voting. I went to my Lake House superior to complain and after that, the government was gunning for me. I was forced to resign. (Yoonoos 1993)

Always a strong foe of government, Yoonoos had a few harrowing experiences, courtesy of President Ranasinghe Premadasa and his "Lawrence Mafia" goon squads. As he told me while he was hospitalized in 1993 because of hypertension, he incurred the wrath of the president himself because of his cartoons and refusing a cushy government job offered to him. In Yoonoos's words:

I wanted a house and went to Mr. Premadasa, told him I was the cartoonist of the opposition *Aththa* and had no roof and it was difficult to live that way. The irony is he provided me a house the same day, the same house destroyed by his stooges later.

I was very harsh against Premadasa. I knew he didn't like my face. One particular cartoon I drew five years after he gave me the house irritated him. The details were that it was rumored a bomb blast that killed twelve soldiers was the work of Premadasa because he avoided the huge funeral, later, instead organizing and attending a political meeting in the countryside. I drew a cartoon showing the president hiding behind a tree in the jungle. My common

17.6. Yoonoos cartoon about Prime Minister Sirimavo Bandaranaike. Courtesy of Jiffry Yoonoos.

man "Appu Hamuy" asks him what he is doing there. The president replies, there is a big national funeral in the city, and with his finger on his lips, says, "shsss-s-s, don't shout." That cartoon really upset him. He couldn't do anything about it. (Yoonoos 1993)

Yoonoos told of two other incidents that irked Premadasa. In 1990, a minister had requested that Yoonoos join the Associated Newspapers, offering him a hefty "Rs. 15,000 [US$375 at the 1990 rate of exchange] a month, transport provided." Yoonoos said he promptly replied, "Look, sir, I've been a cartoonist for twenty-three years. Everyone knows me as a cartoonist. I'm sorry I can't join Associated," to which the minister said, "Has come from the top." Yoonoos told me that he could "not sell his soul for that price." He said that the minister was angry about the rejection (Yoonoos 1993).

Yoonoos continued with the third incident that led to his physical assault in 1992. In May of that year, Colombo was inundated by a rain unlike any experienced before. While people's homes were ravaged, apparently the

housing minister escaped in a helicopter. Yoonoos drew a cartoon of "Appu Hamuy" standing on the roof of his house, with the flood surrounding him, and cursing the minister in the fleeing helicopter (Yoonoos 1993).

These two Yoonoos cartoons and the job refusal culminated in a violent attack on Yoonoos and his family, which became widely known and which played a major role in the establishment of the now-named Cartoonists Rights Network International, founded by Robert Russell after he met Yoonoos and heard his story (Stransky 2013). As Yoonoos told me:

About three months after the flood incident, one day after my birthday, on August 17, 1992, two large cars screeched to a halt outside my gate. My grill gate was slammed open and they came into my compound. They pushed my son's three-wheeler down, came in, and shouted, "Where is that son of bitch, bitch bastard Yoonoos?" This was in Sinhalese, which is even worse. I was there seated. About twenty to twenty-five people came out of those big cars. One fellow came up to me—the minister's bodyguard—shoved his pistol into my mouth and broke a tooth. And, a second one said, "If you draw any more cartoons against his excellency, the president, and our minister [of housing], I will kill you and your family." The gunman took his pistol out of my mouth, pressed it against my head, and told my wife, "You tell your husband this: 'You have taken this house from his excellency. How dare you attack him, you bugger.'" He got up, pushed my TV, smashed a couple of chairs, turned around and gave me a final threat, and left. (Yoonoos 1993)

Yoonoos went to the police station to file a report after locking the house doors; his wife and children went to her mother's house to stay. But the violence and terror did not end there. The next day, Yoonoos informed the police inspector general and all of the newspapers about the attack and wrote to Premadasa. He then went to check on the house. He described what he found:

> The house was in shambles. Windows shattered. Furniture broken. Door smashed in. I asked, "Who did this?" Two of the thugs who had come the previous day said, "We, you bugger. What have you to say about it?" They started stabbing me—two stitches in the nose. In the hands, ribs. My shirt was completely soaked in blood. I jumped in my car and went to the police station and reported it. I went alone to the accident ward of the hospital. The police did not accompany me. Which meant they were also in on it. They sort of stitched me up—sixteen stitches altogether. The hospital wanted to admit me, but I refused because security was inadequate and went to another hospital. (Yoonoos 1993)

The aftermath of the violence was even more disheartening. Witnesses to the incident shied away from giving evidence, the police were not investigated, and, as Yoonoos said, "nothing happened to anyone" (1993). The deputy inspector general made an effort to help, summoning all police stations to search for the pistol-toting assailant. However, when he was apprehended, he asked to make one phone call. According to Yoonoos, "he made the call and then handed the phone to a policeman, who said, 'yes sir, yes sir' repeatedly, after which he told the thug to go home."

At the time of our interview eleven months later, Yoonoos had no house; he stayed in a small room at *Aththa*, his family elsewhere. His wife brought him meals daily. He continued to graphically blast Premadasa after these ordeals, as well as his successors, saying, "that's my job." He did not attribute his hypertension to serving as a watchdog on the government or his own living conditions (Yoonoos 1993). Yoonoos said that fear dominated Sri Lankan society.

I devote this much attention to Yoonoos because, according to him, this full account had not been given to others before, and more importantly because what transpired in 1992 in Sri Lanka has and does occur elsewhere in other parts of Asia, globally, and most certainly still in Sri Lanka.

Other Terrorist Actions and Threats

Sri Lanka has not been kind to journalists generally; a number of them have been murdered (nineteen between 1992 and 2014), "disappeared," attacked, or threatened, political cartoonists included. The most noted "disappeared" journalist/political cartoonist incident was of Prageeth Eknaligoda, whose vanishing sparked international campaigns and concerns by Cartoonists Rights Network International, Reporters without Borders, Cartooning for Peace, and Amnesty International. Eknaligoda wrote and drew for the website LankaeNews, where he frequently denounced the Mahinda Rajapaksa government, which was in power from 2005 to 2015. It is more likely that he was "disappeared" because of his articles rather than cartoons, but nevertheless he had feared retaliation by President Rajapaksa and his brother Gotabaya, who was defense minister, and did not sign his cartoons that were critical of them. Eknaligoda disappeared after leaving LankaeNews on January 24, 2010, two days before the national elections, a time of widespread violence. His wife Sandhya's pleas for information about him, shouts of protestors asking for justice, and international campaigns did not budge the Rajapaksa authorities. It was when Mahinda Rajapaksa was ousted in the 2015 election, replaced by his former party secretary, Maithripala Sirisena, that a proper investigation was mounted. Nine army intelligence officers were arrested for the kidnapping, but what happened to Eknaligoda is still unknown (D'Almeida 2015) and is likely to remain a mystery, since Gotabaya Rajapaksa was elected president in 2019 (Ethirajan 2020).[2] Ranked fourth in the world on the Impunity Index compiled by the Committee to Protect Journalists, Sri Lanka was described by the CPJ as a place where "journalists are murdered, and their killers go free."

Cartoonists have had to tread cautiously for decades, enduring (coping with) violent actions; blanket censorship, as in May 2000 when newspaper cartoon space was left blank, except for the word "censored" (Constable 2000, A14); verbal threats and intimidation; legal cases; exhibition removals; and fear-induced self-censorship.

Violent acts and threats continued after Yoonoos's ordeal and the Premadasa regime. In May 2006, gunmen killed two people at the *Uthayan* newspaper, the murders suspected to be a result of a cartoon about a pro-government politician. The following year, *Lankadipa* cartoonist Dasa Hapuwalana was physically hit by an inebriated man for "attacking our leader too much" (A. de Silva 2018b, 320). On another occasion, he was attacked in his residence. For more than thirty years, political cartoonists have received threats on their lives. Wijesoma said that he received death threats initially during the 1987–1989 insurrection, from the Liberation Tigers of Tamil Eelam (LTTE), Janatha Vimukthi Peramuna (JVP), and the government-sponsored Praa ("death squad"). The intimidating letters forced him to self-censor, which he considered worse censorship than that administered by others (Wijesoma 1993). Opatha received many threats to his life from the 1970s onward when the JVP was in power (Opatha 1993), as did Winnie Hettigoda most of his entire career.

Hettigoda, a fierce fighter for free expression, used ingenuity and creativeness in his stands against government oppression. In 1990, Hettigoda, who had been a cartoonist for *Divaina* since 1981, mounted a touring

17.7. Political cartoonist/lecturer Winnie Hettigoda, Colombo, February 18, 2018. Photo by Xu Ying. Permission of Winnie Hettigoda.

exhibition of his political cartoons that pro-government students attacked when it was in Colombo. Another newspaper reported the incident but falsely claimed that the student protestors had acted because Hettigoda and his cartoons supported the JVP. Frightened by potential government repercussions, *Divaina* and its parent company released Hettigoda in mid-1991. Soon after, he helped start another paper, *Lakdiva*, at the suggestion of the owner of Prahbath Newspapers; Hettigoda took on the task on the condition that there would not be any editorial interference. When the management reneged on that policy and placed a full-page advertisement for a smut-laden paper, *Thrishule* (Trident), that it had started, Hettigoda and the rest of the editorial staff resigned without informing the owner until they all registered their logos with the trademark registry. Hettigoda said that when the owner was asked why he did not abide by the agreement, he said: "It's my machine, my equipment, my staff. I pay the salaries; I own the paper, so you should do what I like." Hettigoda said that he replied: "All is yours. Machine, newsprint, and the rest, but we are not your property. We belong to the nation" (Hettigoda 1993).

Hettigoda's next move was to start his own newspaper, a daring venture for such a young man. The first time I interviewed Hettigoda was in 1993, when he was holding exhibitions to raise funds for the proposed newspaper; on this occasion, he was in Kandy, the seventh leg of a twenty-five-city tour. He explained his plan and a government effort to block it:

> Ways to raise money for the newspaper is through my exhibitions and festivals. A veteran film director plans to hold a festival and give all proceeds to us. A drama festival too will donate profits to us. All artists are with us. The government gave us a problem. When I wanted to have my festival in a government art gallery in Colombo, the authorities rejected my request. After that, I sent a friend to ask for the use of the hall for a photograph exhibition. Once he got the hall, we put up the cartoons. The government said the license was for a photograph exhibition. "These are not photographs; they are cartoons." I said, "no, they are photographs of cartoons." (Hettigoda 1993)

The five-day exhibition in the capital city raised Rs. 100,030 (about US$2,000); the money "stacked four feet high," Hettigoda said. Attendees were not required to have tickets; they were requested to donate if they agreed with the newspaper project (Hettigoda 1993). They and others obliged, resulting in the publication of a tabloid weekly.

There were other serious run-ins with the authorities. In 1993, after Hettigoda wrote and illustrated an article detailing how a senior politician was killed, he was tracked by the "goon squad" and saved, he said, by the assassination of President Premadasa a week later. Then, in 1996, Hettigoda lost a Rs. 50 million libel suit brought by the minister of industrial development over one of his cartoons published in *Lakdiva* the previous year. The *Halt* cartoon had its usual seven characters waiting at a bus stop, discussing a "son of a major" who had gotten drunk, berated hotel employees, and urinated in the hotel's swimming pool. Newspapers reported the story without directly naming the individual. Hettigoda said he did not give the minister's name, only that he was the son of a major. Implying that he was set up, Hettigoda explained:

> There are a lot of sons of majors in Sri Lanka. Therefore, he couldn't take any legal action against the cartoon. But

the opposition party named the said minister as the person who urinated in the swimming pool. . . . After that, the minister wrote a letter to the editor [of *Lakdiva*]. The editor published the letter in a box [on] the front page. In the correction, [the] editor mentioned the minister's name and he apologized. After that, the minister filed the case blaming us that the cartoon has damaged his image. He used our correction to prove his blame. (Hettigoda 1996; for more on Hettigoda's career, see *The Island* 2019)

When I interviewed Hettigoda in 2018, he was teaching at the Faculty of Visual Arts and submitting one political cartoon weekly to *Lanka*. He was optimistic about his profession but had been disillusioned with fellow cartoonists and the reading public throughout the 2010s. For example, he gave a very vitriolic interview in 2013 during which he said he was "extremely disappointed" with "most" cartoonists who had hit "rock bottom," were devoid of "principles" and "set ideologies," failed to promote "social and political change," and did the "bidding of politicians." He saved some of his venom for the public, whom he called "extremely passive and selfish" and unreceptive to messages of change (Maduwage 2013).

Other cartoonists faced government reprisals over the years. In 2008, Thass, drawing for *Virakesari*, set up an exhibition of his artwork and cartoons at the request of a government department. After hearing that an armed group, believed to be double agents supportive of both the government and the Tamil rebels, visited the exhibition demanding its removal and warning that he might be physically attacked, he closed the exhibition. The cartoons depicted ordinary citizens' situations after the civil war (A. de Silva 2018b, 321).

Self-Censorship and Other Issues

As some have for years, cartoonists in Sri Lanka self-censor. In most cases, this practice results from newspaper policy, political party support, or an editor abiding by management's unwritten rules. For example,

(1) No delay: Navy Commander's car being allowed clear passage at the railway crossing on Duplication Road, watched by his security personnel

(2) Stopped: awaiting all clear signal to proceed to Galle Face Centre Road from Macan Markar Mawatha

(3) Bolt from the blues: a lone motor cyclist riding alongside the Navy Commander's car activates the bomb strapped on his person.

(4) Blown to pieces: the ill-fated car thrown against a lamp post is seen overturned by the impact of the bomb exploding

— Illustration by Wasantha Siriwardena

17.8. Illustrated crime investigative strip, Wasantha Siriwardena, *Lankadipa*. Courtesy of Wasantha Siriwardena.

in 1993, a few important political cartoonists said that they had to self-censor to keep their positions. Wasantha Siriwardena, staff cartoonist for *Lankadipa* and the *Sunday Times* of Wijewa Publications, said that the group's newspapers stayed out of trouble because they did not print sensitive material, which he defined as "being against someone like Premadasa." This type of self-censorship, Annemari de Silva (2018b, 299) called fear-induced or vigilante self-censorship.[3] Siriwardena said that he was required to submit his cartoons to the editor, who, at least once weekly, rejected one, usually because it might be disliked by the government, an ethnic group, or Tamil separatists (Siriwardena 1993a). To the *Times* editor's credit, he occasionally assigned Siriwardena to do investigative cartooning. Siriwardena would go to the site of an important news happening, draw sketches, question the police, and research the backgrounds and find or take photographs of those involved. From that information, he would draw four instructive panels that explained how a particular event unraveled. Certainly, this was an early example of comics journalism (Siriwardena 1993a, 1993b), although not termed as such.

Sri Lanka's history of political cartooning has mostly encompassed a large selection of methods of subjugation—the use of long-term emergency restrictions, a long list of legal regulations, government and party ownership of venues, abundant self-censorship by editors and cartoonists, physical and verbal attacks, killings and disappearances, denial of support for cartoonists and their venues (e.g., threats to deny vital state advertising revenue), and other harassments. Most of the pressures Sri Lankan political cartoonists have faced are outside legal censorship. In her 2017 survey of eight political cartoonists, Annemari de Silva (2018b, 309) concluded:

269

17.9. Delayed election results. M. D. Weeraratne, *Ceylon Today*, February 12, 2018.

"[I]t was the mechanics of the newspaper companies themselves: informal directives communicated to the company hierarchies, the agenda or ideology of the editors, the business interests of the companies, the unofficial connection to political parties, or the advertising interests with state-owned and private companies."

Despite the expected grievous circumstances, some Sri Lankan political cartoonists engaged in what de Silva (2018b, 306) called "toying with the censor" by employing indirect messages, symbols, and metaphors, using social media such as Facebook postings, calling out and mocking censors, and resorting to a so-called genre of silence.

The Sri Lankan comic art scene in the late 2010s appeared not to be as raucous as it had been in the past, particularly during the Premadasa and Rajapaksa administrations. De Silva (2018b) said that the political atmosphere was "more critical and more comfortable." Perhaps it is because, as Hettigoda (2018) surmised, "most cartoons are now pro-government," eliminating the need for retributive actions by the authorities,

17.10. Awantha Artigala's cartoon showing former president Mahinda Rajapaksa hesitating to appear on stage. *Daily Mirror*, February 13, 2018.

although publishers are occasionally warned if they are considered out of line. Or it might be that the cartoonists have found other venues not yet as susceptible to censorship, such as Facebook (A. de Silva 2018b, 325), or that they purposely shy away from the limelight because of previous dangerous circumstances. For example, Thass uses pseudonyms and moved to northern Sri Lanka for less visibility, and Awantha Artigala of the *Daily Mirror* and *Ada* avoids public appearances to maintain a sense of physical anonymity, although he is a bit vulnerable to verbal abuse through social media, having tens of thousands of followers of his Facebook-posted cartoons (A. de Silva 2018b, 321).[4] Udaya Prema of the *Daily Mirror* and *Sunday Time*s has been described as a "ghost, and content to remain one"; he does not post his cartoons on Facebook, does not apply for awards, and seeks no public recognition (*The Island* 2019).

Issues that political cartoonists in Sri Lanka contend with are frequently encountered in most parts of Asia and have remained unresolved in Sri Lanka for generations. Besides governmental and political restrictions and interference, foremost among the problems is the lack of sufficient living expenses for cartoonists (Hettigoda 2018; Karunathilake 2018; A. de Silva 2018a).

Others are a lack of mentorship of, and interest by, young people to become cartoonists (de Silva 2018a; Karunathilake 2018); understanding of, and respect for, cartoonists' undertakings (Karunathilake 2018); no structured cartooning community consisting of organizations and activities (A. de Silva 2018a); and the existence of a political party–obsessed public indifferent to diverse opinions (Karunathilake 2018).

A Brief Conclusion

Aside from the political cartooning situation, the overall comic art scene in Sri Lanka does not have the same verve as it did a generation or more ago, when there were about half a dozen successful weekly comics newspapers, a number of local comic strips, and innovations such as investigative cartooning and the issue-related, group discussion cartoon. On the other hand, contemporary cartooning in Sri Lanka has shed some of the violence and terrorism that accompanied the profession for many years. A fair trade-off, it seems.

Sri Lanka

Notes

1. Sajitha Prematunge (2018) claims that G. S. F. drew a cartoon in 1931 for *Swadesha Mitraya*, mocking a government report.

2. Another artist, Dhammika Bandara of *Vinivida* (Spectrum) magazine, was kidnapped by Premadasa's henchmen, never to be heard from again.

3. An opposite of vigilante self-censorship might be termed ethical or morality self-censorship. This varies according to cultural factors and might include decency, social-cultural-religious taboos, and the like. Of course, these can be deemed vigilante self-censoring if general knowledge or feelings are that if such taboos are not held to, violence is likely to result.

4. Awantha Artigala is a contemporary political cartoonist who has mastered a visual language of symbolism and idiom to critique the government: lions and tigers stand for different ethnoreligious groups, and reversals of colors on a nation's flag indicates a shift in power; politicians are drawn as "well-fed and smug," their constituents as "deprived and quivering" (Daniel 2015).

Bibliography

Art by Ceylonese Artists. 2017. "1904–1990 G. S. Fernando." October 21. https://kalalanka.wordpress.com/type/image/.

Artigala, Awantha. 2017. Interview with Annemari de Silva, Colombo, May 13.

Boronow, Clare. 2013. "Silencing the Media in Sri Lanka: How the Sri Lankan Constitution Fuels Self-Censorship and Hinders Reconciliation." *Virginia Journal of International Law* 53, no. 3: 726–61.

Collette, Aubrey. 1948. *Ceylon since Soulbury*. Part 1: *A History in Cartoons by Collette*. Colombo: Times of Ceylon.

Collette, Aubrey. 1970. *The World of Sun Tan*. Hong Kong: Asia Magazine.

Constable, Pamela. 2000. "Blacked Out in Sri Lanka." *Washington Post*, May 16, A14.

D'Almeida, Kanya. 2015. "In Sri Lanka Cartoonists Aren't Killed—They're Disappeared." Inter Press Service News Agency, January 13. https://www.ipsnews.net/2015/01/in-sri-lanka-cartoonists-arent-killed-theyre-disappeared/.

Daniel, Smriti. 2015. "Awantha Artigala: Sri Lanka's Quiet Cartoonist." July 18. https://smritidaniel.com/2015/07/18/awantha-artigala-sri-lankas-quiet-cartoonist/.

Dayananda, Paliyagoda. 1993. Interview with John A. Lent, Colombo, July 15.

De Chickera, Gihan. 2017. Interview with Annemari de Silva, Colombo, June 16.

De Silva, Annemari. 2018a. Interview with John A. Lent and Xu Ying, Colombo, February 12.

De Silva, Annemari. 2018b. "Political Cartoons and Censorship in Sri Lanka." *International Journal of Comic Art* 20, no. 1 (Spring–Summer): 297–330.

De Silva, Pramod. 2011. "Unique Period of History through Cartoonists' Eyes." *Sunday Observer* (Colombo), March 20. http://archives.sundayobserver.lk/2011/03/20/fea14.asp.

Dorakumbure, W. B. 1990. "Exhibition of Cartoons by Wijesoma." *The Island*, August 21, 6–7.

Ethirajan, Anbarasa. 2020. "How Fear Set In Overnight in Sri Lanka." BBC News, February 20. https://www.bbc.com/news/world-asia-51555853.

Gerreyn, Max. 2019 "My Brother Mark." eLanka, June 30. http://www.elanka.com.au/my-brother-mark-by-max-gerreyn/.

Ghafoor, A. C. A. 2017. "He Offered Bouquets in Exchange for Brickbats Flung at Him." *Sunday Times* (Colombo), April 9.

Gunawardene, Nalaka. 2010. "Long Live Siribiris—and His Creator, Camillus Perera!" Open Minds!, March 10. https://nalakagunawardene.com/2010/03/10/long-live-siribiris-and-his-creator-camillus-perera/.

Gunawardene, Nalaka. 2013. "When Worlds Collide #65: When Making Fun Is No Laughing Matter." *Ceylon Today*, May 5. http://collidecolumn.wordpress.com/2013/05/05/when-worlds-collide-65-when-making-fun-is-no-laughing-matter/.

Hapuwalana, Dasa. 2017. Interview with Annemari de Silva, Colombo, May 16.

Hettigoda, Winnie. 1993. Interview with John A. Lent, Kandy, Sri Lanka, July 18.

Hettigoda, Winnie. 1996. Correspondence with John A. Lent, September 11.

Hettigoda, Winnie. 1997. Correspondence with John A. Lent, April 24.

Hettigoda, Winnie. 2018. Interview with John A. Lent and Xu Ying, Colombo, February 11.

Human Rights Watch. 2013. "Sri Lanka: Reveal Fate of 'Disappeared' Cartoonist." June 9. http://www.hrw.org/news/2013/06/09/sri-lanka-reveal-fate-disappeared-cartoonist.

Island, The. 2019. "Cross Between Career Cartoonist and Academic: Winnie Hettigoda." May 20. www.island.lk/index.php?page_cat=articles-details&page=articles-details&code_title=204541.

Karunathilake, Dharshana. 2018. Interview with John A. Lent and Xu Ying, Colombo, February 15.

Lent, John A. 2001. "Cartooning in Sri Lanka." In *Illustrating Asia: Comics, Humor Magazines and Picture Books*, edited by John A. Lent, 81–99. Honolulu: University of Hawai'i Press.

Maduwage, Shihara. 2013. "Cartoons Contain a Message to the People." *Daily Mirror*, September 23.

Mahindapala, D. H. L. 1993. Interview with John A. Lent, Colombo, July 20.

Medagama, K. M. K. 1993. Interview with John A. Lent, Colombo, July 14.

Mohamed, Ranee. 2006. "Wijesoma Has Made Us Cry." *Sunday Leader* (Colombo), January 22.

Muthiah, S. 1993. Paper presented at the Symposium on Cartoons, Chennai, July 22.

Niranjani, Roland. 2016. "No Justice for Sri Lanka's Missing and Killed Journalists." Union of Catholic Asia News, January 29. https://www.ucanews.com/news/no-justice-for-sri-lankas-missing-and-killed-journalists/75095.

Opatha, S. C. 1993. Interviews with John A. Lent, Colombo, July 17, 20.

Perera, Camillus. 1993. Interview with John A. Lent, Colombo, July 19.

Perera, Camillus. 2017. Interview with Annemari de Silva, Colombo, May 9.

Pradeep, R. 2017. Interview with Annemari de Silva, Colombo, April 25.

Prematunge, Sajitha. 2018. "Them Damned Pictures Are Killing Me." ThinkWorth, October 9. http://thinkworth.wordpress.com/2018/10/09/history-of-cartoons-with-reference-to-sl.

Ratnayake, Janaka. 1993. Interview with John A. Lent, Colombo, July 15.

Rifas, Leonard. 1995. "Cartooning in Sri Lanka: A Precarious Tightrope Act." In *Asian Popular Culture*, edited by John A. Lent, 109–25. Boulder, CO: Westview Press.

Rupasinghe, Bennete. 1993. Interview with John A. Lent, Colombo, July 19.

Samaranayake, Ajith. 2006. "The Passing of Punchisingho." *Sunday Observer* (Colombo), January 22.

Seneviratne, Malinda. 2016. "Camillus: The Compassionate and Trenchant Fellow-Citizen." Malinda Words. http://malindawords.blogspot.com/2016/11/camillus-compassionate-and-trenchant.html.

Seneviratne, Malinda. n.d. "Wijesoma, Nation-Watcher with the Soft Brush and Acute Perception." Infolanka. http://www.infolanka.com/org/srilanka/people/56.htm.

Singhal, Samarth. 2016. "Drawing (on) Politics: Aubrey Collette in Sri Lanka." *Chitrolekha International Magazine on Art and Design* 6, no. 2: 53–66.

Siriwardena, Wasantha. 1993a. Interview with John A. Lent, Colombo, July 16.

Siriwardena, Wasantha. 1993b. Correspondence with John A. Lent, August 26.

Siriwardena, Wasantha. 2016. "Aubrey Collette: Drawing the Best Out of Political Caricature." *Sunday Observer* (Colombo), May 15.

Sri Kantha, Sachi. 2012. "On Sri Lankan Political Cartoonists, Stray Dogs and Hypocrites." Ilankai Tamil Sangam, September 15. https://sangam.org/on-sri-lankan-political-cartoonists-stray-dogs-and-hypocrites/.

Stransky, Olivia. 2013. "Art to Die for: Cartoonists at Risk and Their Defenders." Sampsonia Way, May 15.

Thass. 2017. Telephone interview with Annemari de Silva, June 1.

Union of Catholic Asia News. 2002. "Catholic Cartoonist's Exhibition Marks 30 Years of Popular Cartoon Character." 2002. UCA News, June 25. https://www.ucanews.com/story-archive/?post_name=/2002/06/25/catholic-cartoonists-exhibition-marks-30-years-of-popular-cartoon-character&post_id=20903.

Weeraratna, Senaka. 2015. "Political Cartoons That Made a Difference and Shook the Nation in the 1950s." Lankaweb, August 3. https://www.lankaweb.com/news/items/2015/08/03/political-cartoons-that-made-a-difference-and-shook-the-nation-in-the-1950s/.

Wickramanayake, W. P. 1993. Interview with John A. Lent, Colombo, July 17.

Wijesoma, W. R. 1993. Interviews with John A. Lent, Colombo, July 15, 17.

Yoonoos, Jiffry. 1993. Interview with John A. Lent, Colombo, July 19.

Observing Asian political cartoonists for well over fifty years, I have seen them evolve and devolve; take on the government as ferociously as an angry lion and cower before the authorities as a cuddly kitten; rise to the ranks of national artistic treasures and compete for lowly blue-collar jobs to keep the family rice bowl full.

A number of factors contribute to this wide disparity: the government in power and its propensity to regulate, restrict, or facilitate political cartooning; the strength of political cartooning traditionally; the lenience or restrictiveness of what was inherited from outside; the importance accorded political cartooning by media publishers, editors, and readers; and the different cultural values that bind and guide people to see concepts such as humor, criticism, and respect differently, for instance respect for elders and leaders, saving face, indirect approaches, and others.

Asian Political Cartoons sets out to discuss these factors by addressing two questions and three statements. In no way are these questions and statements to be interpreted as treating Asia as a single geopolitical entity, as clearly expressed in the introduction. Nor are the questions and statements meant for comparative analysis. They are what they were meant to be—common threads not necessarily tying anything together.

With these caveats in mind, among the common threads of most of Asian political cartooning are: (1) Political and social satire (both visual and textual) existed before the arrival of colonists from the West; for example, satire incorporated in twelfth-century Toba scrolls and later *ukiyo-e* prints in Japan, wayang shadow theater in Indonesia, and Kalighat temple drawings in nineteenth-century India; (2) Nearly every Asian country was colonized or occupied by Europeans, Japanese, or Americans, who started cartoon/humor magazines imitative of those in their homelands, such as *Punch* and *Puck*, and usually for the expatriate communities; (3) Nearly everywhere, political cartoons figured prominently in propaganda to support calls for independence, national campaigns, and wartime causes, perhaps helping to explain nationalist leaders such as Indonesia's Sukarno and Vietnam's Ho Chi Minh ranking as their countries'

Conclusions

first political cartoonists, and the strong reactions of those same leaders against cartoons once in power, knowing firsthand their ability to influence; (4) The "freedom to cartoon" has had a roller-coaster ride in nearly all countries, racing, dipping, jerking, and leveling off, depending on who maintains the power controls; (5) Increasingly, political cartoonists are being recognized with prestigious honorary titles conferred by high government officials (e.g., in India, the Philippines, and Malaysia), museums of their works (at least in China, Japan, Malaysia, and South Korea), and in the case of Chai Rachawat, commissions to be the artist for two books written by the king of Thailand; and (6) Self-censorship by editors and cartoonists is widespread throughout the continent, as is the concept of "guided cartooning," steered by authorities and/or media managements away from sensitive topics and toward national goals.

Outside factors have played roles in the development and nourishment of Asian political cartooning, among which are: (1) the abovementioned waves of colonization that brought in cartoon and humor magazines; (2) the experiences of some Asian political cartoonists who lived abroad and studied with and/or observed the work of foreign masters and brought what they learned home: for instance, China's Feng Zikai in Japan; Japan's Kitazawa Rakuten, Thailand's Chai Rachawat, and the Philippines' Nonoy Marcelo in the United States; and India's Abu Abraham in the United Kingdom; (3) the influence of non-Asian political cartoonists, such as that of the United Kingdom's David Low on R. K. Laxman of India, Mexico and the United States' Miguel Covarrubias on a few of China's second-generation cartoonists, and the United States' Pat Oliphant on a number of other artists; and (4) the transfer of comic art philosophies and techniques that likely occurs when foreign cartoonists work for long periods in Asia, such as Australia's Paul Best and the United States' Larry Feign in Hong Kong, Russia's Sapajou in China, the Philippines' Deng Coy Miel and other Filipinos in Singapore, and France's Stephff (Stephane Peray) in Thailand.

Political cartooning has had a halting history in many parts of Asia, hampered by many factors. Among them

are: (1) authoritarian philosophies (e.g., communism, "two-faced democracies," and irresponsible capitalism); (2) extreme forms and practices of religions, leading to threats and killings (e.g., the death and rape threats by followers of an Indian guru against female cartoonist Kanika Mishra), or jailing and exile (e.g., of Bangladeshi cartoonist Arifur Rahman for an alleged insult against Islam); (3) long periods of colonialism, a prime example being the Philippines under about three hundred years of Spanish rule and fifty of American, or as Filipinos used to say, three hundred years in a convent, fifty in Hollywood; (4) war and succeeding periods of occupation, such as the United States in Japan and Korea following World War II and the Korean War, respectively, or Japan throughout World War II; and (5) recurring periods of governance by political dictatorships, monarchies, and military regimes.

As a result of these nagging setbacks, almost all of Asian political cartooning faces hard times and a bleak future. In recent years, new and reconfigured old policies, modi operandi, and philosophies have made the careers of many political cartoonists marginal at best and impossible at worst. The stumbling blocks that have been stacked higher recently are: (1) already-in-place regulations and restrictions, some inherited from colonialism, such as the printing press and publications, internal security, and sedition laws from the British, used and misused in Malaysia against Zunar and elsewhere; and adjusted and new regulations to plug overlooked gaps and account for the internet, such as the vaguely stated Act 57 in Bangladesh, the Communications and Media Act in Malaysia, and stricter cyberspace laws in China; (2) political correctness and many religious and ethnic sensitivities gone awry; (3) dwindling number of venues, as many print media establishments succumb to stiff competition from virtual media and other new distractions, or reduce their size, in the process squeezing out political cartoons or allocating the scarce space to more lucrative advertising; (4) diminished appreciation and understanding of political cartoons by editors unaware of, or ignoring, the importance of the cartoons, or protecting their positions by playing it safe and banning anything remotely contro-versial, or using cartoons simply as filler material; and (5) conglomerate publishers, increasingly prevalent on the Asian continent, bent on protecting the vested inter-ests of their corporations and others interlocked with them from potentially harmful cartoons, as evidenced in at least India, Indonesia, Malaysia, the Philippines, Japan, and South Korea.

Generally, political cartoonists in Asia continue to keep their profession alive by meeting crippling set-backs with ingenious comebacks, while seeking other means to make a living. Some strategies they have used are: (1) employing other platforms to get their messages across, such as the Korean cartoonists who, through graphic novels, attacked Samsung for its industrial ill-ness epidemic, related the horrible stories of wartime comfort women, and exposed hidden atrocities cov-ered up by long dictatorial reigns; Chinese cartoonist Badiucao, who uses the internet to criticize Chinese authorities from his Australian base; Vietnamese veteran cartoonist Ly Truc Dung, who shares his most brutal cartoons with friends on Facebook; Hong Kong profes-sional and amateur cartoonists who plaster the walls of the city with protest cartoons directed at mainland authorities; and Indonesian art students and other art-ists who come up with clever approaches to what I call "participatory cartooning"; (2) using layered hidden meanings to bypass censorship, the concealed meanings placed in titles of cartoons, such as in the abovemen-tioned four-panel Korean strips whose names directly or indirectly imply strength, unity, or resistance; in sym-bols, such as the sewn-shut mouth of a cartoon charac-ter by Thailand's Prayoon as an act of protest; in plots, such as Chai Rachawat's popular comic strip locale turned into a wasteland when Chai, in 1992, vowed not to draw the strip until the dictatorial powers of Thailand were replaced; in language, through proverbs, rhymed sentences, and bon mots such as in pre-independence Malaysia and China; and in characters, such as the tart-mouthed political strip character Auntie Walsun in Korea; (3) developing new philosophies and schemes to deal with government, such as the "Indonesian Way" of

eliciting a smile from the authorities, the public, and the cartoonist, at the same time getting a criticism or point across; (4) hiding facts behind fiction in comic books and graphic novels, as was accomplished by members of comics collectives in India; and (5) finding other ways to make a living to offset the low pay for political cartoons, forcing many cartoonists to take another job such as graphic artist, betel nut salesman, hairdresser, ferry boat operator, or advertising artist, or a chosen profession such as medical doctor, engineer, architect, or teacher, engaging in political cartooning as a side job or hobby. Some, such as veteran Taiwanese political cartoonist Ling Qun, come up with clever business schemes that are tied in with their drawings.

The future of political cartooning in Asia is assured as long as there are imperfect governments and people's will to dissent. In fact, the future is here already as cartoonists, both professional and amateur, are rapidly turning to the internet and social media to dispense their visual comments and criticism. As more coun-tries join heavily wired South Korea and Indonesia, the cartoonists' reach will be much broader than with only printed newspapers and magazines—that is, if govern-ments and other agents of authority do not interfere. That is a big "if."

275

Two hundred and nine of the many interviews conducted by John A. Lent (in some cases, with Xu Ying) between 1986 and 2019 are cited in this book. Other interviews I conducted on Asian comic art are not germane to political cartoons, and they are not listed here. Also not in this list, but cited in the text, are interviews done by former graduate students under my supervision: Hsiao Hsiang-wen (Taiwan), Fungma Fudong (Nepal), Monsinee Keeratikrainon (Thailand), and research colleague Annemari de Silva (Sri Lanka).

China

Chen, Yuli. Cartoonist; cofounder and coleader, Qiu County Farmers Frog Cartoon Group. Qiuxian, China, May 28–30, 2009.

Ding, Cong. Veteran political cartoonist; imprisoned and banished to the countryside for twenty-two years because of his cartoons. Beijing, December 20, 2002.

Feng, Yiyin. Cartoonist; daughter of Feng Zikai. Shanghai, January 10, 2002.

He, Wei. Veteran cartoonist; art editor, *Workers' Daily*; organizer, Beijing Workers Cartoon Group. Beijing, May 24, 2009.

Jiang, Yousheng. Veteran cartoonist; army cartoonist during World War II; cofounder, *Satire and Humor*. Beijing, December 17, 2002.

Li, Qingai. Cartoonist; cofounder and coleader, Qiu County Farmers Frog Cartoon Group. Qiuxian, China, May 28–30, 2009.

Liao, Bingxiong. Veteran political cartoonist; member of National Salvation Cartoon Propaganda Corps, World War II. Guangzhou, January 4–5, 2002.

Te, Wei. Political cartoonist; founder and director, Shanghai Animation Film Studio; leader, National Salvation Cartoon Propaganda Corps during World War II. Shanghai, June 16, 2001.

Zheng, Huagai. Veteran cartoonist; organizer, Military Camp Humor Cartoon Group; cartoon researcher; military colonel. Beijing, December 16, 2002; June 12, 2005.

Hong Kong

Apink. Editor, *Mild Comix.* Hong Kong, July 12, 1992.

Best, Paul. Political cartoonist, *South China Morning Post.* Hong Kong, July 12, 1992.

Dunn, Napier. Political cartoonist, *Mercury.* Durban, South Africa, July 11, 1996.

Feign, Larry. Political strip cartoonist, *Hongkong Standard*; creator of the strip *The World of Lily Wong*. Hong Kong, July 11, 1992.

Ma Long [Ma Shing-yuen]. Editor, *Fan Dou*; co-organizer and leader, Century Culture Ltd. Hong Kong, July 12, 1992; March 20, 2012.

Zunzi [Wong Kei-Kwan]. Veteran political activist; cartoonist, *Ming Pao* and *Apple Daily*. Drexel Hill, Pennsylvania, July 30, 1991; Hong Kong, March 20, 2012; May 24, 2018.

Japan

Aki, Ryūzan. Veteran cartoonist. Tokyo, November 6, 1993.

Hayakawa, Sadabumi. Cartoon editor, Kyodo Illustration. Tokyo, February 4, 2019.

Hazama, Ryuji. Veteran Kyodo Illustration political cartoonist. Tokyo, February 4, 2019.

Kato, Yoshiro. Political cartoonist; creator of the *Mappira-Kun* strip; president, Japan Cartoonists Association. Tokyo, November 6, 1993.

Kosuge, Riyako. Political cartoonist, Kyodo Illustration. Tokyo, February 4, 2019.

Kurata, Shin [Sin]. Veteran political cartoonist, *Akabata Shimbun*. Tokyo, February 6, 2019.

Matsuzawa, Hidekazu. Kyodo Illustration political cartoonist. Tokyo, February 4, 2019.

Nishida, Toshiko. Correspondence, January 13, 2019.

Nishizawa, Yuzi. Veteran cartoonist. Tokyo, November 6, 1993.

Sasaki, Tomoko. Chief editor, Kyodo Illustration. Tokyo, February 4, 2019.

Satō, Sampei. Political/strip cartoonist; creator of *Yūhi-kun*. Tokyo, November 8, 1993.

Sugiura, Yukio. Veteran political cartoonist; erotic cartoonist; co-organizer, Shin Manga-ha Shūdan. Tokyo, November 6, 1993.

Suzuki, Yamato. Veteran cartoonist. Tokyo, November 6, 1993.

Tokoro, Yukiyoshi. Veteran political cartoonist, *Mainichi Shimbun*. Tokyo, February 5, 2019.

Toshi, Hiko. Veteran Kyodo Illustration political cartoonist. Tokyo, February 4, 2019.

Korea (South)

Ahn, Ui-Sup. Veteran political/strip cartoonist; creator, *Dookobi* strip. Seoul, July 3, 1992.

Cho, Joo-Chung. Magazine cartoonist. Seoul, July 3, 1992.

Cho, Kwan-Je. Head, Bucheon Cartoon Information Center. Seoul, August 16, 2003.

Choi, Kyu-Seok. Political/graphic novelist. Seoul, August 11, 2018.

Chong, Un-Gyong. Political cartoonist, *JoongAng Ilbo*; creator, *Auntie Walsun* strip. Seoul, July 7, 1992.

Gendry-Kim, Keum Suk. Award-winning political/graphic novel cartoonist. Seoul, August 8, 2018.

Kim, Jae-Jung. Director, Seoul Animation Center. Seoul, August 15, 2003.

Kim, Pan-Kook. Political/strip cartoonist; creator, *Ch'onggaeguri* strip. Seoul, July 2, 1992.

Kim, Song-Hwan. Veteran strip/political cartoonist, *Chosun Ilbo*; creator, *Gobau*. Seoul, July 4, 1992.

Kim, Soo-Bak. Political/graphic novel cartoonist. Seoul, August 6, 2018.

Kim, Sung-Hee. Political/graphic novel cartoonist. Seoul, August 6, 2018.

Lee, Hee-Jae. Veteran political/graphic novel cartoonist. Seoul, August 10, 2018.

Lee, Won-Bok. Cartoon researcher; professor. Seoul, July 2, 1992.

Lim, Cheong-Sun. Cartoon professor, Kongju National Junior College. Seoul, July 5, 1994.

Park, Jae-Dong. Veteran political cartoonist, *Hankyoreh*; animator. Seoul, July 7, 1992; July 3–5, 1994; August 15, 2003; August 10, 2018.

Park, Kun-Woong. Political/graphic novel cartoonist. Seoul, August 9, 2018.

Park, Soo-Dong. Cartoonist; creator, *Goindol*. Seoul, July 7, 1992.

Yi, Wonsoon. Cartoonist, *Seoul Shinmun*. Seoul, July 6, 1994.

Yoon, Young-Ok. Political/strip cartoonist; creator, *Kat'uri* strip. Seoul, July 3, 1992.

Mongolia

Erdenebalsuren, Luvsangaldan [Dan Erdenebal]. Producer/director, Nomadic Comics. Ulaan Baatar, July 27, 30, 2018.

Erdenebayar, Nambaral. Pioneer comic book creator. Ulaan Baatar, July 27, 30, 2018.

Tsogtbayar, Samandariin [Satso]. Veteran political cartoonist; painter; director, Hiimori Publishing House. Ulaan Baatar, July 31, 2018.

Taiwan

Ao, Yao-hsiang. Cartoonist, *China Evening Times* and *Children's Daily*. Taipei, July 10, 1992.

Chao, Ning [Johnny]. Former political cartoonist; professor, National Taiwan Normal University. Taipei, August 8, 1986.

Hoong, Tei-lin. Researcher; owner, comics library. Taipei, July 26, 2005.

Hsiao, Yen-chung. Freelance cartoonist, *China Times* and *United Daily News*. Taipei, July 10, 1992.

Jen [Chung Sung-wei]. Political cartoonist, *Liberty Times*. Taipei, February 13, 2019.

Ji, Ching. Former staff cartoonist, *United Daily News*. Taipei, July 25, 2005; February 16, 2019.

L. C. C. [Lo Ching-chung]. Political cartoonist, *China Times* and *Independence Evening Post*; part owner of the first comic strip weekly, *Cartoon Show*. Taipei, July 9, 1992.

Lao, Chung. Cartoonist; pioneer female cartoonist, *United Daily News*. Taipei, July 10, 1992.

Li, Shan. Veteran political cartoonist; former president, Taiwan Cartoonists Association. Taipei, July 9, 1992; July 25, 28, 2005.

Li, Ying-hao. Archivist, Cartoon Library. Taipei, July 28, 2005.

Ling Qun [Yang Hsin-i]. Veteran political cartoonist, *United Daily News*; organizer, Taiwan International Cartoon Contest; founder, China Cartoonists Association. Taipei, February 13, 2019.

Tang, Jian-feng. Political cartoonist; former president, Taiwan Cartoonists Association. Taipei, July 28, 2005; February 11, 2019.

Wang, Peng. Veteran political cartoonist. Taipei, July 9, 1992; July 28, 2005.

Zola, Zu. Freelance political cartoonist, *United Daily News* and *China Times*; college instructor. Taipei, February 11, 2019.

Cambodia

Weeks, John. Comics archivist/organizer; founder/director, Our Books. Phnom Penh, June 19, 22, 2010.

Indonesia

Badrudin, Ramli. Cartoonist, *HumOr*. Jakarta, July 25, 28, 1992.

Darmawan, Hikmat. Researcher; cofounder, Akademi Samali. Jakarta, July 11, 2013.

Gunawan, Iwan. Freelance cartoonist; organizer, *Sequen*; director, Institut Kesenian Jakarta. Jakarta, July 16, 2013.

Koendoro, Dwi. Veteran sociopolitical strip cartoonist; creator, *Pailul dan Panji Koming* strip; pioneer animator; founder and head, Citra Audivistama. Jakarta, July 27, 1992; Petaling Jaya, Malaysia, September 14, 2004; Guiyang, China, September 7, 2007.

Larasati, Dwinita. Pioneer diary comics creator; founder/director, Curhat Anak Bangsa. Singapore, February 23, 2011; Bandung, Indonesia, July 13, 2017.

Mahtum. President, *HumOr* magazine. Jakarta, July 28, 1992.

Masdiono, Toni. Freelance cartoonist; researcher; lecturer. Guiyang, China, July 13, 2008.

Pramono [Pramono R. Pramoedjo]. Political cartoonist, *Suara Pembaruan*; president, Indonesian Cartoonists' Association. Jakarta, July 26, 1992.

Rahadian, Beng. Political/comic strip cartoonist; creator, *Lotif* strip; cofounder, Akademi Samali. Jakarta, July 16, 2013.

Setiawan, Arwah. Founder/director, Lembaga Humor Indonesia; publisher, *Astaga* humor magazine. Jakarta, July 29, 1992.

Sudarno, Dominto M. Managing editor, *HumOr*; secretary, Indonesian Cartoonists' Association. Jakarta, July 28, 1992.

Sudarta, G. M. Veteran political cartoonist, *Kompas*; longtime creator of the strip *Oom Pasikom*. Jakarta, July 28, 1992.

Sunarto, Priyanto. Veteran political cartoonist, *Tempo*. Jakarta, July 15, 2013.

Sunarto, Wagiyono. Cartoon scholar; rector, Institut Kesenian Jakarta. Jakarta, July 9, 2013.

Malaysia

Deen [Nordin Misnan]. Cartoonist, *Gelihati* humor magazine. Kuala Lumpur, August 6, 1993.

Jaafar Taib. Veteran cartoonist; painter; founder/head, *Gila-Gila* humor magazine. Kuala Lumpur, July 21, 2000.

Lat [Mohd. Nor Khalid]. Veteran sociopolitical cartoonist; cofounder, Persatuan Kartunis Selangor dan Kuala Lumpur; creator, *Scenes of Malaysian Life*, *Kampung Boy*; animator. Shah Alam, Malaysia, November 17, 1986; Kuala Lumpur, July 22, 2000.

Muhamad Azhar Abdullah. Cartoonist; creator, *Urban Comics*; researcher; founder, Persatuan Penggiat Komik Malaysia. Bangi, Malaysia, January 14, 2009.

Muliyadi Mahamood. Cartoonist; professor; top comics researcher; cofounder, Persatuan Kartunis Selangor dan Kuala Lumpur. Kuala Lumpur, August 8, 1993; July 21, 2000; Shah Alam, Malaysia, July 9, 2012.

Rejabhad. Veteran political cartoonist; organizer/editor, early humor magazine, *Ha Hu Hum*. Kuala Lumpur, July 21, 2000.

Sanusi Junid, Tan Sri. Former minister of agriculture; secretary of the dominant political party, United Malays National Organisation; founder, *Mat Jenin* humor magazine. Kuala Lumpur, July 21, 2000.

Zunar [Zulkifli Anwar Ulhaque]. Veteran political cartoonist; fighting victim of government reprisals; cofounder, Persatuan Kartunis Selangor dan Kuala Lumpur. Kuala Lumpur, August 7, 1993; Shah Alam, Malaysia, October 9, 2016; correspondence, 2009–2014.

279

Myanmar

Aw Pi Kyeh. Veteran cartoonist; chair, Myanmar Cartoonists Association; motivational speaker; engineer. Yangon, February 22, 2018.

Crab [Su Myat Htwe]. Freelance cartoonist; business department employee. Yangon, February 24, 2018.

Joker [Nyan Myint]. Freelance cartoonist; betel nut merchant. Yangon, February 21, 2018.

Kyaw Thu Yein. Freelance cartoonist; physician. Yangon, February 25, 2018.

Maung Maung Fountain. Freelance cartoonist. Yangon, February 23, 2018.

Nay Myo Aye. Freelance cartoonist, *7 Day News*; tattoo artist. Yangon, February 20, 2018.

Shwe Bo [Aung Bo Bo]. Freelance cartoonist; men's hairdresser. Yangon, February 21, 2018.

Win Aung. Veteran freelance cartoonist. Yangon, February 20, 2018.

The Philippines

Alcala, Larry. Political cartoonist, *Weekly Graphic*; strip cartoonist; pioneer animator. Manila, September 26, 1988.

Avendano, Noel. Cartoonist, *Manila Chronicle*. Manila, July 17, 1992.

Hartendorp, A. V. H. Former editor, *Philippine Magazine*. Manila, September 14, 1964.

Isaac, Norman B. Political/comic strip cartoonist, *Manila Bulletin Today*. Manila, July 16, 1992.

Marcelo, Nonoy. Political cartoonist, *Manila Chronicle*; strip artist, *Ikabod* and *Tisoy*. Manila, September 29, 1988; July 17, 1992.

Miel, Deng Coy. Political cartoonist, *Philippine Star*. Manila, July 16, 1992.

Santiago, Roni. Political comic strip cartoonist. Pasig City, Philippines, October 17, 2009.

Yonzon, Hugo, III. Veteran cartoonist; cofounder/owner, *Mango Comics*; longtime president, Samahang Kartunista ng Pilipinas. Manila, July 12, 2008.

Singapore

Cheah, Sin Ann. Former art supervisor, *Straits Times*; creator, *House of Lim* strip. Singapore, July 23, 1992; July 18, 2000; November 25, 2016.

Francisco, Manny. Political cartoonist, *Straits Times*. Singapore, November 26, 2016.

Heng, Kim Song. Veteran political cartoonist, *Lian He Zao Pao*. Singapore, July 22, 1992; November 30, 2016.

Ilio, Ludwig. Cartoonist, *Straits Times*, *Business Times*. Singapore, November 25, 2016.

Liew, Sonny. Award-winning cartoonist; author of *The Art of Charlie Chan Hock Chye*. Singapore, December 1, 2016.

Lim, Cheng Tju. Comic art historian; school principal. Singapore, July 24, 1992; July 17, 2000; Shah Alam, Malaysia, October 9, 2016; Singapore, December 3, 2016.

Lou, Ken. Freelance cartoonist; architect. Singapore, July 23, 1992.

Low, Don. Web/print designer-cartoonist. Singapore, December 2, 2016.

Miel, Deng Coy. Staff cartoonist, *Straits Times*. Singapore, November 26, 2016.

Ruiz, José. Political cartoonist, *Straits Times*. Singapore, July 23, 1992.

Tan, James. Veteran freelance cartoonist. Singapore, December 2, 2016.

Wong, Dan. Freelance online cartoonist; creator, *A Good Citizen*. Singapore, November 30, 2016.

Thailand

Arun [Arun Watcharasawat]. Veteran political cartoonist, *Nation's Review*, *Bangkok Post*. Bangkok, August 1, 1993.

Bancha Sangthunchai. Political cartoonist, Manager Group. Bangkok, December 1, 2006.

Chai Rachawat [Somchai Katanyutanan]. Veteran political cartoonist, *Thai Rath*; creator, *Poo Yai Ma Kap Tung Ma Muen* strip; commissioned artist for King Bhumibol's books. Bangkok, August 1, 1993; December 4, 2006; July 11, 2014.

Kamin [Chukiat Jaroensuk]. Head of political cartoonists team, Manager Group. Bangkok, December 1, 2006.

Muen [Chuchart Mueningul]. Veteran political cartoonist, *Matichon Daily*, *Prachachart Weekly*. Bangkok, August 1, 1993.

Pon. Political cartoonist, *Kaosod*, Matichon newspapers; creator, *Nuna Kubpa Jam* strip. Bangkok, December 4, 2006.

Sudjai Bhromkoed. Organizer/head, Cartoonthai Institute. Bangkok, December 4, 2006.

Teerapongsack Sungkatip. Political cartoonist, Manager Group. Bangkok, December 1, 2006.

Yodpongsakul. Cartoonist; creator, Manager Group's strip, *Rip Ginger*. Bangkok, December 1, 2006.

Yoot [Yoottachai Kaewdee]. Political cartoonist, *Bangkok Post*. Bangkok, August 4, 1993.

Vietnam

Hung Nguyen Long. Graphic designer; head, Areka Animation Studio, Vietnam Graphic Company. Hanoi, March 1, 2018.

Kong Ngoan. Cartoonist; head of painting department, *Nhan Dan*. Hanoi, August 11, 1993.

Le Phuong [Leo]. Cartoonist, *Tuoi Tre Cuoi* magazine covers. Hanoi, March 1, 2018.

Ly Truc Dung. Veteran cartoonist; organizer/chair, Bamboo Dragon Cup competition. Hanoi, March 2, 2018.

Nguyen Thanh Chung. Editor, *Tienphong Chu Nhat*. Hanoi, August 10, 1993.

Nguyen Thanh Phong. Former political cartoonist; graphic novelist; cofounder, Comicola Publishing. Hanoi, February 27, 2018.

Phuong Ha. International department editor, *Nhan Dan*. Hanoi, August 11, 1993.

Bangladesh

Alam, Saiful. Veteran political cartoonist; imprisoned for political views. Dhaka, July 25, 1993; October 19, 2016.

Amil, Sadatuddin Ahmed [Sadat]. Staff political cartoonist, *Daily Star*. Dhaka, October 20, 2016.

Benu, Zahid Hasan. Political cartoonist, *Naya Diganta*. Dhaka, October 15, 20, 2016.

Bhattacharjee, Shishir. Veteran political cartoonist, *Vorer Kagoj*. Dhaka, July 27, 1993; October 19, 2016.

Chakoborty, Biplob Kumar. Staff cartoonist, *Kaler Kantho*. Dhaka, October 15, 2016.

Chowdhury, Md. Zonayed Azim. Former political cartoonist, *Alokito Bangladesh*. Dhaka, October 20, 2016.

Habib, Ahsan. Veteran cartoonist; longtime head of *Unmad*. Dhaka, July 25, 1993; October 17, 2016.

Haque, Mehedi. Political cartoonist; founder, BANCARAS, Dhaka Comics, and Akantis Comic Art School; executive editor, *Unmad*. Dhaka, October 14, 20, 2016.

Harun-Or-Rashid, Mohammad. Organizer/head, *Cartoon* magazine. Budapest, August 22, 1990; Dhaka, July 24, 25, 1993.

Huda, Asiful. Veteran political cartoonist, *Amar Desh*; playwright; actor; commercial designer; animator. Dhaka, July 27, 1993; October 18, 2016.

Islam, Nazrul. Veteran political cartoonist; college lecturer. Dhaka, July 25, 1993.

Kasem, Kazi Abul. Veteran political cartoonist, *Daily Azad*; career started in 1930 in Calcutta. Dhaka, July 26, 1993.

Khan, Sharier. Veteran political/strip cartoonist, *Daily Star*. Dhaka, October 17, 2016.

Kuddus, M. A. Senior political cartoonist, *Daily Ittefaq*. Dhaka, October 15, 2016.

Manik, Md. Humaun Kabir. Cartoonist; graffiti artist; cofounder, Nerd Rabbit Animation Studio. Dhaka, October 20, 2016.

Mitu, Nasreen Sultana. Female political cartoonist, *Daily New Age*; college teacher. Dhaka, October 14, 2016.

Rahman, Asifur [Rats Asif]. Cartoonist, *Unmad*. Dhaka, October 17, 2016.

Rahman, Samir Asran. Founder/head, Mighty Punch comics. Dhaka, October 20, 2016.

Ranabi [Rafiqun Nabi]. Veteran political cartoonist; creator, social commentary strip *Tokai*; painter; art professor. Dhaka, July 26, 1993.

Ratan, Md. Kamruzzaman. Cartoonist; graffiti artist; cofounder, Nerd Rabbit Animation Studio. Dhaka, October 20, 2016.

Sahid Ullah, Mohammad. Cartoonist. Correspondence, July 25, 2012.

Sayeed, Khondokar Abu. Cartoonist; founder/head, in-home art school. Dhaka, July 26, 1993.

Tanmoy [Syed Rashad Imam]. Political cartoonist; graphic novelist; organizer, Common People. Dhaka, October 17, 19, 2016.

India

Abraham, Abu. Veteran political cartoonist, *Shankar's Weekly*; staff cartoonist, London *Observer* and *Guardian*; member of Parliament, India. Trivandrum, July 12, 1993.

Dar, Sudhir. Veteran cartoonist, *Pioneer*, the *Statesman*. New Delhi, July 7, 1993.

Etteth, Ravi Shankar. Political cartoonist, *India Today*. New Delhi, July 7, 1993.

Gopalakrishnan, Gokul. Freelance cartoonist; police inspector. Thrissur, India, March 19, 20, 23, 2009.

Keshav, Venkata Raghavan P. Longtime political cartoonist, the *Hindu*. Chennai, July 21, 1993.

Kumar, Rajeesh. Art director, Campfire Books. New Delhi, July 8, 2009.

Kutty, P. K. S. Longtime political cartoonist, *Aaj Kaal*. Correspondence, January 6, 1995.

Laxman, R. K. Longtime political cartoonist, *Times of India*; creator, "Common Man." Philadelphia, June 26, 1987; Mumbai, July 10, 1993.

Madhan. Cartoonist; joint editor, *Ananda Vikatan*. Chennai, July 21, 1993.

Muthiah, S. Journalist; author. Chennai, July 22, 1993.

Nair, Raju. Longtime staff political cartoonist, *Deepika Daily*. Trivandrum, July 13, 1993; correspondence, August 28, 1993.

Ninan, Ajit. Staff political cartoonist, *Times of India*. New Delhi, July 7, 2009.

Pran [Pran Kumar Sharma]. Veteran cartoonist; creator, popular strip, *Chacha Chaudhary*. New Delhi, July 5, 1993; Drexel Hill, Pennsylvania, June 5–6, 2006; New Delhi, July 7, 10, 11, 2009.

Puri, Rajinder. Veteran political cartoonist/activist, many newspapers; founder, *Stir* magazine; founder/leader, three political parties. New Delhi, July 5, 1993; July 7, 2009.

Ramaswamy, Cho. Founder/head, *Thuglak* humor magazine. Chennai, July 21, 1993.

Rupam [Ramesh Chande]. Longtime political cartoonist, *Janmabhoomi*. Mumbai, July 10, 1993.

Sawant, Suresh. Veteran freelance cartoonist. Mumbai, July 10, 1993.

Shetty, Prakash. Political/pocket cartoonist, the *Week*. Kottayam, July 12, 1993.

Tailang, Sudhir. Longtime political cartoonist, *Hindustan Times*; cartoonist, *Asian Age*. New Delhi, July 6, 1993; July 9, 2009.

Unny, E. P. Longtime political cartoonist, *Economic Times*. New Delhi, July 7, 1993; July 7, 2009.

Vins [Vijay Narain Seth]. Political cartoonist, *Business World*. Mumbai, July 8, 1993.

Yesudasan, C. J. Staff political cartoonist, *Malayala Manorama*; creator, pocket cartoon, *Kittuvammavan*. Correspondence, October 4, 1993.

Iran

Alidoosti, Fa'ez. Cartoonist; spokesperson for the White Crow cartoonist group. Tehran, October 2, 1999.

Ataeiazar, Elham. Female cartoonist working with four magazines and *Etemad Meli Daily*. Tehran, December 22, 2013.

Baniasadi, Mohammad Ali. Press cartoonist; winner of international cartoon prizes. Tehran, October 3, 1999.

Kermani, Parvin. Iran's first female cartoonist, beginning in 1969 with *Gol Agha and Tofigh Weekly*. Tehran, December 22, 2013.

Kowsar, Nikahang. Cartoon editor of the dailies *Asad* and *Akhbar-e Eghtesad*; cartoonist for *Aftab-e Emroos*; arrested; in exile. Tehran, October 7, 1999.

Mehrabi, Massoud. Prize-winning cartoonist; owner/director, *Film* and *Film International*. Tehran, October 3, 1999.

Neyistani, Touka. Press cartoonist; winner of international cartoon prizes; architect; in self-exile. Tehran, October 6, 1999.

Nikche, Zeynab. Female cartoonist; painter; animator; children's book illustrator. Tehran, December 22, 2013.

Niroumand. Mohammad-Hossein. Director of the Tehran International Cartoon Biennial; editor of *Kayhan Caricature*. Tehran, October 2, 1999.

Tabatabei, Massoud Shojai. Longtime editor of *Kayhan Caricature*; founder of the House of Cartoons. Tehran, October 1, 2, 1999.

Vaziritabar, Farzane. Cartoonist; sculptor. Tehran, December 22, 2013.

Zamanfar, Shiva. Female caricaturist. Tehran, December 22, 2013.

Nepal

Ashok [Ashok Man Singh]. Cartoonist; painter; cofounder, *Kamana* film magazine. Kathmandu, October 24, 27, 2016.

Baral, Dharma Raj. Former secretary, HaSaNe; former editor in chief, *Muskan* humor magazine. Osaka, July 26, 2000.

Ghimire, Yubaraj. Editor in chief, Nepal News Network International, *Annapurna Post*. Kathmandu, October 27, 2016.

Khokana [Mohan Shyam Maharjan]. Veteran freelance political cartoonist. Kathmandu, October 27, 2016.

Panday, Ram Kumar. Humor scholar; founder/president, HaSaNe; founder, Nepal's first humor magazine, *Kaliyug*. Osaka, July 27, 2000; Kathmandu, October 23, 27, 2016.

Shrestha, Abin. Senior political cartoonist; chief subeditor, Kantipur newspapers; president, Cartoonists' Club of Nepal. Kathmandu, October 25, 27, 2016.

Sri Lanka

Dayananda, Paliyagoda. Artist, *Bindu*. Colombo, July 15, 1993.

De Silva, Annemari. Independent cartoon researcher. Colombo, February 12, 2018.

Hettigoda, Winnie. Veteran political cartoonist, *Divaina, Lakdiva, Lanka*; art lecturer. Kandy, Sri Lanka, July 18, 1993; Colombo, February 11, 2018; correspondence, September 11, 1996; April 24, 1997.

Karunathilake, Dharshana. Freelance political cartoonist, *Lakbima*. Colombo, February 15, 2018.

Mahindapala, D. H. L. Editor in chief, *Ceylon Observer*. Colombo, July 20, 1993.

Medagama, K. M. K. Editor, *Jataka Kata* magazine. Colombo, July 14, 1993.

Opatha, S. C. Veteran political cartoonist, *Ceylon Daily Mirror, Ceylon Observer, Daily News*; owner, ad agency. Colombo, July 17, 20, 1993.

Perera, Camillus. Political, pocket, satirical strip, and newspaper cartoonist; founder, Camillus Publications. Colombo, July 19, 1993.

Ratnayake, Janaka. Chief artist, *Chitra Mithra*, Upali Group. Colombo, July 15, 1993.

Rupasinghe, Bennete. Colombo, July 19, 1993.

Siriwardena, Wasantha. Staff political cartoonist, Wijewa newspapers. Colombo, July 16, 1993; correspondence, August 26, 1993.

Wickramanayake, W. P. Freelance political, strip, and comics newspaper cartoonist. Colombo, July 17, 1993.

Wijesoma, W. R. Longtime political cartoonist, Times Group, Lake House Group, Upali Group; introduced first pocket cartoon; creator, *Punchisingho*. Colombo, July 15, 17, 1993.

Yoonoos, Jiffry. Longtime political cartoonist, Lake House Group, *Aththa*; victim of government violence. Colombo, July 19, 1993.

283

Index

290

Index

Professor Emeritus John A. Lent has pioneered in teaching and researching during his sixty-three-year career in the fields of mass communication and popular culture in Asia and the Caribbean, comic art and animation, and development communication. He has authored or edited eighty-five books, started and edited three journals including the *International Journal of Comic Art*, and founded at least six academic international associations and the first university communication school in all of Malaysia.

About the Author

www.ingramcontent.com/pod-product-compliance
Lightning Source LLC
Chambersburg PA
CBHW061234270326

41929CB00031B/3483